Twin Cities Golf Guide

Paul Kangas

PK Publishing
PMB 257
4737 County Road 101
Minnetonka, MN 55345

Table of Contents

Foreward

Welcome to the <u>Twin Cities Golf Guide</u>. Golfing has become a very popular recreational activity for many Twin Cities residents during our beautiful summers. We all enjoy being outdoors in summertime and golf is a great venue to get some exercise, enjoy the outdoors and have some fun. The goal of this book is to help golfers of all abilities enjoy the game a little more.

With so many courses within 45 minutes the big question is where to play? You could just grab the phone book, call the first course you see and make a tee time. How much does the round cost? How well are their greens maintained? Do they have a driving range? How do I get there? These questions cannot be answered by simply looking in the phone book. This book is designed to help you make a more informed decision on which courses you would like to play.

With so many people enjoying the game of golf, many courses are crowded and the pace of play has slowed. This increase in slow play may be due in part to the lack of comparative information available on golf courses. Some courses are better suited to beginners while others may be more enjoyable for an experienced golfers. Regardless of your skill level, my hope is that this book can be a resource for you when its time to make that tee time.

Taking a step back for a second, let me give you a little background on me. I am a guy who loves the game of golf. My handicap hovers around 10 so I am by no means a professional golfer, but I do understand what makes a golf course enjoyable to play. Most of the people I talked to during these past two years have said that the same things are important to them. Some things which are not as important for experienced golfers may be more important to the average golfer and vice-versa.

The information in this book is the culmination of two years of research, interviews, calculations and playing golf courses. One consultant (Todd Loncorich) and I played all 79 eighteen hole regulation courses (par 70 or better) within 40 miles of downtown Minneapolis and St. Paul and rated them on a number of criteria. These criteria include: tee boxes, fairways, greens, layout, amenities, overall and value. The criteria and their subcategories were weighted and an overall rating was calculated for each course. (For more on the rating process please see the rating sections of the book on ***pages 12-13, 15-20***.) While this rating system is somewhat subjective, each course is rated on the same criteria, thereby providing the most fair means of comparison.

There are a number of 9 hole courses and 18 hole subpar 70 courses which are listed in this book but were not played or rated. I have included information on all of these courses as well as information on golf practice facilities in the area. It is my sincere hope that you find this guide a valuable resource in helping you enjoy the game of golf a little more. Although a lot of time and work went into this book, it was a labor of love. I would like to thank Todd for all of his help. A very special thanks goes to my wife Kelly for her patience, support and help in proofreading and editing. Happy Golfing!!

Etiquette Corner

With so many people playing the game today, longer and longer rounds have become common place. All of the following etiquette suggestions came from course managers, golf professionals and everyday golfers. Please help eliminate slow play and make the game more enjoyable for everyone by remembering the following golf etiquette:

- Limit yourself to one or two practice swings. Improving one's game should be done on the practice range.
- If a lost ball cannot be found in two or three minutes, play another ball.
- Do not calculate or write scores on the green, do it on the next tee.
- Play "ready golf". Get to the ball, be sure no one is in your line and hit.
- Be ready to putt when it's your turn. Do not wait to read your putt until everyone is waiting for you to putt.
- Repair your ball marks on the green. Do not leave them for someone else to fix or putt over.
- Get to the course in plenty of time. Do not arrive 5 minutes before your tee time. Late arrivals contribute to slow play for everyone.
- Rake bunkers when you are done and enter bunkers from the low side
- Leave your golf bag on the side of the green closest to the next hole.
- The person with the closest shot to the pin tends it. The first person who "holes out" replaces the pin.
- Play from the tee level that matches your ability level. Most newer courses have four or five ability levels to choose from. Playing from the wrong ability level is one of the largest contributing factors to slow play.
- Help others by watching their ball to prevent long searches for lost balls.
- Replace your divots!
- Refrain from talking when others are hitting or putting and do not stand in their line of view.
- Refrain from hitting extra balls when others are waiting on you.
- If you are driving a cart, practice the 90 degree rule when possible and take the clubs with you that you might need.

By following these simple rules, everyone will have more fun and that is what the game of golf is all about.

Alphabetical Listing of Courses

18 hole Regulation Courses

Course	Page #	Map #	Rating
Afton Alps	21-22	4	81.53
Baker National	23-34	1	99.55
Bellwood Oaks	25-26	4	90.55
Bluff Creek	27-28	3	85.60
Braemar	29-30	3	101.43
Brookview	31-32	1	93.68
Bunker Hills	33-34	1	102.65
Carriage Hills	35-36	4	76.90
Cedar Creek	37-38	1	99.38
Chaska Town Course	39-40	3	108.65
Chisago Lakes	41-42	2	99.05
Chomonix	43-44	2	99.05
Columbia	45-46	2	90.20
Como	47-48	2	87.53
Creeksbend	49-50	3	102.85
Crystal Lake	51-52	4	98.75
Dahlgreen	53-54	3	99.25
Daytona	55-56	1	91.38
Deer Run	57-58	3	94.80
Eagle Valley	59-60	4	99.70
Edinburgh	61-62	1	101.25
Elk River	63-64	1	94.95
Elm Creek	65-66	1	82.10
Falcon Ridge	67-68	2	85.83
Fountain Valley	69-70	4	88.48
Fox Hollow	71-72	1	104.90
Francis A. Gross	73-74	2	87.50
Goodrich	75-76	2	81.00
Greenhaven	77-78	1	94.80
Greenwood	79-80	2	78.20
Hampton Hills	81-82	1	75.75
Heritage Links	83-84	3	97.25
Hiawatha	85-86	4	91.43
Hidden Greens	87-88	4	84.40
Hidden Haven	89-90	2	88.60
Highland Park	91-92	4	81.75
Hollydale	93-94	1	87.08
Inverwood	95-96	4	103.70
Island View	97-98	3	93.30

Course	Page #	Map #	Rating
Keller	99-100	2	97.95
Lakeview	101-102	1	79.28
Legends	103-104	3	101.98
Links at Northfork	105-106	1	104.60
Majestic Oaks Gold	107-108	2	95.28
Majestic Oaks Platinum	109-110	2	102.73
Manitou Ridge	111-112	2	100.38
Meadowbrook	113-114	3	90.95
Mississippi Dunes	115-116	4	105.15
Monticello	117-118	1	92.20
New Prague	119-120	3	95.40
Oak Glen	121-122	2	105.18
Oak Marsh	123-124	2	101.75
Oneka Ridge	125-126	2	91.90
Phalen Park	127-128	2	92.60
Pheasant Acres	129-130	1	93.20
Pioneer Creek	131-132	1	106.83
Prestwick	133-134	4	108.08
Refuge	135-136	1	104.98
Ridges at Sand Creek	137-138	3	109.53
River Oaks	139-140	4	99.80
Rum River Hills	141-142	1	78.80
Rush Creek	143-144	1	105.70
Sanbrook	145-146	2	81.23
Sawmill	147-148	2	102.15
Shamrock	149-150	1	76.48
Southern Hills	151-152	4	95.15
Stonebrooke	153-154	3	93.85
StoneRidge	155-156	2	101.10
Sundance	157-158	1	87.93
Tanners Brook	159-160	2	98.53
Theodore Wirth	161-162	1	88.98
Timber Creek	163-164	1	92.70
University of Minnesota	165-166	2	84.23
Valley View	167-168	3	88.60
Valleywood	169-170	4	87.53
Viking Meadows	171-172	2	90.75
Wild Marsh	173-174	1	105.10
Wilds	175-176	3	94.50
Willingers	177-178	3	103.25

18 hole subpar 70 and 9 hole Courses

MAPS

This map section will make it easier for you to find courses. The Twin Cities area was divided into four sections: NW, NE, SW and SE. These four maps show the general locations of courses. For detailed maps and directions to each course look for the pages in the book that list that course's information.

Map 1 - NW   Map 2 - NE

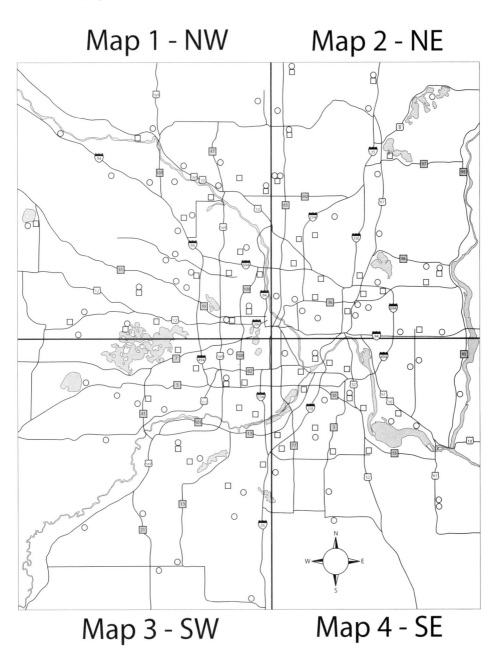

Map 3 - SW   Map 4 - SE

Map 1 - NW

- (2) Baker National
- (6) Brookview
- (7) Bunker Hills
- (9) Cedar Creek
- (18) Daytona
- (21) Edinburgh
- (22) Elk River
- (23) Elm Creek
- (26) Fox Hollow
- (29) Greenhaven
- (31) Hampton Hills

- (37) Hollydale
- (41) Lakeview
- (43) Links at Northfork
- (49) Monticello
- (55) Pheasant Acres
- (56) Pioneer Creek
- (58) Refuge
- (61) Rum River Hills
- (62) Rush Creek
- (65) Shamrock
- (69) Sundance

- (71) Theodore Wirth
- (72) Timber Creek
- (77) Wild Marsh

- [5] Baker Evergreen
- [6] Begin Oaks
- [12] Brookland
- [13] Brookview
- [14] Buffalo Heights
- [15] Bunker Hills
- [18] Centerbrook

- [27] French Lake Open
- [30] Hayden Hills
- [42] New Hope
- [46] Orono
- [48] Pinewood
- [49] Red Oak
- [51] Rivers Edge
- [53] Theodore Wirth
- [57] Woodland Creek

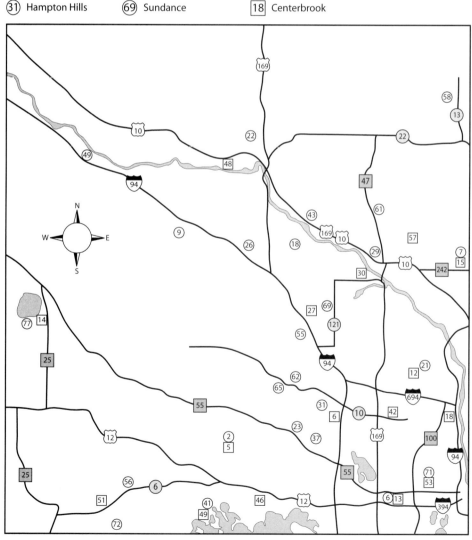

7

Map 2 - NE

⑪ Chisago Lakes	㊺ Majestic Oaks Gold	⑰ Tanners Brook	24 Falcon Ridge
⑫ Chomonix	㊺ Majestic Oaks Platinum	㊂ University of Minnesota	28 Gem Lake Hills
⑬ Columbia	㊻ Manitou Ridge	㉟ Viking Meadows	34 Island Lake
⑭ Como	㊶ Oak Glen	3 Applewood Hills	35 Kate Haven
㉔ Falcon Ridge	㊺ Oak Marsh	9 Bridges of Moundsview	38 Majestic Oaks
㉗ Francis A Gross	㊾ Oneka Ridge	10 Brightwood Hills	39 Maple Hills
㉘ Goodrich	㊻ Phalen Park	16 Castlewood	43 Oak Glen
㉚ Greenwood	㊿ Sanbrook	17 Cedarholm	44 Oakdale Greens
㉟ Hidden Haven	㊿ Sawmill	20 Cimarron	52 Sanbrook
㊵ Keller	㉞ StoneRidge	22 Country View	55 Vikingwoods

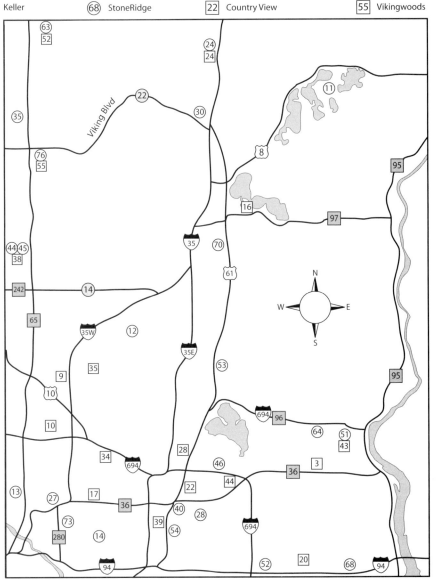

8

Map 3 - SW

(4) Bluff Creek   (39) Island View   (78) Wilds   [26] Fred Richards

(5) Braemar   (42) Legends   (79) Willingers   [29] Glen Lake

(10) Chaska Town Course   (47) Meadowbrook   [32] Hyland Greens

(15) Creeksbend   (50) New Prague   [8] Braemar   [36] Lone Pine

(17) Dahlgreen   (59) Ridges at Sand Creek   [19] Chaska Par 30   [40] Meadowwoods

(19) Deer Run   (67) Stonebrooke   [21] Cleary Lake   [45] Orchard Gardens

(32) Heritage Links   (74) Valley View   [23] Dwan   [56] Waters Edge

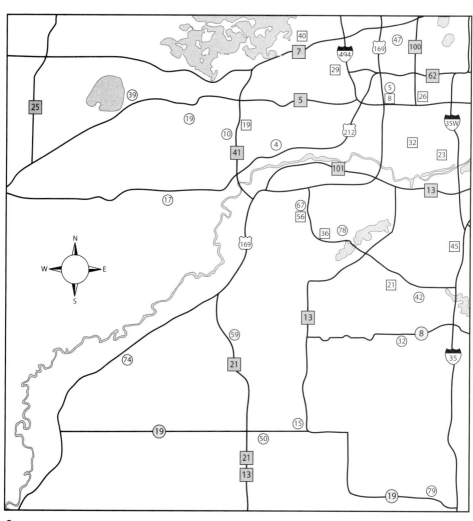

9

Map 4 - SE

① Afton Alps

③ Bellwood Oaks

⑧ Carriage Hills

⑯ Crystal Lake

⑳ Eagle Valley

㉕ Fountain Valley

㉝ Hiawatha

㉞ Hidden Greens

㊱ Highland Park

㊳ Inverwood

㊽ Mississippi Dunes

㊻ Prestwick

㊿ River Oaks

⑯ Southern Hills

⑦ Valleywood

1 All Seasons

2 Apple Valley

4 Arbor Pointe

7 Birnamwood

11 Brockway

25 Fort Snelling

31 Highland Park

33 Inverwood

37 Lost Spur

41 Mendota Heights

47 Parkview

50 Rich Valley

54 Thompson Oaks

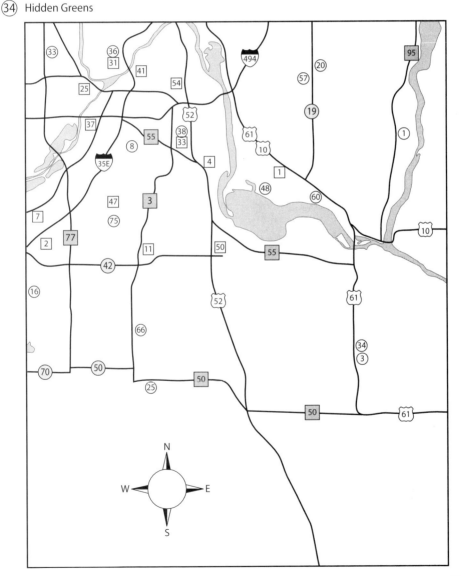

How to Use This Book

There is quite a bit of information supplied on each course. This section will help you understand how to utilize each section.

Course Information

This section is self-explanatory. It contains information about rates, reservation policies, leagues, amenities and management. It is my intention to keep all of the information in it up-to-date.

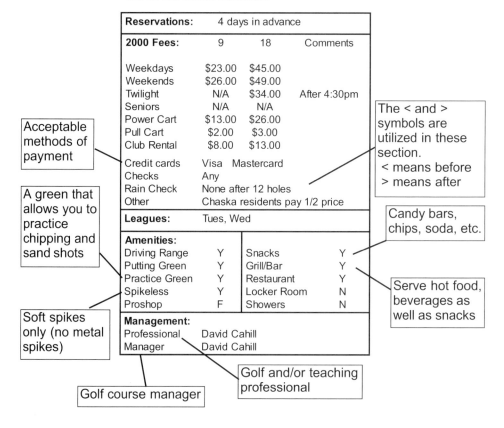

Chaska Town Course
3000 Town Course Drive
Chaska, MN 55318
952-443-3748

Course Information

Reservations:	4 days in advance		
2000 Fees:	9	18	Comments
Weekdays	$23.00	$45.00	
Weekends	$26.00	$49.00	
Twilight	N/A	$34.00	After 4:30pm
Seniors	N/A	N/A	
Power Cart	$13.00	$26.00	
Pull Cart	$2.00	$3.00	
Club Rental	$8.00	$13.00	
Credit cards	Visa Mastercard		
Checks	Any		
Rain Check	None after 12 holes		
Other	Chaska residents pay 1/2 price		
Leagues:	Tues, Wed		

Amenities:

Driving Range	Y	Snacks	Y
Putting Green	Y	Grill/Bar	Y
Practice Green	Y	Restaurant	Y
Spikeless	Y	Locker Room	N
Proshop	F	Showers	N

Management:

Professional	David Cahill
Manager	David Cahill

Acceptable methods of payment

The < and > symbols are utilized in these section.
< means before
> means after

A green that allows you to practice chipping and sand shots

Candy bars, chips, soda, etc.

Serve hot food, beverages as well as snacks

Soft spikes only (no metal spikes)

Golf course manager

Golf and/or teaching professional

Course Overview:

The course overview offers a brief glimpse into what the course is like. It tells you my impressions of the course, whether the course is better suited to beginners or advanced golfers and some of the unique aspects of the course. It will also show the overall rating for each golf course (out of 120).

Chaska Town Course is a very challenging and well laid out golf course surrounded by native grasslands and flowers. Driving accuracy is a premium on this course. Long hitters may be rewarded with short approach shots but stray from the beautifully kept fairways and the rough will get you. Playing this course intelligently will make for a very enjoyable round. This is one of my favorite courses to play in the Twin Cities Area. The course will challenge golfers of all ability levels, however, beginning golfers may find this course a struggle.

Rating   108.65

Course Rating

This is the main section of this book. What is it that make one course better or more fun to play than another? Is it putting on greens like Augusta or hitting from fairways like carpet? This rating system takes into account the many factors that determine which golf courses people like to play. The overall ratings offer a comparison of the courses. How does this rating system work?

Each golf course is rated on seven major categories: Tees, Fairways, Greens, Layout, Amenities, Overall and Value. Each of the major categories are then broken down into criteria. For instance in the category of greens the criteria are: condition, speed, size & variety, slope and fringe. Each of the criteria are scored from 1 to 5. A five meaning that there is no room for improvement and a one meaning either very poor or nonexistent. A rating of three is average, which means that one can reasonably expect a public course to meet this standard.

Each of the categories and criteria are weighted by their relative importance. For example most golfers would agree that the category of greens is more important than the amenities. Likewise when considering the importance of the criteria for each category, for example fairways, the condition of the fairways is more important than whether or not there is more than one cut of rough. To reach a final score for each category, the scores for each criteria are multiplied by the weighted relative importance of that criteria. Similarly each major category is multiplied by its weighted relative importance to reach an overall rating for the course. The ratings serve as a comparison between the different courses. A perfect score would be 120.

The next section of the book, **pages 15-20**, will outline the expectations for each of the categories and criteria. The goal of this book is to be as objective as possible when rating each course; however, we did not get out a ruler to measure the height of the rough or bring along a portable stimp-meter to measure the speed of the greens. We did try to be fair in our assessments of each criteria, and used the same criteria for every course.

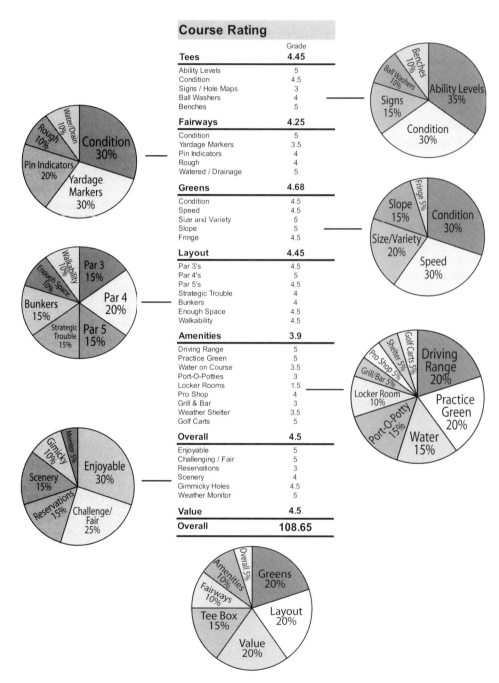

Course Rating

	Grade
Tees	**4.45**
Ability Levels	5
Condition	4.5
Signs / Hole Maps	3
Ball Washers	4
Benches	5
Fairways	**4.25**
Condition	5
Yardage Markers	3.5
Pin Indicators	4
Rough	4
Watered / Drainage	5
Greens	**4.68**
Condition	4.5
Speed	4.5
Size and Variety	5
Slope	5
Fringe	4.5
Layout	**4.45**
Par 3's	4.5
Par 4's	5
Par 5's	4.5
Strategic Trouble	4
Bunkers	4
Enough Space	4.5
Walkability	4.5
Amenities	**3.9**
Driving Range	5
Practice Green	5
Water on Course	3.5
Port-O-Potties	3
Locker Rooms	1.5
Pro Shop	4
Grill & Bar	3
Weather Shelter	3.5
Golf Carts	5
Overall	**4.5**
Enjoyable	5
Challenging / Fair	5
Reservations	3
Scenery	4
Gimmicky Holes	4.5
Weather Monitor	5
Value	**4.5**
Overall	**108.65**

Scorecard and Map:

Including a scorecard from the course gives you a better idea of how the course is laid out. The scorecard includes the yardages for every tee box available as well as the rating and slope from each particular tee box. The maps are not to scale but do show you exactly how to get to the course.

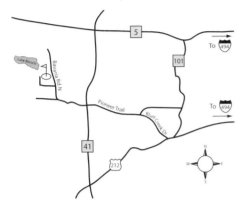

From I-494 take Hwy 5 west 8.25 miles to Hwy 41. Go south 2.5 miles to Pioneer trail. Go west and follow the signs to the course.

Hole by Hole Commentary:

Have you ever played a new course and hit a drive down the middle of the fairway thinking you hit the perfect tee shot, only to find that you are blocked from the green by a tree? How about hitting a blind approach shot to a green only to discover that you hit it on the bottom tier of a two tiered green and the pin is on the top level? The hole by hole commentary is a helpful guide to avoid these situations when playing a course for the first time. The following example shows only the first few holes of a course.

Hole Commentary

1.   A lot of room on the right. Aim just right of bunker on the left at 150 yards FG. Long hitters may want to use a three-wood.
2.   The huge fairway allows plenty of room to swing away on this long par 4. Bunkers on left from 150-100 yards FG. Avoid the deep grass bunker to the right side of green.
3.   A long straight drive can reach the green but beware of woods and greenside pond on left. Smart play is to right of oak tree to 75 yards FG. Bunkers front right of green.
4.   Don't miss short or left of this large green.
5.   Creek on left crosses fairway 150 yards FG. Smart play is to aim for 150 marker to right and hit to between 115-130 yards FG. Green has two tiers.
6.   Long green front to back with bunkers left and right. Wind is always a factor.

In an effort to be consistent most yardages are from the green and denoted by FG. The only exception would be a yardage marked from the men's tee box denoted by FT.

Tee Boxes:

Every hole begins with the tee shot. Having to play from a tee box which matches your ability level is very important. Nothing is more disheartening than seeing the red, white and blue tees with 15 yards of each other hole after hole. The perspective you get from the tee box as well as the condition of the tee box are extremely important to any golfer's confidence level. If you feel like you know where you want to hit the ball and get a good look at it from the tee, your anxiety level drops and you will be more likely to hit a good tee shot. Getting off the tee well makes for a much more enjoyable round.

Ability levels (35%): Every golf course should have at least three separate tees for different player ability levels. The women's tee box should be a separate tee box. Having one long tee box and trying to cram all the different men's and women's ability levels on that tee box is not acceptable. Many courses now have as many as five ability levels with separate tee boxes on most holes for each ability levels. It is important for all golfers to be able to play from a tee box which matches their ability level and it also speeds up the game.

Condition (30%): Tee boxes should be level and preferably elevated to give the golfer a better look at the hole and a feeling of confidence. The women's tee box should be in the same condition as the men's tee box, not just set in the middle of the fairway as an afterthought. The grass should be cut uniformly to a height similar to that of the fairways. The tee boxes should be moved regularly to avoid having too many bare spots or divot holes. You should also be able to tee you ball up without needing a hammer to get the tee in the ground.

Signs (15%): The layout of the course should be accurately depicted whether on the scorecard or signs on the tee box. Showing where things like sand, water, trees and out of bounds are gives a golfer a feeling of how the hole is shaped. Hazards that cross the fairway should be noted, for example "220 yards to the water, 250 to carry." Yardages for each men's and women's ability level should be easy to find. Tee boxes should have an official Center of Green marker which is easily visible, especially on par 3's so you can accurately judge yardages.

Ball Washers (10%): There is no excuse not to have a ball washer on every tee. Since most golfers cannot afford to use a new ball on every hole, having a ball washer ensures that at least they can be clean and look new.

Benches (10%): There should be a bench on every hole. On days when the pace of play is slower and it's hot out, it's nice to be able to sit down and wait instead of standing in the hot sun.

How would you like to stand on the tee box of this hole?
The world's longest par 3 is the 270 yard sixteenth at the International Golf Club in Bolton, Massachusetts.

Fairways:

Now that you have teed off it is time to find your ball. The fairway tends to be elusive at times so when you hit the fairway you expect it to be in good condition. Every week professional golfers play on fairways that most golfers would love to be able to putt on. When your ball does stray from the fairway, you should be able to find it without uncovering old cars or other long lost artifacts. None of us qualified for this years' US Open and we do not need the practice. Having rough from which one can reasonably advance the ball is important. Now that you found your ball, how far is it to the hole? Having to spend several minutes searching for a yardage marker wastes time. The course should be marked so you can quickly determine your yardage, which also speeds up play. Along with knowing the yardage, knowing the pin placement is crucial to club selection. For this reason accurate pin indicators are a necessity.

Condition (30%): The fairways should be cut to a uniform height on every hole. Winter kill or diseases are sometimes unavoidable but these areas should be clearly marked and quickly repaired quickly. There should not be any bare patches. When you hit the fairway you want to enjoy the experience.

Yardage Markers (30%): There should at the very least be easily visible markers at 100, 150 and 200 yards. Preferably there would also be markers at 75, 125, 175, 225 and on longer holes 250. All sprinkler heads should be marked and a yardage book is a bonus. GPS and yardage maps on the carts are nice but do nothing for the golfer who likes to walk instead of ride.

Pin indicators (20%): Along with knowing the yardage, it is important that the pins indicate whether the hole is front, middle or back. Some greens are large enough that different hole locations could result in as much as a three club difference in club selection. Color coding the flags is preferable to a flag on the pin indicating hole location. Regardless which system is used, it should be accurate.

Rough (10%): The rough should be cut evenly throughout the course and should be cut to a fair height. The rough is supposed to be less desirable than the fairway, but you should be able to take one or two extra clubs and advance the ball toward the hole. There should be more than one cut of rough, which is a consistent width throughout the golf course.

Watered/Drainage (10%): The course should be properly watered so there are no fairways with dry areas. On the other hand, there should be plenty of drainage so that there is not normally standing water on the course, especially from over-sprinkling.

Who needs a fairway when you hit the ball this far?
The longest officially recorded drive is 406 yards! Jack Hamm of Denver, Colorado accomplished this in 1986 in an official long drive competition.

Greens:

Finally you have reached the green! What could be more frustrating than putting on the first hole and coming up 5 feet short, then going to the second hole and blasting one 10 feet by the hole? Consistency in the condition and speed of the greens is the critical for golfers of all abilities. Professionals putt on greens so consistent and well maintained, most golfers would feel guilty even walking on them. Having greens that roll true and feel like you are putting on a glass surface gives everyone a chance to make more putts. Even if the greens are a little slower, consistency is the key. While some uphill, downhill and sidehill putts are expected, it is nice to have a few straight and level putts also. Playing a course where all of the greens are either postage stamps or national parks is not enjoyable. A good variety of sizes and shapes, all of which match the holes, helps to make the entire round more enjoyable.

Condition (30%): All of the greens should have consistent grass quality and height, with no dead patches. They should be cut at least every other day so they are never spiked up or bumpy. Putts should roll, not bounce to the hole. Old hole locations should be hardly noticeable and well repaired. The key is for all of greens to be consistent.

Speed (30%): This is a constant source of frustration for the average golfer. All of the greens should be similar in speed. Faster greens are the easiest to putt on. If they are a little faster or slower it's okay, as long as they are consistent throughout the course.

Size and Variety (20%): There should be a good variety in the greens with regard to size and shape. No one likes to play greens that are all round carbon copies of each other. Larger, undulating greens put some challenge into the game that most golfers enjoy. The greens should also fit the layout of the hole.

Slope (15%): Once again, variety is important. Having multitiered greens once in a while can add to the enjoyment of a round, but not every hole. All of the greens should have slope and undulations. There should be opportunities to hit putts which are uphill, downhill, left-breaking, right-breaking and others which are more level. Variety is the key!

Fringe (5%): There should be at least one cut of fringe which is well maintained and well defined. The fringe should be about a yard in width and should allow you the option to putt from it.

Don't play quarters on the practice green with these four!
Fewest putts for 18 holes:
Men - 15, by Richard Stanwood and Ed Drysdale.
Women - 17, by Joan Joyce and Beverly Whitaker.

Layout:

Now the major components which go into making an enjoyable golf hole have been discussed, let's step back and look at the overall layout of the golf course. Course layout is often times a determining factor in whether or not a golfer will play a course again. There's nothing more dissatisfying than finishing a round and feeling like you played the same hole eighteen times. Variety is what makes a golf course fun to play. A course which has holes designed to force a player to strategize how they are going to play the hole makes the game challenging yet enjoyable. Playing a round of golf feeling like you need a helmet and riot gear because balls are flying everywhere is not an experience anyone wants to have. A great course layout can often overshadow some shortcomings the course may have.

Interesting holes (50%): Having holes which are longer, shorter, dogleg, have hazards, etc. make a round of golf interesting and more fun! Everyone wants to play holes which are different, scenic, challenging and just plain fun.

      Par 3's (15%) A variety of long, middle and short tee shots.

      Par 4's (20%) A good variety of length, layout and trouble.

      Par 5's (15%) Risk and Reward!

Strategic Trouble (20%): Everyone who loves golf enjoys the challenge of the game. Most golfers will appreciate a course that is challenging yet fair. Having water along one side of a hole is challenging. Putting a bunker in the middle of the fairway between 220 and 260 yards is not challenging but unfair and does nothing to increase the enjoyment of the game. Whenever there is trouble, a golfer should always have a bailout area, where they may not have the best shot but at least it's out of trouble.

Enough Space (15%): Fore! On some courses you hear that more than anything else on the course. The layout of a course should minimize the possibility of hitting someone in another fairway. Too many courses have golfers packed in like sardines.

Bunkers (10%): Whether surrounding a green or strategic placed off the fairway, bunkers are a part of the game. The bunkers should be well placed in a position which penalizes a poor shot, not a good one. All of the bunkers should be well maintained. Playing from a bunker which looks like someone just finished a sand volleyball game is not acceptable. It's hard enough for most golfers to get out of a nice bunker.

Walkability (5%): Every course should be designed to minimize long walks between holes. Golf is a game that is meant to be walked if one is able. Many of the courses which are being built today are forgetting that and have 10 minute walks between holes or actually require the use of a cart.

Whoever laid out this course must have been a masochist!
The longest Golf course in the world is the International Golf Club in Bolton Massachusetts. This par 77 courses measures a whopping 8,325 yards.

Amenities:

All other facets of a course being equal, many golfers will choose a course which offers them amenities that other courses do not. A driving range and practice green are important for most golfers to prepare for the round. Water, other beverages and snacks should be available on the course. Should nature call (or use a megaphone), it should not take an act of God to find a restroom or weather shelter nearby. Many people today play business golf and find that it is much nicer to change clothes in a locker room than the parking lot. Every golf course should have a pro shop with at least the basic essentials, more selection is better. When the round is over, nothing soothes frustrations better than your favorite beverage and something to eat. These may not seem like the most important things a golf course has to offer but not having these amenities could be reason enough not to play a course twice.

Driving Range (25%): The driving range should have good grass to hit balls from and be large enough to accommodate all of the days golfers. Having to wait a long time to hit balls or hitting from mats is no fun.
Putting Green (25%): A must! It should be large enough to accommodate a number of people and be cut the same as the greens on the course. It should also have some sloped areas to simulate conditions on the course.
Water on The Course (15%): There should be water available to drink on at least every third hole. Dehydration can ruin a round very quickly. Coolers placed strategically can serve more than one hole.
Portable Restrooms (15%): There should be at least one per nine holes. When nature calls, it should not be long distance. A restroom should be reasonably accessible (within a five minute walk) from any point on the course and should service multiple holes if possible.
Locker Rooms (10%): Locker rooms are increasingly important since many people rush to the course from work and need a place to chance. Having showers in the locker rooms is a plus.
Pro Shop (5%): Every course should have the basics like balls and gloves. Having a good selection of clubs, shoes and golf apparel is a plus.
Grill/Bar (5%): They should have a good selection at a fair price and should provide prompt service. Having ample seating inside and additional seating outside is important after walking for 18 holes.
Weather Shelters (5%): When weather comes in fast you should be able to get to a shelter on foot or by cart in no more than five minutes.
Golf Carts (5%): There are people who cannot or choose not to walk. The power carts should be in good shape and electric carts are a plus. Running out of gas or battery charge should never happen to anyone.

They better have Dom Perignon in all the water coolers on this course:
The most expensive country club in the world is the Koganei Country Club in Tokyo, Japan. Membership here costs $2,344,000!

Overall:

There are some things which a course does or does not offer that do not fall into other categories, but can be very important. Finishing a round and feeling like you just got beat up is no fun nor is the feeling like the course was too easy. Needing to know the secret handshake or password just to get a tee time is a not good. Viewing nice scenery on the course can make it that much more enjoyable to play.

Enjoyable (30%): This is an overall feeling that we were left with after the round was over. Many things go into determining whether the round was enjoyable.
Challenging/Fair (25%): This is a measure of whether or not the course challenges the golfer without getting ridiculous. Strategic placing of bunkers, hazards, water, etc. can lead to a more enjoyable round. Conversely having challenges which are unfairly placed can lead to a round filled with frustration.
Reservations (15%): For those who like to play different courses, making tee times can be extremely frustrating. City courses who give priority to residents is understandable, but some courses have reservation policies which seem to make it impossible to play their course.
Scenery (15%): This is a bonus. No one wants to look at a junk yard of old cars for three or four holes. Playing a course that offers scenic views of the surrounding area and displays the natural beauty of the course gives a golfer a warm, fuzzy feeling that makes them want to come back
Gimmicky Holes (10%): For instance a par three that measures 160 yards and drops 150 feet without letting you know what the hole actually plays. That does not add to the enjoyment of a round.
Weather Monitor (5%): It is always nice to know if we are going to get rained on out on the course. Having a weather monitor easily visible is a plus. A lightning detector is a must!

Value:

This is a subjective number but it really means what do you get for your money. A course that costs $60 and ranks highly in many of the categories could be considered a decent value, whereas a course which costs $60 but is ranked at or below average may not be a good buy. Money will always be a factor in determining where we golf, but it is never the only factor.

Afton Alps Golf Course

6600 Peller Avenue South
Hastings, MN 55033
651-436-1320
www.aftonalps.com

Course Information

Reservations:	3 days in advance		

2000 Fees:	9	18	Comments
Weekdays	$12.00	$18.00	
Weekends	$15.00	$23.00	
Twilight	N/A	N/A	
Seniors	$11.00	$16.00	Sa,Su $15/$23
Power Cart	$12.00	$21.00	
Pull Cart	$2.50	$2.50	
Club Rental	$7.00	$7.00	
Credit cards	Visa Mastercard		
Checks	Any		
Rain Check	18 hole<5 holes, 9 hole<14 holes		
Other			

Leagues:	Various

Amenities:			
Driving Range	N	Snacks	Y
Putting Green	Y	Grill/Bar	Y
Practice Green	N	Restaurant	N
Spikeless	Y	Locker Room	Y
Proshop	B	Showers	N

Management:	
Manager	Penny Brown
Professional	None

Afton Alps is a golf course with two very different 9 holes. The front nine is quite flat, with the exception of two holes. It is wide open leaving plenty of room for error. The back nine is much shorter but accuracy is more critical. This nine is cut into the slopes of the ski hill and offers some incredible views of the St. Croix valley. The fairways are more narrow, there is much more trouble and there are some significant elevation changes. The scenery on the back nine really make this course. The course is well suited for beginner to intermediate golfers.

Rating   81.53

Course Rating

Tees	Grade 2.28
Ability Levels	1
Condition	2.5
Signs / Hole Maps	2.5
Ball Washers	3.5
Benches	4.5

Fairways	3.15
Condition	2.5
Yardage Markers	3
Pin Indicators	4
Rough	3
Watered / Drainage	4

Greens	3.03
Condition	3
Speed	3
Size and Variety	3
Slope	3.5
Fringe	2

Layout	2.9
Par 3's	3
Par 4's	2.5
Par 5's	2
Strategic Trouble	3
Bunkers	2
Enough Space	5
Walkability	4

Amenities	2.68
Driving Range	1
Practice Green	3
Water on Course	3
Port-O-Potties	3.5
Locker Rooms	3
Pro Shop	1.5
Grill & Bar	4
Weather Shelter	3.5
Golf Carts	3

Overall	3.35
Enjoyable	3
Challenging / Fair	2.5
Reservations	3
Scenery	5
Gimmicky Holes	4
Weather Monitor	4.5

Value	4
Overall	81.53

Hole	Blue	Red	Par	Handicap
1	345	208	4	3
2	175	138	3	15
3	308	267	4	17
4	460	395	5	1
5	332	289	4	13
6	463	395	5	7
7	493	439	5	5
8	295	288	4	9
9	189	160	3	11
Out	3060	2579	37	
10	348	297	4	14
11	282	263	4	12
12	159	146	3	16
13	260	216	4	10
14	328	276	4	4
15	128	115	3	18
16	448	377	5	2
17	304	272	4	8
18	276	260	4	6
In	2533	2222	35	
Total	5593	4801	72	
Slope	110	114		
Rating	67.3	68.1		

Hole Commentary

1. Dogleg is 115 yards FG. OB and trees right with trees left of fairway. Favor left side of fairway from 150-100 yards FG, past that and you're down a hill.
2. Bunker front left with water long and right.
3. Bunker on the left side of the fairway about 100 yards FG. Bunkers front left and right of the green.
4. Pond on the right 200 yards FT with OB right also. Favor left side of fairway. Inside 225 yards you can see the hole. Fairway opens up from 200-150 yards FG and slopes to the left. Bunker left of the green.
5. Wide open driving hole with OB far left by the road. Bunker front right so don't miss right.
6. Very open driving hole with OB right of the fairway. Bunker front right of green with creek over and right of green.
7. Water on the right from 240 -190 yards FG. Bunker front left of the green with water right of the green.
8. Trees guard left side so favor right side of fairway. There is water if you hit too far right also. Bunker front right of green, no other trouble around the green.
9. Longer par 3 over a creek. Bunker front left with some room to bail out anywhere else.
10. OB along right side of hole so favor left side with plenty of area to hit to. Bunker front right of the green with OB left of the green.
11. Hit your tee shot to 150-120 yards FG and favor the middle to left side of fairway. Downhill approach to a small green with trouble over and left. Favor right side and roll ball onto green.
12. Can't see putting surface. Don't miss right or over, left and short are ok. Hit short of the middle right side and it will roll on the green.
13. Pond to the right at 100 yards FG. Favor left side of fairway and hit to 100-75 yards FG. No room to miss this green. Hit ball short and let it roll on.
14. Hit to the right side toward the birch trees to about 160 yards FG. Hit it short and left it run onto the green, don't miss right.
15. Short par 3 with bunkers short left and right of the green. Can't miss this green anywhere but short. Aim for the middle of the green.
16. Fairway slopes severely left until you get inside 200 yards FG. Safest play is to hit 170 yards to top of hill on right side. Hit your second to the middle to left side of fairway.
17. Aim for the middle to left side of the fairway to about 100 yards FG. Green is tucked behind trees to the right.
18. Don't use the driver. Hit a club that will get you to the dogleg at 150 yards FG. Approach is uphill and requires extra club to reach a wide open green.

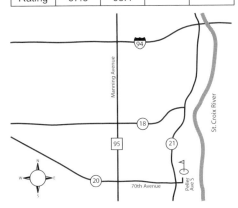

From I-94 take Manning Avenue south 7 miles. Go east on CR 20 for 3 miles. Cross CR 21 and take a left on Peller Avenue South to the course.

Baker National Golf Course

2935 Parkview Drive
Medina, MN 55340
763-473-0800
www.hennepinparks.org/golf/baker

Course Information

Reservations:	3 days in advance		
	www.teemaster.com		
2000 Fees:	9	18	Comments
Weekdays	$18.00	$32.00	
Weekends	$18.00	$32.00	
Twilight	N/A	N/A	
Seniors	$16.00	$27.00	M-Th & F/S/S
Power Cart	$15.00	$25.00	after 3:00
Pull Cart	$3.00	$3.00	
Club Rental	$7.75	$7.75	
Credit cards	Visa Mastercard Discover		
Checks	Any		
Rain Check	18 hole<4 holes, 9 hole<13 holes		
Other	Patron discounts available		
Leagues:	Various		

Amenities:			
Driving Range	Y	Snacks	Y
Putting Green	Y	Grill/Bar	Y
Practice Green	Y	Restaurant	N
Spikeless	Y	Locker Room	Y
Proshop	F	Showers	Y

Management:	
Manager	Jeff May
Professional	Lisa Masters

Baker National sits in the middle of Baker National Park. It is one of only 47 golf courses in the nation to be recognized by Audubon International. The course has blended great golf with maintaining the existing environment. You will see different side of nature on every hole. The scenery on this course can make even a rotten round seem not so bad. The course can be quite challenging if aren't hitting the ball straight. The course will challenge golfers of all ability levels.

Rating   99.55

Course Rating

Tees	Grade 4.4
Ability Levels	4
Condition	5
Signs / Hole Maps	4
Ball Washers	4
Benches	5

Fairways	3.9
Condition	4
Yardage Markers	4
Pin Indicators	4
Rough	3
Watered / Drainage	4

Greens	4.1
Condition	3
Speed	4
Size and Variety	5
Slope	5
Fringe	5

Layout	3.5
Par 3's	3.5
Par 4's	3.5
Par 5's	3.5
Strategic Trouble	4
Bunkers	3
Enough Space	4
Walkability	3

Amenities	3.9
Driving Range	4
Practice Green	5
Water on Course	3
Port-O-Potties	3
Locker Rooms	5
Pro Shop	4
Grill & Bar	3
Weather Shelter	3
Golf Carts	4

Overall	4.35
Enjoyable	4
Challenging / Fair	5
Reservations	3
Scenery	5
Gimmicky Holes	5
Weather Monitor	4

Value	4
Overall	**99.55**

Hole	Black	White	Par	Men Handicap	Yellow	Par	Women Handicap
1	466	440/417	4	3	417/367	5	5
2	159	146	3	17	130	3	15
3	446	425	4	1	378	5	7
4	530	473	5	9	399	5	1
5	348	324	4	15	280	4	13
6	468	447	5	7	382	5	3
7	162	139	3	13	109	3	17
8	396	379/345	4	5	289	4	11
9	409	384	4	11	355	4	9
Out	3384	3157/3100	36		2739/2689	38	
10	512	491/453	5	10	431	5	4
11	410	379	4	2	330	4	10
12	181	150	3	18	130	3	18
13	538	528	5	8	410	5	2
14	422	359	4	4	300	4	8
15	182	180/142	3	12	157	3	14
16	348	328	4	14	274	4	12
17	360	327	4	16	270	4	16
18	425	395	4	6	354	4	6
In	3378	3137/3061	36		2656	36	
Total	6762	6294/6161	72		5395/5345	74	
Slope	135	131			128		
Rating	73.9	71.8			72.7		

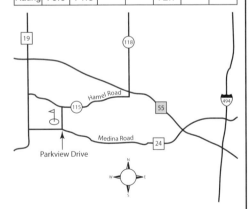

From I-494, take Highway 55 west 2 miles to CR 24. Go west (south) 8 miles to Parkview Drive (CR 201). Go north 1/2 mile, course is on the left.

Hole Commentary

1. Elevated tee shot, avoid right side due to trees. Bunker far left runs from 215-175 yards FG. Multi-tiered green with upper left and lower right portions.
2. Large bunker guards entire front of green and over green is OB. Multi-tiered green.
3. Driving through chute of trees, favor left side of fairway. Bunker on right from 200-175 FG. Large bunker left of green, don't go over.
4. Bunker sits on left side at 300 yards FT on this uphill hole. Two-tiered green is guarded by front bunker. OB over the green.
5. Avoid the marsh on the right. Bunker front right of green with big trouble over.
6. Tough par 5 where accuracy is key. Favor right side of fairway. Marsh runs all the way to hole on right and behind the green. Only bail out is left of this wide but shallow green.
7. You have to know where the pin is on this three-tiered green to avoid impossible putts.
8. Dogleg left with bunker 170-140 yards FG on left side of fairway. Favor right side of fairway. Green slopes front to back so holding the green can be difficult.
9. Blind uphill tee shot to a very wide, forgiving fairway. Aim for center and swing away. Bunker on left at 175 yards FG, the fairway narrows at that point. Bunker guards entire right side of green.
10. Hit away on this par 5 with a good long tee shot allowing you to go for green in two. Green is well-bunkered front, left and right with trees over the two-tiered green.
11. Fairway narrows with longer tee shots, 150 yards being the most narrow, favor right side. Uphill approach requires ½ extra club.
12. Pot-bunkers guard this downhill par 3 green. Water under overhanging tree on left.
13. Marsh on both sides of fairway that pinches in at 250 yards FT on this par 5. Bunker guards right side at 200 yards FG. Small green slopes front to back, long approaches are tough to hold the green.
14. Hitting over a marsh, the widest part of fairway is at 170 yards FG. From 150-110 yards fairway gets very narrow, favor left side.
15. Hitting over a marsh to long, diagonal green. Plenty of green to hit.
16. Dogleg left with marsh along entire left side of hole. Bunkers on right from 100-75 yards FG. Stay to right of pin on approach.
17. Uphill par 4 with bunker on left at 150 yards FG. Multi-tier green with multiple breaks can present a challenge.
18. Great view of the hole from tee box. Bunkers on right at 150 yards FG and left at 125 yards FG pinch fairway. Trees over green and bunker front left of green.

Bellwood Oaks
Golf Course
13239 210th Street East
Hastings, MN 55033
651-437-4141

Course Information

| Reservations: | Weekdays - 5 days in advance |
| | Weekends - 8:00 am Tuesday |

2000 Fees:	9	18	Comments
Weekdays	$12.00	$20.00	
Weekends	$14.00	$23.00	
Twilight	N/A	N/A	
Seniors	$11.00	$18.00	
Power Cart	$12.00	$24.00	
Pull Cart	$2.00	$2.00	
Club Rental	$7.00	$7.00	
Credit cards	Visa Mastercard		
Checks	Any		
Rain Check	Pro-rated		
Other			

| Leagues: | Mon - Thur |

Amenities:			
Driving Range	N	Snacks	Y
Putting Green	Y	Grill/Bar	N
Practice Green	N	Restaurant	N
Spikeless	Y	Locker Room	N
Proshop	B	Showers	N

Management:	
Manager	Dan Raskob
Professional	None

Bellwood Oaks is nestled in a stretch of rolling countryside. The course is fairly wide open but does have it's share of challenges also. There are small to mid-sized trees lining most of the fairways. Water comes into play on a few holes but you can spray the ball without getting in too much trouble on many holes. This is probably the best value in the Twin Cities area and is well worth the drive. The course will challenge golfers of all ability levels.

Rating   90.55

Course Rating

Tees	Grade 3.5
Ability Levels	3
Condition	4
Signs / Hole Maps	3
Ball Washers	4
Benches	4

Fairways	3.3
Condition	3
Yardage Markers	4
Pin Indicators	2
Rough	4
Watered / Drainage	4

Greens	3.05
Condition	4
Speed	2
Size and Variety	3
Slope	3
Fringe	4

Layout	3.25
Par 3's	3
Par 4's	3.5
Par 5's	2
Strategic Trouble	3
Bunkers	3
Enough Space	4
Walkability	5

Amenities	2.35
Driving Range	1
Practice Green	3
Water on Course	3
Port-O-Potties	3
Locker Rooms	2
Pro Shop	2
Grill & Bar	2
Weather Shelter	2
Golf Carts	3

Overall	3.55
Enjoyable	4
Challenging / Fair	3
Reservations	4
Scenery	4
Gimmicky Holes	2
Weather Monitor	4

Value	5
Overall	90.55

Hole	Blue	White	Par Men	Men Handicap	Red	Par Women	Women Handicap
1	387	369	4	8	353	4	8
2	503	482	5	16	462	5	15
3	387	379	4	4	362	4	5
4	160	146	3	10	135	3	17
5	380	372	4	6	242	4	6
6	182	171	3	12	150	3	9
7	301	290	4	18	245	4	18
8	434	409	4	2	312	4	7
9	500	480	5	14	460	5	10
Out	3234	3098	36		2721	36	
10	494	478	5	13	460	5	12
11	393	380	4	5	364	4	4
12	360	352	4	15	291	4	16
13	372	363	4	7	294	4	13
14	481	461	5	17	433	5	11
15	405	387	4	9	306	4	14
16	424	410	4	1	385	5	2
17	226	204	3	3	156	3	1
18	386	374	4	11	297	4	3
In	3541	3409	37		2986	38	
Total	6775	6507	73		5707	74	
Slope	123	121			126		
Rating	72.5	71.2			72.3		

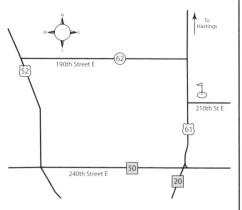

From 494 take Hwy 61 south 20 miles, through Hastings to 210th Street. Go east 1/2 mile to the course.

Hole Commentary

1. Three bunkers guard the fairway to the right on this opening hole but you need to favor the middle to right of the fairway past 170 yards FG for the best approach to the green.
2. Field left, bunkers at 284 yards FG both left and right. Bunker guards green front and along the right. You can run the ball up on the approach shot.
3. Dogleg right, water on right from 170 - 130 yards FG. Bunker right front of green.
4. Keep your tee shot below the hole or face a very quick downhill putt on this uphill par 3.
5. A good tee shot through the opening in the trees will make for a short approach shot.
6. Large bunker guards the entire front and left of this par 3.
7. Favor the right side of this fairway or the trees on the left side of the fairway will block your approach shot.
8. Swing away, bushes on the right are a free drop and the best approach to the green is from the right side.
9. Bunkers at 267 yards FG guard the fairway on this reachable par 5. Hole starts to dogleg right at 150 yards.
10. Water on the right runs from 240 – 150 FG so it is reachable. Two bunkers guard front of green.
11. 90° dogleg right. The fairway runs between the single tree with a ring around it on the right and the two trees with rings around them further ahead to the left. Aim just left of tree with rings on the right and hit it 230 yards FT.
12. Big tree overhangs right side, so aim just left of that tree. A fade is the perfect shot and will set up a short approach.
13. Dogleg right par 4. Smart play is to aim just left of trees and hit to 130-150 yards FG favoring the right side. If you're a long hitter aim over or just right of the tallest tree.
14. Bunker on right from 260 - 240 FG and one on the left at 220 yards FG. Water from 125-100 yards FG on the right. Long fade into hole can reach the green in two.
15. Two bunkers at 160 yards FG guard this straight, up-hill par 4. Take an extra club on your second shot.
16. A little more room on the right than it appears from the tee. Aim for right side of fairway for best approach to green. Once again an extra club may be wise for uphill approach.
17. A bunker short and a hill for a backstop on this long par 3. Be sure you leave the ball below the hole or you will have a very fast downhill putt.
18. Bunkers right at 165 yards FG and the left at 150 yards FG guard the fairway on the home hole. Hit a good drive and you can set yourself up for a nice finish to the round.

Bluff Creek Golf Course

1025 Creekwood
Chanhassen, MN 55318
952-445-5685

Course Information

Reservations:	Weekdays - 1 week in advance
	Weekends - Monday
	www.teemaster.com

2000 Fees:	9	18	Comments
Weekdays	$18.00	$27.00	
Weekends	$18.00	$33.00	
Twilight	N/A	$15.00	After League
Seniors	$12.00	$20.00	M-Th < 3:00PM
Power Cart	$16.00	$28.00	$12/$20 Sr.
Pull Cart	$2.00	$3.00	
Club Rental	$11.00	$17.00	
Credit cards	Visa Mastercard		
Checks	Any		
Rain Check	18 hole<3 holes, 9 hole<12 holes		
Other	M-Th < 9am, 20% discount on		
	greens fees (holidays excluded)		
Leagues:	Mon - Thur		

Amenities:			
Driving Range	Y	Snacks	Y
Putting Green	Y	Grill/Bar	N
Practice Green	N	Restaurant	N
Spikeless	Y	Locker Room	N
Proshop	B	Showers	N

Management:	
Manager	Dave Kirkbride
Professional	None

Set high on the bluffs overlooking the Minnesota River valley, Bluff Creek offers some great views. The course has many elevation changes to challenge golfers. The 12th hole finds golfers hitting over a ravine to a small, well bunkered green. If you hear strange crying noises by the 8th hole, don't call 911 it is just the peacocks. The course was not in the best shape when I played it, but the golf was still good. The course is well suited for beginner to intermediate golfers.

Rating   85.60

Course Rating

Tees	Grade 3.45
Ability Levels	3
Condition	3
Signs / Hole Maps	4
Ball Washers	4
Benches	5

Fairways	3.15
Condition	2.5
Yardage Markers	3
Pin Indicators	4
Rough	3
Watered / Drainage	4

Greens	3.2
Condition	3
Speed	3.5
Size and Variety	3
Slope	3
Fringe	4

Layout	3.3
Par 3's	3.5
Par 4's	3.5
Par 5's	3.5
Strategic Trouble	3
Bunkers	2
Enough Space	4
Walkability	4

Amenities	2.7
Driving Range	4
Practice Green	4
Water on Course	3
Port-O-Potties	1
Locker Rooms	1
Pro Shop	2
Grill & Bar	2
Weather Shelter	1
Golf Carts	3

Overall	3.55
Enjoyable	3
Challenging / Fair	3
Reservations	5
Scenery	3
Gimmicky Holes	5
Weather Monitor	4

Value	3.5
Overall	85.60

Hole	Blue	White	Red	Par	Handicap
1	535	528	453	5	8
2	388	382	339	4	10
3	186	182	149	3	14
4	413	400	302	4	2
5	171	164	129	3	16
6	413	407	359	4	6
7	415	408	350	4	4
8	481	475	382	5	18
9	376	368	324	4	12
Out	3378	3314	2787	36	
10	492	479	381	5	5
11	170	163	135	3	7
12	364	358	312	4	1
13	149	140	111	3	17
14	511	505	447	5	11
15	404	398	328	4	3
16	477	470	427	5	13
17	206	200	145	3	9
18	377	371	325	4	15
In	3150	3084	2611	36	
Total	6528	6398	5398	72	
Slope	119	118	118		
Rating	70.8	70.2	70.7		

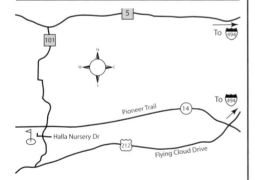

From I-494 take Hwy 5 west 5 miles to Hwy 101 south. Go south 3 miles to Halla Nursery Drive (just past the Halla Nursery on the right.) Course is 1/4 mile on Halla Nursery Drive.

Hole Commentary

1. A big draw over the trees on the left is best shot but brings those trees into play. Safe shot is to hug trees on left and hit the shot 240 yards. Too far and you'll end up down a steep hill. There is a tall pole which marks location of green on downhill approach shot. Take one less club for downhill approach.
2. Favor the center of fairway for the best approach to this uphill par four. Bunker and trees guard the right side of the fairway.
3. Bunkers right and front left of green.
4. Aim just to the right of the trees on the left side of the fairway and avoid trees on the right further up. Don't go long on the approach shot.
5. Downhill par three, wind direction and speed will determine club selection. Swing easy if there is no wind to avoid overshooting green.
6. Trees on the left are OB. Fairway slopes left to right so aim to left side of fairway. Approach shot is long shot, don't go long or left.
7. The bridge is at 150 yards FG with OB left, the fairway ends at 170 yards FG. There normally is no water under the bridge, just long grass which can be hard to hit from. Best shot is to hit tee shot to 160-170 yards FG.
8. Pond on the left is 175 yards FT and runs for about 25 yards. Plenty of fairway to aim for, favor right side of fairway.
9. OB along left side of hole by the road. Favor right side of fairway for best approach to the green. Big gully is 100 yards FG on the left side of fairway so long hitters beware.
10. Favor right side of fairway to avoid being blocked out by trees on the left. Bunkers guard far right side of fairway at about 260 yards FG. Don't go long on the approach.
11. Downhill par three, can't see much of the putting surface. Take a ½ less club.
12. Signature hole requires a tee shot to the left side of the fairway. Anything to the right will be blocked by the trees on the right. No bail-out area on this hole on the approach shot. Miss-hit balls will find trouble.
13. Uphill par 3, take one extra club.
14. Downhill tee shot, favor the right side of the fairway but avoid hitting too far right because of trees. Long hitters beware of the pond at 290 yards FT on the left. Approach shot requires one extra club.
15. Water juts in on right side of the hole at 200 yards FG, runs down right side of the fairway.
16. Pond runs on right side of hole from 290-240 yards FG and bunker on the left at about 270 yards FG.
17. Long par three, running the ball up to the green on the left side is a good play.
18. Bunker on far left side of fairway on this finishing par four. Straight away hole which gives a chance to finish strong.

Braemar Golf Course

6364 John Harris Drive
Edina, MN 55439
952-826-6799

Course Information

Reservations:	1 day in advance		
	www.teemaster.com		
2000 Fees:	9	18	Comments
Weekdays	$18.00	$30.00	
Weekends	$18.00	$30.00	
Twilight	N/A	N/A	
Senior	N/A	N/A	
Power Cart	$14.00	$24.00	$15 single Hcp
Pull Cart	$2.50	$2.50	
Club Rental	$8.00	$8.00	
Credit cards	Visa Mastercard		
Checks	Any		
Rain Check	18 hole<3 holes, 9 hole<12 holes		
Other	Patron discounts available		
Leagues:	Various		

Amenities:			
Driving Range	Y	Snacks	Y
Putting Green	Y	Grill/Bar	Y
Practice Green	Y	Restaurant	Y
Spikeless	Y	Locker Room	Y
Proshop	F	Showers	Y

Management:	
Professional	Joe Greupner
Manager	John Valliere

Braemar is built on 500 acres of rolling hills, scenic lakes and oak ridges. It is easy to forget that you not out in a secluded wilderness, but are only 20 minutes from downtown Minneapolis. There are 27 holes of golf. Each of the three 9 holes offers something different for the golfer. The course is kept in great shape with very nice greens. It can be tough to get a tee time without being a resident of Edina but it is worth trying. Although not overly long, the course is filled with plenty of challenges. The course will challenge golfers of all ability levels.

Rating   101.43

Course Rating

Tees	Grade 4.03
Ability Levels	4
Condition	4
Signs / Hole Maps	3.5
Ball Washers	4
Benches	5

Fairways	3.95
Condition	4
Yardage Markers	3.5
Pin Indicators	4
Rough	4
Watered / Drainage	5

Greens	4.25
Condition	4
Speed	4.5
Size and Variety	4.5
Slope	4
Fringe	4

Layout	4.03
Par 3's	4
Par 4's	4
Par 5's	3.5
Strategic Trouble	4
Bunkers	4
Enough Space	4.5
Walkability	4.5

Amenities	4.25
Driving Range	5
Practice Green	4.5
Water on Course	3.5
Port-O-Potties	3.5
Locker Rooms	5
Pro Shop	4
Grill & Bar	4.5
Weather Shelter	4
Golf Carts	3.5

Overall	3.85
Enjoyable	4
Challenging / Fair	4
Reservations	2
Scenery	4
Gimmicky Holes	5
Weather Monitor	5

Value	4
Overall	101.43

Hole	Blue	White	Red	Gold	Hcp White front/back	Hcp Red front/back	Par Men	Par Women
1	458	445	372	346	5/6	13/14	4	4
2	546	530	395	366	1/2	3/4	5	5
3	179	160	140	120	15/16	17/18	3	3
4	432	426	400	371	3/4	5/6	4	5
5	414	406	376	303	7/8	9/10	4	4
6	411	402	382	370	13/14	11/12	4	4
7	177	165	160	118	17/18	15/16	3	3
8	395	380	330	290	9/10	7/8	4	4
9	488	471	405	364	11/12	1/2	5	5
Red	3500	3385	2960	2648			36	37
10	460	381	359	337	3/4	11/12	4	4
11	343	337	332	297	15/16	9/10	4	4
12	141	120	115	98	17/18	17/18	3	3
13	358	351	335	312	13/14	7/8	4	4
14	485	476	456	406	7/8	1/2	5	5
15	411	396	388	316	1/2	3/4	4	5
16	420	413	384	348	5/6	5/6	4	4
17	236	182	152	119	9/10	15/16	3	3
18	316	300	221	162	11/12	13/14	4	4
White	3170	2956	2742	2395			35	36
19	372	361	322	313	11/12	9/10	4	4
20	181	164	140	128	15/16	15/16	3	3
21	377	351	322	295	7/8	11/12	4	4
22	195	185	164	142	13/14	13/14	3	3
23	511	497	443	404	5/6	5/6	5	5
24	504	484	444	390	3/4	1/2	5	5
25	146	129	101	85	17/18	17/18	3	3
26	388	377	280	213	1/2	7/8	4	4
27	486	468	403	372	9/10	3/4	5	5
Blue	3160	3016	2619	2342			36	36
R/W	6670	6341	5702	5043			71	73
Slope	125	122	126	118				
Rating	71.9	70.4	72.7	69.1				
W/B	6330	5972	5361	4737			71	72
Slope	126	123	120	113				
Rating	70.5	68.8	71.0	68.0				
B/R	6660	6401	5579	4990			72	73
Slope	129	127	125	119				
Rating	72.2	71.0	72.5	69.5				

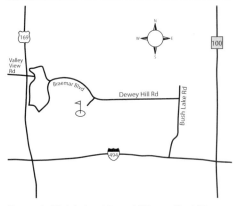

From I-494 take Hwy 169 north 1/2 mile to Valley View Road. Go east to the T in the road and follow the signs to the course. You will be staying on Valley View Road until you hit Braemar Blvd.

Hole Commentary

1. Driving range right of fairway is OB. Water to the right at 100 yards. Bunker front left of green.
2. Water left of the hole from 250 yards FG and cuts close to fairway both left and right at 150 yards FG. Bunker guards front right of green.
3. Medium length par 3 with bunker guarding right side and trouble left and over green.
4. Trees right and left of fairway. Bunker guards front left side of green.
5. Large trees right of fairway and smaller trees left. Avoid big bunker front left side of green.
6. Elevated tee shot with water to the left at 200 yards FG. Water right and over the green with bunkers right and left of green.
7. Longer par 3 over a creek with bunkers guarding front right and left side of the green.
8. Water to the right by the bridge. Aim just left of bunker on right from 170-145 yards FG. Bunkers guard green front left and over.
9. Fairway ends from 200 - 140 yards FG over creek. Bunker front right and far left of the green. Back part of green slopes away.
10. Straightforward tee shot. Bunkers guard front left and right side of this green with a swale in the middle.
11. Have to hit ball to right side of fairway to avoid being blocked by willow tree on left at 100 yards FG. Bunker guards left side of green.
12. Severe downhill par 3 makes club selection crucial. Bunkers guard front left and right of green.
13. Straight par 4 with wetlands on the far right side inside 150 yards FG. Bunker front right of green. Don't miss right or over green.
14. Bunkers left and right of the fairway at 220 yards FG. Favor left side of fairway. Water left of green with bunkers left, right and over green.
15. Bunker on left side of fairway at 200 yards FG. Bunker front left and right of green. Green slopes away from you.
16. Marsh on right side of the fairway. Green protected left and right by bunkers and over by marsh.
17. Hitting over wetland to a well protected green.
18. Tee shot over wetlands and creek with water left of the entire hole. Multiple level green well bunkered.
19. Favor left side on tee shot. Large bunker guards front right side of green. Don't miss long.
20. Slightly downhill par 3 with left side of green protected by bunkers.
21. Aim just left of the trees on the right and hit to 150-100 yard FG. Approach is uphill and requires extra club. Green protected by bunker front right of green with trouble over.
22. Downhill par 3. Wind will determine club selection. Bunkers left, right and over green.
23. Favor left side of fairway to have a chance at the green in two. Trees on right start at 200 yards FT. Bunkers on right side of the fairway inside 200 yards.
24. Tight driving hole with trees and wetlands left and right. Creek cuts across fairway at 150 yards FG. Bunker guards front left side of green.
25. Water surrounds this green and leaves little room for error. Bunkers right and over green.
26. Favor right side of fairway on tight driving hole. Hit your drive to between 200-150 yards FG. Inside that and fairway gets very narrow. Don't miss left or long.
27. Sign tells you distance to water, you can't clear the water. Multi-level green with bunkers guarding front left and right side of green.

Brookview Golf Course

200 Brookview Parkway
Golden Valley, MN 55426
763-512-2300
www.ci.golden-valley.mn.us/brookviewgolf

Course Information

Reservations:	2 days in advance		
	www.teemaster.com		

2000 Fees:	9	18	Comments
Weekdays	$15.50	$28.00	
Weekends	$15.50	$28.00	
Twilight	N/A	$15.50	Sa, Su >3:30pm
Seniors	*	*	w/ patron card
Power Cart	$15.00	$25.00	
Pull Cart	$2.50	$2.50	
Club Rental	$10.00	$14.00	
Credit cards	Visa Mastercard		
Checks	Local Checks Only		
Rain Check	Ask		
Other	Patron discounts available		

Leagues:	Various

Amenities:			
Driving Range	Y	Snacks	Y
Putting Green	Y	Grill/Bar	N
Practice Green	N	Restaurant	Y
Spikeless	Y	Locker Room	Y
Proshop	S	Showers	Y

Management:	
Manager	Kris Tovson
Professional	Jeff Orthun

Brookview is a challenging, mature course with some tree-lined fairways, fairly small greens, and an abundance of water hazards. Bassett Creek flows through the course, crossing six holes. Other water hazards come into play on 11 additional holes. The course is really packed into a small area and is a favorite spot for geese. It is a fairly short course but the water hazards require that you hit the ball straight. If you are not a patron card holder it can be tough to get a tee time. The course is well suited for beginner to intermediate golfers.

Rating   93.68

Course Rating

Tees	Grade 3.5
Ability Levels	3
Condition	3.5
Signs / Hole Maps	4
Ball Washers	4
Benches	4

Fairways	4
Condition	4
Yardage Markers	4
Pin Indicators	4
Rough	4
Watered / Drainage	4

Greens	3.73
Condition	4
Speed	4
Size and Variety	3
Slope	3.5
Fringe	4

Layout	3.78
Par 3's	3.5
Par 4's	3.5
Par 5's	3
Strategic Trouble	4
Bunkers	4
Enough Space	4
Walkability	5

Amenities	3.68
Driving Range	4.5
Practice Green	3.5
Water on Course	3.5
Port-O-Potties	4
Locker Rooms	3
Pro Shop	3
Grill & Bar	3
Weather Shelter	3.5
Golf Carts	3.5

Overall	3.83
Enjoyable	3.5
Challenging / Fair	3.5
Reservations	3
Scenery	5
Gimmicky Holes	5
Weather Monitor	4

Value	3.5
Overall	93.68

Hole	Blue	White	Red	Par	Men Handicap	Women Handicap
1	360	354	330	4	11	9
2	465	460	444	5	9	1
3	544	520	412	5	3	3
4	173	166	120	3	13	15
5	318	310	240	4	17	13
6	375	331	323	4	5	11
7	399	394	363	4	1	5
8	203	193	164	3	7	17
9	308	304	301	4	15	7
Out	3145	3032	2697	36		
10	380	372	345	4	2	6
11	358	351	301	4	12	12
12	159	155	145	3	16	18
13	346	336	326	4	8	8
14	337	324	303	4	14	16
15	561	547	426	5	6	4
16	534	509	475	5	4	2
17	135	126	111	3	18	14
18	414	357	334	4	10	10
In	3224	3077	2766	36		
Total	6369	6109	5463	72		
Slope	127	124	124			
Rating	70.3	69.1	71.4			

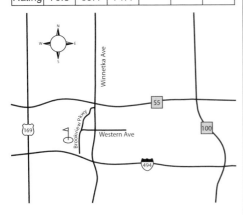

West of Hwy 100 and east of Hwy 169 on Hwy 55. Take Winnetka Avenue south to Brookview Parkway. Go west, the course is 1/2 mile on the right.

Hole Commentary

1. Elevated tee shot with OB along the left and water on the right inside of 100 yards FG. Approaching the green there is a bunker right of the green with water further right.
2. OB along the fence to the left and water to the right in the driving area. Large bunker in front of the green on the left and a smaller bunker front left.
3. OB along the fence to the left but a fairly open driving hole. Two bunkers guard left side of green and one front right. Uphill approach requires extra club.
4. Creek runs in front of green with bunkers right and bunker left of the green.
5. Hitting over a creek, best play is to hit to between 100-80 yards FG. Those who try for green have trees right and left and severe slopes to contend with.
6. Water to the right if you hit drive too far and water far left of fairway. Hit to the 150-100 yard area for best approach to uphill green.
7. Water and trees left and trees right call for accurate drive. Fairway slopes left so favor right side of fairway. Water cuts across fairway in front of green.
8. Longer par 3, slightly downhill. Don't miss this green long.
9. Short par 4 with water to the right of the fairway on the drive and water left from 150 yards to the green. Accuracy more important than length. Bunkers over and right of green.
10. Favor left side of fairway, anything too far right is trouble. Approach is uphill and requires extra club. Bunkers front left and right of green.
11. Water starts 115 yards in front of green and cannot be carried so lay up to a comfortable distance. Two bunkers left and one bunker front right of green.
12. Mid-length par 3 that is well bunkered.
13. Bunkers on the right end at 80 yards FG so stay left. Not much trouble around this two-tiered green, don't go too far right.
14. Aim just right of the water on the left that runs from 150-60 yards FG. Water on the right also from 100-40 yards FG.
15. Elevated tee shot with water to the left of the fairway and plenty of room to the right. Creek crosses the fairway at 130 yards FG. Bunkers front left and right of the green and one back left.
16. Favor left side of fairway as slope kicks everything right. Creek crosses the fairway at 150 yards FG. Approach is uphill and requires extra club.
17. Straight forward par 3 with little trouble around the green.
18. Water both left and right on the tee shot. Water ends at 160 yards FG on the left side. Green well guarded by bunkers left and right.

Bunker Hills
Golf Course

Hwy 242 & Foley Blvd
Coon Rapids, MN 55448
763-755-4141

Course Information

Reservations:	4 days in advance after 9am www.teemaster.com		
2000 Fees:	9	18	Comments
Weekdays	$17.00	$34.00	
Weekends	$17.00	$34.00	
Twilight	N/A	N/A	
Seniors	N/A	N/A	
Power Cart	$13.00	$26.00	
Pull Cart	$3.00	$3.00	
Club Rental	$10.00	$10.00	
Credit cards	Visa Mastercard Discover		
Checks	Any		
Rain Check	18 hole<4 holes, 9 hole<12 holes		
Other			
Leagues:	Wed, Thur		

Amenities:			
Driving Range	Y	Snacks	Y
Putting Green	Y	Grill/Bar	Y
Practice Green	Y	Restaurant	Y
Spikeless	Y	Locker Room	Y
Proshop	F	Showers	Y

Management:	
Manager	Richard Tollette
Professional	Richard Tollette

Bunker Hills is spread out over 290 acres with mature trees lining most holes. Water comes into play on 11 of 27 holes. The course lives up to it's name as the large greens are well-protected by large, well kept bunkers. The tees, greens and fairways are all bent-grass. The course can play as long as 6938 yards for the men and as short as 5509 yards for the women. Bunker Hills plays host to numerous tournaments throughout the year. The course will challenge golfers of all ability levels.

Rating   102.65

Course Rating

Tees	Grade 4.35
Ability Levels	4
Condition	4
Signs / Hole Maps	5
Ball Washers	5
Benches	5
Fairways	**3.8**
Condition	4
Yardage Markers	4
Pin Indicators	3
Rough	4
Watered / Drainage	4
Greens	**4.45**
Condition	5
Speed	4
Size and Variety	4
Slope	5
Fringe	4
Layout	**4.1**
Par 3's	4
Par 4's	4.5
Par 5's	4
Strategic Trouble	4
Bunkers	4
Enough Space	5
Walkability	3
Amenities	**3.85**
Driving Range	3
Practice Green	4
Water on Course	4
Port-O-Potties	4
Locker Rooms	5
Pro Shop	3
Grill & Bar	4
Weather Shelter	4
Golf Carts	4
Overall	**4.1**
Enjoyable	4
Challenging / Fair	4
Reservations	4
Scenery	4
Gimmicky Holes	5
Weather Monitor	4
Value	**4**
Overall	**102.65**

Hole	Blue	White	Gold	Par	Men Handicap	Red	Par	Women Handicap
1	410	390	375	4	5	370	4	2
2	413	386	337	4	2	332	4	3
3	372	358	298	4	6	293	4	9
4	501	479	470	5	4	429	5	4
5	437	414	370	4	1	358	4	1
6	180	160	146	3	8	141	3	8
7	380	361	306	4	7	301	4	5
8	180	160	145	3	9	140	3	7
9	545	525	500	5	3	430	5	6
North	3418	3233	2947	36		2794	36	
10	430	410	395	4	2	390	4	1
11	368	347	283	4	4	278	4	2
12	164	142	135	3	9	96	3	9
13	474	451	446	5	5	405	5	5
14	370	350	335	4	7	330	4	7
15	515	495	480	5	6	475	5	4
16	220	200	185	3	8	180	3	8
17	450	430	400	4	1	320	4	6
18	390	370	355	4	3	350	4	3
East	3381	3195	3014	36		2824	36	
19	425	405	390	4	3	385	4	1
20	530	510	500	5	6	430	5	7
21	195	175	160	3	8	140	3	4
22	360	340	325	4	9	320	4	9
23	550	530	520	5	2	430	5	6
24	440	420	405	4	1	400	5	8
25	400	380	365	4	4	360	4	2
26	240	220	185	3	5	180	3	5
27	380	360	345	4	7	340	4	3
West	3520	3340	3195	36		2985	37	
N/E	6799	6428	5961	72		5618	72	
Slope	132	129	124			131		
Rating	72.5	70.8	68.7			72.2		
E/W	6901	6535	6209	72		5509	73	
Slope	132	129	126			131		
Rating	73:5	71.8	70.3			73.9		
W/N	6938	6573	6142	72		5779	73	
Slope	133	130	126			134		
Rating	73.4	71.8	69.8			73.3		

Hole Commentary

North – East – West (27 holes)

1. Bunker on the left side of fairway from 250-215 yards FG. Best to approach green from right side of fairway, as there is a bunker on the front left.
2. Pronounced dogleg right, lined with pines on all sides. 225 yards to the corner, which you must make. Smart shot is a long iron or 3 / 5 wood off the tee.
3. Very narrow fairway lined with tall trees left and right. Favor left side of fairway to have a chance at green in two. Two dry bowls, front right and left of green prevent you from rolling it on.
4. Easy par 5 if you can maneuver the sharp dogleg right corner at 230 yards FT. At the corner, fairway slopes right, and may prevent you from going for the green in two. Fairway narrows from 150 yards FG in.
5. Tough bending dogleg left with length and narrow approach to green. Hole favors a right-to-left player. Go over small trees at corner to cut some distance.
6. Hitting to a green 46 yards long, so pay attention to pin location. Green is shared with another hole.
7. Slight dogleg left, pines on both sides of fairway. Water short of the 50-yard wide green. Best approach is from right side unless pin position is far right.
8. Water short and left should not be in play. Front right trap will probably cause the most problems.
9. Very wide fairway is forgiving so swing away. Long hitters can reach green in 2 with a good second.
1. Slight dogleg left. Fairway bunkers on both sides of fairway from 200 – 250 yards FT. Green is 50 yards deep.
2. Narrow fairway and a shorter hole may lend itself to an iron off the tee. Green slopes back to front.
3. Very deep green with bunkers front, left and right. Choose the right club and aim for the large green.
4. A short par 5 should allow you to score, just keep the ball in play. Trees on right side and around the green can force you to waste a shot chipping out.
5. Fairway slopes right, toward water. Bunker on left is at 225 yards FT. Approach from left side of fairway.
6. Wide fairway gives you a chance to swing away. Bunker on left from 250 – 200 yards FG. Birdie hole!
7. Green is actually up-hill from tee box. Bunkers at the front right and left will catch short shots.
8. 430 is a long par 4 but fortunately, the fairway is wide open with no trouble.
9. Aim between water on left and bunker on right which meet at about 220 FT. Make it past and it's a piece of cake.
1. Slight dog-leg left. Fairway bunker on the right is 240 FT. Want to approach green from right side.
2. Favor left side off the tee to avoid the water on the right. Fairway bunker on left is 260 yards FT. Hit 2nd shot to left side to avoid front-right bunker.
3. Green is surrounded by bunkers. Play safely to the green and worry about the pin position second.
4. Easiest hole on this 9. Bunker 215 yards FT on left. Bunkers front left and right will catch short shots.
5. Water left off the tee, trees right. Long hitters want to play to left side to have a shot at green in two.
6. #1 handicap hole on this 9, mainly for length. Hole is straight away. OB along the left.
7. OB along the left, water on the right off the tee. Water is 240 yards FT. Approach green straight-up.
8. Carry the water and avoid the bunkers on front left and right. Safe shot is to the left.
9. The two fairway bunkers on each side of the fairway cause problems from 210 – 270 yards FT. A conservative shot plays short of trouble and leaves 150 yards to green.

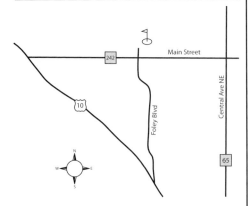

From I-694 take Hwy 65 (Central Avenue) north 9 miles to Hwy 242. Go west 2 1/4 miles to Foley Blvd. Take a right on Foley and follow the signs to the course.

Carriage Hills Country Club

3535 Wescott Woodlands
Eagan, MN 55123
651-452-7211

Course Information

Reservations:	7 days in advance		
2000 Fees:	9	18	Comments
Weekdays	$14.00	$22.00	
Weekends	$16.00	$27.00	
Twilight	N/A	N/A	
Seniors	$10.50	$14.00	M-F < 3pm
Power Cart	$11.00	$22.00	$10/$20 Sr.
Pull Cart	$2.00	$2.00	
Club Rental	$5.00	$5.00	
Credit cards	Visa Mastercard		
Checks	Local Checks Only		
Rain Check	18 hole<4 holes, 9 hole<13 holes		
Other			
Leagues:	Mon - Thur		

Amenities:			
Driving Range	Y	Snacks	Y
Putting Green	Y	Grill/Bar	N
Practice Green	N	Restaurant	N
Spikeless	O	Locker Room	N
Proshop	B	Showers	N

Management:	
Manager	Ronnie Rahn
Professional	None

Carriage hills is a course that could be improved with a little work. The course combines rolling hills with mature trees and a few water hazards. The layout includes some interesting holes like the 16th and some poor ones like the 17th. When I played the course, the bunkers had not been raked recently and the fairways were not in the best condition. There are only two ability levels to tee from. They are making improvement like the addition of a driving range in 2002. The course is well suited for beginner to intermediate golfers.

Rating   76.90

Course Rating

Tees	Grade
	1.9
Ability Levels	1
Condition	2
Signs / Hole Maps	1
Ball Washers	4
Benches	4

Fairways	**2.15**
Condition	2.5
Yardage Markers	2
Pin Indicators	1
Rough	3
Watered / Drainage	3

Greens	**2.95**
Condition	3
Speed	3.5
Size and Variety	2
Slope	3
Fringe	3

Layout	**3.23**
Par 3's	3.5
Par 4's	3
Par 5's	3
Strategic Trouble	3
Bunkers	2
Enough Space	4
Walkability	5

Amenities	**2.55**
Driving Range	1
Practice Green	4
Water on Course	2
Port-O-Potties	4
Locker Rooms	2
Pro Shop	2
Grill & Bar	3
Weather Shelter	1
Golf Carts	3

Overall	**3.1**
Enjoyable	3
Challenging / Fair	2
Reservations	4
Scenery	3
Gimmicky Holes	5
Weather Monitor	3

Value	**3.5**
Overall	**76.90**

Hole	Men	Par	Men Handicap	Women	Par	Women Handicap
1	400	4	4	387	4	4
2	434	5	14	351	5	6
3	148	3	16	138	3	18
4	295	4	18	206	4	16
5	324	4	10	222	4	12
6	508	5	2	399	5	2
7	369	4	8	357	4	8
8	310	4	12	287	4	10
9	183	3	6	158	3	14
Out	2971	36		2505	36	
10	330	4	3	311	4	11
11	370	4	5	357	4	3
12	325	4	15	318	5	5
13	533	5	1	397	5	1
14	146	3	7	134	3	7
15	346	4	13	284	4	15
16	158	3	11	129	3	9
17	430	5	9	410	5	17
18	316	4	17	306	4	13
In	2873	35		2510	36	
Total	5831	71		5015		
Slope	108			109		
Rating	67.2			68.2		

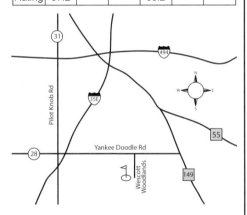

From I-494 take I-35E south 2.25 miles to Yankee Doodle Road. Go east 1.25 miles to Wescott Woodlands. Go south to the course.

Hole Commentary

1. You won't get a good look at the hole until you get inside 130 yards FG. No room to bail out around green

2. Hit too far left on this dogleg left and you'll be blocked out by a tree. Approach is uphill, take at least one extra club. Fairway slopes left so aim for right side. Water on right from 130 - 100 yards FG. A split level green.

3. A downhill par 3 where wind and shot trajectory will determine club selection.

4. The fairway funnels balls toward the middle. No trouble around green.

5. Hole runs along the road and everything slopes to the left so favor right side of fairway. Too far left could lead to an awkward shot. Don't go over this green

6. A blind tee shot with OB along the right. Fairway slopes left to right. Most drives will leave you with a downhill lie. Creek at bottom of hill is at 210 yards FG. Approach shot is uphill.

7. OB along the entire right side of this hole, so be careful not to cut corner too much. The hole turns right at 150 yards FG by the big tree on the right side. Water just left of green.

8. OB along entire right side of this dogleg left par 4. Aim just right of tree on left side. A bunker guards front right portion of green.

9. A very straight forward par 3 with tree trouble over the green

10. Big hitters hit straight away, other aim toward left side of fairway. Hole flattens out at 120 yards. A big bunker front right of green.

11. A dogleg to the left with plenty of room to hit out to the right, if you try to cut corner you could have tree trouble. Green guarded by a small bunker to the right.

12. A tricky hole. It's 174 yards to the water and 293 yards to carry. OB left of the fairway. Aim for right side of fairway and hit to 160 - 130 yards FG. Anything left will be blocked by tree on left side. Don't go right of green.

13. Hit to the right of fairway. Once you get past tree on left, not much trouble. There is a little water on the right side. Approach shot is uphill requiring extra club but don't go long.

14. A nice par 3 that should be an easy par or birdie opportunity. Beware of the wind.

15. Straight forward par 4 with plenty of hitting area. Only trouble is water over the green.

16. Very nice par 3 over water. Bunker guards front right side of green, not a large green.

17. A deceptive par 5, double dogleg. It is 168 to the first dogleg left, 107 to the dogleg right and 146 to the pin from there. The trees make it very hard to cut the corners, play it as a three shot hole.

18. Favor right side of fairway with OB along the left. Green is very open, should be a great chance to end with a birdie if played right.

Cedar Creek Golf Course

5700 Jason Avenue
Albertville, MN 55301
763-497-8245
www.cedarcreekmn.com

Course Information

Reservations:	5 days in advance www.ezlinks.com		
2000 Fees:	9	18	Comments
Weekdays	$16.00	$26.00	9 holes > 3pm
Weekends	$16.00	$32.00	9 holes > 3 pm
Twilight	N/A	N/A	
Seniors	*	*	* see other
Power Cart	$13.00	$26.00	
Pull Cart	$3.00	$3.00	
Club Rental	$5.00	$10.00	
Credit cards	Visa Mastercard Discover AmEx		
Checks	Any		
Rain Check	18 hole<3 holes, 9 hole<12 holes		
Other	Sr.'s 1/2 off greens fees w/ patron card. M-Th < 11am, F-Su >2pm		
Leagues:	Wed, Thur		

Amenities:			
Driving Range	Y	Snacks	Y
Putting Green	Y	Grill/Bar	Y
Practice Green	N	Restaurant	N
Spikeless	Y	Locker Room	N
Proshop	F	Showers	N

Management:	
Manager	Ross Johnson
Professional	Ross Johnson

Cedar Creek is one of the newer courses in the Twin Cities, opening in 1999. There are 19 ponds and 4 carries over wetlands. The course is very short, playing 6060 yards from the back tees. The water hazards, bunkers and some tight fairways require you to be accurate. You will likely be hitting metal woods and long irons instead of your driver on many holes. It is worth the drive to play. The course will challenge golfers of all ability levels.

Rating   99.38

Course Rating

Tees	Grade 4.15
Ability Levels	3.5
Condition	4.5
Signs / Hole Maps	4.5
Ball Washers	4
Benches	5
Fairways	**3.95**
Condition	4
Yardage Markers	3.5
Pin Indicators	5
Rough	3
Watered / Drainage	4
Greens	**4.2**
Condition	4
Speed	4
Size and Variety	4.5
Slope	4.5
Fringe	4.5
Layout	**3.83**
Par 3's	4
Par 4's	3.5
Par 5's	3.5
Strategic Trouble	4
Bunkers	4
Enough Space	4
Walkability	4
Amenities	**3.35**
Driving Range	3.5
Practice Green	4.5
Water on Course	3
Port-O-Potties	3
Locker Rooms	1
Pro Shop	4
Grill & Bar	4
Weather Shelter	3
Golf Carts	4
Overall	**4.23**
Enjoyable	4
Challenging / Fair	4
Reservations	4
Scenery	4.5
Gimmicky Holes	5
Weather Monitor	5
Value	**4**
Overall	**99.38**

Hole	Blue	White	Red	Par	Handicap
1	480	465	410	5	6
2	375	360	305	4	10
3	370	310	300	4	8
4	150	150	80	3	16
5	315	305	240	4	12
6	145	130	100	3	14
7	530	520	460	5	4
8	145	125	100	3	18
9	385	365	315	4	2
Out	2895	2730	2310	35	
10	520	485	450	5	3
11	320	310	250	4	15
12	465	455	395	5	5
13	345	325	275	4	11
14	385	375	335	4	7
15	170	160	105	3	17
16	320	305	270	4	13
17	195	185	155	3	9
18	445	385	270	4	1
In	3165	2985	2505	36	
Total	6060	5715	4815	71	
Slope	117	114	106		
Rating	68.4	66.8	65.4		

Take I-94 north 14.5 miles from the I-694/I-494 interchange to the Albertville exit 202. Go west to CR 19. Go south 1 mile to CR 18. Take CR 18 west 1 mile, the course is on the right.

Hole Commentary

1. Bunkers left and right of fairway from 230 - 210 yards FG. Hazard area to the right of fairway at 150 yards FG. Two bunkers guard right side of green.
2. OB along left side of the hole. At 120 yards FG on the right there is a small area of water. A steep hill with OB awaits you over the green.
3. Water on left from 170 - 15 yards FG. Bunkers on right from 150 - 80 yards FG. Past the bunkers on the right is a marsh area. Bunker guards left side of green.
4. Woods guard left side of hole, bunker front of the hole. Don't go left of this long green.
5. OB along right side of the hole with plenty of room to the left. Bunkers left and right of the green with OB right of the green.
6. Two bunkers guard left side of hole and water sits over and left of green on this par 3.
7. Driving range on left is OB. Bunker on left from 270 - 240 FG. Bunker on right at 110 yards FG. Two bunkers guard left of green and prevent running ball onto green. Water over the green and trouble right of the green.
8. Big bunker guards front left side of multi-tiered green. Water over the green.
9. Water all along left side of hole up to 20 yards FG. Don't go over or left of green.
10. Water on left ends at 220 yards FG. Water on right from 250 - 140 yards FG. Water on left again from 100 yards to the green prevents running ball onto green. On second shot, aim toward left side of fairway. Bunkers right of green and a pot bunker front left of green.
11. Aim over or just right of bunkers on left from 150 - 100 yards FG. OB along entire left side of hole. Two bunkers left, one bunker right of green. Water long and right.
12. Hitting over a marsh that also runs along the entire left side of the hole. Bunker on right from 240 - 200 yards FG. Marsh cuts close to fairway at 100 yards FG. Bunkers right and left of green with water left and over.
13. Water along the left side of the hole. Bunker on left from 105 to 80 yards FG. Marsh both left and right of the green.
14. Bunker on left from 160 - 120 yards FG. Marsh cuts close to hole at 100 yards FG. Bunker guards right side of green.
15. Multi-tiered green with the back portion sloping away from you toward the marsh.
16. Water on left side of hole from 150 yards to the hole. Aim just right of 150 stake, don't go left of that. Green slopes away from you.
17. Water left of and over the green. Anything other than short will be trouble.
18. Water along the right ends at 150 yards FG. Water on left starts at 150 yards FG, runs to the hole and gets closer to the fairway as you get closer to the hole.

Chaska Town Course

3000 Town Course Drive
Chaska, MN 55318
952-443-3748

Course Information

Reservations:	4 days in advance		
2000 Fees:	**9**	**18**	**Comments**
Weekdays	$23.00	$45.00	
Weekends	$26.00	$49.00	
Twilight	N/A	$34.00	After 4:30pm
Seniors	N/A	N/A	
Power Cart	$13.00	$26.00	
Pull Cart	$2.00	$3.00	
Club Rental	$8.00	$13.00	
Credit cards	Visa Mastercard		
Checks	Any		
Rain Check	None after 12 holes		
Other	Chaska residents pay 1/2 price		
Leagues:	Tues, Wed		

Amenities:			
Driving Range	Y	Snacks	Y
Putting Green	Y	Grill/Bar	Y
Practice Green	Y	Restaurant	Y
Spikeless	Y	Locker Room	N
Proshop	F	Showers	N

Management:	
Professional	David Cahill
Manager	David Cahill

Chaska Town Course is a very challenging and well laid out golf course surrounded by native grasslands and flowers. Driving accuracy is a premium on this course. Long hitters may be rewarded with short approach shots but stray from the beautifully kept fairways and the rough will get you. Playing this course intelligently will make for a very enjoyable round. This is one of my favorite courses to play in the Twin Cities Area. The course will challenge golfers of all ability levels, however, beginning golfers may find this course a struggle.

Rating   108.65

Course Rating

	Grade
Tees	**4.45**
Ability Levels	5
Condition	4.5
Signs / Hole Maps	3
Ball Washers	4
Benches	5
Fairways	**4.25**
Condition	5
Yardage Markers	3.5
Pin Indicators	4
Rough	4
Watered / Drainage	5
Greens	**4.68**
Condition	4.5
Speed	4.5
Size and Variety	5
Slope	5
Fringe	4.5
Layout	**4.45**
Par 3's	4.5
Par 4's	5
Par 5's	4.5
Strategic Trouble	4
Bunkers	4
Enough Space	4.5
Walkability	4.5
Amenities	**3.9**
Driving Range	5
Practice Green	5
Water on Course	3.5
Port-O-Potties	3
Locker Rooms	1.5
Pro Shop	4
Grill & Bar	3
Weather Shelter	3.5
Golf Carts	5
Overall	**4.5**
Enjoyable	5
Challenging / Fair	5
Reservations	3
Scenery	4
Gimmicky Holes	4.5
Weather Monitor	5
Value	**4.5**
Overall	**108.65**

Hole	Black	Green	White	Red	Par	Handicap
1	415	388	374	301	4	11
2	451	426	408	330	4	1
3	287	269	254	204	4	13
4	144	124	120	78	3	15
5	351	331	304	253	4	7
6	187	154	146	117	3	17
7	521	500	495	424	5	5
8	403	383	364	295	4	9
9	561	538	511	461	5	3
Out	3320	3113	2976	2463	36	
10	413	394	379	300	4	10
11	453	443	425	336	4	4
12	190	171	162	104	3	18
13	381	358	297	201	4	12
14	217	151	140	100	3	16
15	496	482	472	390	5	8
16	319	299	276	219	4	14
17	481	450	401	310	4	6
18	547	521	510	430	5	2
In	3497	3269	3062	2390	36	
Total	6817	6382	6038	4853	72	
Slope	125	121	118	112		
Rating	73.4	71.4	69.9	69.0		

Hole Commentary

1. Lot's of room on the right. Aim just right of bunker on the left at 150 yards FG. Long hitters may want to use a three-wood.
2. The huge fairway allows plenty of room to swing away on this long par 4. Bunkers on left from 150-100 yards FG. Avoid the deep grass bunker to the right side of green.
3. A long straight drive can reach the green but beware of woods and greenside pond on left. Smart play is to right of oak tree to 75 yards FG. Bunkers front right of green.
4. Don't miss short or left of this large green.
5. Creek on left crosses fairway 150 yards FG. Smart play is to aim for 150-yard marker to right and hit to between 130-115 yards FG. Green has two tiers.
6. Long green front to back with bunkers left and right. Wind always a factor.
7. Favor left side from tee and on approach. Bunkers on right at 290 and 150 yards FG. Safe play is to lay up to 100 yards FG. Bunkers left and waste area right of green.
8. Straightforward hole with bunker on right at 150 yards FG. Avoid left side.
9. Bunker at dogleg is 285 yards FG. Big hitters aim for siren, otherwise stay left of bunker. Approach narrow green from right side. Green protected by three bunkers in front.
10. Bunkers from 190-135 yards FG on the left are definitely in play. Stay below the hole on this green fronted by a bunker.
11. Tough hole requiring a long drive. Favor left to middle of fairway, avoid right side which can be jail. Water runs up to the green on left.
12. Plenty of room to bail out right. Many balls find the bunker in front of green.
13. Play it smart and hit straight shot to 150–120 yards FG. Bunker on left is at 100 yards FG. Green slopes away with hazard right.
14. Bail out left, avoid being short or right.
15. Play it as a three shot hole. Creek crosses fairway from 200-160 yards FG. Hit second shot to 100-75 yards FG. Pond in front of green, so bail out is long and right.
16. Tempting to go for green but even a good long tee shot could end up in trouble. Smart play is to aim over left side of fairway bunker to 80 yards FG.
17. Very long and difficult hole. Avoid bunker on right at 240 yards FG. Three good shots to reach green are better than one bad one. Green is guarded on all sides.
18. Signature hole. Pebble Beach in Minnesota. Play conservative and par is attainable. Get greedy and look out for double digits! Bunkers straight away at 285 yards FG, on right at 250 yards FG and 125 yards FG. Green protected by bunkers left and right and water short.

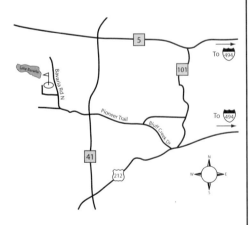

From I-494 take Hwy 5 west 8.25 miles to Hwy 41. Go south 2.5 miles to Pioneer trail. Go west and follow the signs to the course.

Chisago Lakes Golf Course

P.O. Box 529
Lindstrom, MN 55045
651-257-1484
www.chisagolakesgolf.com

Course Information

Reservations:	Weekdays - 6 days in advance Weekend - Tuesday		
2000 Fees:	9	18	Comments
Weekdays	$14.00	$22.00	
Weekends	$17.00	$26.00	
Twilight	N/A	$15.00	After 5 pm
Seniors	$12.00	$19.00	M-Th, 62+
Power Cart	$14.00	$24.00	
Pull Cart	$2.00	$3.00	
Club Rental	$5.00	$7.00	
Credit cards	Visa Mastercard		
Checks	Local Checks Only		
Rain Check	18 hole<3 holes, 9 hole<12 holes		
Other	Patron cards available		
Leagues:	Mon, Tues, Wed, Fri		

Amenities:			
Driving Range	Y	Snacks	Y
Putting Green	Y	Grill/Bar	Y
Practice Green	Y	Restaurant	Y
Spikeless	Y	Locker Room	Y
Proshop	F	Showers	Y

Management:	
Manager	Todd Kueppers
Professional	Todd Kueppers

Chisago Lakes is a well hidden secret for the residents who live nearby. The course is generally in very good condition. The course is set on gently rolling terrain and lined with mature trees. Water comes into play on a number of the holes including the 5th where you hit over water to a green protected by a tree in front. On most holes there is plenty of room to swing away, but a few holes do require very accurate shot making. The course will challenge golfers of all ability levels.

Rating   99.05

Course Rating

Tees	Grade 3.55
Ability Levels	4
Condition	3
Signs / Hole Maps	3
Ball Washers	4
Benches	4

Fairways	3.1
Condition	3
Yardage Markers	2
Pin Indicators	4
Rough	4
Watered / Drainage	4

Greens	3.8
Condition	4
Speed	3.5
Size and Variety	4
Slope	4
Fringe	3

Layout	3.78
Par 3's	4
Par 4's	4
Par 5's	3.5
Strategic Trouble	4
Bunkers	3
Enough Space	4
Walkability	4

Amenities	4.0
Driving Range	5
Practice Green	5
Water on Course	3
Port-O-Potties	3
Locker Rooms	4
Pro Shop	3
Grill & Bar	4
Weather Shelter	3
Golf Carts	4

Overall	3.9
Enjoyable	4
Challenging / Fair	3
Reservations	4
Scenery	4
Gimmicky Holes	5
Weather Monitor	5

Value	5
Overall	**99.05**

Hole	Blue	White	Red	Par	Men Handicap	Women Handicap
1	401	381	335	4	8	6
2	410	400	341	4	4	14
3	498	489	464	5	12	2
4	420	402	366	4	2	8
5	148	134	106	3	18	16
6	345	333	320	4	6	10
7	171	164	139	3	14	18
8	368	363	342	4	16	12
9	498	494	410	5	10	4
Out	3259	3160	2823	36		
10	526	498	433	5	7	3
11	362	350	336	4	15	13
12	360	345	333	4	13	7
13	364	362	328	4	3	5
14	468	464	446	5	1	1
15	186	184	174	3	9	15
16	416	402	346	4	5	9
17	192	154	142	3	17	17
18	396	380	353	4	11	11
In	3270	3139	2891	36		
Total	6529	6299	5714	72		
Slope	119	117	124			
Rating	71.2	70.3	72.7			

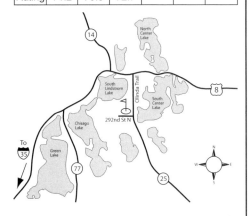

Take I-35 north 5 miles from the I-35W I-35E split to Hwy 8 exit 132. Go east 12 miles to CR 25. Go south 1.2 miles to 292nd Street N. Take a right, the course is on the left.

Hole Commentary

1. OB runs along the left side of hole. Water comes into play on the left from 130 - 75 yards FG and on the far right from 130 - 80 yards FG. Big bunker guards right side.
2. OB along the left side of hole. Slight dogleg left. No real trouble up by the green other than over the green.
3. Bunker on the left side of fairway. Water runs from 80 yards FG on the right all the way behind the green. Don't go right or over green.
4. Blind tee shot over a hill. Water along right side of this hole. Inside 200 yards FG the fairway slopes toward the green and from 150 - 100 yards FG it slopes severely. Water right of the green and a bunker left. OB over the green.
5. Par 3 over water with a tree in front of the green. There is room over tree to hit green.
6. An interesting hole with water along the right side of fairway. Best shot is left side of the fairway around or inside 150 yards FG. Going over the water is no advantage.
7. A long green with water left of green.
8. A dogleg to the right so hit tee shot to left side of fairway. OB runs on right side of fairway. Only real trouble is to right of green.
9. Par 5 heading toward clubhouse. OB along the right side of hole. On your second shot there's water from 100 - 65 yards FG on the right. A big bunker over this green.
10. OB along the entire right side of hole. A straightforward par 5 with no real trouble around the green. Good chance for birdie.
11. Favor left side of fairway. Pond on the right runs from 210 - 150 yards FG. A small, round green with water over and trees to the left.
12. Water just past Women's tee box. A straightforward hole with a bunker guarding the front right of the green.
13. Best shot is to aim toward the 150-yard pole with a little fade. Trees all along right side of the hole. Don't go over or right of green.
14. Dogleg right par 5. Driver not the best shot since some people could hit through the fairway where there is OB. The corner is 260 yards FG. Nothing in front of green, don't go left or over.
15. Long par 3 with a big bunker guarding the front right side of green. Don't go over green.
16. Water to the right off the tee. Aim left of trees on right, plenty of room to the left. Water right of green and over. Bunker guards front left side of green.
17. Uphill par 3 to a very long green. Need to know where the pin is located, could change club selection by one or two clubs. Green slopes severely back to front.
18. Water down the right side from 250 - 220 yards FG. Favor left to center of the fairway. Bunker guards the front left of the green. Don't go over or too far left of green.

Chomonix Golf Course
646 Sandpiper Drive
Lino Lakes, MN 55014
651-482-8484

Course Information

Reservations:	4 days in advance www.ezlinks.com		
2000 Fees:	9	18	Comments
Weekdays	$17.00	$25.00	
Weekends	$17.00	$27.00	
Twilight	N/A	N/A	
Seniors	$12.00	$16.00	
Power Cart	$14.00	$24.00	
Pull Cart	$3.00	$3.00	
Club Rental	$6.00	$10.00	
Credit cards	Visa Mastercard Discover		
Checks	Local Checks Only		
Rain Check	18 hole<4 holes, 9 hole<13 holes		
Other	Patron discounts available		
Leagues:	Mon - Thur		

Amenities:			
Driving Range	Y	Snacks	Y
Putting Green	Y	Grill/Bar	Y
Practice Green	N	Restaurant	Y
Spikeless	Y	Locker Room	N
Proshop	S	Showers	N

Management:	
Manager	Bill Hauck
Professional	Bill Hauck

Chomonix sits in the middle of the Rice Creek-Chain County Regional Park. The course offers the best of nature. You are likely to see wildlife including an occasional fox out on the course. The course is kept in better than average condition, although there were some rough spots. With mature trees and water on a number of holes the course can be challenging. The price is right, the scenery is beautiful and it is well worth playing. The course will challenge golfers of all ability levels.

Rating   99.05

Course Rating

Tees	Grade 3.7
Ability Levels	3.5
Condition	3.5
Signs / Hole Maps	3.5
Ball Washers	4
Benches	5
Fairways	**3.05**
Condition	3
Yardage Markers	3.5
Pin Indicators	2
Rough	3.5
Watered / Drainage	3.5
Greens	**3.9**
Condition	4
Speed	4
Size and Variety	3.5
Slope	4
Fringe	4
Layout	**4.1**
Par 3's	4
Par 4's	4
Par 5's	4
Strategic Trouble	4
Bunkers	4
Enough Space	4.5
Walkability	4.5
Amenities	**3.85**
Driving Range	4
Practice Green	5
Water on Course	3.5
Port-O-Potties	3
Locker Rooms	4
Pro Shop	3.5
Grill & Bar	3.5
Weather Shelter	3.5
Golf Carts	3
Overall	**4.15**
Enjoyable	4
Challenging / Fair	4
Reservations	4
Scenery	4
Gimmicky Holes	5
Weather Monitor	5
Value	**4.5**
Overall	**99.05**

Hole	Blue	White	Red	Par	Men Handicap	Women Handicap
1	525	515	497	5	3	1
2	215	205	143	3	7	15
3	415	403	333	4	5	7
4	469	445	398	5	15	11
5	168	164	118	3	17	17
6	424	404	261	4	1	3
7	387	372	265	4	13	13
8	366	354	289	4	11	9
9	369	357	341	4	9	5
Out	3338	3219	2645	36		
10	378	363	348	4	14	12
11	510	498	443	5	6	6
12	424	389	304	4	4	4
13	182	172	157	3	16	18
14	511	501	440	5	2	2
15	155	148	115	3	18	16
16	335	302	280	4	12	14
17	395	385	375	4	10	8
18	358	348	338	4	8	10
In	3258	3116	2810	36		
Total	6586	6325	5445	72		
Slope	128	125	125			
Rating	72.2	70.9	72.3			

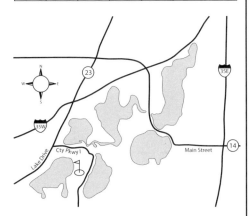

From I-494 take I-35W north 10 miles to CR 23, exit 36. Go south 1.1 miles to Aqua Lane. Go east 1 mile to the course.

Hole Commentary

1.   Bunkers on both side of fairway at 250 yards FG. Left side is all OB. There is a pond to the right of green and a big bunker guards the front right of the green.

2.   Water runs all along the right side of hole. Approaching green, bunker on front left side.

3.   Water runs along the right side of this hole. Big trouble over this green, so don't hit it long.

4.   A difficult driving hole with water along the right side and trees on the left with not a lot of fairway to hit. Bunkers guard the front left and right of the green and over the green is trouble.

5.   The tee box is sheltered on this downhill par 3 so look to the treetops for the wind. Bunkers left and right, over the green is OB.

6.   Blind uphill tee shot with plenty of landing area. Left and right are OB. To the right and over this hole are also OB.

7.   Favor left side of fairway as all balls seem to want to go right. A large bunker sit 10 yards in front of green.

8.   Favor the right side of the fairway since left is all OB on this dogleg left. Don't want to miss this green with trouble all around it.

9.   OB along the entire left side of the fairway on this tricky dogleg right. The corner where the hole doglegs right is at 150 yards FG, you need to stay left if you can't get the ball to that point. OB left and over the green.

10.   Very straightforward hole with a bunker to the right at 200 yards FG. A bunker right of the green and trouble over the green.

11.   A dogleg to the left with OB along the left side of the hole. Avoid the left side on your drive. A bunker guards backside of the green.

12.   Water just off to the right from 150 yards FT up to where the trees start. Multi-tiered green with trouble left and over the green and a large bunker guarding the front right of green.

13.   Nice par 3. Can't go right or long on this hole. A bunker guards the left side of green.

14.   Hitting over a creek, favor left side of the fairway to have a view of the green, otherwise you'll be blocked out by a stand of trees on the right. Left of the fairway is OB. Green is guarded by a bunker on front left and OB over.

15.   Very pretty par 3 to the green surrounded by marsh.

16.   This hole doglegs to the left with houses and OB along the left. There is also water on the left from 180 - 80 yards FG. A bunker guards the front right side of the small green.

17.   Mounds on right help keep errant shots in play on this straight par 4. Plenty of trouble over the green with a bunker guarding the right side of green.

18.   OB along the right side of the hole. Large bunkers guard the front left and right side of green with plenty of room over the green.

Columbia Golf Course

3300 Central Avenue NE
Minneapolis, MN 55418
612-789-2627
www.minneapolisparks.com

Course Information

Reservations:	4 days in advance www.teemaster.com		
2000 Fees:	9	18	Comments
Weekdays	$17.00	$24.00	
Weekends	$17.00	$26.00	
Twilight	N/A	$17.00	After 4 pm
Seniors	N/A	$15.00	w/ Sr. patron
Power Cart	$13.00	$24.00	card
Pull Cart	$2.00	$3.00	
Club Rental	$4.00	$7.50	
Credit cards	Visa Mastercard AmEx Discover		
Checks	Any		
Rain Check	18 hole<4 holes, 9 hole<13 holes		
Other	M-Th < 1pm, w/ 2 or 4-some is $27.50 including cart.		
Leagues:	Mon - Thur		

Amenities:			
Driving Range	Y	Snacks	Y
Putting Green	Y	Grill/Bar	Y
Practice Green	N	Restaurant	N
Spikeless	Y	Locker Room	Y
Proshop	B	Showers	Y

Management:	
Manager	Tim Kuebelbeck
Professional	None

Established in 1919, Columbia Golf Course is one of the oldest in Minnesota. Built on gently rolling terrain, there are many mature trees on the course as well as some smaller trees. A number of holes feature water but much of the course is wide open. The grass is usually in good shape but you may find some dry or bare patches out there. The practice facility is top notch. The course is well suited for beginner and intermediate golfers.

Rating   90.20

Course Rating

Tees	Grade **3.1**
Ability Levels	3
Condition	3
Signs / Hole Maps	2
Ball Washers	3.5
Benches	5

Fairways	**3.5**
Condition	3.5
Yardage Markers	3
Pin Indicators	4
Rough	3.5
Watered / Drainage	4

Greens	**3.65**
Condition	4
Speed	4
Size and Variety	3
Slope	3
Fringe	4

Layout	**3.5**
Par 3's	3.5
Par 4's	3.5
Par 5's	3
Strategic Trouble	3.5
Bunkers	3
Enough Space	4
Walkability	4.5

Amenities	**3.85**
Driving Range	5
Practice Green	3
Water on Course	4
Port-O-Potties	3.5
Locker Rooms	4
Pro Shop	3
Grill & Bar	4
Weather Shelter	4
Golf Carts	3.5

Overall	**3.6**
Enjoyable	3.5
Challenging / Fair	3.5
Reservations	3
Scenery	4
Gimmicky Holes	4.5
Weather Monitor	3.5

Value	**3.5**
Overall	**90.20**

Hole	Blue	White	Red	Par	Men Handicap	Women Handicap
1	379	365	285	4	11	11
2	390	380	248	4	3	5
3	148	129	100	3	17	17
4	513	500	442	5	5	1
5	202	191	154	3	13	13
6	422	407	375	4	1	7
7	504	480	370	5	7	3
8	165	154	137	3	15	15
9	346	336	272	4	9	9
Out	3069	2942	2383	35		
10	340	330	249	4	12	12
11	547	532	476	5	8	4
12	187	170	135	3	16	16
13	410	400	355	4	6	8
14	334	321	305	4	14	14
15	518	508	463	5	4	2
16	450	436	375	4	2	6
17	120	102	100	3	18	18
18	396	380	311	4	10	10
In	3302	3179	2769	36		
Total	6371	6121	5152	71		
Slope	M 122 W 131	M 119 W 128	M 111 W 117			
Rating	M 70.0 W 75.8	M 68.8 W 74.5	M 64.6 W 69.3			

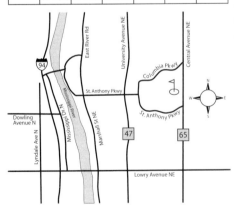

From I-94 take Lowry Avenue east 1.75 miles to Central Avenue NE (Hwy 65). Go north 1 mile, the course is on the left.

Hole Commentary

1. Shorter downhill par 4 with bunker on right side at 150 yards FG that narrows fairway considerably. No trouble around green.
2. Not much trouble on the drive except water far right from 170-120 yards FG. Approach shot to elevated green requires extra ½ club. Bunker guards front right of green.
3. Bunker guards front and right of green and trouble over this par 3.
4. Favor left side of fairway on this par 5. Water from 170-40 yards FG on left side of hole. Don't want to go long or left of the green.
5. Downhill par three with bunker guarding right side and trees over this green.
6. Favor the left side of the fairway on this dogleg left to cut some distance. Water along right side by the hole and over the hole.
7. Water runs along the right side on most of this par 5. Fairly wide open driving hole. Bunkers guard front, right and back of green.
8. Large bunker guards front right of this par 3. Don't go over this green.
9. Dogleg left par 4 with big valley on left side of fairway. Aim up right side of fairway. Fairway turns right at 150 yards FG. Bunker guards front left of green.
10. Favor center to left side of fairway to avoid trees. Tee shot to 120-100 yards FG will put you in great position. Bunker guards left of green and over the green is big trouble.
11. OB on far right side of hole. Marsh on left side of hole runs from 270-100 yards FG. Marsh on right from 230-100 yards FG. Bunkers guard left and right of green.
12. Bunkers guard entire right and left side of the green on this par 3.
13. OB along left side of hole. Water on right from 175-50 yards FG. Bunkers guard right side of green.
14. Past the trees the fairway is fairly wide open with bunker at 100 yards FG on right side. Should be good hole to make birdie on. Bunkers guard left and right of green.
15. Long hitters can favor left side of fairway on this dogleg left. Otherwise favor center to right side to avoid being blocked by trees. Hole turns left at 250 yards FG. Not much trouble approaching green. Bunkers guard front left and right side of green.
16. Elevated tee shot but green is back up the hill. Pond on right side at 240 yards FG. Favor left side of fairway. Approach shot is uphill so take extra club.
17. Large bunkers guard front and front left of green on this par 3. Don't miss this green.
18. Elevated tee box where you can swing away. No problems on second shot. Bunker guards right side of green

Como Golf Course

1431 North Lexington Parkway
St. Paul, MN 55103
651-488-9673
www.ci.stpaul.mn.us/depts/parks

Course Information

Reservations:	Weekdays - 1 week in advance Weekend - Thursday www.teemaster.com		
2000 Fees:	9	18	Comments
Weekdays	$18.00	$25.00	
Weekends	$18.00	$25.00	
Twilight	$16.00	$16.00	after 4 pm
Seniors	*	*	* see other
Power Cart	$15.00	$23.00	
Pull Cart	$3.00	$3.00	
Club Rental	$6.00	$6.00	
Credit cards	Visa Mastercard		
Checks	Any		
Rain Check	18 hole<9 holes, 9 hole<14 holes		
Other	Sr. rates available with resident Sr. card		
Leagues:	Tues, Wed, Thur		

Amenities:			
Driving Range	N	Snacks	Y
Putting Green	Y	Grill/Bar	Y
Practice Green	N	Restaurant	N
Spikeless	Y	Locker Room	Y
Proshop	S	Showers	Y

Management:	
Manager	John Shimpach
Professional	John Shimpach

One of the St. Paul city course, Como Golf Course doubles as a snow tubing area in the winter because of its many hills. Most of the holes feature elevation changes, some of the elevation changes being severe. Because of this, club selection can be difficult. The grass was in average condition when I played it. It seems to be packed into a very small area. The course is well suited for beginner to intermediate golfers.

Rating   87.53

Course Rating

Tees	Grade 3.0
Ability Levels	3
Condition	3
Signs / Hole Maps	2
Ball Washers	4
Benches	3.5
Fairways	**3.45**
Condition	3
Yardage Markers	3.5
Pin Indicators	4
Rough	3
Watered / Drainage	4
Greens	**3.33**
Condition	3.5
Speed	3
Size and Variety	3
Slope	4
Fringe	3.5
Layout	**3.68**
Par 3's	3.5
Par 4's	3.5
Par 5's	3
Strategic Trouble	4
Bunkers	4
Enough Space	4
Walkability	4
Amenities	**2.83**
Driving Range	1
Practice Green	3.5
Water on Course	2.5
Port-O-Potties	2.5
Locker Rooms	5
Pro Shop	4
Grill & Bar	4
Weather Shelter	3
Golf Carts	2.5
Overall	**3.98**
Enjoyable	3.5
Challenging / Fair	3.5
Reservations	5
Scenery	4
Gimmicky Holes	5
Weather Monitor	4
Value	**3.5**
Overall	**87.53**

Hole	Blue	White	Red	Par	Men Handicap	Women Handicap
1	345	337	320	4	9	9
2	325	300	270	4	15	13
3	345	330	288	4	13	7
4	310	304	300	4	17	11
5	335	330	325	4	7	5
6	166	158	129	3	11	17
7	425	410	335	4	1	1
8	515	489	435	5	3	3
9	200	185	140	3	5	15
Out	2966	2843	2542	35		
10	370	360	350	4	6	8
11	287	277	257	4	16	14
12	364	344	295	4	10	12
13	145	135	130	3	18	18
14	364	348	333	4	8	10
15	338	314	276	4	4	6
16	140	128	110	3	14	16
17	355	350	345	4	2	2
18	492	482	439	5	12	4
In	2855	2738	2535	35		
Total	5821	5581	5077	70		
Slope	117	115	115			
Rating	67.6	66.5	69.0			

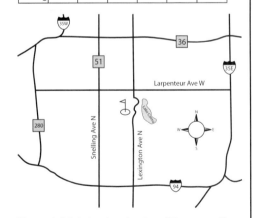

From I-94 take Lexington Pkwy north for 2 miles. The course is on the left in the Como Park area.

Hole Commentary

1. Wide open downhill par 4. Bunkers guard front left and far right side of the green.
2. Hitting on top of a hill. Stray too far from the fairway and you may find yourself 50 feet down the hill. Bunkers left at 130 yards FG and right from 100-80 yards FG. Don't miss green long.
3. Favor left side of the fairway, it slopes left to right. Water right of fairway at 170 yards FG. Approach shot is uphill, take enough club. Bunker guards front right side of green.
4. Favor left side of the fairway to avoid the overhanging tree on the right side. Bunker on left side at 50 yards FG. No good place to miss this green surrounded by bunkers.
5. Aim for the bunker on the left side that runs from 110-90 yards FG. Bunkers guard front left and back right side of green. OB left and over green. Easy to come up short.
6. Downhill par 3 with water along the right side. Not a lot of room to miss this green.
7. Trees along left side of the hole. Approach shot is uphill so take enough club to reach the green guarded by bunkers both left and right.
8. Favor left side of fairway as everything slopes right. Water on right runs from 130 yards to the green. Safe play is to lay-up short of 130 yards. There's room to miss green long or left.
9. Bunkers guard both left and right side of the green on this longer par 3.
10. Trees along left side with a bunker on the right at 150 yards FG. You'll need an extra club to reach elevated green protected by bunkers front left and right of the green.
11. Short, downhill par 4 that can be difficult with a severe uphill approach shot. Not much trouble around this green.
12. OB along the left side of the hole. The hole doglegs left at 150 yards FG. If you hit to left side you must get inside 120 yards FG or be blocked out by trees. Bunkers left and right of the green.
13. Bunkers guard the green left and right.
14. OB left and right of the fairway. Must stay on left side of fairway to have a shot at the green. Hole turns at 150 yards FG. Bunker guards front left of the green.
15. This hole is shaped around the lake on the right side. Avoid the water and it's a short and fairly simple hole. Green is protected by water on almost all sides.
16. Short par 3 with water to the right of the green. There is room to miss left.
17. Uphill par 4 with OB along the right side of the hole. Must hit your tee shot to center of fairway to avoid being blocked by trees.
18. Wide open driving hole on this short par 5. Approach to green is difficult with water in front of and right of green. Not a lot of area to miss around the green

Creeksbend
Golf Course
26826 Langford Avenue
New Prague, MN 56071
952-758-7200

Course Information

Reservations:	5 days in advance
	www.teemaster.com

2000 Fees:	9	18	Comments
Weekdays	$15.00	$23.00	
Weekends	$18.00	$29.00	
Twilight	N/A	$27.00	Incl. pow cart
Seniors	$17.00	$23.00	$18/$29 wkend*
Power Cart	$15.00	$25.00	
Pull Cart	N/A	$4.00	
Club Rental	N/A	$7.50	
Credit cards	Visa Mastercard Discover		
Checks	Any		
Rain Check	Pro-rated		
Other	M-Th < 10:30 am - $27 incudes		
	cart. * Sr. wkend rate includes cart		

Leagues:	Various

Amenities:			
Driving Range	Y	Snacks	Y
Putting Green	Y	Grill/Bar	Y
Practice Green	Y	Restaurant	N
Spikeless	Y	Locker Room	Y
Proshop	F	Showers	Y

Management:	
Manager	Joe Kreuser
Professional	Joe Kreuser

Creeksbend features 230 acres of woodland, rolling hills, a winding creek, numerous bunkers and over 80 acres of ponds and wetlands. The course offers nice scenery and challenging golf. It is not a long course but offers many holes with risk/reward. If you play smart you should shoot a good score and have a fun round. A great old renovated barn serves as the clubhouse where you can enjoy the 19th hole. Well worth the drive. The course will challenge golfers of all ability levels.

Rating   102.85

Course Rating

	Grade
Tees	**4.25**
Ability Levels	4
Condition	4
Signs / Hole Maps	5
Ball Washers	4
Benches	5
Fairways	**3.8**
Condition	4
Yardage Markers	3
Pin Indicators	4
Rough	4
Watered / Drainage	5
Greens	**3.85**
Condition	4
Speed	3
Size and Variety	4
Slope	5
Fringe	4
Layout	**4.1**
Par 3's	4.5
Par 4's	4
Par 5's	3.5
Strategic Trouble	4
Bunkers	4
Enough Space	5
Walkability	4
Amenities	**3.45**
Driving Range	3
Practice Green	4
Water on Course	4
Port-O-Potties	3
Locker Rooms	3
Pro Shop	4
Grill & Bar	4
Weather Shelter	2
Golf Carts	4
Overall	**3.8**
Enjoyable	4
Challenging / Fair	4
Reservations	3
Scenery	4
Gimmicky Holes	4
Weather Monitor	3
Value	**5**
Overall	**102.85**

Hole	Blue	White	Red	Par	Men Handicap	Women Handicap
1	374	331	280	4	7	3
2	450	431	288	5	1	7
3	150	142	121	3	13	9
4	383	361	297	4	3	5
5	343	329	310	4	17	15
6	328	293	216	4	15	17
7	161	152	119	3	9	1
8	356	346	294	4	5	13
9	468	447	398	5	11	11
Out	3013	2832	2323	36		
10	380	359	315	4	12	8
11	513	488	435	5	6	4
12	358	333	267	4	4	2
13	204	195	156	3	2	12
14	449	438	376	5	4	6
15	189	176	106	3	16	14
16	367	342	285	4	18	18
17	396	372	316	4	10	16
18	396	339	287	4	8	10
In	3252	3042	2543	36		
Total	6265	5874	4866	72		
Slope	127	M 124 W 126	114			
Rating	70.0	M 68.3 W 73.4	68.5			

Hole Commentary

1. Plenty of room to drive the ball, just avoid far right which is OB. Creek runs in front of green from left to right so beware.
2. Favor right side of fairway as hill kicks balls left. Second shot is likely a blind shot so aim between the oak trees. The green is large and has many tricky breaks.
3. Uphill par 3 so take a little extra club. Don't go right or come up short.
4. Bunker guards right side of fairway at 150 yards FG, aim for little red building across the road.
5. Bunkers left and right of fairway at 150 yards FG. Aim toward right side of clubhouse on drive. Take less club on approach since it's downhill and long is trouble.
6. Blind tee shot, aim just left of trees by the red tee box on the hill. Approach shot should be short so put it close and avoid left and over.
7. Forget about the trees and other trouble and just hit your 155-yard club.
8. Aim just left of the fairway bunker on the right which is at 170-150 yards FG. Uphill approach so club selection is important.
9. A reachable par 5 with a good drive. Bunker on left at 240 yards FG. Pond on left is 100 yards FG with OB over, approach with a wood or long iron can be difficult.
10. Aim to middle of fairway and let hill kick ball right. Approach is actually downhill so us a little less club and don't go over, it's big trouble.
11. Longest par 5 but still an easy hole with not much trouble. Swamp areas on right and left from 200-160 yards FG. Can't go left or over this green.
12. Best play on this tricky par 4 is to the right of the water and hit it to between 130-100 yards FG for an easy approach.
13. Longer par 3 surrounded by water and usually into the wind. Choose your club wisely.
14. A risk/reward par 5. Favor left side and hit tee shot to top of hill, about 260 yards FT. Marsh starts at 160 yards from the hole. Best play is to hit second shot to right of trees to about 80-50 yards FG. Green surrounded by trees, water and marsh.
15. Easy to leave the ball short especially with wind. With no trouble over, don't under-club.
16. Aim between bunkers at 150 yards FG. A little less club is required on approach with trouble over and a pond on the right side of green.
17. Favor the left side of fairway since hill will kick balls right. Bunker on left at 180 FG. Green is just over hill, over this green is big trouble.
18. Nice finishing hole over the marsh. Favor left side of fairway because of hill. Water on right from 110-80 yards FG. Elevated green requires ½ extra club.

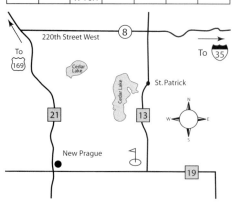

The course is 13 miles south of Prior Lake on Hwy 13. From Hwy 169 take Hwy 21 south 3.3 miles to CR 8. Go east 5.3 miles to Hwy 13. Go south 5 miles, the course is on the right. From I-35 W take CR 70 (turns into CR 8) west 10.5 miles to Hwy 13 then south to the course.

Crystal Lake Golf Club

16725 Innsbrook Drive
Lakeville, MN 55044
952-432-6566
www.crystallakegolf.com

Course Information

Reservations:	3 days in advance		
2000 Fees:	9	18	Comments
Weekdays	$18.00	$26.00	
Weekends	$20.00	$33.00	
Twilight	N/A	N/A	
Seniors	N/A	$21.00	M-Th
Power Cart	$9.00	$13.00	Per person
Pull Cart	$3.00	$4.00	
Club Rental	$7.00	$10.00	
Credit cards	Visa Mastercard Discover AmEx		
Checks	Any		
Rain Check	Pro-rated		
Other			
Leagues:	Tues, Thur		

Amenities:			
Driving Range	Y	Snacks	Y
Putting Green	Y	Grill/Bar	Y
Practice Green	N	Restaurant	N
Spikeless	O	Locker Room	N
Proshop	S	Showers	N

Management:	
Professional	Paul Strande
Manager	Lorie Kjergaard

Crystal Lake is one of the new breed of golf courses being built with large homes surrounding it. The people here really work hard to make you want to come back. I saw the beverage cart out here more than on any other course and the people were friendly. The course was in very good shape with a variety of interesting holes. Water comes into play on 11 of 18 holes so it is no pushover, even though it is not very long. The course will challenge golfers of all ability levels.

Rating   98.75

Course Rating

	Grade
Tees	**4.45**
Ability Levels	5
Condition	4
Signs / Hole Maps	4
Ball Washers	4
Benches	5
Fairways	**3.6**
Condition	4
Yardage Markers	3
Pin Indicators	4
Rough	3.5
Watered / Drainage	3.5
Greens	**4.0**
Condition	4
Speed	3.5
Size and Variety	5
Slope	4
Fringe	3
Layout	**3.75**
Par 3's	4
Par 4's	3.5
Par 5's	3
Strategic Trouble	4
Bunkers	4
Enough Space	5
Walkability	3
Amenities	**3.55**
Driving Range	3
Practice Green	4.5
Water on Course	3.5
Port-O-Potties	4
Locker Rooms	1
Pro Shop	4
Grill & Bar	4
Weather Shelter	3.5
Golf Carts	5
Overall	**4.1**
Enjoyable	4.5
Challenging / Fair	4
Reservations	3
Scenery	4
Gimmicky Holes	5
Weather Monitor	4
Value	**4**
Overall	**98.75**

Hole	Back	Middle	Forward	Par	Men Handicap	Women Handicap
1	490	464	382	5	12	6
2	180	147	110	3	16	10
3	397	369	286	4	4	16
4	396	373	311	4	14	14
5	355	329	269	4	10	12
6	419	389	329	4	2	2
7	334	304	256	4	6	4
8	127	109	94	3	18	18
9	525	492	410	5	8	8
Out	3223	2978	2447	36		
10	366	341	286	4	11	7
11	374	347	364	4	9	9
12	168	146	111	3	15	15
13	516	489	407	5	1	1
14	145	137	107	3	17	17
15	364	335	284	4	13	3
16	380	347	299	4	7	11
17	379	341	291	4	5	5
18	376	366	309	4	3	13
In	3083	2849	2358	35		
Total	6306	5827	4805	71		
Slope	128	124	116			
Rating	70.7	68.6	68.5			

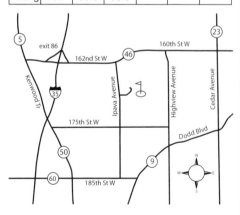

From I-35 take 162nd Street W east 1.1 miles to Ipava Avenue. Go south 0.6 miles to Innsbrook Drive. Go east to the course.

Hole Commentary

1.   Water runs along left side on this par 5, ending at 180 yards FG. Favor left side of fairway. Trees jut in on the right at 160 yards FG. Water on left from 80-40 yards FG. Must fly ball onto green.

2.   Large bunker guards front right and bunker guards over green. Don't go right.

3.   Far right is OB on this dogleg left. Bunkers left and right pinch fairway from 150 - 100 yards FG. Favor left side of fairway. Over green leaves tough recovery shot.

4.   Plenty of room to swing away. Water on right side of hole from 170 yards FG to the green. Bunkers guard entire right side of green.

5.   Candy cane pole marks water on right side of fairway which runs from 150 yards FG to the green. Green guarded by bunkers on left side. Green slopes front to back.

6.   OB runs entire left side of this par 4. Bunkers on left are from 160 - 100 yards FG. Bunkers guard front left and right of green.

7.   Straight uphill par 4. Approach requires extra club to hit this green which breaks in multiple directions.

8.   Short par 3 with a multi-tiered green and a severe slope from right to left.

9.   Bunkers on left and right side of hole end at 230 yards FG. Favor left side of fairway. Water in front right and bunkers on left guard green.

10.   Water on far right side runs from 175 yards FG to the green. Bunker guards left side of long but narrow green.

11.   Hitting over the marsh which ends at 200 yards FG on this par 4. Bunker on left at 150 yards FG, at which point hole doglegs severely left. Don't go over or right of this green.

12.   Well bunkered par three with creek in front to catch short shots. Very long green.

13.   Can be a reachable par 5. Creek cuts across fairway at 220-210 yards FG. Need to hit to 200 yards FG to be safe. Fairway narrows inside 150 yards FG. Favor left side on approach to avoid trees on right.

14.   Very well bunkered green which is deep and at the back slopes front to back.

15.   Trouble all along the left side of this fairway so favor right side. Bunker left and woods right and over this green.

16.   Water on the right at 200 yards FG and a pond to the left at 200 yards FG. Creek runs across fairway at 100 yards FG, stay to the left side of the fairway to avoid the creek.

17.   Bunkers on the right from 130 - 90 yards FG. Long green is guarded by bunkers on the right side.

18.   Bunkers on left at 150 yards FG and on the right at 120 yards FG. Long hitters should aim over top or just right of bunker on left. Bunker on right side of multi-level green.

Dahlgreen Golf Club

6940 Dahlgren Road
Chaska, MN 55318
952-448-7463

Course Information

Reservations:	Weekdays - 5 days in advance Weekend - Wednesday		
2000 Fees:	9	18	Comments
Weekdays	$18.00	$28.00	
Weekends	N/A	$35.00	* see other
Twilight	N/A	N/A	
Seniors	N/A	$16.00	M-Th < 11:30
Power Cart	$15.00	$25.00	$12,$18 Sr.
Pull Cart	$2.00	$4.00	
Club Rental	$5.00	$10.00	
Credit cards	Visa Mastercard Discover AmEx		
Checks	Any		
Rain Check	18 hole<5 holes, 9 hole<14 holes		
Other	* weekends >2pm, $12-9 $28-18.		
Leagues:	Tues, Thur, Fri		

Amenities:			
Driving Range	Y	Snacks	Y
Putting Green	Y	Grill/Bar	Y
Practice Green	N	Restaurant	Y
Spikeless	Y	Locker Room	Y
Proshop	F	Showers	Y

Management:	
Manager	Dave Tessman
Professional	Peer Finstad

Dahlgreen Golf club can be a difficult courses if you are not hitting the ball straight. The course is well kept and grass was in great shape all around the course. Besides great golf Dahlgreen offers you peace and quiet in the countryside. There are a number of elevation changes on the course including the 10th hole with a steep drop and a great view of the surrounding area. Water on 7 holes and numerous bunkers add to the challenge. The course will challenge golfers of all ability levels.

Rating   99.25

Course Rating

Tees	Grade **4.1**
Ability Levels	4
Condition	4
Signs / Hole Maps	4
Ball Washers	4
Benches	5

Fairways	**3.7**
Condition	4
Yardage Markers	3
Pin Indicators	4
Rough	4
Watered / Drainage	4

Greens	**4.3**
Condition	5
Speed	4
Size and Variety	4
Slope	4
Fringe	4

Layout	**3.85**
Par 3's	3
Par 4's	4
Par 5's	4
Strategic Trouble	4
Bunkers	4
Enough Space	4
Walkability	4

Amenities	**3.4**
Driving Range	2
Practice Green	4
Water on Course	3
Port-O-Potties	3
Locker Rooms	5
Pro Shop	4
Grill & Bar	5
Weather Shelter	3
Golf Carts	4

Overall	**4.15**
Enjoyable	4
Challenging / Fair	4
Reservations	4
Scenery	4
Gimmicky Holes	5
Weather Monitor	5

Value	**4**
Overall	**99.25**

Hole	Blue	White	Gold	Red	Par	Men Handicap	Women Handicap
1	346	336	312	302	4	13	9
2	180	165	152	120	3	17	17
3	523	493	448	383	5	7	5
4	375	365	302	262	4	9	7
5	477	465	385	340	4	1	1
6	181	171	155	115	3	15	15
7	506	495	370	355	5	5	13
8	451	416	341	266	4	3	3
9	367	360	344	300	4	11	11
Out	3406	3266	2809	2448	36		
10	373	362	332	328	4	12	14
11	550	525	475	429	5	8	4
12	170	158	140	108	3	14	18
13	417	411	396	320	4	2	8
14	177	170	160	152	3	16	10
15	400	392	375	300	4	10	16
16	414	400	380	351	4	4	2
17	466	460	402	382	5	18	12
18	388	383	362	295	4	6	6
In	3355	3261	3022	2665	36		
Total	6761	6527	5831	5113	72		
Slope	130	128	121	120			
Rating	72.5	71.5	68.3	69.3			

Hole Commentary

1.   Favor middle of fairway to avoid trees on left. Bunker guards front left of green.
2.   Straightforward par 3 with bunker guarding front left of green.
3.   Big dogleg to the right. Aim just left of the trees on the right and hit the ball 230-240 yards FT. Too far or short and you will have tree trouble. No trouble on the approach shot.
4.   Straight away par 4, just swing away. Pond on right runs from 160-130 yards FG.
5.   Very long dogleg par 4. Favor the left side to avoid being blocked out by the trees on the right. The green is downhill so take that into account when selecting club.
6.   Straightforward par three with water in front and bunkers left and right.
7.   Water comes into play on the left side from 225-185 yards FG for long hitters. Only chance to go for green in two is from left side of fairway because of trees on right side of green. The pond in front of green is at 80 yards FG.
8.   Aim for the silo in the distance on this par 4. Bunkers guard the right side of this green.
9.   Shorter par 4 with a bunker guarding the fairway on the right. Favor left side of fairway and don't go over on the approach.
10.   Favor the right side of the fairway on this straight downhill tee shot. OB runs along left.
11.   Swing away on the tee shot for this par 5. Water comes into play on the second shot at 140 yards FG and cuts across the fairway.
12.   Slightly downhill par three with water guarding the front right of the green.
13.   Favor left side of fairway as balls will kick to the right in the fairway. Approach shot is downhill so take a little less club.
14.   Uphill par 3, cannot see the putting surface. Take an extra club, no trouble long.
15.   Straight dogleg right par 4. Bunker on the right at 170 yards FG makes cutting the corner tough. If you decide to cut the corner aim over top of small trees on the right and hit ball to 120 yards FG. Smart play is just to left of trees on the right and hit ball to 160 yards FG.
16.   Dogleg left par 4 with a bunker guarding left side of fairway at 200 yards FG. Best shot is to favor left side of fairway. Green is downhill so take ½ less club than normal. Rolling the ball up to green is not a bad play.
17.   Favor the left side of the fairway on this uphill par 5 to have a shot at the green in two. Narrow chute on the left side of the green allows you to roll the ball on the green. Large bunker guards the entire right side of the green. Over the green is not a problem.
18.   Favor the left of the fairway to avoid trees on the right. Hitting to an elevated green so take an extra club. Do not go right or over the green because of steep hill.

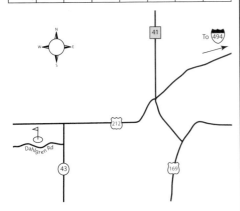

From I-494 go west 15.5 miles on Hwy 212, through Chaska to CR 43. Go south 1/2 mile to Dahlgreen Road. Go west 1/2 mile, the course is on the right.

Daytona Country Club

14730 Lawndale Lane
Dayton, MN 55327
763-427-6110
www.daytonacc.com

Course Information

Reservations:	7 days in advance		

2000 Fees:	9	18	Comments
Weekdays	$17.75	$26.00	
Weekends	$18.00	$30.00	9 hole > 3pm
Twilight	N/A	N/A	
Seniors	$13.00	$16.50	
Power Cart	$7.00	$12.50	
Pull Cart	$2.00	$4.00	
Club Rental	$8.00	$10.00	
Credit cards	Visa Mastercard Discover AmEx		
Checks	Any		
Rain Check	18 hole<5 holes, 9 hole<14 holes		
Other			

Leagues:	Various		

Amenities:			
Driving Range	Y	Snacks	Y
Putting Green	Y	Grill/Bar	Y
Practice Green	N	Restaurant	Y
Spikeless	Y	Locker Room	Y
Proshop	S	Showers	Y

Management:			
Manager	Bruce McCann		
Professional	None		

Daytona Country Club sits in the middle of the countryside and offers peace and quiet to it's golfers. Gentle rolling hills and tree lined fairways create a challenge for golfers. Water comes into play on 10 of the 18 holes with several holes having multiple water hazards. The grass was all in good shape on the course. A brand new clubhouse offers the best in dining and refreshments after a round. The course will challenge golfers of all ability levels.

Rating   91.38

Course Rating

Tees	Grade 3.93
Ability Levels	3.5
Condition	4
Signs / Hole Maps	4
Ball Washers	4
Benches	5

Fairways	3.4
Condition	4
Yardage Markers	4
Pin Indicators	1
Rough	4
Watered / Drainage	4

Greens	3.48
Condition	4
Speed	3.5
Size and Variety	2.5
Slope	3.5
Fringe	4

Layout	3.63
Par 3's	3
Par 4's	3.5
Par 5's	3.5
Strategic Trouble	3.5
Bunkers	3.5
Enough Space	4
Walkability	5

Amenities	3.3
Driving Range	3.5
Practice Green	3.5
Water on Course	2.5
Port-O-Potties	3
Locker Rooms	4.5
Pro Shop	3.5
Grill & Bar	4
Weather Shelter	2
Golf Carts	3

Overall	3.8
Enjoyable	3.5
Challenging / Fair	3
Reservations	5
Scenery	3.5
Gimmicky Holes	5
Weather Monitor	4.5

Value	3.5
Overall	91.38

Hole	Blue	White	Par	Handicap	Red	Par	Handicap
1	513	495	5	9	424	5	8
2	222	172	3	13	160	3	16
3	369	365	4	7	306	4	12
4	577	522	5	11	395	5	6
5	303	294	4	17	273	4	14
6	386	377	4	5	309	4	10
7	389	384	4	3	326	4	4
8	370	358	4	1	286	4	2
9	176	160	3	15	140	3	18
Out	3305	3127	36		2619	36	
10	365	351	4	10	320	4	1
11	401	376	4	2	351	5	15
12	197	152	3	18	134	3	17
13	552	544	5	12	401	5	13
14	404	398	4	4	304	4	7
15	200	176	3	16	167	3	11
16	390	325	4	14	280	4	5
17	549	542	5	6	447	5	9
18	370	361	4	8	342	4	3
In	3428	3225	36		2746	37	
Total	6733	6352	72		5365	73	
Slope	125	121			117		
Rating	71.6	69.8			71.0		

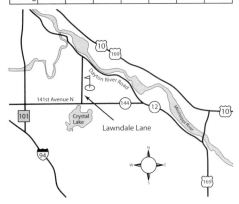

From I-94 take Hwy 101 north 1 mile to 141st Avenue N. Go east 2.4 miles to Lawndale Lane. Go north, the course is on the right.

Hole Commentary

1. Straightforward par 5 with a bunker on the right at 225 yards FG. A bunker guards left side of green, No trouble other than that.
2. Longer par 3, no trouble around the green.
3. Bunker on the left at 150 yards FG. Past 150 yards on the right there is hazard on the right. Two bunkers guard right side of green.
4. OB along right side of the hole but plenty of fairway to aim for. Look at the hole location from the tee since your approach will be a blind shot over the hill to the green which is back down the hill.
5. Dogleg right par 4. Hole is in line with bunker on right at 100 yards FG. The longer you hit a ball, the more directly you can go at the hole. OB right of hole. No room over green.
6. Dogleg left par 4. Favor right side of fairway to avoid tree on left at 150 yards FG. Bunker guards right side of green.
7. Plenty of room to hit left, don't miss right in the hazard. Water right and left of fairway at 50 yards FG. Hazard over the green.
8. Uphill tee shot on this dogleg left. Hit to top of hill to have good look at green. Creek runs in front of green so don't miss short.
9. Bunker guards right portion of green. Trouble also awaits you over the green.
10. It is 240 yards FT to the dogleg, which is protected by two bunkers and a large tree. Approach shot is uphill and requires extra club. Going over green is trouble.
11. 90° dogleg right with no chance to cut the corner. Water along right side of hole. Hole turns right at 150 yards FG and there is hazard left of the fairway to the hole. Approach is severely uphill so take extra club.
12. Longer downhill par 3 with no trouble around the green.
13. OB runs along the entire right side of this dogleg left par 5. Hole turns right at 230 yards FG and OB runs along the left up to the hole.
14. Favor right side of fairway with hazard left. Take extra club on approach to uphill green.
15. Downhill par 3 with trouble over the green. Wind makes it easy to come up short.
16. Uphill par 4 with OB along the entire left side of the hole. Approach is uphill and requires extra club. Bunker guards left side of green. OB over and left of green.
17. Left of the fairway is out of play along most of the hole. Creek crosses fairway at 220 yards FG with marsh both left and right. Approach is again uphill and requires extra club to reach it. Don't go left or over the green.
18. Uphill dogleg right. Must hit your drive to 150 yards FG to get a look at the hole and avoid trees on right. Approach is uphill and requires extra club. Bunker guards front right of green.

Deer Run Golf Club

8661 Deer Run Drive
Victoria, MN 55386
952-443-2351
www.deerrungolf.com

Course Information

Reservations:	5 days in advance
	www.teemaster.com

2000 Fees:	9	18	Comments
Weekdays	$19.00	$29.00	
Weekends	$19.00	$35.00	
Twilight	N/A	$19.00	wknds > 5pm
Seniors	N/A	$25.00	(M-Th < Noon
Power Cart	N/A	$26.00	includes cart)
Pull Cart	$3.00	$3.00	
Club Rental	N/A	N/A	
Credit cards	Visa Mastercard AmEx		
Checks	Any		
Rain Check	9 hole rain check only		
Other	Memberships available		

Leagues:	Tues, Wed, Thur

Amenities:			
Driving Range	Y	Snacks	Y
Putting Green	Y	Grill/Bar	Y
Practice Green	Y	Restaurant	Y
Spikeless	Y	Locker Room	Y
Proshop	S	Showers	Y

Management:	
Manager	Tom Abts
Professional	Tom Abts

Deer run is a well kept course with beautiful homes surrounding it. There are a number of elevation changes to make things interesting. It is not a long course and offers you the chance to score well if you can keep the ball in play. The course offers peace and quiet for a relaxing round of golf. The golf carts are equipped with detailed layouts of the holes. The course is well suited for beginning to intermediate golfers.

Rating   94.80

Course Rating

Tees	Grade 3.6
Ability Levels	3
Condition	4
Signs / Hole Maps	3
Ball Washers	4
Benches	5

Fairways	3.7
Condition	4
Yardage Markers	3
Pin Indicators	4
Rough	4
Watered / Drainage	4

Greens	3.95
Condition	4
Speed	4
Size and Variety	4
Slope	4
Fringe	3

Layout	3.83
Par 3's	4.5
Par 4's	4
Par 5's	3
Strategic Trouble	4
Bunkers	4
Enough Space	4
Walkability	3

Amenities	4.1
Driving Range	4
Practice Green	5
Water on Course	5
Port-O-Potties	4
Locker Rooms	3
Pro Shop	3
Grill & Bar	4
Weather Shelter	3
Golf Carts	3

Overall	3.3
Enjoyable	3
Challenging / Fair	3
Reservations	4
Scenery	4
Gimmicky Holes	3
Weather Monitor	3

Value	3.5
Overall	94.80

Hole	Black	White	Gold	Red	Par	Men Handicap	Women Handicap
1	381	371	311	301	4	15	15
2	156	149	129	129	3	17	17
3	416	401	361	332	4	1	9
4	498	495	444	432	5	7	1
5	383	375	312	312	4	3	5
6	196	186	178	178	3	13	3
7	361	351	305	296	4	5	13
8	472	463	377	377	5	11	11
9	369	353	343	248	4	9	7
Out	3232	3144	2760	2605	36		
10	434	424	325	278	4	2	16
11	361	351	343	343	4	12	2
12	350	340	332	332	4	14	8
13	339	329	244	244	4	10	10
14	184	176	122	122	3	8	14
15	365	361	346	327	4	6	6
16	138	130	123	123	3	18	12
17	317	307	280	280	4	16	18
18	534	519	419	419	5	4	4
In	3022	2937	2534	2468	35		
Total	6254	6081	5294	5073	71		
Slope	122	M 121 W 130	M 115 W 122	119			
Rating	70.3	M 69.5 W 74.8	M 66.5 W 70.7	69.5			

Hole Commentary

1. Aim at the left side of the fairway. Hit tee shot to between 100-130 yards FG. Avoid bunker at 110 yards FG on left side of fairway.
2. Wind determines club selection on this downhill par 3. No wind, one less club. A lot of wind could require 1 or 2 extra clubs.
3. Favor left-center of fairway. Bunkers on left are at 170 and 150 yards FG. Extra club required for approach.
4. Not much trouble except for water on far right side. No reason not to go for green in two, don't go long or too far left because of OB.
5. Favor right side of fairway on tee shot. Take a little extra club on the uphill approach but don't go long because of OB.
6. Easy to leave the ball short when the wind blows on this hole. OB runs far left of hole.
7. Accuracy important on this tee shot. Nothing but trouble right. Safe shot is to hit to about 150 - 140 yards FG.
8. Another reachable par 5 with water on the right and OB on far left side of fairway. Approach shot is difficult to get ball on putting surface because of bunker guarding entire right side of green. Green slopes front to back.
9. Aim tee shot just to the right of the tree on left. Try to hit ball between 150-100 yards FG. Past that more trouble comes into play. Short, right and long all trouble on approach.
10. Uphill par four. Aim just right of bunker on left at 190 yards FG. Uphill approach shot requires one extra club and pay attention to pin placement because of large green.
11. Bunker at 140 yards FG on right and OB far left and right. Favor right side of fairway.
12. No real trouble on this tee shot unless you go way left or right. Better short than long on the approach shot because of trees over green.
13. Tricky downhill hole where tee shot placement is important. Between 150-80 yards FG you will have a tough downhill lie. Either lay-up to 150 yards FG or hit it to 60-80 yards FG, anything past 60 yards will be in the water.
14. Tough uphill par 3, especially with any wind. OB and sand right of hole and OB over.
15. Water all along left side of hole and OB right but the hole opens up to the right when you get past 150 yards FG.
16. Short uphill par 3 that may require extra club depending on the wind. Trouble over.
17. Can get close to this green but bunkers on left from 130 - 110 yards and 65-40 yards FG. OB along right side. Best play is to hit to about 100 yards FG. OB over green.
18. Wide fairway with plenty of landing area. Trees on left, bunker on right at 120 yards FG and water right of that at 100 yards FG make long approach shot difficult. Left of trees on the left is OB.

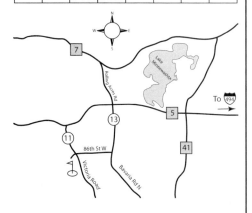

From I-494 take Hwy 5 west 12 miles to CR 11. Go south 3/4 mile, the course is on the right.

Eagle Valley Golf Course

2600 Double Eagle Lane
Woodbury, MN 55129
651-714-3750
www.eaglevalleygc.com

Course Information

Reservations:	3 days in advance www.teemaster.com		
2000 Fees:	9	18	Comments
Weekdays	$17.00	$28.00	
Weekends	$17.00	$31.00	
Twilight	N/A	N/A	
Seniors	*	*	* see other
Power Cart	$16.00	$27.00	
Pull Cart	$3.25	$3.25	
Club Rental	$6.00	$12.00	
Credit cards	Visa Mastercard		
Checks	Any		
Rain Check	18 hole<5 holes, 9 hole<14 holes		
Other	Avail w/ Sr. resident card		
Leagues:	Tues, Wed		

Amenities:			
Driving Range	Y	Snacks	Y
Putting Green	Y	Grill/Bar	Y
Practice Green	N	Restaurant	N
Spikeless	Y	Locker Room	N
Proshop	F	Showers	N

Management:	
Professional	Shaun Peltier
Manager	Shaun Peltier

For those of you who like water, this is a course for you. Water or wetlands come into play on 12 of the 18 holes on Eagle Valley. The course is surrounded by large homes. The greens, fairways and tee boxes were all in very good shape with few bare or dead patches. They have a very large and nice practice facility to hone your skills. Eagle Valley provides very nice scenery as well as great golf. The course will challenge golfers of all ability levels.

Rating   99.70

Course Rating

Tees	Grade 4.3
Ability Levels	5
Condition	4
Signs / Hole Maps	3
Ball Washers	4
Benches	5
Fairways	**4.0**
Condition	4
Yardage Markers	4
Pin Indicators	4
Rough	4
Watered / Drainage	4
Greens	**3.3**
Condition	4
Speed	2
Size and Variety	4
Slope	4
Fringe	2
Layout	**3.98**
Par 3's	4
Par 4's	4.5
Par 5's	3.5
Strategic Trouble	4
Bunkers	3
Enough Space	5
Walkability	4
Amenities	**3.9**
Driving Range	4
Practice Green	5
Water on Course	5
Port-O-Potties	3
Locker Rooms	1
Pro Shop	5
Grill & Bar	3
Weather Shelter	3
Golf Carts	5
Overall	**3.9**
Enjoyable	4
Challenging / Fair	4
Reservations	3
Scenery	4
Gimmicky Holes	4
Weather Monitor	5
Value	**4.5**
Overall	**99.70**

Hole	Black	Blue	White	Red	Par	Men Handicap	Women Handicap
1	537	521	503	456	5	6	6
2	420	402	393	337	4	8	8
3	379	358	338	298	4	12	14
4	419	403	376	317	4	2	2
5	135	125	113	85	3	18	18
6	443	419	391	339	4	4	4
7	170	150	120	97	3	16	16
8	349	335	304	260	4	14	12
9	403	373	361	285	4	10	10
Out	3255	3086	2899	2474	35		
10	502	482	473	422	5	9	7
11	427	410	399	315	4	11	11
12	454	422	363	343	4	1	1
13	179	170	155	127	3	17	17
14	548	525	501	404	5	5	5
15	366	345	317	260	4	15	13
16	204	191	164	148	3	13	15
17	534	519	506	417	5	3	3
18	423	404	381	297	4	7	9
In	3637	3468	3259	2733	37		
Total	6892	6554	6158	5207	72		
Slope	127	124	M 121 W 128	116			
Rating	73.0	71.4	M 69.6 W 74.8	69.5			

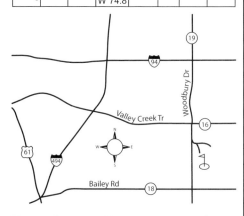

From I-94 take Woodbury Drive (CR 19) 2.7 miles to Eagle Valley Drive. Go east about 2 blocks to Double Eagle Lane. Go south to the course.

Hole Commentary

1.   Straight away opening par 4 with water front and right of the green.
2.   This hole drops off significantly at 150 yards FG. Beware of water over the hill on the right at 100 yards FG and left at 80 yards FG. If you hit from the top of hill take one less club.
3.   Aim just to the right of the trees on the left of the fairway. The first bunker on the left is at 150 yards FG and the second is at 120 yards FG. Water on the right is at 100 yards FG.
4.   Bunker on the right runs from 200-160 yards FG and water on the left starts at 160 yards FG and goes all the way to the hole. Aim at the left side of the fairway.
5.   Bunkers guard the front and back of this wide but shallow green. Take par and run.
6.   Aim for big tree in the distance and you'll be in perfect position on your approach shot. Bunker on the left side grabs a lot of shots.
7.   Trouble abounds if you don't hit this green with water left and a bunker right.
8.   Long hitters can go for this green if they aim over the left edge of the trees on the right. The smart play is to hit the ball to 100 yards FG so you can play a wedge into the green.
9.   There is a swale in the middle of this green so be sure you know where the pin is located.
10.   Water runs all along the right of the fairway so favor the left side on your drive. Beware of the bunker lurking on the left at 250 yards FG.
11.   The trees in the distance are the end of the fairway at 110 yards FG on the dogleg left. Aim at the left side of the fairway and hit a shot to 150-120 yards FG. There is a bunker at 180 yards FG on the left so beware!
12.   Favor the left side of the fairway and avoid the water on the right. Par is a good score.
13.   Wind plays a big factor in club selection. Best play with a lot of wind could be to hit a low shot and roll it up on the green.
14.   Better left than in the trees on the right on this par 5. There is plenty of room to miss around the smaller green if you go for it in two.
15.   Not a very large landing area so hit to 150-100 yards FG. Take an extra club on your uphill approach shot to an undulating green.
16.   Once again the wind will play with the ball on this downhill par 3. Normally hit 1 or 2 less clubs depending on the wind.
17.   Favor the left side of the fairway on this uphill par 5. Trees and a marsh guard the right side from 200 yards FG and in. Take an extra club on your uphill approach shot.
18.   Water on the right is hard to see but runs from 200-120 yards FG. The water on the left ends at 180 yards FG and starts again at 100 yards FG. Can be a tough finishing hole.

Edinburgh USA

8700 Edinbrook Crossing
Brooklyn Park, MN 55443
763-315-8550

Course Information

Reservations:	4 days in advance > 2:00 pm www.ezlinks.com		
2000 Fees:	9	18	Comments
Weekdays	N/A	$45.00	
Weekends	N/A	$45.00	
Twilight	N/A	$21.00	
Seniors	N/A	$33.00	
Power Cart	$15.00	$30.00	
Pull Cart	N/A	$2.50	
Club Rental	N/A	$10.00	
Credit cards	Visa Mastercard		
Checks	Local Checks Only		
Rain Check	Pro-rated		
Other			
Leagues:	Tues		

Amenities:			
Driving Range	Y	Snacks	Y
Putting Green	Y	Grill/Bar	Y
Practice Green	N	Restaurant	Y
Spikeless	Y	Locker Room	Y
Proshop	F	Showers	Y

Management:	
Manager	Donald Berry
Professional	Donald Berry

Opened in 1987, Edinburgh USA is a challenging course that has attracted beautiful neighborhoods. Designed by Robert Trent Jones Jr., the course has hosted numerous LPGA tournaments and has received national acclaim rapidly. The course has an established feel, as mature trees were preserved and incorporated into the holes. Fairways are bent-grass and in excellent condition. Water and bunkers are prevalent on many holes and every fairway seems to slope toward the water. The course will challenge golfers of all ability levels.

Rating   101.25

Course Rating

Tees	Grade **4.55**
Ability Levels	5
Condition	4
Signs / Hole Maps	4
Ball Washers	5
Benches	5

Fairways	**4.1**
Condition	4
Yardage Markers	5
Pin Indicators	3
Rough	4
Watered / Drainage	4

Greens	**4.25**
Condition	4.5
Speed	4
Size and Variety	4.5
Slope	4
Fringe	4

Layout	**3.93**
Par 3's	3
Par 4's	4
Par 5's	5
Strategic Trouble	3.5
Bunkers	4
Enough Space	4
Walkability	4

Amenities	**4.4**
Driving Range	5
Practice Green	5
Water on Course	4
Port-O-Potties	3.5
Locker Rooms	5
Pro Shop	4
Grill & Bar	4
Weather Shelter	3.5
Golf Carts	4

Overall	**3.9**
Enjoyable	5
Challenging / Fair	3
Reservations	3
Scenery	4
Gimmicky Holes	4
Weather Monitor	4

Value	**3.5**
Overall	**101.25**

Hole	Black	Blue	White	Red	Par	Handicap
1	510	492	474	440	5	5
2	193	176	133	93	3	17
3	420	393	360	304	4	3
4	514	484	448	425	5	7
5	335	315	282	258	4	11
6	195	178	141	124	3	9
7	440	404	369	341	4	1
8	165	150	125	101	3	13
9	520	508	486	449	5	15
Out	3292	3100	2818	2635	36	
10	335	313	267	242	4	14
11	435	415	404	376	4	6
12	550	515	479	438	5	10
13	414	390	372	347	4	8
14	203	185	164	123	3	16
15	544	528	482	446	5	2
16	165	145	118	106	3	18
17	394	374	343	317	4	4
18	397	370	352	325	4	12
In	3437	3235	2981	2720	36	
Total	6729	6335	5799	5255	72	
Slope	141	137	132	129		
Rating	73.1	73.1	68.8	70.9		

Hole Commentary

1. Dogleg left. At 250 yards FT, there are trees and bunkers right. A perfect tee shot is a draw between the two. The corridor to the 2-tiered green is lined with trees

2. Elevated green off the back that slopes to trees. Hole difficulty depends on pin placement.

3. Slight dog leg right with water right, bunkers left. Water comes into play closer to the green on the right. Green is 2-tiered.

4. Dogleg right, fairway slopes to water on the right. Bunkers left at 250 yards FT. Play safely off the tee. On approach fairway slopes to water on the left and hill / OB on the right

5. Bunkers line the fairway and surround the green. Aim for elevated fairway left for the best approach to the green.

6. Green is tucked to the right behind water. Trees and sand to the left.

7. Water far left and bunkers and OB to the right. Green is elevated with a bunker in front right and left and trees long. Green is 2 tiered.

8. Water should not come into play unless you are short or right. Bunkers left and right.

9. Straight par 5 with trees far right and a bunker in center of fairway. Aim left of bunker. Avoid large bunker in fairway on second shot. Approach elevated green from left.

10. A longer drive will have leave a short chip to an elevated green surrounded by bunkers.

11. Trees left and right so proper aim is crucial. A fade off tee to left side is ideal. Mounds in the rough all the way down may give you an awkward second shot.

12. Don't go left on the drive or the fairway may kick the ball right in the water. Avoid the bunkers on the left and thick trees on the right on your approach.

13. Straight hole with thick trees right and left. Keep it in play. Don't challenge the thick trees!

14. Straight par 3 with bunkers front right and left. Green slopes back to front.

15. Aim for the left side of the narrow fairway with thick trees to the right. Don't get too close to the large, mature trees on the corner. Bunkers at the corner to catch errant shots. Bunkers front right and left.

16. Steeply elevated green with a very deep bunker on the right. Trouble anywhere but on the green. Don't miss it!

17. Signature hole of the course. Tee shot to an island fairway surrounded with water. Hit a normal drive to fairway. The longer the drive, the shorter the second shot over water to the green. Bunkers short right and long left.

18. Slight dog-leg left with thick trees left and bunkers on the right. Large elevated green shared with 9.

From I-694 take Hwy 252 north 2.9 miles to 85th Avenue N (CR 109). Go west 1.4 miles to Edinbrook Crossing. Go north to the course.

Elk River County Club
20015 Elk Lake Road
Elk River, MN 55330
763-441-4111

Course Information

Reservations:	7 days in advance		
2000 Fees:	9	18	Comments
Weekdays	$17.00	$31.00	
Weekends	$19.00	$34.00	
Twilight	N/A	N/A	
Seniors	$12.50	$18.50	
Power Cart	$13.00	$26.00	
Pull Cart	$3.25	$3.25	
Club Rental	$8.00	$8.00	
Credit cards	Visa Mastercard Discover AmEx		
Checks	Local Checks Only		
Rain Check	18 hole<6 holes, 9 hole<13 holes		
Other	M-Th < 11am - $124 per foursome including carts		
Leagues:	Various		

Amenities:			
Driving Range	Y	Snacks	Y
Putting Green	Y	Grill/Bar	Y
Practice Green	N	Restaurant	N
Spikeless	Y	Locker Room	N
Proshop	F	Showers	N

Management:	
Professional	Kevin Carter
Manager	Kevin Carter

Elk River Country Club offers a relaxing atmosphere just outside the metro area. There is nothing spectacular about the course but it was an enjoyable round of golf. Water comes into play on 10 of the 18 holes. The grass could have been better maintained in spots but overall the course was in good shape. All of the par 5's are relatively short and should afford you the opportunity to score well. The course is well suited for beginner to intermediate golfers.

Rating   99.05

Course Rating

	Grade
Tees	**4.08**
Ability Levels	3.5
Condition	5
Signs / Hole Maps	3
Ball Washers	4
Benches	5
Fairways	**3.4**
Condition	4
Yardage Markers	4
Pin Indicators	1
Rough	4
Watered / Drainage	4
Greens	**3.63**
Condition	4.5
Speed	3.5
Size and Variety	2.5
Slope	3.5
Fringe	4
Layout	**4.0**
Par 3's	4
Par 4's	4.5
Par 5's	3
Strategic Trouble	4
Bunkers	4
Enough Space	4
Walkability	4.5
Amenities	**3.65**
Driving Range	4.5
Practice Green	5
Water on Course	3
Port-O-Potties	3
Locker Rooms	1
Pro Shop	4
Grill & Bar	4
Weather Shelter	3
Golf Carts	4
Overall	**4.13**
Enjoyable	3.5
Challenging / Fair	4
Reservations	5
Scenery	4.5
Gimmicky Holes	5
Weather Monitor	3
Value	**3.5**
Overall	**94.95**

Hole	Blue	White	Par	Handicap	Red	Par	Handicap
1	425	415	4	1	390	5	5
2	170	135	3	17	135	3	17
3	335	320	4	15	275	4	13
4	180	165	3	13	155	3	15
5	470	445	5	5	425	5	1
6	375	350	4	7	325	4	9
7	370	330	4	11	310	4	11
8	510	480	5	3	385	5	3
9	415	400	4	9	395	5	7
Out	3250	3040	36		2795	38	
10	530	510	5	2	415	5	4
11	205	195	3	12	135	3	18
12	380	365	4	8	295	4	12
13	295	290	4	18	275	4	14
14	470	450	5	6	435	5	6
15	180	165	3	16	160	3	16
16	375	365	4	10	355	4	2
17	340	330	4	14	325	4	10
18	455	430	4	4	400	5	8
In	3230	3100	36		2795	37	
Total	6480	6140	72		5590	75	
Slope	121	118			122		
Rating	71.1	69.6			72.3		

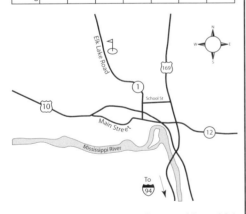

From I-94 go north 7 miles on Hwy 101 to Hwy 10. Go west 1.7 miles to CR 1. Go north 3 miles, the course is on the right.

Hole Commentary

1. Tight driving hole with OB left where the driving range is. The fairway is most level from 150 – 120 yards FG. Green is downhill so take a little less club. Don't go over the green.
2. Short par 3. The green has two tiers, pay attention to the pin location.
3. Short par 4 with hazard along right side of the hole and OB left. Can be an easy hole but being too aggressive will lead to high scores.
4. Slightly uphill par 3 over a small ravine. Plenty of room to miss anywhere but short.
5. Favor left side of fairway, it slopes toward the right. Landing area to the right is at 215 yards FG. Longer hitters may want to hit further left to cut off distance, but accuracy is essential. Need to be on right side of the fairway to have a shot at the green. OB left and over the hole.
6. Favor the left side of the fairway. If you hit too far and to the right you will run out of fairway. Take extra club for the uphill approach shot. Don't go right or long of the green.
7. Avoid hitting too far right as trees line that side of the fairway. Don't miss this green right.
8. Tricky dogleg left which turns left at 200 yards FG. At that point the hazard area on the right cuts closer to the fairway. Water from 90-60 yards FG on the left.
9. Favor the right side of the fairway as it slopes severely to the left. There is area to miss around this green.
10. Dogleg right par 5. Aim just over or left of the trees on the right side. Water both right and left where the fairway starts. Water on the left sits at 125 yards FG. Water over the green.
11. Longer par 3 with a bunker guarding front right side of hole. Don't go too far over.
12. Water on left from 170 - 150 yards FG and again 20 yards in front of green. Not much trouble around green except trees on right.
13. Tree on the right sits at 115 yards FG. Must hit left of the tree to avoid being blocked out from the green. Fairway slopes to the left. Inside of 100 yards FG the fairway slopes down to hole. No room to miss the green.
14. Water on left runs from 240 - 150 yards FG so favor center to right side of fairway. Water along the left side of the green.
15. Longer par 3. Bunkers front left and right of green. Not a lot of room to miss over the green.
16. Favor right side of fairway to avoid water on left from 140 - 80 yards FG. Green surrounded by trees except left of the green.
17. Tight hole with trees left and right in the hitting area. Favor right side of fairway. Past 150 FG the hole opens up slightly. Don't miss green over.
18. Very wide fairway with plenty of landing area so swing away. Don't miss this green long.

Elm Creek Golf Links

18940 Highway 55
Plymouth, MN 55446
763-478-6716

Course Information

Reservations:	14 days in advance		
	www.teemaster.com		
2000 Fees:	9	18	Comments
Weekdays	$15.50	$25.00	
Weekends	$17.50	$29.00	
Twilight	N/A	N/A	
Seniors	$11.50	$18.00	*see other
Power Cart	$14.00	$25.00	
Pull Cart	$2.00	$4.00	
Club Rental	$10.00	$15.00	
Credit cards	Visa Mastercard		
Checks	Any		
Rain Check	18 hole<3holes, 9 hole<12 holes		
Other	Senior rate M-Th anytime, Fri. <		
	11:00am Sa,Su < 3:00 pm		
Leagues:	Mon - Thur		

Amenities:			
Driving Range	N	Snacks	Y
Putting Green	Y	Grill/Bar	Y
Practice Green	N	Restaurant	N
Spikeless	O	Locker Room	N
Proshop	S	Showers	N

Management:	
Manager	Dave Kirkbride
Professional	Dave Kirkbride

Elm Creek combines rolling terrain, mature trees and a meandering creek as a backdrop for golf. On most holes there is plenty of room to hit the fairways and there is not a lot of trouble in front of the greens. There are quite a few elevation changes, especially on the tough downhill par 3 ninth hole. The course is not long but there are areas where you can get into trouble if you don't stay in the fairway. The course is well suited for beginner to intermediate golfers.

Rating   82.10

Course Rating

Tees	Grade
Tees	**3.45**
Ability Levels	3
Condition	3
Signs / Hole Maps	4
Ball Washers	4
Benches	5
Fairways	**2.4**
Condition	3
Yardage Markers	2
Pin Indicators	1
Rough	3
Watered / Drainage	4
Greens	**3.0**
Condition	3
Speed	3
Size and Variety	3
Slope	3
Fringe	3
Layout	**3.35**
Par 3's	3.5
Par 4's	3
Par 5's	2.5
Strategic Trouble	3
Bunkers	4
Enough Space	3
Walkability	5
Amenities	**2.1**
Driving Range	1
Practice Green	2
Water on Course	2
Port-O-Potties	4
Locker Rooms	1
Pro Shop	3
Grill & Bar	2
Weather Shelter	2
Golf Carts	3
Overall	**3.35**
Enjoyable	3
Challenging / Fair	3
Reservations	4
Scenery	3
Gimmicky Holes	5
Weather Monitor	3
Value	**3.5**
Overall	**82.10**

Hole	Blue	White	Yellow	Par	Men Handicap	Red	Par	Women Handicap
1	392	375	360	4	13	335	4	13
2	390	367	350	4	3	340	4	5
3	325	295	275	4	5	265	4	3
4	420/390	385	375	4	7	370	5	11
5	445	442	435	5	17	400	5	7
6	150	135	130	3	11	123	3	15
7	322	300	290	4	15	240	4	17
8	350	343	333	4	1	255	4	9
9	177	162	152	3	9	145	3	1
Out	2971	2804	2700	35		2473	36	
10	350	350	346	4	14	325	4	16
11	380	340	330	4	8	320	4	6
12	161	150	140	3	16	125	3	18
13	630/570	540	500	5	2	375	5	2
14	409	380/360	345	4	10	315	4	10
15	361	342	332	4	12	295	4	4
16	390	375	370	4	6	285	4	12
17	138	132	113	3	18	106	3	14
18	445/410	360	315	4	4	255	4	8
In	3264	2969	2791	35		2401	35	
Total	6235	5773	5491	70		4874	71	
Slope	132	128	126			117		
Rating	70.4	68.8	67.6			68		

Hole Commentary

1. Dogleg left par 4 with plenty of room to bail out so go ahead and swing away.
2. Favor the left side of the fairway to avoid being blocked by the trees on the right on your approach shot. The hill is at 150 yards FG and the bunker on the left is at 80 yards FG.
3. Short, uphill par 4. In order to have a flat lie for your approach shot hit your tee shot to about 100 yards FG or all the way to 40 yards FG, in-between you'll have an uphill lie.
4. Don't go right on this uphill par 4. Favor left side of the fairway for a shorter approach shot.
5. Favor the left side of the fairway to have a straight approach on this downhill par 5 but avoid the bunker on the left at 175 yards FG. Trees right of the hole and water left and long.
6. The 150 yard marker is on the upper tee box. Favor the left side as the hill kicks balls right on this downhill par 3.
7. Tee box and hole are set up to send balls right into bunker at 100 yards FG or the trees. Big hitters may be able to drive the green.
8. The marsh on the left runs from 160-125 yards FG so favor the right side of the fairway. The bunker left is at 125 yards FG but left side of the fairway gives the best angle to the green.
9. Very intimidating downhill par 3. Tee boxes tend to send balls to the right into the creek. Take one less club since it's downhill.
10. Dogleg left so aim just right of the trees on the left and big hitters beware, OB runs along the right side of the hole and is reachable at only 220 yards FT.
11. Hole doglegs 90° right at top of hill with a creek at the bottom. Hit your ball to 160-140 yards FG and favor the left side. Too far right and the trees will block your shot. Approach shot is downhill so take one less club.
12. Don't go left on this downhill par 3. Hitting it right, the hill will kick the ball back to the left.
13. Favor left side of the fairway. The hole is straight so hit down the middle of the fairway on your blind second shot. Bunker guards the front right portion of a green which slopes front to back and has no room over the green.
14. Just avoid the water! Bunkers guard the left and back of the green.
15. Water comes into play on the left with plenty of room to bail out to the right. Water right and bunker left of the green on this hole.
16. The fairway narrows the longer you hit it with OB along the right side. A bunker runs from 140-120 FG on the left. The smart play is to hit to the 150 yard marker favoring the left side of the fairway.
17. Nice downhill par 3. Take one less club.
18. Favor the left side on this tee shot over the meandering Elm Creek. Take an extra half club on the uphill approach shot.

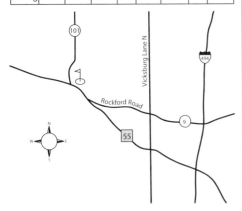

From I-494 take Hwy 55 west 4 miles. Entrance to the course is on the right, just past the bridge.

Falcon Ridge
Golf Course

33942 Falcon Avenue North
Stacy, MN 55079
651-462-5797 or 877-535-9335
www.falconridgegolf.net

Course Information

Reservations:	7 days in advance		
	www.teemaster.com		
2000 Fees:	9	18	Comments
Weekdays	$12.00	$20.00	
Weekends	$14.00	$24.00	
Twilight	N/A	N/A	
Seniors	*	*	* see other
Power Cart	$12.00	$24.00	
Pull Cart	$3.00	$3.00	
Club Rental	$6.00	$6.00	
Credit cards	Visa Mastercard Discover		
Checks	Any		
Rain Check	18 hole<4 holes, 9 hole<13 holes		
Other	Sr. (Age 58+) M-F, $20/golfer w/cart		
Leagues:	Mon - Thur		

Amenities:			
Driving Range	Y	Snacks	Y
Putting Green	Y	Grill/Bar	N
Practice Green	N	Restaurant	N
Spikeless	Y	Locker Room	N
Proshop	S	Showers	N

Management:	
Manager	Patrick Smith
Professional	Patrick Smith

Falcon Ridge offers a variety of hole layouts. Some holes are wide open while other have mature trees or water to catch errant shots. The grass was just in average condition around the course. Overall the course was average but it was enjoyable to play. Since the course is very short, golfers should have the opportunity to score well. The course is well suited for beginner to intermediate golfers.

Rating   85.83

Course Rating

Tees	Grade 2.48
Ability Levels	2
Condition	2.5
Signs / Hole Maps	2.5
Ball Washers	3
Benches	3.5

Fairways	2.85
Condition	3
Yardage Markers	2.5
Pin Indicators	2.5
Rough	3
Watered / Drainage	4

Greens	3.33
Condition	3.5
Speed	3.5
Size and Variety	3
Slope	3
Fringe	3.5

Layout	3.15
Par 3's	3.5
Par 4's	3
Par 5's	2
Strategic Trouble	3.5
Bunkers	2
Enough Space	4
Walkability	5

Amenities	2.63
Driving Range	3
Practice Green	3.5
Water on Course	2.5
Port-O-Potties	3
Locker Rooms	1
Pro Shop	3.5
Grill & Bar	1
Weather Shelter	1
Golf Carts	2.5

Overall	3.55
Enjoyable	3
Challenging / Fair	3
Reservations	5
Scenery	3.5
Gimmicky Holes	5
Weather Monitor	2.5

Value	4.5
Overall	**85.83**

Hole	Back	Front	Women	Par	Men Handicap	Women Handicap
1	334	328	310	4	15	15
2	481	465	421	5	7	7
3	193	179	159	3	11	11
4	287	283	275	4	17	17
5	465	456	356	5	1	1
6	147	141	127	3	9	9
7	318	306	299	4	5	5
8	409	397	352	4	13	13
9	400	383	371	4	3	3
Out	3034	2938	2670	36		
10	481	471	375	5	4	8
11	221	213	197	3	12	12
12	293	287	278	4	16	4
13	234	226	214	4	6	6
14	303	295	281	4	10	16
15	164	158	138	3	18	18
16	299	293	285	4	2	14
17	292	286	276	4	14	2
18	466	460	356	5	8	10
In	2753	2689	2400	36		
Total	5787	5627	5070	72		
Slope	115	114	120			
Rating	68.0	68.0	70.3			

Hole Commentary

1.   Very straightforward hole. Not much trouble in the fairway or around the green.
2.   There's a bunker just to the right of the fairway at 200 yards FG and water along the left from 150 - 100 yards FG on this par 5. Once again not much trouble around green.
3.   A longer par 3 with trouble all around the green. The only place to miss is short.
4.   A very short par four. A small bunker sits left of the green with trouble over the green.
5.   Water runs along the left side of the fairway up to 170 yards FG. Water on the right from 270 - 200 yards FG. Not a lot of trouble around the green.
6.   Water in front of green and trouble to the right. Long or left the only good misses.
7.   Creek runs all along the left side of this hole and cuts across fairway just in front of the green. Long and right are definitely trouble.
8.   Trouble all along the left side of this fairway. The hole doglegs to the right at about 170 yards FG. Don't go left or over the green.
9.   Dogleg right with a creek running near the fairway on the right from 200 yards FG all the way behind the hole. Trees on the left side at 120 yards FG block tee shots hit to the left side.
10.   Water on left side comes into play inside 230 yards FG. A creek that runs 10 yards in front of the green prevents you from running the ball on the green. Trouble over and right.
11.   Trees on right side can make a far right pin placement difficult. Don't go right or over green.
12.   Nice dogleg to the right the hole which really turns right after 150 yards FG. Not much trouble unless you go over the green.
13.   Very short par 4 dogleg left. A tee shot to 100 yards FG will leave a short approach. If you get greedy and try to hit a draw it better not go straight or it will be in the trees it really isn't worth the risk.
14.   Hit your tee shot to 125 yard FG to have a clear shot at the green. Avoid left side of the fairway, especially from 125 yards FG and in. A bunker guards the front of green.
15.   Easy par 3 unless you hit it too far to the right of the green.
16.   Hit to the left side of the fairway from 130 - 100 yards FG on this dogleg right. Hit short of that and you may be blocked out by the trees on the right. Don't go right of the green.
17.   Anything inside 150 yards FG is a good shot on this dogleg right and will give a clear view of the green. Don't go over or right.
18.   There's water just off the tee box to the right on this par 5. A second area of water to the right from 270 - 230 yards FG means you want to stay to the left side of this fairway. Creek cuts across fairway at 170 yards FG. Bunker guards front left of the green.

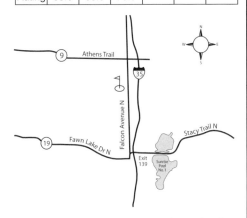

Take I-35 north 12.6 miles from the I-35W/I-35E split to CR 19 exit 139. Go west to Falcon Avenue (CR 78). Go north 3 miles, the course is on the left.

Fountain Valley Golf Club

2830 220th Street West
Farmington, MN 55024
651-463-2121

Course Information

Reservations:	7 days in advance		
2000 Fees:	9	18	Comments
Weekdays	$14.00	$20.00	
Weekends	$15.00	$25.00	
Twilight	N/A	N/A	
Seniors	$10.00	$14.00	M-F < noon
Power Cart	$13.00	$26.00	
Pull Cart	$2.00	$2.00	
Club Rental	$5.00	$10.00	
Credit cards	Visa Mastercard		
Checks	None		
Rain Check	Only when lightning occurs		
Other			
Leagues:	Tues, Wed		

Amenities:

Driving Range	Y	Snacks	Y
Putting Green	Y	Grill/Bar	Y
Practice Green	Y	Restaurant	N
Spikeless	Y	Locker Room	N
Proshop	S	Showers	N

Management:

Manager	Bryce & Carole Olson
Professional	Sue Bremer

Fountain Valley is a very wide open course on most of the holes. The course has a number of trees but not many mature trees. There are some bunkers and a few water hazards to add to the challenge. The grass on the course was not always the best with some bare spots and a lot of weeds but your ball is always playable. Being away from the suburban area, Fountain Valley offers a very peaceful setting for golf at a fair price. The course is well suited for beginner to intermediate golfers.

Rating   88.48

Course Rating

Tees	Grade 2.95
Ability Levels	3
Condition	3
Signs / Hole Maps	1
Ball Washers	4
Benches	4.5
Fairways	**3.35**
Condition	3
Yardage Markers	3
Pin Indicators	4
Rough	3.5
Watered / Drainage	4
Greens	**3.13**
Condition	3.5
Speed	3
Size and Variety	2.5
Slope	3
Fringe	4.5
Layout	**3.53**
Par 3's	3
Par 4's	3.5
Par 5's	3.5
Strategic Trouble	4
Bunkers	3
Enough Space	3
Walkability	5
Amenities	**3.3**
Driving Range	3
Practice Green	4
Water on Course	4
Port-O-Potties	4
Locker Rooms	1
Pro Shop	3
Grill & Bar	3
Weather Shelter	3
Golf Carts	3
Overall	**3.73**
Enjoyable	3
Challenging / Fair	3.5
Reservations	5
Scenery	3
Gimmicky Holes	5
Weather Monitor	5
Value	**4.0**
Overall	**88.48**

Hole	Blue	White	Red	Par	Men Handicap	Women Handicap
1	385	375	370	4	8	8
2	438	433	360	4	2	12
3	125	115	100	3	18	18
4	360	351	345	4	14	14
5	150	139	129	3	16	16
6	520	507	430	5	10	6
7	400	385	375	4	4	2
8	350	341	335	4	12	10
9	560	551	465	5	6	4
Out	3288	3197	2909	36		
10	370	365	360	4	5	9
11	365	353	345	4	7	11
12	165	155	145	3	17	17
13	485	477	470	5	11	1
14	350	288	288	4	13	13
15	562	550	460	5	3	3
16	200	175	170	3	15	15
17	425	417	370	4	1	5
18	350	341	335	4	9	7
In	3272	3121	2943	36		
Total	6560	6318	5852	72		
Slope	119	M 117 W 128	122			
Rating	71.5	M 70.3 W 76.0	73.4			

Hole Commentary

1. Uphill par 4 with a bunker on the right side at 100 yards FG.
2. OB runs along the left side otherwise it's a straightforward hole. There is also OB over the green.
3. Short par 3 with bunkers guarding the green all around it.
4. Bunker in the middle of the fairway at 130 yards FG.
5. Uphill par three that may require an extra club depending on the wind direction. Bunkers guard front right and front left of the green.
6. Bunker on right 200 yards FT. Set of bunkers on the right from 200-150 yards FG.
7. OB runs along the left side of fairway. Favor left side of fairway and avoid bunker at 150 yards FG on right side of fairway. Do not go over this green.
8. Favor the left side of the fairway to avoid being blocked by the trees on the right. Bunkers surround this green.
9. Bunker on the right side 250 yards FT, otherwise swing away on the tee shot. Good chance to make birdie on this hole.
10. Favor left side of fairway to avoid being blocked by the trees on the right. May need a little extra club on the approach shot.
11. Nice downhill, dogleg left par 4. Blind uphill approach shot to the green.
12. Longer par three with big bunkers that guards the left and front right of the green.
13. OB runs along the left side of the fairway and bunkers that sit on the left and right side of the fairway at 250 yards FG. Can reach the green in two but there is water front right of the green, OB over the green and left of the green.
14. Bunker juts in from the right side of the fairway at 110 yards FG. Long grass over and bunkers short guard this green.
15. Long straight par 5. Trees on the left come into play at 250 yards FG and a marsh on the right is at 200 yards FG. OB all along the left inside of 200 yards FG.
16. Wind will play with the ball on this wide open par 3. Bunkers guard left and right side of green.
17. Marsh runs along the left side from 250 - 210 yards FG. Long grass over and right of green will cause trouble.
18. Water comes in from the left and right making the fairway narrow from 100 yards FG to the green. Bunkers guard left and right of green and over the green is OB.

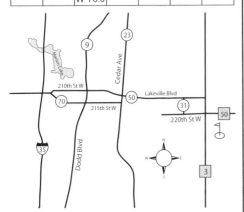

From I-35 go east 4 miles on CR 70, exit 71. Follow the signs for CR 50 and go east 4 miles to Hwy 3. Go south 3/4 miles to CR 50. Go east 3/4 mile, the course is on the right.

Fox Hollow Golf Club

4780 Palmgren Lane NE
Rogers, MN 55374
763-428-4468

Course Information

Reservations:	3 day in advance www.teemaster.com		
2000 Fees:	9	18	Comments
Weekdays	$21.00	$32.00	M - Th
Weekends	$21.00	$42.00	
Twilight	N/A	N/A	
Seniors	N/A	$20.00	M-Th < 10am
Power Cart	$13.00	$26.00	
Pull Cart	$4.00	$4.00	
Club Rental	$10.00	$10.00	
Credit cards	Visa Mastercard AmEx		
Checks	Local Checks Only		
Rain Check	Before the 12th tee		
Other	$37 < 10am Fri, > 3pm Sa,Su		
Leagues:	Various		

Amenities:			
Driving Range	Y	Snacks	Y
Putting Green	Y	Grill/Bar	Y
Practice Green	Y	Restaurant	Y
Spikeless	Y	Locker Room	Y
Proshop	F	Showers	Y

Management:	
Manager	Doug Dieter
Professional'	Mark Sverkerson

Fox Hollow now offers 27 holes of golf having just added 9 holes in 2001 which are reversible. The course is set in the Crow River Valley. The river borders the course on several holes and actually surrounds the 3rd green, an island in the river. Bent grass landing areas provide a nice place from which to hit approach shots. The course was in beautiful condition when I played it. It is not that far outside of the main Twin Cities loop and is well worth the drive. The course will challenge golfers of all ability levels.

Rating   104.90

Course Rating

	Grade
Tees	**4.45**
Ability Levels	5
Condition	4
Signs / Hole Maps	4
Ball Washers	4
Benches	5
Fairways	**4.25**
Condition	4.5
Yardage Markers	4
Pin Indicators	4
Rough	4
Watered / Drainage	5
Greens	**4.2**
Condition	4
Speed	4.5
Size and Variety	4.5
Slope	4
Fringe	3
Layout	**3.95**
Par 3's	4
Par 4's	4
Par 5's	3.5
Strategic Trouble	4.5
Bunkers	3
Enough Space	4
Walkability	5
Amenities	**4.18**
Driving Range	5
Practice Green	4
Water on Course	4
Port-O-Potties	3.5
Locker Rooms	5
Pro Shop	3
Grill & Bar	4
Weather Shelter	4
Golf Carts	4
Overall	**4.1**
Enjoyable	4.5
Challenging / Fair	4
Reservations	3
Scenery	4
Gimmicky Holes	5
Weather Monitor	4
Value	**4.5**
Overall	**104.90**

Hole	Blue	White	Yellow	Red	Par	Men Handicap	Women Handicap
1	396	383	363	317	4	5	6
2	350	304	291	248	4	8	8
3	170	156	142	97	3	3	9
4	515	457	449	407	5	6	5
5	513	497	467	427	5	4	2
6	428	405	377	327	4	2	4
7	413	397	371	333	4	1	1
8	192	161	148	138	3	7	3
9	375	365	359	295	4	9	7
Front	3352	3125	2967	2589	36		
1	406	389	365	330	4	4	3
2	501	490	453	410	5	7	5
3	179	158	141	129	3	8	8
4	459	417	337	329	4	2	7
5	541	523	502	420	5	6	6
6	156	131	102	88	3	9	9
7	353	330	320	297	4	1	1
8	372/352	326/304	290/258	278/250	4	5	2
9	394	380	358	311	4	3	4
Back	3361	3144	2868	2592	36		
1	569	383	496	457	5	4	3
2	344	304	321	299	4	7	6
3	185	156	152	125	3	8	8
4	570	457	516	448	5	1	5
5	420	497	371	345	4	3	4
6	155	405	120	100	3	5	7
7	534	397	497	419	5	6	2
8	190	161	132	90	3	2	9
9	318	365	297	257	4	9	1
Gold	3285	3125	2902	2540	36		
1	346	337	305	265	4	8	5
2	175	160	150	95	3	6	9
3	527	517	485	419	5	3	2
4	210	195	180	145	3	1	4
5	407	387	363	322	4	7	6
6	550	522	495	430	5	2	3
7	386	372	343	308	4	9	7
8	195	175	150	123	3	5	8
9	529	505	470	430	5	4	1
Black	3325	3170	2941	2537	36		
G/Fr	6637	6250	5869	5129	72		
Slope	132	128	125	124			
Rating	72.3	70.5	68.5	70.0			
G/Ba	6646	6264	5770	5132	72		
Slope	134	130	127	121			
Rating	72.4	70.6	68.3	70.3			
Bl/Fr	6677	6295	5908	5126	72		
Slope	135	131	128	124			
Rating	72.4	70.7	69.0	70.0			
Bl/Ba	6686	6314	5809	5219	72		
Slope	137	133	130	122			
Rating	72.5	70.8	68.5	70.3			

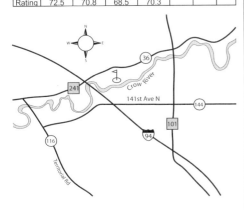

Take I-94 north 11.6 miles from the I-694/I-494 split to exit 205. Go east 1 mile on CR 36, the course is on the right.

Hole Commentary

Original 18, Gold 9

1. Bentgrass landing area ends 130 yards FG. Can cut corner right, don't leave it short in grass bunkers.
2. Landing areas from 130-115 and 75-60 yards FG. Water right and bunkers left of fairway. Green is well bunkered with water over.
3. Par 3 going over the Crow River. Short is the only place to miss-hit tee shot.
4. River along right side of hole. Small pond guards left front of green to discourage going for green in two.
5. Can cut corner but putting ball in bunkers will make hole difficult. Best play is just right of bunkers (270-150 yards FG) on left. Multi-level green.
6. OB all along right side of hole, landing area runs from 200-100 yards FG. Aim for 150 yard pole. Don't go over well bunkered green.
7. Two landing areas; upper from 210-160 yards FG and lower from 170-150 yards FG. Lower area slopes to marsh. Don't go long on approach.
8. Watch the wind on this short par 3. Check pin location as green has two distinct levels.
9. Landing area ends at about 70 yards FG. Favor right side of fairway to get good look at hole.
10. Dogleg left. Landing area 200-130 yards FG. Big hitters can cut corner just right of trees on left.
11. Bunkers left from 245-225 yards FG guard fairway. Water on left from 150 yards FG to the hole. Landing area from 105-40 yards FG. Right is bailout.
12. Don't come up short. Long and left are the only places to bail out on this par 3.
13. Bunkers left from 220-170 yards FG. Landing area ends at 150 yards FG.
14. Water 220-240 yards FT on right. 2nd shot is blind uphill shot favor left-center of fairway. Top of hill is 150 yards FG. Bunkers left and right from 90 yards FG in.
15. Short downhill par 3 requires smooth swing. Water left of hole.
16. Hit tee shot within 120 yards FG to avoid being blocked by trees. Landing area runs from 100-55 yards FG. Water short and left with trees right.
17. Two fairways to hit with creek splitting them; left from 160-120 yards FG and right from 115-65 yards FG. Right is better. Small green, only bailout is short.
18. Landing areas from 205-145 and 140-110 yards FG with bunkers left of that. Bunker on right at 150 yards FG. Three separate area of green, be accurate.
1. Bunkers left from 300-260 yards FG and water right from 250-170 yards FG. Bunker right from 150-120 yards FG. Elevated green, bunkers right and left.
2. Water right from 105 yards FG to the green. Bunker left and marsh over green. Stay left.
3. Downhill par 3 surrounded by bunkers.
4. Don't go left. Bunker right at top of hill. On second shot favor center to left side with marsh right from 150-50 yards FG. Bunker left, 75 yards FG to green.
5. Open driving hole with water left 225-150 yards FG. Water right 175-150 yards FG. Bunker left from 85-50 yards FG. Bunker left of green.
6. Water left and bunkers right of green. Green is 60 yards long, cannot see most of green from tee.
7. Avoid right side with water along right side. Bunkers from 242-210 yards FG left and right. Bunker left and trouble over green.
8. Water in front of 60-yard wide horseshoe shaped green.
9. Don't overdrive the fairway that ends at 80 yards FG. Hit to 100-80 yards FG. Water on three side of the green with a bunker right.

Francis A. Gross
Golf Course
2201 St. Anthony Blvd.
St. Anthony, MN 55418
612-789-2542
www.minneapolisparks.com

Course Information

Reservations:	4 days in advance		
2000 Fees:	9	18	Comments
Weekdays	$17.00	$24.00	
Weekends	$17.00	$26.00	
Twilight	$17.00	$17.00	After 4 pm
Seniors	N/A	$15.00	* see other
Power Cart	$13.00	$24.00	
Pull Cart	$2.00	$3.00	
Club Rental	$4.00	$7.50	
Credit cards	Visa Mastercard AmEx Discover		
Checks	Any		
Rain Check	18 hole<4 holes, 9 hole<13 holes		
Other	M-Th < 1pm, w/ 2 or 4-some is $27.50 including cart. *Sr. discount available w/ patron card		
Leagues:	Various		

Amenities:			
Driving Range	N	Snacks	Y
Putting Green	Y	Grill/Bar	Y
Practice Green	N	Restaurant	N
Spikeless	Y	Locker Room	Y
Proshop	B	Showers	Y

Management:	
Manager	Steve Walters
Professional	None

Gross Golf Course is undergoing some major changes. It is one of the older courses in the Twin Cities and these changes will help modernize it. The course is full of mature trees on every hole. Despite the numerous trees on the course, you will almost always have an opportunity to advance your ball. With the addition of new water hazards the course will be more challenging and more fun. Even though it is just minutes from downtown Minneapolis, it feels very secluded on the golf course. The course will challenge golfers of all ability levels.

Rating   87.50

Course Rating

Tees	Grade **2.4**
Ability Levels	1.5
Condition	3
Signs / Hole Maps	1.5
Ball Washers	3.5
Benches	4
Fairways	**3.65**
Condition	3.5
Yardage Markers	3.5
Pin Indicators	4
Rough	3.5
Watered / Drainage	4
Greens	**3.23**
Condition	3.5
Speed	3.5
Size and Variety	2
Slope	4
Fringe	3.5
Layout	**3.45**
Par 3's	3
Par 4's	3
Par 5's	2.5
Strategic Trouble	4
Bunkers	3.5
Enough Space	4
Walkability	5
Amenities	**3.23**
Driving Range	1
Practice Green	4.5
Water on Course	3
Port-O-Potties	3.5
Locker Rooms	5
Pro Shop	2
Grill & Bar	4
Weather Shelter	3
Golf Carts	4
Overall	**3.65**
Enjoyable	3.5
Challenging / Fair	3.5
Reservations	3
Scenery	3.5
Gimmicky Holes	5
Weather Monitor	5
Value	**4.0**
Overall	**87.50**

Hole	Blue	White	Gold	Red	Par	Men Handicap	Women Handicap
1	359	351	341	329	4	13	7
2	402	386	284	280	4	5	9
3	191	179	120	116	3	9	17
4	413	405	370	368	4	3	3
5	354	347	343	340	4	17	11
6	385	365	224	220	4/3	11	15
7	208	198	176	174	3	15	13
8	384	378	353	328	4	7	5
9	532	520	485	480	5	1	1
Out	3228	3129	2696	2635	35/34		
10	497	491	470	431	5	6	2
11	214	186	158	158	3	10	14
12	150	150	150	150	3	18	18
13	395	380	279	275	4	4	6
14	404	396	284	280	4	2	4
15	360	356	356	352	4	12	10
16	377	357	263	260	4	8	8
17	176	159	153	123	3	16	16
18	343	328	290	288	4	14	12
In	2916	2803	2403	2317	34		
Total	6144	5932	5099	4952	69/68		
Slope	118	M 116 W 122	M 108 W 112	111			
Rating	68.6	M 69.7 W 73.2	M 63.9 W 68.6	67.7			

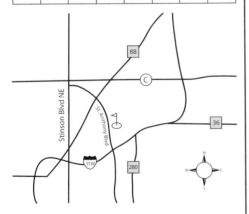

From I-35W take the Industrial Park / St. Anthony Blvd. exit. Go north 1/2 mile, the course is on the right.

Hole Commentary

1. Straightforward opening par 4 with plenty of fairway to hit to. Approach shot is slightly uphill with a bunker guarding the right side of the green.
2. Fairway slopes left to right with a bunker on the right from 200 - 150 yards FG. Fairway ends at 120 yards FG and starts up again at 85 yards FG. Two bunkers left and one bunker right of the green.
3. Uphill par 3 to a green guarded in front right by a bunker. Over or left can be trouble.
4. Bunker right of fairway from 150-130 yards FG. Favor left side of fairway. One bunker guards front right, two bunkers guard left side of the green.
5. Favor left side of fairway as OB runs along the right side of the hole. Bunkers both left and right of the green with OB right of the green.
6. Wide open hole with only trees left and right on the hole. Green is guarded by a bunker on the front right side with water over and OB right of bunker.
7. Long par 3 with bunkers guarding both left and right side of the green.
8. Favor left side of fairway but avoid bunker on left from 160 - 140 yards FG. Water right of the fairway inside 100 yards FG. Bunker guards left side of green with OB right.
9. Bunkers on right side of the fairway at 280 and 220 yards FG. Avoid the trees and it's an easy hole. Bunkers guard front of the green both left and right.
10. Straightforward hole that gets narrow from 150 - 100 yards FG. Bunker on the right inside 100 yards FG. Green guarded front left by a bunker.
11. Long par 3, bunkers guarding front right side and one guarding right side of green. Don't miss green left or long.
12. Slightly uphill par 3, trouble over and left.
13. Bunker on the left at 70 yards FG is the only trouble on the drive. Bunker guards right side of the green.
14. Water left of the hole from 100 yards FG to the green. Bunker guards left side of green with tree trouble right and over green.
15. Favor the right side to avoid the tree overhanging the fairway on the left at 100 yards FG. Avoid bunker on the right at 150 yards FG. Not much trouble around the green.
16. Favor left side of the fairway and stay out of the trees and the hole should be fairly easy. Bunker guards right side of the green.
17. Big bunker guards front and left side of the green with another bunker right of the green.
18. Bunker on the left is at 120 yards FG. Bunkers both left and right in front of the green. Don't miss this green in any direction.

Goodrich Golf Course

1820 North Van Dyke Road
Maplewood, MN 55109
651-748-2525
www.co.ramsey.mn.us/parks/golf_courses

Course Information

Reservations:	4 days in advance		

2000 Fees:	9	18	Comments
Weekdays	$15.00	$24.00	
Weekends	$15.00	$24.00	9 hole > 2pm
Twilight	N/A	$15.00	After 5 pm
Seniors	N/A	*	* see other
Power Cart	$14.00	$23.00	
Pull Cart	$2.00	$4.00	
Club Rental	$8.00	$12.00	
Credit cards	Visa Mastercard		
Checks	Local Checks Only		
Rain Check	18 hole<6 holes, none after 10th		
Other	Sr. discount available with Sr. card		
Leagues:	Mon - Fri		

Amenities:			
Driving Range	N	Snacks	Y
Putting Green	Y	Grill/Bar	N
Practice Green	N	Restaurant	N
Spikeless	Y	Locker Room	N
Proshop	B	Showers	N

Management:	
Professional	Mike Diebel
Manager	Mike Diebel

Goodrich is a wide open golf course where it is difficult to get into too much trouble. There are bunkers, 5 holes with water and mature trees but there uis plenty of room to mishit shots. The course is fairly flat and many of the holes look similar. It could be kept in a little better shape but the ball was always playable. A new clubhouse should be ready for the 2002 golf season. The course is well suited for beginner to intermediate golfers.

Rating   82.05

Course Rating

Tees	Grade
	2.975
Ability Levels	2.5
Condition	3.5
Signs / Hole Maps	1
Ball Washers	4
Benches	5

Fairways	**2.9**
Condition	3.5
Yardage Markers	2
Pin Indicators	2
Rough	3.5
Watered / Drainage	5

Greens	**2.725**
Condition	3
Speed	3
Size and Variety	1.5
Slope	3
Fringe	3.5

Layout	**3.75**
Par 3's	4
Par 4's	4
Par 5's	3
Strategic Trouble	3
Bunkers	4
Enough Space	4
Walkability	4.5

Amenities	**3.075**
Driving Range	1
Practice Green	4
Water on Course	4
Port-O-Potties	4.5
Locker Rooms	2
Pro Shop	3
Grill & Bar	2
Weather Shelter	4
Golf Carts	3

Overall	**3.275**
Enjoyable	3
Challenging / Fair	3
Reservations	3
Scenery	3.5
Gimmicky Holes	5
Weather Monitor	3

Value	**3.0**
Overall	**82.05**

Hole	Blue	White	Women	Par	Men Handicap	Women Handicap
1	530	510	475	5	11	3
2	368	361	320	4	9	5
3	160	150	115	3	17	17
4	420	406	315	4	7	9
5	385	360	333	4	3	7
6	522	490	410	5	1	1
7	195	172	144	3	15	15
8	193	173	141	3	13	13
9	388	370	295	4	5	11
Out	3161	2992	2548	35		
10	402	392	362	4	6	4
11	330	315	304	4	12	14
12	405	390	345	4	2	2
13	469	457	355	5	14	6
14	345	336	290	4	16	12
15	216	175	140	3	4	16
16	370	344	307	4	8	10
17	158	153	148	3	18	18
18	372	346	325	4	10	8
In	3067	2908	2576	35		
Total	6228	5900	5124	70		
Slope	110	107	113			
Rating	68.6	67.2	69.3			

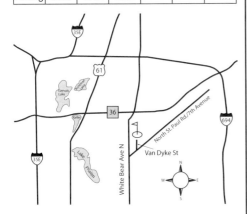

From I-694 take White Bear Avenue south 3.2 miles to North St. Paul Rd. Go east 1/3 mile, the course is on the left.

Hole Commentary

1. OB along the right side of the hole. Bunker on the left is at 300 yards FG. Water on right side from 250 - 230 yards FG cannot be seen on tee box. Don't miss the green right or over.
2. Water to the right off the tee box. Bunkers left and right at 140 yards FG. Bunker guards right front of the green. Don't miss long.
3. Slightly uphill par 3 over a pond. Plenty of area to miss the green.
4. Straightforward par 4 with bunker on right at 200 yards FG. Don't miss over the green.
5. No trouble on the tee shot. Bunker guards front right side of the green. Don't miss left or long.
6. OB along right side of the hole. Oak trees line the fairway on both sides. From 200-120 yards FG the fairway narrows. Fairway slopes toward green from 150-100 yards FG. Bunker guards front left side of green. Don't miss right or over.
7. Bunkers guard front right side and one left of green.
8. Bunkers both left and right of the green.
9. OB along the right side of this hole. Bunker on the left at 160 yards FG. Large bunkers guard front right and left of the green.
10. Favor the right side of the fairway for best approach to green. Not much trouble around the green.
11. Very straight forward hole with little trouble. Bunker in front of the green.
12. Bunker on left from 160-140 yards FG. Bunker guards front left side of the green.
13. Bunker on the right is 280 yards FG. Want to get to the top of the hill. The green is guarded by two bunkers in the front right of the green.
14. Slightly downhill par 4 with water just off to the right on the tee shot. Bunker on left is at 130 yards FG with a bunker behind it on the right side at 90 yards FG. Don't go over or left of the green.
15. Big bunker guards front left side of the green on this longer par 3.
16. Wide open fairway on tee shot. Bunker guards right side of the green.
17. Bunker guards front right side of the green on this mid-length par 3.
18. Bunker on the left is at 200 yards FG. Two bunkers guard front left of green with one bunker right. Don't miss over or right.

76

Greenhaven Golf Course

2800 Greehaven Road
Anoka, MN 55303
763-427-3180

Course Information

Reservations:	Weekday - Sat after 10:00 am	
	Weekend - Wed after 7:00 am	

2000 Fees:	9	18	Comments
Weekdays	$15.00	$26.50	
Weekends	$15.00	$29.75	
Twilight	N/A	N/A	
Seniors	N/A	$15.00	M, W, Th, F
Power Cart	$12.55	$24.50	
Pull Cart	$3.00	$3.00	
Club Rental	$7.00	$10.00	
Credit cards	Visa Mastercard		
Checks	Any		
Rain Check	Ask		
Other			

Leagues:	Tues - Fri

Amenities:			
Driving Range	Y	Snacks	Y
Putting Green	Y	Grill/Bar	Y
Practice Green	N	Restaurant	Y
Spikeless	Y	Locker Room	Y
Proshop	F	Showers	Y

Management:	
Manager	Jon Bendix
Professional	Jon Bendix

Greenhaven is a very affordable, well maintained course with many mature trees that define the holes. Greens are soft and hold your approach shots. Water, hills and trees make for an enjoyable challenge. The only drawback is the length: at 6,069 yards, today's equipment takes the distance factor out of the course. Focus on your accuracy and choose the smart shot over the macho one. On many holes hitting driver will only get you into trouble. The course is well suited for beginner to intermediate golfers.

Rating 94.80

Course Rating

Tees	Grade 4.0
Ability Levels	3
Condition	4
Signs / Hole Maps	5
Ball Washers	5
Benches	5

Fairways	3.55
Condition	2.5
Yardage Markers	4
Pin Indicators	4
Rough	4
Watered / Drainage	4

Greens	3.3
Condition	3.5
Speed	2
Size and Variety	4
Slope	4
Fringe	5

Layout	3.18
Par 3's	3
Par 4's	2
Par 5's	2.5
Strategic Trouble	3
Bunkers	4
Enough Space	5
Walkability	4

Amenities	3.95
Driving Range	2
Practice Green	5
Water on Course	4
Port-O-Potties	4
Locker Rooms	5
Pro Shop	4
Grill & Bar	5
Weather Shelter	4
Golf Carts	4

Overall	3.9
Enjoyable	4
Challenging / Fair	4
Reservations	4
Scenery	3
Gimmicky Holes	4
Weather Monitor	5

Value	4.5
Overall	94.80

Hole	Blue	Yellow	Par	Handicap	Red	Par	Handicap
1	431	422	4	5	401	5	5
2	356	346	4	9	319	4	9
3	179	165	3	17	150	3	17
4	540	522	5	3	416	5	1
5	440	425	4	1	402	5	3
6	397	377	4	7	336	4	7
7	493	486	5	11	416	5	13
8	171	158	3	15	136	3	15
9	359	345	4	13	335	4	11
Out	3366	3246	36		2911	38	
10	361	347	4	16	325	4	12
11	189	179	3	12	158	3	14
12	307	300	4	18	231	4	18
13	484	471	5	2	436	5	2
14	172	161	3	6	154	3	8
15	360	350	4	10	348	4	10
16	501	489	5	4	426	5	4
17	203	192	3	8	187	3	6
18	344	334	4	14	242	4	16
In	2921	2823	35		2507	35	
Total	6287	6069	71		5418	73	
Slope	121	M 119 W 118			110		
Rating	69.1	M 68.2 W 75.1			71.5		

Hole Commentary

1. Straight shot from a slightly elevated tee box. Approach the hole from the left side, as there is a bunker on the front right.
2. Short, slight dog-leg right. Focus on an accurate tee shot. Lake on the left should not be in play.
3. Downhill par 3. Oak tree on the right side of the fairway should not be in play.
4. Signature hole for Greenhaven. OB right, lake left all the way. Decide what distance you want for each shot and aim accordingly.
5. #1 handicap hole on the course, mainly for it's relative length. Rough is dotted with small trees that may come into play. Second shot requires long iron so stay in the fairway.
6. Elevated tee box, fairway bunker on the right side at driving distance. Approach from the left. Don't miss to elevated right side.
7. Long, bending par 5 to the left. OB on the right side all the way down. Stay to the left of the large tree on the right. Flat green.
8. Flat green, hit from a slightly elevated tee box. Bunker on the front right side.
9. Slight dogleg right. Fairway bunker at the corner on the right side. Uphill all the way.
10. Slight dogleg left. Play to the right side of the fairway for the best approach to the green. Bunker on the front-left.
11. Hit your 180-yard club straight and easy. Bunkers on both sides of the green.
12. Tee off from an elevated tee box. Careful walking to the tee box if there are people teeing off – they will not see you. Hole plays short at 300 yards and from an elevated tee box. Bunker 50 yards FG on the left.
13. Long bending par 5 to the left. Trees prevent you from cutting the corner too much. Bunker on the front left of the green, so approach from the right. Green is elevated at the back, so do not go over! It will cost you.
14. Uphill, elevated green. OB right and behind the green. Green is like an upside down saucer. Putts break away from the center of the green.
15. Slight dogleg right. Bunker at the front-right of the green and back left, so approach from the left side. Green slopes back to front.
16. Tee shots in fairway make for easy hole. Go left or right and add a stroke or two. Don't bring large hill on the left into play. Fairway bunkers at 250 FG on both sides of the fairway can cause problems for your 2nd shot.
17. The 8th handicap hole, but impossible if you miss the green right or long. Green is elevated and surrounded by trees.
18. Sharp dogleg left. Not a long hole, but requires accuracy off the tee. You need to make the corner to have an approach to the green because of large mound on the front left.

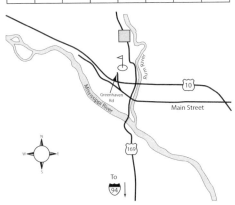

From I-694 take Hwy 169 north 8.8 miles to Hwy 10. Go west and take the first exit. The entrance to the course is at the bottom of the exit.

Greenwood Golf Links

4520 East Viking Blvd.
Wyoming, MN 55092
651-462-4653

Course Information

| Reservations: | Weekdays - 1 day in advance |
| | Weekend - 2 days in advance |

2000 Fees:	9	18	Comments
Weekdays	$12.00	$19.00	
Weekends	$14.00	$23.00	
Twilight	N/A	N/A	
Seniors	$8.00	$14.00	
Power Cart	$12.00	$24.00	
Pull Cart	$2.50	$5.00	
Club Rental	$4.00	$8.00	
Credit cards	Visa Mastercard Discover AmEx		
Checks	Any		
Rain Check	18 hole<4 holes, 9 hole<13 holes		
Other			
Leagues:	Tues - Thur		

Amenities:			
Driving Range	N	Snacks	Y
Putting Green	Y	Grill/Bar	N
Practice Green	N	Restaurant	N
Spikeless	Y	Locker Room	N
Proshop	B	Showers	N

Management:	
Manager	Adam Bright
Professional	Ross Johnson

Greenwood is a golf course in need of help. Much of the course is cut out of swamp land so the fairways are narrow and the grass is not the best. Doing some small things like new signs showing how the holes are laid out would help. Parts of the course look like they have been neglected for a while. New management took over in 2001. Hopefully they can make some changes to increase the challenge and layout of the course. This course is well suited for beginning golfers.

Rating   78.20

Course Rating

Tees	Grade 2.8
Ability Levels	2.5
Condition	3
Signs / Hole Maps	1.5
Ball Washers	4
Benches	4

Fairways	2.55
Condition	3
Yardage Markers	2
Pin Indicators	2
Rough	3.5
Watered / Drainage	3

Greens	3.35
Condition	4
Speed	3.5
Size and Variety	2.5
Slope	3
Fringe	3

Layout	3.18
Par 3's	3.5
Par 4's	3.5
Par 5's	2.5
Strategic Trouble	3
Bunkers	1.5
Enough Space	4
Walkability	5

Amenities	1.9
Driving Range	1
Practice Green	2.5
Water on Course	2
Port-O-Potties	3
Locker Rooms	1
Pro Shop	2
Grill & Bar	2
Weather Shelter	1
Golf Carts	2

Overall	2.8
Enjoyable	2.5
Challenging / Fair	2.5
Reservations	3
Scenery	3.5
Gimmicky Holes	3
Weather Monitor	3

Value	3.0
Overall	78.20

Hole	Blue	White	Red	Par	Handicap
1	490	490	470	5	5
2	280	280	248	4	9
3	475	475	441	5	7
4	340	340	307	4	1
5	311	311	271	4	13
6	297	297	277	4	15
7	275	275	260	4	17
8	206	206	186	3	3
9	228	228	147	3	11
Out	2902	2902	2607	36	
10	472	465	426	5	6
11	251	234	191	4	12
12	91	86	82	3	14
13	112	107	78	3	10
14	111	97	90	3	18
15	471	464	382	5	2
16	299	294	265	4	16
17	581	571	481	5	4
18	228	218	189	4	8
In	2616	2536	2184	36	
Total	5518	5438	4791	72	
Slope	105	M 103 W 116	109		
Rating	67.2	M 66.5 W 71.0	67.3		

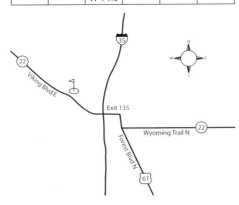

Take I-35 north 8.6 miles from the I-35W/I-35E split to Viking Boulevard, exit 135. Go west 1/2 mile, the course is on the right.

Hole Commentary

1. Dogleg left with OB all along the right side of the hole. Plenty of room to hit left. Pond on the left at 100 yards FG. No trouble around green.
2. OB and water right off the tee. Hole doglegs 90° at 150 yards FG. No way to cut the corner. Hit it too far and you may not find your ball in long weeds. Bunker right of green.
3. Water left and right of fairway on the entire hole. Teeing off through a chute of trees over a creek. Need to be accurate, don't go over.
4. Water left and right of fairway on the entire hole. Don't go right or over the green.
5. Hit your tee shot to the left side of fairway inside 150 yards FG to have a shot at green. Creek runs in front of green, OB over green.
6. Dogleg left par 4. Water to the left just before you cross the road. Bunker guards left side of green.
7. Favor right side of fairway with bunkers down the left. Stands of pine trees surround the green, don't miss green long.
8. Long par 3 with little trouble other than the length.
9. Long par 3 over a pond. Bunkers front right and over green. Green slopes severely toward front of green.
10. Dogleg right par 5 with a narrow fairway lined by trees on both side. Favor left side of fairway to have a chance in two. The hole turns right at 150 yards FG.
11. Short dogleg left par 4. Hit tee shot to a comfortable distance for a wedge shot to the green.
12. Short par 3 in the trees. Not much room to miss around the green.
13. Par 3, this one over water. Not much room to miss the green.
14. A third consecutive par 3, this one surrounded by trees.
15. Blind tee shot on a dogleg left par 5. Aim just right of trees on the left. From 220 yards FG you can see the green. Don't go over the green.
16. Short par 4 with water both left and right of the fairway. Fairway gets narrow around 150 yards FG.
17. Straight par 5 with water on the right all along the hole. Fairway narrows and splits around 250 yards FG. Fairway opens up inside 225 yards FG. Again at 150 yards FG a patch of grass splits the fairway.
18. Very short par 4 through a very narrow chute of trees. Have to hit it straight or you'll be in the trees. There is room to miss short or right of the green.

Hampton Hills
Golf Club

5313 North Juneau Lane
Plymouth, MN 55446
763-559-9800

Course Information

Reservations:	Fri, Sat, Sun & Holidays		
2000 Fees:	9	18	Comments
Weekdays	$15.00	$21.00	
Weekends	$18.00	$25.00	
Twilight	N/A	$10.00	Sa,Su > 5 pm
Seniors	$8.00	$10.00	Before 2 pm
Power Cart	$12.00	$20.00	
Pull Cart	$2.00	$2.00	
Club Rental	$3.00	$3.00	
Credit cards	None		
Checks	Local Checks Only		
Rain Check	18 hole<4 holes, 9 hole<13 holes		
Other			
Leagues:	Various		

Amenities:			
Driving Cage	Y	Snacks	Y
Putting Green	Y	Grill/Bar	Y
Practice Green	N	Restaurant	N
Spikeless	O	Locker Room	N
Proshop	B	Showers	N

Management:	
Manager	Dian Whelan
Professional	Mike Svendahl

Hampton Hills is a course that needs some help. Much of the course is cut out of marsh land and the ground and grass is in average to poor condition. The layout of the course is fine but everything from the tees to the greens could use some work. It is a peaceful setting with elevations changes and nice scenery but the subpar condition of the course is a minus. The course is usually easy to get on to and is fine for practicing your game. The course is well suited for beginning golfers.

Rating 75.75

Course Rating

Tees	Grade 2.85
Ability Levels	3
Condition	2
Signs / Hole Maps	2
Ball Washers	4
Benches	5

Fairways	1.95
Condition	2
Yardage Markers	2
Pin Indicators	1
Rough	2.5
Watered / Drainage	3

Greens	2.55
Condition	2.5
Speed	2.5
Size and Variety	2
Slope	3
Fringe	4

Layout	3.38
Par 3's	3
Par 4's	3
Par 5's	2.5
Strategic Trouble	4
Bunkers	3
Enough Space	4
Walkability	5

Amenities	2.35
Driving Range	1.5
Practice Green	3
Water on Course	3
Port-O-Potties	3
Locker Rooms	1
Pro Shop	2
Grill & Bar	2
Weather Shelter	2
Golf Carts	3

Overall	2.9
Enjoyable	2
Challenging / Fair	2
Reservations	5
Scenery	3
Gimmicky Holes	5
Weather Monitor	2

Value	3.0
Overall	**75.75**

Hole	Men	Women	Par	Men Handicap	Women Handicap
1	470	428	5	12	5
2	141	126	3	16	18
3	413	400	4	5	9
4	512	440	5	9	1
5	192	182	3	3	13
6	286	276	4	17	14
7	489	355	5	2	2
8	400	359	4	8	8
9	369	302	4	1	3
Out	3272	2868	37		
10	244	234	4	18	15
11	333	275	4	6	11
12	461	408	5	11	10
13	245	240	4	14	12
14	397	282	4	4	4
15	468	380	5	10	6
16	161	145	3	15	16
17	140	135	3	13	17
18	414	354	4	7	7
In	2863	2453	36		
Total	6315	5321	73		
Slope	111	122			
Rating	69.9	70.2			

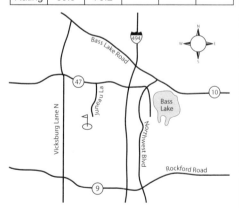

From I-494 take Bass Lake Road (CR 10) east 1/2 mile to Northwest Blvd. (CR 61). Go south 1/4 mile to CR 47. Go west 1.2 miles to Juneau Lane. Go south 1 mile to the course.

Hole Commentary

1.   Dogleg right from an elevated tee box. Do not go right on this tee shot, anything to the left is okay but not right. Do not go over the green, the hill drops off severely.
2.   Downhill par 3, favor the right side since the hill will kick balls back to the left.
3.   Downhill par 4 with OB running the entire left side of the hole. The creek runs from 200 yards FG on left side to 100 yards FG on right side. Bunker guards right side of green.
4.   OB runs along the left side and a creek runs along the right side of this fairway all the way to the hole. No real trouble around green.
5.   Trouble surrounds this tough par 3. Only place to bail out is short.
6.   Short dogleg left par 4 which can be reached by longer hitters. Aim just right of tree on left side. Multi-level green with front upper left portion and lower right portion.
7.   Creek runs far right and OB runs far left of hole. Water guards entire front of green so approach shots must clear water. Not much trouble going over green.
8.   Elevated tee box with trees on left side and a creek running 100 yards FG. No real trouble around the green.
9.   Aim just right of trees on left side. Approach shot is up a hill so take an extra club. Leaving the shot short makes for a tough chip.
10.   Short par 4 that is definitely reachable but there is trouble left and over this green. Can be an easy birdie or a frustrating bogey or worse.
11.   Just don't go right on this hole. Anything left should be okay unless you are a long hitter. A lone tree sits at 80 yards FG on the left side and can alter shots hit from over there.
12.   Dogleg left par 5. Aim toward left side of fairway to have best chance at going for green in two. On approach, trees to the right are the only real trouble.
13.   Another short, reachable par 4 with trouble in front of, left of and over the green. Creek runs 20 yards in front of green. Hit to just in front of creek or go for the green.
14.   Marsh runs along left side of hole and it's OB. Not much trouble around this green except too far right.
15.   Hitting out of chute of trees with OB running entire left side of fairway. Creek on right starts at 200 yards FG and cuts across fairway at 30 yards in front of green.
16.   Par 3 with trouble over the green and OB far left of the green.
17.   Slightly uphill par three with trouble right and over the green. Hit it short and you'll have a tough recovery shot.
18.   Slight dogleg left par 4. Need to get to 150 yards FG to see the pin which is slightly downhill. Only real trouble is left of the green.

Heritage Links
Golf Club
8075 Lucerne Blvd.
Lakeville, MN 55044
952-440-4653
www.heritagelinks.com

Course Information

Reservations:	7 days in advance www.teemaster.com		
2000 Fees:	9	18	Comments
Weekdays	$17.00	$27.00	
Weekends	$19.00	$33.00	
Twilight	N/A	$17.00	
Seniors	$11.00	$18.00	weekdays
Power Cart	$18.00	$25.00	
Pull Cart	$3.00	$3.00	
Club Rental	$10.00	$10.00	
Credit cards	Visa Mastercard		
Checks	Any		
Rain Check	18 hole<5 holes, 9 hole<14 holes		
Other			
Leagues:	Tue, Wed, Thur		

Amenities:			
Driving Range	Y	Snacks	Y
Putting Green	Y	Grill/Bar	Y
Practice Green	N	Restaurant	N
Spikeless	Y	Locker Room	N
Proshop	B	Showers	N

Management:	
Manager	Mark Zweber
Professional	Tim Vernon

Heritage Links has two distinctive 9 holes. The front nine has a links style feel to it with water and rolling terrain. The back nine is more wooded, lined with trees, water, bunkers and great elevation changes. The entire course consists of 45 bunkers with water coming into play on 16 of 18 holes. The scenery is great and the golf even better. The course will challenge golfers of all ability levels.

Rating   97.25

Course Rating

Tees	Grade 4.6
Ability Levels	5
Condition	4
Signs / Hole Maps	5
Ball Washers	4
Benches	5

Fairways	2.3
Condition	3
Yardage Markers	2
Pin Indicators	1
Rough	3
Watered / Drainage	3

Greens	4.25
Condition	4
Speed	5
Size and Variety	4
Slope	4
Fringe	3

Layout	3.95
Par 3's	4
Par 4's	4
Par 5's	3
Strategic Trouble	4
Bunkers	4
Enough Space	4
Walkability	5

Amenities	3.2
Driving Range	3
Practice Green	4
Water on Course	4
Port-O-Potties	3
Locker Rooms	2
Pro Shop	2
Grill & Bar	3
Weather Shelter	3
Golf Carts	3

Overall	3.65
Enjoyable	4
Challenging / Fair	4
Reservations	3
Scenery	3
Gimmicky Holes	4
Weather Monitor	3

Value	4
Overall	97.25

Hole	Black	Gold	Blue	Handicap	Par	White	Handicap
1	374	351	340	16	4	311	9
2	575	555	536	8	5	486	1
3	451	434	410	10	4	367	5
4	191	165	150	14	3	119	17
5	553	544	491	2	5	416	3
6	385	360	323	4	4	257	7
7	225	203	177	18	3	151	15
8	381	355	333	12	4	290	11
9	399	387	365	6	4	300	13
Out	3534	3354	3125		36	2697	
10	319	305	291	15	4	266	10
11	193	176	158	3	3	138	16
12	427	399	373	17	4	324	8
13	270	256	242	5	4	216	12
14	138	133	124	11	3	84	18
15	383	373	357	1	4	257	14
16	575	553	535	7	5	464	2
17	381	376	343	13	4	323	6
18	452	395	381	9	4	376	4
In	3138	2966	2804		35	2448	
Total	6672	6320	5929		71	5145	
Slope	125	121	118			116	
Rating	72.3	70.7	69.0			70.4	

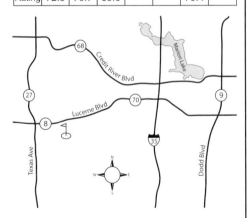

From I-35 take CR 70 (exit 81) west 3.3 miles, the course is on your left.

Hole Commentary

1. Ideal tee shot is left side of the fairway between the fairway bunker and 150-yard marker. Avoid long or right on approach.
2. Favor left center of fairway to avoid hidden bunkers on right side of fairway. Aim at right-hand tower on second shot. Water runs on the left side of the fairway from 80 yards FG in.
3. Aim at the 150-yard marker on the tee shot. Beware of marsh on the right side of fairway.
4. Depending on the wind you may want to hit ½ less club since the tee is elevated. A bunker short and marsh long will grab errant shots.
5. Aim your tee shot just right of the left bunker for the best angle on your second shot. A hidden pond lurks over the right side of the fairway. Aim at the right tower on your second shot whether you go for it or not since the marsh guards the left side of the green.
6. Don't go right! Best approach to this peninsula green is from the left side. Tough approach shot as right, long and short are wet.
7. Bunker guards left side of this long par 3.
8. The smart play here is to hit a club that gets you to 150-yard marker. There is no reward for trying to drive over the creek. The approach shot is uphill, pick your club wisely.
9. Aim between left fairway bunker and the 150-yard marker. A bunker and marsh guard right side for drives of 250 yards or longer.
10. Hit a club that will get you to 120 yards from the green. To carry the creek requires 250 yards and there is no reward for doing so.
11. Beautiful, elevated par 3 to a clover shaped green. The wind will play with your ball so choose your club accordingly.
12. Favor the left side but beware of OB on the left. The water comes into play at 280 yards FG so long hitters beware. Two green side bunkers guard this narrow green.
13. Risk/Reward! The landing area is 180 FT. Long hitters can go for the green but trees right and over, a deep bunker in front and a drop off right will make you think twice.
14. Elevated and protected tee box make club selection crucial. Short is better than long!
15. Right is okay. Approach shot is downhill, it plays shorter than it looks. Green protected in front by marsh, over by a steep bank.
16. There is OB left and for long hitters a marsh comes into play on the right. Aim for the tower in the distance. The lay-up area has two bunkers guarding it and a marsh runs along the right side of this hole from 100 yards FG and in.
17. The smart play is to hit to the 150-yard marker. Hitting over the marsh is possible but leaves you with a difficult, steep, side-hill lie.
18. Favor the right side as two ponds protect a narrow landing area 216 to 225 yards FT. Take an extra club to this elevated green.

Hiawatha Golf Course

4553 Longfellow Avenue South
Minneapolis, MN 55407
612-724-7715
www.minneapolisparks.com

Course Information

| Reservations: | 4 days in advance |
| | www.teemaster.com |

2000 Fees:	9	18	Comments
Weekdays	$17.00	$24.00	
Weekends	$17.00	$26.00	9 holes > 2pm
Twilight	N/A	$17.00	After 4 pm
Seniors	N/A	$15.00	* see other
Power Cart	$13.00	$24.00	
Pull Cart	$2.00	$3.00	
Club Rental	$4.00	$7.50	

Credit cards	Visa Mastercard AmEx Discover
Checks	Any
Rain Check	18 hole <4 holes, 9 hole <13 holes
Other	M-Th < 1pm, w/ 2 or 4-some is
	$27.50 including cart. *Sr. discount
	avail. w/ patron card

Leagues:	Various

Amenities:			
Driving Range	Y	Snacks	Y
Putting Green	Y	Grill/Bar	Y
Practice Green	N	Restaurant	N
Spikeless	Y	Locker Room	Y
Proshop	B	Showers	Y

Management:	
Manager	Steve Skaar
Professional	Lee Toftner

Hiawatha is a long course, generally flat with mature trees and small greens. Two fairways and four tees border Lake Hiawatha. Minnehaha Creek flows into Lake Hiawatha through the back nine holes. There are 12 ponds and 30 bunkers strategically placed throughout the golf course. The course was in slightly better than average condition. There is a very nice driving range and practice facility on the course. The course is well suited for beginning to intermediate golfers.

Rating   91.43

Course Rating

Tees	Grade 3.83
Ability Levels	4.5
Condition	3.5
Signs / Hole Maps	2
Ball Washers	4
Benches	5

Fairways	3.3
Condition	3.5
Yardage Markers	3
Pin Indicators	3
Rough	3.5
Watered / Drainage	4

Greens	3.35
Condition	3.5
Speed	3.5
Size and Variety	2.5
Slope	3.5
Fringe	4.5

Layout	3.68
Par 3's	4
Par 4's	3
Par 5's	3.5
Strategic Trouble	3.5
Bunkers	3.5
Enough Space	4
Walkability	5

Amenities	3.8
Driving Range	4.5
Practice Green	4.5
Water on Course	2.5
Port-O-Potties	3.5
Locker Rooms	5
Pro Shop	2
Grill & Bar	3.5
Weather Shelter	2
Golf Carts	4.5

Overall	3.65
Enjoyable	3.5
Challenging / Fair	3.5
Reservations	3
Scenery	3.5
Gimmicky Holes	5
Weather Monitor	5

Value	3.5
Overall	91.43

Hole	Blue	White	Gold	Par	Handicap	Red	Par	Handicap
1	473	447	423	5	13	381	4	3
2	518	509	420	5	11	410	5	5
3	129	121	112	3	17	92	3	17
4	317	287	273	4	15	242	4	13
5	416	402	379	4	3	316	4	9
6	368	338	320	4	9	254	4	11
7	540	526	507	5	7	456	5	1
8	200	190	164	3	5	130	3	15
9	418	372	362	4	1	339	4	7
Out	3379	3192	2960	37		2620	36	
10	501	471	439	5	18	390	4	2
11	388	378	322	4	6	316	4	8
12	168	151	142	3	8	136	3	16
13	485	476	441	5	10	403	5	4
14	350	297	278	4	12	247	4	14
15	164	155	130	3	16	120	3	18
16	412	385	365	4	2	333	4	6
17	395	383	324	4	4	292	4	10
18	371	323	284	4	14	265	4	12
In	3234	3019	2725	36		2502	35	
Total	6613	6211	5685	73		5122	71	
Slope	126	122	117			118		
Rating	71.2	69.4	67.0			69.2		

From I-35 take 46th Street east 1.4 miles to the course.

Hole Commentary

1. Plenty of room to hit to on this par 5. Water left of the fairway at 100 yards FG. Bunker left of the green and water right of the green.
2. Aim just left of lone tree on right side of fairway. Bunkers left of fairway sit at 260 yards FG. Bunkers guard front left and right side of green.
3. Bunkers guard left and right side of the green on this uphill par 3.
4. Make sure you hit the fairway on this short par 4 to set up a short wedge to the green. Bunkers on left as you approach the green. Don't go over green.
5. Straightforward par 4 with water far left of the fairway inside 100 yards FG. Don't miss this green left or over.
6. Water left of fairway ends at 150 yards FG, water on right ends at 100 yards FG. Bunkers both left and right as you approach the green.
7. Water just off the tee to the right and a larger pond of water to the left of the fairway. Past the water there isn't any trouble with a wide-open green.
8. Bunkers guard both left and right side of the green. Don't go long or right of this green.
9. Straightforward par 4 with water right of the hole from 200-160 yards FG. Bunker guards front left side of green.
10. Bunkers left of fairway from 230-210 yards FG, right of fairway from 215-200 yards FG. OB over the green and waste area right of green.
11. Dogleg left with Lake Hiawatha on your left. Water on right from 175-130 yards FG. Bunker on left from 120-100 yards FG. Aim over or just right of that bunker on left side. Not a lot of room to miss the green.
12. Short par 3 over the creek. Bunker both left and right of the green. Don't go over the green.
13. OB along left side of the hole. Pole on right side of fairway marks 200 yards to the creek that runs 75 yards in front of green. Bunker guards front right side of green.
14. Water to the right of hole from 160-110 yards FG with a bunker past the water. Bunker guards right side of this green.
15. Green is guarded by bunkers both front right and front left. Don't go over this green.
16. Dogleg right with the driving range and OB left. Water cuts across the fairway 70 yards in front of green. No trouble around the green.
17. Driving range is OB left of the fairway. Water on the right from 210-145 yards FG and water on left from 165-140 yards FG. Bunkers guard both left and right side of green.
18. Slightly uphill and fairly wide-open par 4. Bunker guards front right side of the green.

Hidden Greens Golf Course

12977 200th Street East
Hastings, MN 55033
651-437-3085

Course Information

| Reservations: | Weekdays - 2 days | | |
| | Weekend - 9 am Tuesday | | |

2000 Fees:	9	18	Comments
Weekdays	$10.00	$18.00	M - Th
Weekends	$14.00	$22.00	
Twilight	N/A	N/A	
Seniors	N/A	N/A	
Power Cart	$11.00	$22.00	
Pull Cart	$2.00	$2.00	
Club Rental	$3.00	$3.00	
Credit cards	Visa Mastercard		
Checks	Local Checks Only		
Rain Check	None		
Other			

Leagues:	Tues - Thur

Amenities:			
Driving Range	Y	Snacks	Y
Putting Green	Y	Grill/Bar	Y
Practice Green	N	Restaurant	N
Spikeless	Y	Locker Room	N
Proshop	B	Showers	N

Management:	
Manager	Leonard Swanson
Professional	None

The name tells the story of Hidden Greens. Many of the greens cannot be seen from the tee box. The course has mature pine trees that line the fairways and may make it necessary to hit directly back to the fairway if you hit into them. It is a short course where playing smart will lead to good scores. There are a few bunkers and water hazards to add challenge. While it could have been in better condition, you cannot beat the price for a fun round of golf. The course is well suited for beginner to intermediate golfers.

Rating   85.98

Course Rating

Tees	Grade 3.0
Ability Levels	3.5
Condition	3
Signs / Hole Maps	4
Ball Washers	4
Benches	4

Fairways	2.7
Condition	3
Yardage Markers	3
Pin Indicators	1
Rough	4
Watered / Drainage	3

Greens	2.55
Condition	3
Speed	2
Size and Variety	2
Slope	3
Fringe	4

Layout	3.15
Par 3's	3.5
Par 4's	3
Par 5's	2.5
Strategic Trouble	4
Bunkers	1
Enough Space	4
Walkability	5

Amenities	2.85
Driving Range	2
Practice Green	3
Water on Course	4
Port-O-Potties	3
Locker Rooms	3
Pro Shop	2
Grill & Bar	3
Weather Shelter	2
Golf Carts	3

Overall	3.5
Enjoyable	3
Challenging / Fair	3
Reservations	4
Scenery	4
Gimmicky Holes	5
Weather Monitor	3

Value	4.5
Overall	85.98

Hole	Blue	White	Red	Par	Handicap
1	388	369	351	4	8
2	313	290	257	4	10
3	537	527	470	5	4
4	388	372	347	4	12
5	371	331	311	4	14
6	521	501	438	5	6
7	152	142	132	3	18
8	291	281	262	4	2
9	194	164	146	3	16
Out	3155	2977	2714	36	
10	486	476	406	5	5
11	180	158	148	3	17
12	413	391	356	4	3
13	351	336	318	4	11
14	315	295	273	4	8
15	310	293	283	4	13
16	413	395	341	4	1
17	174	153	133	3	15
18	492	480	407	5	7
In	3134	2977	2665	36	
Total	6289	5954	5379	72	
Slope	121	118	123		
Rating	70.2	68.8	70.6		

Hole Commentary

1. Hit your tee shot to 130 – 120 yards FG and favor the left side of the fairway to avoid being blocked out by tree on the right.
2. This par 4 is a quick 90° dogleg at 110 yards FG. The hole is located behind trees on left as hole bends. Only a big draw has a chance at the green and not a good one. Best play is to 100 – 80 yards FG.
3. Long, straight par 5. Stay out of the trees and keep right from 150 yards FG and in to avoid the over hanging tree on left.
4. Tee shot favoring right middle of fairway will give you the best angle to the green.
5. A fade is the best tee shot, hit the ball to 150 yards FG for good approach to green.
6. Favor the right side of fairway on tee shot but be careful not to go too far right and be blocked by pine trees. Only trouble by the green is long and right.
7. Water runs along left and backside of this downhill par 3.
8. Short par 4 with a creek dissecting the fairway from 170 yards FG at the bridge to 120 yards FG on left of fairway. Smart play is to hit tee shot to 130 yards FG. Creek runs in front of and right of the hole so bail out left.
9. Hole is located in collection area so one extra club won't hurt on this uphill par 3.
10. Favor the right side of the fairway on the tee shot to have a chance to go for it in two. Green is two-tiered so know where the pin is located.
11. Don't go long or right on this nice par 3.
12. Left is out-of play so avoid that side. Straightforward par 4.
13. Hit tee shot from 150 – 120 yards FG and favor the left side of the fairway to avoid the overhanging trees on the right.
14. Dogleg left par 4. Hit tee shot from 100 – 70 yards FG. Only a long draw has a chance to hit the green from the tee box
15. Aim just to the left of the trees on the right and hit your ball to 100 yards FG for best approach. Left side of fairway is better than right side due to overhanging trees on the right. Avoid the pond to right of trees on the right.
16. You have two choices. Tee shot to left side of fairway allows a chance to go for the green in two but approach is over water. Tee shot aimed at right side of fairway will put you in good position to lay up to a comfortable distance for the approach shot.
17. Don't go over or right on this par 3.
18. Favor the left side of the fairway for a chance to go for this finishing par 5 in two. No real danger by the hole so go for the green and end the round on a good note.

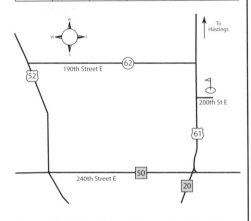

From 494 take Hwy 61 south 19 miles, through Hastings. Go east on 200th Street 1/2 mile to the course.

Hidden Haven Golf Club

20520 NE Polk Street
Cedar, MN 55011
763-434-6867

Course Information

Reservations:	3 days in advance		

2000 Fees:	9	18	Comments
Weekdays	$14.00	$24.00	
Weekends	$15.00	$26.00	
Twilight	N/A	$6.00	1 hr < sunset
Seniors	$13/14	$22/24	wkday/wkend
Power Cart	$12.00	$24.00	
Pull Cart	$3.00	$4.00	
Club Rental	$5.00	$8.00	
Credit cards	Visa Mastercard Discover		
Checks	Local Checks Only		
Rain Check	Ask		
Other			

Leagues:	Various

Amenities:			
Driving Range	N	Snacks	Y
Putting Green	Y	Grill/Bar	Y
Practice Green	Y	Restaurant	Y
Spikeless	Y	Locker Room	N
Proshop	F	Showers	N

Management:	
Manager	Mark Hetland
Professional	Mark Hetland

Hidden Haven has two very different 9 holes. The front nine is very new and in great shape with nice greens and grass. The back nine is older, tighter and not in as good of shape, especially the fairways. Water comes into play on 8 holes, most notably the 14th hole with water on both side of the fairway. Even though the back nine needs some work it was a fun course to play with some interesting holes. The course is well suited for beginner to intermediate golfers.

Rating   88.60

Course Rating

Tees	Grade 2.58
Ability Levels	1.5
Condition	3
Signs / Hole Maps	3
Ball Washers	4
Benches	3

Fairways	3.05
Condition	2.5
Yardage Markers	3.5
Pin Indicators	3
Rough	3
Watered / Drainage	3.5

Greens	3.8
Condition	3.5
Speed	3
Size and Variety	5
Slope	4.5
Fringe	3.5

Layout	3.98
Par 3's	4
Par 4's	3.5
Par 5's	3
Strategic Trouble	4
Bunkers	4.5
Enough Space	5
Walkability	4.5

Amenities	2.98
Driving Range	1
Practice Green	4
Water on Course	3.5
Port-O-Potties	4
Locker Rooms	1
Pro Shop	3.5
Grill & Bar	4.5
Weather Shelter	3
Golf Carts	4

Overall	3.73
Enjoyable	4
Challenging / Fair	3.5
Reservations	2.5
Scenery	4
Gimmicky Holes	5
Weather Monitor	3.5

Value	3.5
Overall	88.60

Hole	White	Handicap	Red	Handicap	Par
1	338	7	281	2	4
2	422	3	353	3	4
3	121	17	85	8	3
4	515	1	384	1	5
5	316	13	271	6	4
6	296	9	264	7	4
7	143	11	105	9	3
8	362	5	314	4	4
9	355	15	311	5	4
Out	2868		2365		35
10	377	6	316	5	4
11	137	16	113	9	3
12	308	18	268	8	4
13	447	4	406	6	5
14	361	10	341	2	4
15	311	14	276	7	4
16	446	8	414	1	5
17	223	2	180	4	3
18	328	12	298	3	4
In	2938		2631		36
Total	5806		4996		71
Slope	119		111		
Rating	67.7		64.1		

Hole Commentary

1.   Water all along right side of hole, plenty of room right. Water cuts just in front of green so you can't come up short. OB long, marsh right.
2.   Water off the tee box to the right with trees after the water ends so favor center to left side of fairway. Bunkers guard left and over green.
3.   Short par 3. Trees can cause problems depending on pin placement.
4.   OB far left of the hole. There is water right from 150 - 100 yards FG. Green slopes away from you, trouble left and over the green.
5.   Water to the right from 150-100 yards FG. Bunkers guard both left and right side of the green. Trouble over the narrow green.
6.   OB left of the fairway. Playing for position is smart play from 150-100 yards FG. Don't miss the green in any direction.
7.   Short par 3 with bunkers fronting green, trouble right and over the green.
8.   Water right from 220-120 yards FG, plenty of room left. Green guarded by bunker on left side. Green has collection area in middle right portion that can lead to tough putts.
9.   Plenty of room on this dogleg left par 4. Water in front of green on the left. Green has many undulations that make long putts difficult.
10.   Tee shot through very narrow area between trees. Bunker right from 130-100 yards FG. Fairway gets narrow from 150-100 yards FG. Bunkers front right, left and back right.
11.   The putting surface is hidden on this par 3. Can't miss this green in any direction.
12.   Short par 4 with OB right of fairway and trees left. Bunkers front left and back right of green. Green slopes severely toward the front.
13.   Water to the left of the hole ends at 220 yards FG. Trees right make it a tighter driving hole. Fairway ends at 200 yards FG and starts again at 100 yards FG. Bunkers left and right with trouble over the green.
14.   Water to the left from 180 yards FG up to the green and on the right from 200-60 yards FG. Bunkers guard front left and right of green with tree trouble over the green.
15.   OB far right of hole. Bunker sits out 100 yards FG on right. Bunkers front left and right of the green with OB left, right and over the green.
16.   Short par 5 is made more difficult by trees crossing the fairway at 150 yards FG, leaving only a narrow chute to the green. Lay back far enough behind trees to give yourself a shot over or around trees. OB right of green, bunker in front left of green.
17.   Long par 3 with bunkers right and left back of green. Tree trouble over the green.
18.   Short par 4, stay back at least 120 yards FG so you have options to get past the tree in the middle and on the left at 90 yards FG.

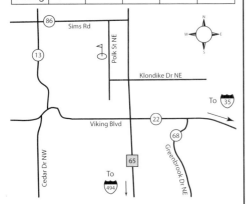

From I-694 take Hwy 65 north 18.5 miles to Klondike Dr. NE. Go west 1/2 mile to Polk St. NE. Go north 1/2 mile, the course is on the right. From I-35 take Viking Blvd. (CR 22) west 14 miles to Hwy 65. Go north 1 mile to Klondike Dr, same directions as above.

Highland Park Golf Course

1403 Montreal Avenue
St. Paul, MN 55116
651-695-3774
www.ci.stpaul.mn.us/depts/parks

Course Information

Reservations:	Weekdays - 7 days		
	Thursday for weekend/holidays		
	www.teemaster.com		

2000 Fees:	9	18	Comments
Weekdays	$18.00	$25.00	
Weekends	$18.00	$25.00	
Twilight	N/A	$16.00	after 4 pm
Seniors	*	*	* see other
Power Cart	$15.00	$23.00	
Pull Cart	$3.00	$3.00	
Club Rental	$6.00	$6.00	
Credit cards	Visa Mastercard		
Checks	Any		
Rain Check	Ask		
Other	Sr. discount available w/ Sr. card		

Leagues:	Various

Amenities:			
Driving Range	Y	Snacks	Y
Putting Green	Y	Grill/Bar	Y
Practice Green	Y	Restaurant	N
Spikeless	Y	Locker Room	Y
Proshop	S	Showers	N

Management:	
Manager	Bob Cotie
Professional	Bob Cotie

Highland park is one of the St. Paul city courses. The course is set on a hill and offers elevation changes on many of the holes. Although there are mature trees on the course it is very wide open. Not a long course, if you play smart you should score well. The course was good shape when I played it. The city of St. Paul is looking at redesigning the entire course in the future. The course is well suited for beginner to intermediate golfers.

Rating   81.75

Course Rating

Tees	Grade 2.65
Ability Levels	2
Condition	3
Signs / Hole Maps	1
Ball Washers	4
Benches	5

Fairways	3.3
Condition	3
Yardage Markers	3
Pin Indicators	4
Rough	3.5
Watered / Drainage	3.5

Greens	2.78
Condition	3.5
Speed	2
Size and Variety	2.5
Slope	3
Fringe	3.5

Layout	3.13
Par 3's	4
Par 4's	2.5
Par 5's	2.5
Strategic Trouble	3
Bunkers	2
Enough Space	4
Walkability	5

Amenities	3.15
Driving Range	4
Practice Green	4
Water on Course	3
Port-O-Potties	2
Locker Rooms	2
Pro Shop	3.5
Grill & Bar	4
Weather Shelter	2
Golf Carts	2.5

Overall	3.3
Enjoyable	3
Challenging / Fair	2
Reservations	5
Scenery	3
Gimmicky Holes	5
Weather Monitor	4

Value	3.5
Overall	81.75

Hole	Blue	White	Par	Handicap	Red	Par	Handicap
1	489	479	5	9	464	5	1
2	195	182	3	11	177	3	13
3	409	404	4	1	344	4	5
4	519	513	5	3	504	5	3
5	164	155	3	17	131	3	11
6	472	472	5	5	407	5	9
7	298	288	4	13	280	4	15
8	324	311	4	15	302	4	7
9	181	165	3	7	137	3	17
Out	3051	2969	36		2746	36	
10	414	410	4	2	348	4	2
11	136	130	3	14	124	3	16
12	383	378	4	12	372	4	8
13	320	308	4	6	296	4	4
14	404	374	4	4	303	4	14
15	494	489	5	16	438	5	10
16	329	324	4	18	316	4	6
17	236	220	3	10	217	4	18
18	498	495	5	8	440	5	12
In	3214	3128	36		2854	37	
Total	6265	6097	72		5600	73	
Slope	111	110			118		
Rating	69.0	68.4			71.1		

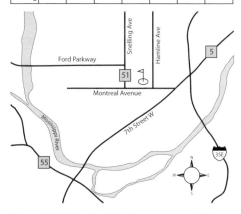

From I-35E take 7th Street west 1/3 mile to Montreal Avenue (CR 51). Go west 0.4 miles to Hamline Ave. Go north 1 block, the course is on the left.

Hole Commentary

1. Straightforward par 5 with mature trees lining the fairway inside 200 yards FG. Bunker right of the hole.
2. Downhill par 3 but take enough club. Green is much more level than it appears. Don't go over this green.
3. Uphill par 4 with OB far left by the street. Take enough club on the uphill approach. Better short than long on your approach. Don't miss green left.
4. Dogleg left par 5 with trees on both sides of the fairway. Favor right side of fairway but stay out of the trees. Large tree overhangs fairway at the dogleg 150 yards FG. Bunker right side of fairway at 150 yards FG. OB on the left from 200 yards FG to the green. Bunkers left and right of green.
5. Slightly uphill par 3, easy to come up short. Bunker right of the green.
6. Downhill par 5 with OB left and mature trees right. Should be reachable in two shots. Bunker left of the green with little trouble right or long.
7. Swing away, the green may be reachable by longer hitters. Hit into the trees on the right and par will be difficult. Bunker left of green.
8. Long hitters may not want to hit driver. Tree trouble left and right. Hit inside 150 yards FG and you will have a downhill lie on your approach. Creek runs in front of the green with a bunkers left and right of the green.
9. Deceptively long par 3. Many balls find the bunker in front right of green.
10. OB along the left by the driving range. Tree in the middle of the fairway at 120 yards FG forces you to choose a side of the fairway. Don't go over this green.
11. Short par 3 with a large bunker in front of green and trouble right of green.
12. Straight forward par 4 with little trouble on the drive. No trouble around green except long.
13. Dogleg left par 4 with a creek running left of the fairway to the hole, then running in front of the green. Favor right side of fairway and hit to 100 - 75 yards FG. Bunkers right of green.
14. Uphill par 4 with little trouble other than trees on right side. No trouble around green.
15. Downhill dogleg left par 5. Favor right to middle of fairway to avoid waste area left of hole at 150 yards FG. Bunkers left and right of the green.
16. Uphill par 4 with no trouble on the drive other than trees. No trouble around the green.
17. Long par 3 with a bunker and trees short and right.
18. OB to the left where the driving range is inside of 200 yards FG. Not much trouble around the green, right may have tree trouble.

Hollydale Golf Club
4710 Holly Lane North
Plymouth, MN 55446
763-559-9847

Course Information

Reservations:	Weekdays -1st come/1st served
	Weekend - Tues 7:30am

2000 Fees:	9	18	Comments
Weekdays	$16.50	$23.50	
Weekends	$18.00	$27.00	
Twilight	N/A	N/A	
Seniors/Jr	$14.00	$18.00	M-F < 11am
Power Cart	$13.00	$24.00	
Pull Cart	$2.00	$3.00	
Club Rental	$4.00	$4.00	
Credit cards	None		
Checks	Local checks only		
Rain Check	18 hole<4 holes, 9 hole<13 holes		
Other			

Leagues:	Various

Amenities:			
Driving Range	Y	Snacks	Y
Putting Green	Y	Grill/Bar	N
Practice Green	N	Restaurant	N
Spikeless	Y	Locker Room	N
Proshop	B	Showers	N

Management:	
Manager	Dave Deziel
Professional	None

For the most part Hollydale is a very wide open golf course with plenty of room to mishit. The greens were in good shape but they were all small round greens. There was some variety in hole layout, with some small elevation changes. Water comes into play on 7 holes but for the most part is not a factor. There are very few bunkers on the course to add some challenge. Being a short course and very wide open, most people should have the opportunity to score well. The course is well suited for beginner to intermediate golfers.

Rating   87.08

Course Rating

Tees	Grade
	3.1
Ability Levels	3
Condition	3
Signs / Hole Maps	2
Ball Washers	3.5
Benches	5

Fairways	**3.05**
Condition	3.5
Yardage Markers	2
Pin Indicators	3
Rough	3.5
Watered / Drainage	4.5

Greens	**3.05**
Condition	4
Speed	3
Size and Variety	1.5
Slope	3
Fringe	4

Layout	**3.4**
Par 3's	3
Par 4's	3
Par 5's	3
Strategic Trouble	4
Bunkers	3
Enough Space	3.5
Walkability	5

Amenities	**3.23**
Driving Range	4
Practice Green	3
Water on Course	3
Port-O-Potties	3
Locker Rooms	4
Pro Shop	3
Grill & Bar	2
Weather Shelter	3.5
Golf Carts	3

Overall	**3.33**
Enjoyable	3
Challenging / Fair	2.5
Reservations	5
Scenery	3
Gimmicky Holes	5
Weather Monitor	2

Value	**4.0**
Overall	**87.08**

Hole	Blue	White	Par	Handicap	Red	Par	Handicap
1	392	377	4	5	327	4	5
2	382	377	4	7	327	4	1
3	183	176	3	9	136	3	11
4	484	474	5	11	421	5	3
5	167	155	3	17	125	3	17
6	539	531	5	3	443	5	9
7	333	323	4	13	270	4	7
8	421	415	4	1	360	5	13
9	301	291	4	15	271	4	15
Out	3202	3082	36		2680	37	
10	342	330	4	8	304	4	6
11	425	415	4	2	330	5	10
12	219	204	3	4	142	3	18
13	296	292	4	16	242	4	16
14	158	153	3	18	146	3	8
15	504	494	5	14	438	5	2
16	349	328	4	6	278	4	12
17	499	489	5	12	444	5	4
18	166	156	3	10	124	3	14
In	2958	2861	35		2488	36	
Total	6160	5980	71		5128	73	
Slope	121	M 119 W 130			120		
Rating	70.1	M 69.4 W 74.7			69.9		

Hole Commentary

1. Favor left side of fairway to avoid tree trouble on right side. Bunker on right is at 170 yards FG. Bunker guards right side of green.
2. Slight dogleg left with not much trouble other than the trees on the hole.
3. Straightforward par 3 with not much trouble around the green.
4. Straight uphill par 5 with water on the left at 270 yards FG. Approach shot is blind so aim just right of furthest clump of trees on left side. Don't go right of green.
5. Mid-length downhill par 3 with little trouble around the green.
6. Water runs the entire left side of the hole. Can cut some distance off by aiming left and hitting approach from rough. Pond on left sits at 270 yards FG.
7. OB left side of the hole. Approach shot is uphill and generally crosswind so choose club accordingly. No real trouble around the green.
8. Wide-open dogleg right par 4 so get out the big lumber. Green is wide open.
9. Smart play is to favor left side of fairway or trees will block approach shot. Need to be aware of OB along left side of fairway.
10. Water on the right side at about 70 yards FG is the only real trouble on this par 4. Bunker guards front and left side of green.
11. Dogleg left with trees lining the fairway. Stay out of the trees and there's no other trouble on the hole or around the green.
12. Longer par 3 with water on front and left of green to catch errant shots.
13. Great chance to score on this short par 4 with little trouble on drive or around the green.
14. Par 3 with water just off the tee box that should not come into play.
15. The hole turns right and heads downhill at about 250 FT. Large tree at the edge of the fairway is at 200 yards FG and in the rough so you must stay right of that. Left and over the green is water.
16. Dogleg right par 4. The approach shot is somewhat blind since you can't see the putting surface. There is some trouble past the green so avoid going over the green.
17. Downhill, dogleg right par 5. Clump of trees on the right is at 200 yards FG and the hole turns right from there. Must hit past or left of those trees. Creek runs behind the green so don't go too long.
18. Downhill par 3 with water on the left side of the hole.

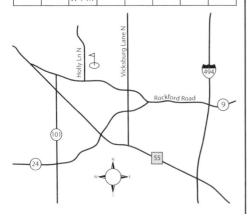

From I-494 take Rockford Road west 1 mile to Old Rockford Road. Go west 1.2 miles to Holly Lane. Go north 0.4 miles the course is on the right.

Inver Wood Golf Course

1850 70th Street
Inver Grove Heights, MN 55077
651-457-3667

Course Information

Reservations:	3 days in advance		

2000 Fees:	9	18	Comments
Weekdays	$17.00	$28.00	
Weekends	$17.00	$28.00	
Twilight	N/A	N/A	
Seniors	N/A	N/A	
Power Cart	$16.00	$26.00	
Pull Cart	$2.75	$2.75	
Club Rental	N/A	$9/$12	
Credit cards	Visa Mastercard		
Checks	Local checks only		
Rain Check	18 hole<4 holes, 9 hole<13 holes		
Other			

Leagues:	Mon, Tues, Thur

Amenities:			
Driving Range	Y	Snacks	Y
Putting Green	Y	Grill/Bar	Y
Practice Green	N	Restaurant	N
Spikeless	O	Locker Room	N
Proshop	F	Showers	N

Management:	
Manager	Al McMurchie
Professional	Al McMurchie

Inverwood Golf Course will challenge your golf game from hole 1 to 18. Gently rolling hills, mature trees lining most fairways and plenty of bunkers and water hazards await you. Be sure to play from the appropriate tee box or it could be a long and frustrating round. There is a great variety of length and layout to the holes making it a very enjoyable golf course to play. The setting is beautiful and the course in great shape. The course will challenge golfers of all ability levels.

Rating   103.70

Course Rating

Tees	Grade **4.45**
Ability Levels	5
Condition	4
Signs / Hole Maps	4
Ball Washers	4
Benches	5

Fairways	**3.95**
Condition	4
Yardage Markers	4
Pin Indicators	4
Rough	3.5
Watered / Drainage	4

Greens	**4.05**
Condition	4
Speed	3.5
Size and Variety	5
Slope	4
Fringe	4

Layout	**4.05**
Par 3's	4
Par 4's	4
Par 5's	4
Strategic Trouble	4
Bunkers	4
Enough Space	5
Walkability	3.5

Amenities	**3.93**
Driving Range	5
Practice Green	5
Water on Course	4
Port-O-Potties	3
Locker Rooms	2.5
Pro Shop	3.5
Grill & Bar	3.5
Weather Shelter	2.5
Golf Carts	3

Overall	**4.2**
Enjoyable	4
Challenging / Fair	4
Reservations	4
Scenery	5
Gimmicky Holes	4.5
Weather Monitor	4

Value	**4.5**
Overall	**103.70**

Hole	Blue	White	Gold	Red	Par	Men Handicap	Women Handicap
1	536	526	466	444	5	7	5
2	349	334	292	259	4	11	13
3	363	334	324	285	4	9	9
4	352	328	316	282	4	15	11
5	409	383	372	326	4	5	7
6	206	160	151	118	3	13	15
7	537	512	500	450	5	3	3
8	453	428	418	368	4	1	1
9	167	134	124	114	3	17	17
Out	3372	3139	2963	2646	36		
10	512	484	432	416	5	2	2
11	351	325	314	276	4	14	10
12	240	176	144	123	3	8	16
13	351	305	295	228	4	12	18
14	540	512	461	434	5	4	4
15	389	361	353	308	4	6	6
16	385	359	350	307	4	18	14
17	190	172	154	134	3	16	12
18	394	361	329	303	4	10	8
In	3352	3055	2832	2529	36		
Total	6724	6194	5795	5175	72		
Slope	135	131	M 127 W 131	124			
Rating	72.5	70.3	M 68.4 W 73.7	70.3			

Hole Commentary

1.   Favor the left side of the fairway on this par 5 as everything slopes to the right. Approach to deep but narrow green should be to right side, unless you go for green in two.

2.   Downhill par 4. Water on the right side of fairway from 125 yards FG to the green.

3.   Favor left side of fairway to avoid tree trouble and on right. Bunker guards this narrow but deep elevated green. Extra club may be necessary to reach green.

4.   Favor left side of fairway to avoid tree trouble and water which runs from 150 yards FG to the green. Bunkers on left side of fairway from 125-75 yards FG, the narrowest part.

5.   Favor left side of fairway. Water on right runs from 150-70 yards FG. Multi-level green with multiple breaks.

6.   Check above trees for wind as flag may not be accurate. One small bunker in front of green.

7.   Aim at or left of flag in middle of fairway. Fairway ends at 240 yards FG with bunkers on right from 300-250 yards FG. Approach is downhill to well bunkered green but don't take any less club.

8.   Tough uphill par 4. Favor left side of fairway to avoid tree trouble right. Take extra club as you don't want to be short. Bunkers surround this multi-tiered green.

9.   Slightly downhill par 3 with trouble all around this green.

10.   Tough par 5 with bunkers on the left from 270-230 yards FG. Aim just right of bunkers on left. Hole is behind trees on left, favor right side on approach. Bunkers guard left side of green.

11.   Avoid bunkers on left from 150-120 yards FG and on right from 105-80 yards FG. Uphill approach to green guarded by bunkers on left. Don't go right or over this green.

12.   Fantastic elevated par 3 with a great view. Take one less club due to elevation.

13.   Have to hit past 150 yards FG to clear the water. Aim for between 120-75 yards FG. May need extra club to reach elevated green.

14.   Great view from elevated tee box, avoid left side. Fairway narrows where bunker juts in on right side at 250 yards FG. Bunkers guard approach from 75 yards FG to the green.

15.   Trees pinch in on left at 150 yards FG with overhanging tree on right at 125 yards FG. Green is well bunkered.

16.   Fairway doglegs left starting at 175 yards FG. Favor right side of fairway. Bunkers guard front left and right side of green.

17.   Long par 3 with plenty of trouble.

18.   Aim just left of bunkers on the right that run from 160-140 yards FG or over bunkers inside 140 yards FG. Bunker and lake on left start at 90 yards FG.

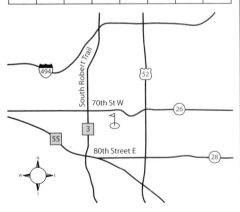

From I-494 take Hwy 3 south 1.75 miles to 70th Street E (CR26). Go east 0.8 miles, the course is on the right.

Island View Golf Club

9150 Island View Road
Waconia, MN 55387
952-442-6116

Course Information

Reservations:	2 days in advance		
2000 Fees:	9	18	Comments
Weekdays	N/A	$42.00	
Weekends	N/A	$46.00	
Twilight	N/A	$25.00	
Seniors	N/A	N/A	
Power Cart	N/A	$28.00	
Pull Cart	N/A	$2.00	
Club Rental	N/A	$10.00	
Credit cards	Visa Mastercard		
Checks	Local Checks Only		
Rain Check	Ask		
Other			
Leagues:	Various		

Amenities:			
Driving Range	Y	Snacks	Y
Putting Green	Y	Grill/Bar	Y
Practice Green	Y	Restaurant	Y
Spikeless	Y	Locker Room	Y
Proshop	F	Showers	Y

Management:	
Manager	Dave Anderson
Professional	Dan Callahan

Don't let the lack of length fool you, Island View is not a push-over. If you play smart and hit for accuracy instead of distance you can score well. If you spray the ball around it could be a long day. There are many trees, bunkers and water hazards which are strategically placed to catch errant tee shots and approach shots. The terrain is rolling hills with fairways well protected by trees. A little pricey but certainly a fun course to play. The course will challenge golfers of all ability levels.

Rating   93.30

Course Rating

Tees	Grade 3.5
Ability Levels	2
Condition	4
Signs / Hole Maps	4
Ball Washers	5
Benches	5

Fairways	3.9
Condition	4
Yardage Markers	4
Pin Indicators	4
Rough	3
Watered / Drainage	4

Greens	3.85
Condition	4
Speed	4
Size and Variety	3
Slope	4
Fringe	5

Layout	3.88
Par 3's	4
Par 4's	3
Par 5's	3.5
Strategic Trouble	4
Bunkers	5
Enough Space	4
Walkability	4

Amenities	4.2
Driving Range	4
Practice Green	5
Water on Course	5
Port-O-Potties	3
Locker Rooms	5
Pro Shop	4
Grill & Bar	5
Weather Shelter	2
Golf Carts	3

Overall	3.7
Enjoyable	4
Challenging / Fair	4
Reservations	2
Scenery	4
Gimmicky Holes	4
Weather Monitor	4

Value	3.0
Overall	**93.30**

Hole	Blue	White	Gold	Red	Par	Men Handicap	Women Handicap
1	486	465	465	448	5	15	5
2	398	364	364	335	4	1	3
3	520	509	509	486	5	3	1
4	161	147	147	131	3	17	17
5	394	378	365	357	4	11	7
6	189	176	167	133	3	9	15
7	400	357	290	290	4	5	11
8	384	355	355	292	4	13	13
9	401	384	312	310	4	7	9
Out	3333	3135	2974	2782	36		
10	364	355	355	338	4	6	6
11	180	174	174	157	3	16	14
12	322	310	310	285	4	14	12
13	345	329	300	263	4	12	10
14	571	558	445	445	5	2	2
15	336	325	325	302	4	10	8
16	145	131	131	129	3	18	18
17	554	543	334	334	5/4	4	4
18	402	392	402	350	4/5	8	16
In	3219	3117	2776	2600	36		
Total	6552	6252	5750	5382	72		
Slope	129	126	M 119 W 128	124			
Rating	71.5	70.1	M 67.8 W 73.1	71.0			

Hole Commentary

1. Favor right side of fairway on the downhill opening par 5. Bunkers on right from 270 to 200 yards FG are in play on the drive.
2. Uphill par 4 usually plays into the wind. Favor the left side of fairway but avoid bunker at 160 yards FG on left. Don't go over green.
3. Favor center of this fairway and avoid the bunkers and water on the right and it is an easy par 5. No trouble running ball onto green.
4. Bunkers guard this green well. Keep an eye on wind direction.
5. OB along the right of the hole. Smart play is to hit a controlled shot to 150-110 yards FG. Water left of green. Wind will determine club selection on downhill approach.
6. Tough par 3 which almost always plays into the wind. Could require a couple of extra clubs.
7. Try to hit as far up the hill as possible and avoid bunkers on right at 150 yards FG. Depending on length of drive, may require and extra club or two to reach the green.
8. Favor right side of fairway. Hitting behind trees on right will cost you a shot. Bunker on left at 120 yards FG. Left and long are bad.
9. Long hitters can cut over the corner on this dogleg right but the fairway can be over-driven. Best play is to aim just left of trees to middle of fairway between 150 - 130 yards FG. Bunker guard right side of fairway past trees.
10. Placement of your tee shot very important. Favor left-middle of fairway to avoid being blocked by trees on either side.
11. Tough par 3 which usually play into the wind. Tree overhanging right side of green makes right pin placement tough. Take one or two extra clubs depending on the wind.
12. Risk/Reward par 4. Best play is to avoid trees on right and bunkers on left and hit to about 100 yards FG.
13. Don't go right. Widest area to drive ball to is at 125 yards FG, after that the fairway narrows. That will give you a short pitch to the green.
14. Long and straight par 5 with OB running the entire left side of the hole. Not much sense in going for green in two with OB just left and over green and water guarding front left of green. Use 2nd shot to set up approach.
15. Once again this is a placement hole. Trees on the left have a tendency to attract balls. Hit a controlled club toward right to middle of fairway between 150-110 yards FG.
16. Watch the wind. Although tee box seems secluded the wind will catch ball above trees.
17. Favor left side of fairway off the tee. Set up approach with 2nd shot as green is guarded and tough to hit in two, keep ball below hole.
18. Avoid bunker on left at 120 yards FG, more room to right past trees. Uphill approach may require extra club.

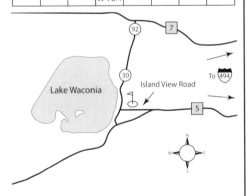

From I-494 take Hwy 5 west 15.8 miles to Island View Road. Take a right, the course is 3/4 mile on the right.

98

Keller Golf Course

2166 Maplewood Drive
Maplewood, MN 55109
651-766-4170
www.co.ramsey.mn.us/parks/golf_courses

Course Information

Reservations:	4 days in advance		
2000 Fees:	9	18	Comments
Weekdays	N/A	$27.00	
Weekends	N/A	$27.00	
Twilight	N/A	$16.00	After 5 pm
Seniors	N/A	$15.50	* see other
Power Cart	$14.00	$23.00	
Pull Cart	$2.00	$4.00	
Club Rental	$8.00	$12.00	
Credit cards	Visa Mastercard		
Checks	Local Checks Only		
Rain Check	18 hole<6 holes, none > 10 holes		
Other	Sr. rate valid w/ Sr. ID card Tu-Th < 11am, F-Su & holidays > 3 pm.		
Leagues:	Mon - Fri		

Amenities:			
Driving Range	Y	Snacks	Y
Putting Green	Y	Grill/Bar	Y
Practice Green	Y	Restaurant	Y
Spikeless	Y	Locker Room	Y
Proshop	F	Showers	Y

Management:	
Professional	Tom Purcell
Manager	Tom Purcell

Keller Golf Course is rich in history and tradition. It has been home to several PGA and LPGA golf tournaments in the past. The gently rolling tree-lined fairways and relatively small and round greens are indicative of 1920's-style golf course architecture. The course is well bunkered and water comes into play on five holes. Keller is a mature and challenging course. The course will challenge golfers of all ability levels.

Rating   97.95

Course Rating

Tees	Grade **3.8**
Ability Levels	4
Condition	4
Signs / Hole Maps	2
Ball Washers	4
Benches	5

Fairways	**4.0**
Condition	4
Yardage Markers	4
Pin Indicators	4
Rough	4
Watered / Drainage	4

Greens	**4.15**
Condition	4
Speed	4.5
Size and Variety	4
Slope	4
Fringe	4

Layout	**3.95**
Par 3's	4.5
Par 4's	4
Par 5's	4
Strategic Trouble	3.5
Bunkers	3
Enough Space	5
Walkability	4

Amenities	**3.13**
Driving Range	3
Practice Green	2.5
Water on Course	3
Port-O-Potties	2.5
Locker Rooms	5
Pro Shop	4
Grill & Bar	4
Weather Shelter	3.5
Golf Carts	2.5

Overall	**3.9**
Enjoyable	4
Challenging / Fair	4
Reservations	3
Scenery	4
Gimmicky Holes	5
Weather Monitor	3

Value	**4.0**
Overall	**97.95**

Hole	Blue	White	Par	Handicap	Red	Par	Handicap
1	332	310	4	15	290	4	7
2	373	334	4	9	287	4	11
3	505	485	5	11	425	5	1
4	150	130	3	13	110	3	15
5	380	371	4	7	300	4	9
6	210	190	3	5	134	3	17
7	420	400	4	3	314	4	13
8	396	382	4	1	340	4	3
9	462	437	5	17	422	5	5
Out	3228	3039	36		2622	36	
10	445	426	4	2	403	5	4
11	392	346	4	10	323	4	12
12	510	475	5	14	430	5	10
13	147	137	3	18	127	3	16
14	350	332	4	12	282	4	8
15	177	155	3	8	125	3	18
16	550	431	5/4	4	411	5	2
17	362	320	4	16	300	4	14
18	405	380	4	6	350	4	6
In	3338	3002	36/35		2751	37	
Total	6566	6041	72/71		5373	73	
Slope	128	123			125		
Rating	71.7	69.4			71.3		

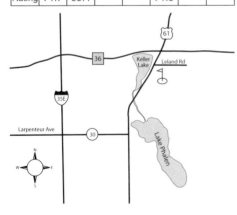

From I-35E take Hwy 36 east 1.75 miles to Hwy 61. Go south 1/4 mile to CR B. Go east, the entrance to the course in on the right.

Hole Commentary

1. Elevated tee shot on dogleg right. Two bunkers right at 105 yards FG yet favor right side of fairway. Either hit to 125 yards or hit past 100 yards FG to have level lie.
2. Elevated tee shot on straight downhill par 4. Bunker on right side of fairway from 125-100 yards FG. Trouble surrounds green.
3. Bunker on right 200 FT. OB along the fence line on left. Approaching green, bunkers guard front left and right with tree trouble over green.
4. Very interesting par 3 with a large tree in front of green. Over the green is trouble.
5. Favor center to left side of fairway on this straightforward par 4. Bunker guards front right with trouble over this green.
6. Long, downhill par 3 with water on the right. Hit the green and be happy with par.
7. Favor the center to left of fairway. Inside 150 yards FG fairway slopes down to green. Bunker front right of green, don't go over.
8. Blind tee shot up hill. Inside 175 yards FG fairway narrows with bunkers right from 160-140 yards FG. Favor left side of fairway.
9. Short uphill par 5. Bunker right at 250 yards FG. Favor right to center of fairway. Uphill approach to a small green with bunker right.
10. Straight, slightly downhill hole. No trouble on tee shot. Bunker guards right side of green, miss left and it's a tough chip back up the hill.
11. Favor center to right side of fairway. Too far left and you'll find tree trouble. Bunker guards left side of green, don't go over.
12. Far right is OB along the hole. Favor left side of fairway. From 150-100 yards FG fairway is severely sloped. Water left and bunker right of the green.
13. Uphill par 3 with bunker right of hole. Take extra club, don't come up short.
14. Downhill, dogleg right par 4. Best shot is between 90-60 yards FG. Green well bunkered in the front. Water far left if you hit too long.
15. Uphill par 3, may want to take extra club but don't go over green. Short better than long.
16. Dogleg left par 5. If you aim up left side need to get past last overhanging tree which is at 240 yards FG. Otherwise hit center to left of fairway. Flag behind green shows green location. Bunkers front left and right of green.
17. Shorter par 4. Favor left side of fairway to avoid hitting over tree by green. Two bunkers guard fairway left and right at 60 yards FG. Left and long are trouble.
18. Bunkers on right of hole from 190-160 yards FG and on right at 150 yards FG. Bunkers guard green right and left.

Lakeview Golf Course

405 North Arm Drive
Mound, MN 55364
952-472-3459

Course Information

Reservations:	Weekdays - 1 week in advance Weekend - Tuesday www.teemaster.com		

2000 Fees:	9	18	Comments
Weekdays	$15.00	$22.00	
Weekends	$17.00	$26.00	
Twilight	N/A	N/A	
Seniors	$11.00	$18.00	weekdays
Power Cart	$14.00	$25.00	
Pull Cart	$2.75	$2.75	
Club Rental	$7.00	$10.00	
Credit cards	Visa Mastercard AmEx		
Checks	Any		
Rain Check	18 hole<3 holes, 9 hole<12 holes		
Other			

Leagues:	Various

Amenities:			
Driving Range	N	Snacks	Y
Putting Green	Y	Grill/Bar	N
Practice Green	N	Restaurant	N
Spikeless	Y	Locker Room	N
Proshop	B	Showers	N

Management:	
Manager	David Eidahl
Professional	None

If you are a beginning golfer or do not like long courses, Lakeview is the place to go. Although it is short, it is not short on trouble. Water comes into play on many holes if you hit an errant shot. Many people could play the course without their driver and score very well. The course could be better maintained, especially the greens and tee boxes. It can be a great confidence builder as long as you keep the ball in play. The course is well suited for beginner to intermediate golfers.

Rating   79.28

Course Rating

Tees	Grade 2.9
Ability Levels	2.5
Condition	2.5
Signs / Hole Maps	2.5
Ball Washers	4
Benches	5

Fairways	3.5
Condition	3
Yardage Markers	4
Pin Indicators	3
Rough	4
Watered / Drainage	4

Greens	2.7
Condition	2.5
Speed	2
Size and Variety	3
Slope	4
Fringe	3

Layout	2.78
Par 3's	3
Par 4's	2.5
Par 5's	2.5
Strategic Trouble	3
Bunkers	1
Enough Space	4
Walkability	4.5

Amenities	2.23
Driving Range	1
Practice Green	2.5
Water on Course	3
Port-O-Potties	3
Locker Rooms	2
Pro Shop	1.5
Grill & Bar	2
Weather Shelter	2
Golf Carts	3

Overall	3.23
Enjoyable	2.5
Challenging / Fair	2.5
Reservations	4.5
Scenery	3.5
Gimmicky Holes	5
Weather Monitor	3

Value	3.5
Overall	79.28

Hole	Blue	White	Red	Par	Men Handicap	Women Handicap
1	341	319	319	4	8	3
2	354	349	338	4	14	13
3	155	145	133	3	10	5
4	324	312	298	4	6	11
5	163	155	146	3	12	15
6	330	323	313	4	16	9
7	500	479	457	5	2	1
8	303	296	270	4	4	7
9	155	155	152	3	18	17
Out	2625	2533	2426	34		
10	175	165	144	3	9	14
11	510	490	430	5	1	2
12	264	251	236	4	13	16
13	273	259	248	4	11	10
14	231	222	213	4	15	12
15	370	359	334	4	5	8
16	391	363	330	4	3	4
17	156	132	123	3	17	18
18	473	462	398	5	7	6
In	2843	2703	2456	36		
Total	5468	5236	4882	70		
Slope	107	104	112			
Rating	66.3	65.3	68.2			

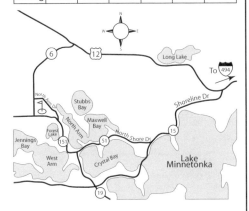

From I-494 take Hwy 12 west 12.5 miles to McCulley Rd. (CR 6). Go south (CR 6 merges with CR 19) 2.25 miles to North Arm Drive. Go east 1/2 mile, course is on the right.

Hole Commentary

1.   Short uphill dogleg left with the green behind the trees on the left. Approach from 120-100 yards FG is best. Not much trouble around green.
2.   Fairway splits with upper right and lower left fairway, either one is fine. No trouble around this green.
3.   Uphill par 3, take extra club. Better off a little short than long. Missing the putting surface in any direction leaves tricky chip shot.
4.   Favor right side of fairway to avoid trees on left side of fairway. Don't want to miss this green too far over.
5.   Do not want to go over or right of the green. Large green to hit to.
6.   Very straightforward hole with little trouble around the green.
7.   Favor right side of fairway with water to the left off the tee, fairway slopes to the left. Inside 150 yards FG the fairway slopes to the right. Two-tiered green, don't miss long or left.
8.   Avoid creek on left side of fairway. Approach is uphill and requires extra club. Back of green drops off steeply. Missing right is ok.
9.   Downhill par 3 with water in front right. There is room to miss short or left although left leaves a tough chip shot.
10.   Mid-length par 3 with water left of green.
11.   Accurate tee shot required to set up approach, left to center of fairway. Approaching the green there is water and a tree 100 yards in front of green to the left. Don't miss this green right or long.
12.   Uphill and short par 4. Green definitely can be driven but miss the green anywhere but short and you will struggle to make par. Smart play is to hit to top of the hill, 100 - 75 yards FG. Water over the green.
13.   Water just off the tee box and to the right of the fairway inside 120 yards FG. If you miss this green, miss short or left.
14.   Once again this green can be driven, but miss the green and it's a tough par. Whether you go for green or lay up short, this should be a birdie hole.
15.   Aim just right of the trees on the left. Plenty of room to bail out left, going right could lead to trouble. Don't want to miss this green in any direction as a difficult recovery shot awaits you.
16.   Fairly wide open driving hole, favor the left side of the fairway. Choose club wisely on approach, going too far over is big trouble.
17.   Downhill par 3, requires less club than what you would normally hit. There is a lake left of the green so don't miss that direction.
18.   This par 5 is wide open and reachable if you hit a good drive. There is OB right of the fairway. There is a little room to miss the green left but don't miss it long or right.

Legends Golf Club

8670 Credit River Boulevard
Prior Lake, MN 55372
952-226-4777
www.legendsgc.com

Course Information

Reservations:	7 days in advance		

2000 Fees:	9	18	Comments
Weekdays	$30.00	$65.00	(9 hole after
Weekends	$30.00	$65.00	twilight only)
Twilight	N/A	$35.00	
Senior	N/A	N/A	
Power Cart	N/A	$15.00	
Pull Cart	$3.00	$3.00	
Club Rental	N/A	$25/35	
Credit cards	Visa	Mastercard	Discover AmEx
Checks	Any		
Rain Check	Ask		

Leagues:	None	

Amenities:			
Driving Range	Y	Snacks	Y
Putting Green	Y	Grill/Bar	Y
Practice Green	Y	Restaurant	Y
Spikeless	Y	Locker Room	Y
Proshop	F	Showers	Y

Management:	
Professional	Howie Samb
Manager	Howie Samb

Legends just opened in August of 2001. The golf course is set amidst an expansive natural setting featuring a 30 acre lake, cascading creek, and scenic wetlands and ponds. There is a tremendous variety of holes, including the par 3's which all feature carries over water. Some of the grass was in poor shape but that is to be expected of such a new course. The clubhouse is spectacular and the Legends Grill has something for everyone after the round. The course will challenge golfers of all ability levels.

Rating   101.98

Course Rating

	Grade
Tees	**4.13**
Ability Levels	5
Condition	5
Signs / Hole Maps	2.5
Ball Washers	4
Benches	1
Fairways	**3.35**
Condition	3.5
Yardage Markers	2.5
Pin Indicators	4
Rough	3.5
Watered / Drainage	4
Greens	**4.48**
Condition	4
Speed	4.5
Size and Variety	5
Slope	5
Fringe	3.5
Layout	**4.75**
Par 3's	5
Par 4's	4.5
Par 5's	5
Strategic Trouble	5
Bunkers	5
Enough Space	5
Walkability	3.5
Amenities	**4.5**
Driving Range	5
Practice Green	5
Water on Course	3.5
Port-O-Potties	4
Locker Rooms	5
Pro Shop	4
Grill & Bar	4.5
Weather Shelter	4
Golf Carts	5
Overall	**5.0**
Enjoyable	5
Challenging / Fair	5
Reservations	5
Scenery	5
Gimmicky Holes	5
Weather Monitor	5
Value	**3.0**
Overall	**101.98**

Hole	Silver	Black	Blue	White	Gold	Par	Handicap
1	396	374	350	332	295	4	11
2	416	409	396	377	302	4	9
3	458	440	421	399	290	4	5
4	530	510	498	463	313	5	3
5	122	115	105	101	89	3	17
6	452	421	392	358	282	4	1
7	182	167	161	151	70	3	13
8	388	369	350	329	235	4	15
9	511	493	474	457	410	5	7
Out	3455	3298	3147	2967	2286	36	
10	390	369	351	327	282	4	10
11	593	573	551	539	444	5	4
12	351	341	321	298	264	4	16
13	184	182	174	159	136	3	14
14	299	290	277	260	249	4	18
15	402	384	362	344	307	4	8
16	621	596	580	518	367	5	2
17	191	181	155	136	73	3	12
18	420	405	386	353	334	4	6
In	3451	3321	3157	2934	2456	36	
Total	6906	6619	6304	5901	4742	72	
Slope	143	140	139	M 134 W 135	120		
Rating	73.3	72.0	70.6	M 68.7 W 74.4	68.0		

From I-35 take 185th Street W (exit 84) west 2.2 miles to Natchez Avenue (CR 91). Go south 1 mile to Credit River Blvd. (CR 68). Go west, course is on the right.

Hole Commentary

1.   Water on the left off the tee box. Long grass to the right ends at 150 yards FG. Very long green, don't miss long or right.
2.   Long dogleg left par 4, favor center to left side of fairway. Two turf hollows guard front right with Legends Lake right of green.
3.   Very long par 4 with wide fairway. Marsh on left and trees right. Bunker straight away is 150 yards FG. Bunker front and trouble over green.
4.   Short dogleg left par 5. Best tee shot is over the bend in cart path on left. Very deep green guarded on both sides by bunkers.
5.   Short par 3 but intimidating. Don't miss the green, hit to the center and take par.
6.   Another longer par 4. Favor left side of fairway. Water on right ends at 223 yards FG and water left ends at 164 yards FG. Green guarded on right by wetlands and bunkers.
7.   Mid-length par 3 plays tough into a wind. Small landing area short and left of green.
8.   Accuracy off tee is critical with trees lining fairway left and right. Left side of fairway gives perfect angle to attack green. Small green protected by bunkers front right and left.
9.   Dogleg left par 5 plays uphill and into wind. Favor right side of fairway and avoid mounds on left. Small green is wide but shallow. Approach is open on right with bunkers left.
10.   Hitting right takes bunker in front of green out of play but brings the water into play. Water on right ends at 150 yards FG. Fairway slopes right to left toward water. Water fronts green on left with mounds of long grass right.
11.   Double dogleg par 5. Hit tee shot over or toward right side of bunker on right. Aim for large oak tree for second landing area. Almost impossible to reach in two. Bunker on right at 360 yards FG, bunkers on left end at 280 yards FG. Water fronts green with bail-out area right.
12.   Can be aggressive and cut off as much of fairway as you like. Fairway slopes right to left. Water fronts green with bunker left.
13.   Tough par 3 over water with bunkers left and right. Try to stay below the hole.
14.   Green falls off sharply in all directions except left. Only chance to go for green is to hit to left side and roll it on. Miss anywhere and it will be tough to make par.
15.   Favor left side of fairway that slopes right. Green fronted by water with bunkers left and over. Water on right from 93 yards FG to the green. Very long green.
16.   Aim at fairway bunker in the distance. On 2nd shot hit over bunkers on left from 220-160 yards FG. Bunkers guard left of green.
17.   Tough par 3 over water with little bail out area, can't be short.
18.   Aim at or left of bunker on right at 153 yards FG. Bunkers left and over green.

Links at Northfork

9333 153rd Avenue NW
Ramsey, MN 55303
763-241-0506

Course Information

Reservations:	7 days in advance		

2000 Fees:	9	18	Comments
Weekdays	N/A	$33.00	
Weekends	N/A	$42.00	
Twilight	N/A	$15/22	walk/ride > 6pm
Seniors/Jr.	N/A	$21.00	
Power Cart	N/A	$12.00	per person
Pull Cart	N/A	$4.00	
Club Rental	N/A	$15.00	
Credit cards	Visa	Mastercard	Discover AmEx
Checks	Ask		
Rain Check	Pro-rated		
Other			

Leagues:	Various		

Amenities:			
Driving Range	Y	Snacks	Y
Putting Green	Y	Grill/Bar	Y
Practice Green	Y	Restaurant	Y
Spikeless	Y	Locker Room	Y
Proshop	F	Showers	N

Management:			
Manager	Mick Mollbergs		
Professional	Nick Ramsey		

The Links at Northfork features a traditional Scottish style layout with mounds, fairway bunkers and deep rough. Bentgrass fairways and greens make for ideal conditions. Deep rough is truly deep – the ball settles under thick grass, which grabs your club as you try and hit out of it. The course is void of trees until you get to hole 14 on the back, therefore you will feel any wind. This is your chance to play in British Open conditions (especially when the wind blows) without the airfare. The course will challenge golfers of all ability levels.

Rating   104.60

Course Rating

Tees	Grade 4.75
Ability Levels	5
Condition	5
Signs / Hole Maps	4
Ball Washers	5
Benches	4

Fairways	4.4
Condition	5
Yardage Markers	4
Pin Indicators	4
Rough	4
Watered / Drainage	5

Greens	4.3
Condition	5
Speed	4
Size and Variety	4
Slope	4
Fringe	4

Layout	3.85
Par 3's	4
Par 4's	4
Par 5's	4
Strategic Trouble	3
Bunkers	4
Enough Space	5
Walkability	3

Amenities	4.5
Driving Range	5
Practice Green	5
Water on Course	5
Port-O-Potties	4
Locker Rooms	4
Pro Shop	3
Grill & Bar	4
Weather Shelter	4
Golf Carts	4

Overall	3.95
Enjoyable	4.5
Challenging / Fair	4
Reservations	4
Scenery	3
Gimmicky Holes	4
Weather Monitor	3

Value	4.0
Overall	104.60

Hole	Championship	Back	Middle	Forward	Par	Handicap
1	525	515	494	457	5	4
2	428	405	385	324	4	10
3	420	395	381	296	4	8
4	190	175	160	109	3	16
5	371	340	335	266	4	14
6	429	400	375	318	4	12
7	155/146	140/129	125/115	79/74	3	18
8	446	425	415	340	4	6
9	514	500	479	403	5	2
Out	3478	3295	3149	2592	36	
10	490	479	471	425	5	3
11	426	408	384	318	4	9
12	207/206	197/194	188/184	154/153	3	15
13	380	365	338	264	4	13
14	557	543	512	416	5	1
15	403	381	362	304	4	11
16	440	401	381	316	4	7
17	176	165	153	109	3	17
18	432	419	406	344	4	5
In	3511	3358	3195	2650	36	
Total	6989	6653	6344	5242	72	
Slope	127	124	M 121 W 130	M 111 W 117		
Rating	73.7	72.4	M 71.0 W 76.6	M 66.0 W 70.5		

Hole Commentary

1. Avoid mounds by playing as straight as possible. Approach green from middle or right.
2. Play over bunker on the left. The longer and further left, the better. Mound on front right side of green will prevent approach from right.
3. Water on the right dictates the safe play is to left side. Too far left and you may have a lost ball in the rough.
4. Water on the right will swallow balls hit that way. Aim for middle of green. Short is safe.
5. Short distance can be deceiving. This severe dog-leg right requires accuracy on both shots. Safe shot is to play a 200-yard club to the corner. On your approach to the green, do not go long and left – OB comes up quick.
6. Mounds and traps at driving distance. Stay in the fairway and approach green straight on.
7. This hole actually has 2 separate greens with water in the middle. Make sure you are hitting to the correct green!
8. Straight, flat hole. Hard to see trouble from the tee box. Approach green from the left side.
9. Hit a good first shot to set up a good second shot, positioning your 3rd shot right in front of the water about 100 yards FG. Don't need to be long. Going for green in 2 is not wise with water short and trouble over green.
10. A big hitter can cut the corner on the left through a waste bunker and have an easy shot for green in 2. Green is 2-tiered.
11. Hole has 2 fairways, choose right fairway as the left one puts a lot of trouble in the form of bunkers between you and the green.
12. This green has two forks that come out on the right and left, with a bunker in the middle.
13. Challenge here is the large tree on left side of the fairway that can knock your drive down or get in the way of second shot. Therefore, approach green from right side of the fairway.
14. Avoid going too far left, as the trees give you no shot. Best play is long and to right side. The last 200 yards to the green are down a fairly narrow tunnel lined by trees. Your goal should be setting up a good 2nd shot to score.
15. This dog-leg left is as challenging as you make it. Hit a 200-225 yard shot straight off the tee. Cutting the corner doesn't pay. Green is up-hill, to the right across a stream, take an extra club.
16. Best shot is to hit it straight and long and catch the downslope of the hill. Wind really affects your shot. 2nd shot will be a tough up-hill blind shot to green, choose club carefully.
17. Only safe place on this hole is the green. Bunker short left and water to the right.
18. Fairway bunkers left, mounds right. This hole requires a drive to left side of fairway to take water out of play. Best approach to the green is from the left.

From I-94 take Hwy 101 north 6.75 miles to Hwy 10. Go east 3.75 miles to 153rd Ave. NW. Go north 3/4 mile, the course is on the right. From I-694 take Hwy 169 north 15.5 miles to 153rd Ave. NW. Follow directions above.

Majestic Oaks
Golf Course - Gold

701 Bunker Lake Blvd.
Ham Lake, MN 55304
763-755-2142

Course Information

Reservations:	4 days in advance		
2000 Fees:	9	18	Comments
Weekdays	$13.00	$24.00	
Weekends	$13.00	$28.00	9 hole > 2pm
Twilight	N/A	$13.00	After 6pm
Seniors/Jr.	$9.00	$16.00	ask for times
Power Cart	$14.00	$25.00	
Pull Cart	$3.00	$3.00	
Club Rental	$10.00	$18.00	
Credit cards	Visa Mastercard Discover AmEx		
Checks	Any		
Rain Check	18 hole<3 holes, 9 hole<12 holes		
Other			
Leagues:	Mon - Thur		

Amenities:			
Driving Range	Y	Snacks	Y
Putting Green	Y	Grill/Bar	Y
Practice Green	Y	Restaurant	Y
Spikeless	Y	Locker Room	Y
Proshop	F	Showers	Y

Management:	
Professional	Bill Folkes
Manager	Bill Folkes

The Gold course is the easier of the two courses at Majestic Oaks. Everything seemed to be a step down from the Platinum course. Despite that, the course was in good condition and the round of golf was enjoyable. Water comes into play on 10 holes and mature trees are abundant. There are a couple of short par 4's that tempt you to hit driver, but play smart or you will likely be looking at a bogey or worse. The course is well suited for beginner to intermediate golfers.

Rating   95.28

Course Rating

Tees	Grade 3.55
Ability Levels	3
Condition	3.5
Signs / Hole Maps	4
Ball Washers	4
Benches	4.5

Fairways	3.15
Condition	3
Yardage Markers	2.5
Pin Indicators	4
Rough	3
Watered / Drainage	4

Greens	3.7
Condition	4
Speed	4
Size and Variety	3
Slope	3.5
Fringe	3.5

Layout	3.73
Par 3's	3.5
Par 4's	3.5
Par 5's	3
Strategic Trouble	3.5
Bunkers	4.5
Enough Space	4.5
Walkability	4

Amenities	4.48
Driving Range	4
Practice Green	5
Water on Course	4.5
Port-O-Potties	4.5
Locker Rooms	5
Pro Shop	4
Grill & Bar	5
Weather Shelter	4.5
Golf Carts	3

Overall	3.68
Enjoyable	3.5
Challenging / Fair	3.5
Reservations	3
Scenery	4
Gimmicky Holes	5
Weather Monitor	4

Value	4.0
Overall	**95.28**

Hole	Back	Middle	Forward	Par	Men Handicap	Women Handicap
1	376	351	283	4	9	5
2	433	404	321	4	1	1
3	489	463	395	5	3	9
4	310	285	266	4	15	13
5	157	140	117	3	17	17
6	336	299	259	4	11	11
7	379	342	289	4	5	3
8	176	150	119	3	13	15
9	509	472	406	5	7	7
Out	3165	2906	2455	36		
10	335	305	256	4	10	12
11	352	328	282	4	6	8
12	516	486	394	5	4	6
13	204	174	135	3	12	14
14	412	387	263	4	2	2
15	365	336	284	4	18	10
16	324	285	244	4	14	18
17	195	170	145	3	16	16
18	528	502	390	5	8	4
In	3231	2973	2393	36		
Total	6396	5879	4848	72		
Slope	123	M 118 W 132	120			
Rating	71.2	M 68.8 W 74.1	68.4			

Hole Commentary

1. Dogleg right with bunkers on the right from 130-50 yards FG, aim just left of these. Bunkers left, right and over green.
2. Favor left side of the fairway. Fairway ends at 150 yards FG and starts again at 125 yards FG. Water left from 150 yards FG to the green. Bunkers surround the green.
3. OB along entire left side of the hole. Cutting corner on left only leads to trouble. Plenty of room to hit to right. Inside 200 yards FG you get a good look at the hole. Two bunkers guard right side of hole. Don't miss green left or over.
4. No reason to cut hole to the left, plenty of area to the right. Water left of fairway from 120 yards FG. Two bunkers right of green.
5. Bunkers over and marsh short of this wide but shallow green.
6. OB along entire left side and trees to the right of the fairway. Smart play is to lay-up to a comfortable wedge area. Long but narrow green with a bunker right of green.
7. OB along left side of the hole. Fairway gets tight inside of 80 yards FG and a creek runs in front of green. Don't go over the green.
8. Par 3 with water running across the hole and nothing but trouble over the green.
9. OB along left side of hole, plenty of area to hit right. Bunkers front left and right of green.
10. Can get close to this par 4 with a good drive. Avoid left side of fairway with the trees over there. Don't hit drive inside 100 yards FG unless you stay right. Bunker over the green.
11. Trees on the right side come into play at about 100 yards FG. Want to stay in middle of fairway to avoid being blocked out by trees on either side. Bunker front left of the green.
12. Double dogleg par 5 with OB and trees left of fairway. Favor right side of fairway but avoid bunkers from 260-220 yards FG. Best 2nd shot lay-up is to 100 - 80 yards FG.
13. Take extra club on this slightly up-hill par 3 and watch the wind.
14. Water across fairway at about 130 yards FG, hit to 150 yards FG. The green is very long so know where the pin is to avoid long putts. Water right of green.
15. Slightly uphill par 4. Avoid left side of fairway or trees will block approach shot. Bunkers surround the green.
16. Driver not the smart play. Best play is to lay-up to a distance where you can spin a wedge shot. Green slopes away from you. Trouble on all sides of the green.
17. Bunkers guard all sides of this green. Wind will affect club selection.
18. Swing away on this straight par 5. Can be reached in two with two good shots. Good chance for birdie to finish the round. Bunkers surround this green.

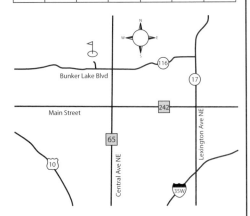

Bunker Lake Blvd

Main Street

116

17

242

65

10

35W

Central Ave NE

Lexington Ave NE

From I-694 take Hwy 65 (Central Avenue) north 15.5 miles to Bunker Lake Blvd. (CR 116). Go west 1/2 mile, the course is on the right.

Majestic Oaks
Golf Course - Platinum
701 Bunker Lake Blvd.
Ham Lake, MN 55304
763-755-2142

Course Information

Reservations:	4 days in advance		

2000 Fees:	9	18	Comments
Weekdays	$15.00	$29.00	
Weekends	$15.00	$33.00	9 hole>3pm
Twilight	$13.00	$13.00	After 6pm
Seniors/Jr.	$10.00	$18.00	ask for times
Power Cart	$14.00	$25.00	
Pull Cart	$3.00	$3.00	
Club Rental	$10.00	$18.00	
Credit cards	Visa Mastercard Discover AmEx		
Checks	Any		
Rain Check	18 hole<3 holes, 9 hole<12 holes		
Other			

Leagues:	Various

Amenities:			
Driving Range	Y	Snacks	Y
Putting Green	Y	Grill/Bar	Y
Practice Green	Y	Restaurant	Y
Spikeless	Y	Locker Room	Y
Proshop	F	Showers	Y

Management:	
Professional	Bill Folkes
Manager	Bill Folkes

The platinum course is the premiere course at Majestic Oaks. The course lives up to its name with beautiful oak trees lining many of the fairways. Water comes into play on only 8 holes but a multitude of bunkers around the greens are strategically placed to catch errant approach shots. The course was in great shape with nice grass and quick greens. The golf course hosts many company outings throughout the year. The course will challenge golfers of all ability levels.

Rating   102.73

Course Rating

	Grade
Tees	**4.23**
Ability Levels	4.5
Condition	4
Signs / Hole Maps	4
Ball Washers	4
Benches	5
Fairways	**3.55**
Condition	4
Yardage Markers	2.5
Pin Indicators	4
Rough	4
Watered / Drainage	4
Greens	**4.23**
Condition	4.5
Speed	4
Size and Variety	4.5
Slope	4
Fringe	3.5
Layout	**4.2**
Par 3's	4
Par 4's	4
Par 5's	4
Strategic Trouble	4.5
Bunkers	3.5
Enough Space	5
Walkability	5
Amenities	**4.48**
Driving Range	4
Practice Green	5
Water on Course	4.5
Port-O-Potties	4.5
Locker Rooms	5
Pro Shop	4
Grill & Bar	5
Weather Shelter	4.5
Golf Carts	3
Overall	**4.15**
Enjoyable	4
Challenging / Fair	4.5
Reservations	3
Scenery	4.5
Gimmicky Holes	5
Weather Monitor	4
Value	**4.0**
Overall	**102.73**

Hole	Championship	Back	Middle	Forward	Par	Men Handicap	Women Handicap
1	540	506	490	430	5	7	3
2	375	353	338	302	4	15	11
3	415	395	338	315	4	9	9
4	220	175	155	130	3	13	15
5	396	376	354	310	4	11	5
6	545	537	508	480	5	1	1
7	422	389	357	300	4	3	7
8	150	139	125	95	3	17	17
9	420	401	369	278	4	5	13
Out	3483	3271	3033	2640	36		
10	415	389	369	325	4	2	8
11	427	400	381	325	4	12	10
12	200	174	158	142	3	16	18
13	509	475	460	402	5	14	4
14	412	390	342	284	4	10	12
15	188	164	148	132	3	18	14
16	550	525	490	425	5	4	2
17	400	377	362	256	4	8	16
18	429	396	369	337	4	6	6
In	3530	3290	3079	2628	36		
Total	7013	6561	6112	5268	72		
Slope	129	125	M 121 W 136	M 113 W 126			
Rating	73.9	71.4	M 69.8 W 76.3	M 65.9 W 71.6			

Hole Commentary

1. Favor right side of fairway to avoid trees on the left. On your approach there is water left of the fairway from 100 FG to the green. Bunkers front left, front right and left of green.
2. Aim just right of the bunker on the left from 130 - 100 yards FG. OB left of the fairway. Bunkers front left and right of green.
3. OB far left of hole with bunkers on the left from 200 - 150 yards FG. Water right of fairway from 180 yards FG to the green. Bunker guards left side of green. Trouble over green.
4. Longer, uphill par 3 with bunkers front left, right and one long right. OB far left of green.
5. Water on right of the fairway and OB left of the fairway. Hole turns left at 150 yards FG, aim just right of the trees on the left.
6. OB and trees left so favor middle to right side of fairway. Water on right is reachable by long hitters and runs all the way to the hole. Bunkers surround this green.
7. Dogleg right par 4 with bunker on the right at 150-100 yards FG, hit left of that bunker.
8. Can't see the putting surface but bunkers surround green.
9. Favor center to right side of fairway. Approach is uphill and requires extra club. Bunkers left and right of green.
10. Tough driving hole, turning right at 150 yards FG. Too far left or right can be tree trouble. Bunkers front left and right of green.
11. Bunkers to the left from 170 - 150 yards FG with water right of fairway inside 150 yards FG. Two bunkers left and right of this green.
12. Shorter uphill par 3 with bunkers surrounding the green.
13. Flat landing area where hole turns left is from 220 - 200 yards FG. Inside 150 yards FG the fairway gets tight. Bunkers surround green.
14. Water on the right from 170 yards FG to the green, plenty of room left. Two bunkers left and one front right of the green.
15. Water left and right on your tee shot with bunkers surrounding the green.
16. Water along the entire left side of the fairway. Bunkers left and right of the fairway from 280-240 yards FG. Water gets close to fairway at 160 yards FG. Bunkers surrounding green make it almost impossible to run ball onto green.
17. Hitting over a marsh but a fairly open tee shot. Bunkers left and right of the green. Don't miss the green over and left.
18. Split fairway with a bunker right in the middle from 175-140 yards FG. More room to hit right of the bunker than left. Bunkers front, left and right of the green. Not a lot of room to miss long.

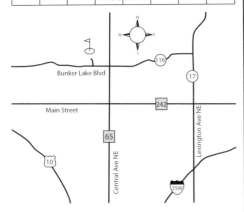

From I-694 take Hwy 65 (Central Avenue) north 15.5 miles to Bunker Lake Blvd. (CR 116). Go west 1/2 mile, course is on the right.

Manitou Ridge
Golf Course

3200 North McKnight Road
White Bear Lake, MN 55110
651-777-2987
www.co.ramsey.mn.us/parks/golf_courses

Course Information

Reservations:	4 days in advance		
2000 Fees:	9	18	Comments
Weekdays	$15.00	$25.00	
Weekends	$15.00	$25.00	9 hole > 2pm
Twilight	N/A	$15.00	After 5pm
Seniors	N/A	*	avail w/ Sr. card
Power Cart	$14.00	$23.00	
Pull Cart	$2.00	$4.00	
Club Rental	$8.00	$12.00	
Credit cards	Visa Mastercard		
Checks	Local Checks Only		
Rain Check	18 hole<6 holes, none > 10 holes		
Other	$12.50 twilight > 6pm.		
Leagues:	Mon - Thur		

Amenities:			
Driving Range	Y	Snacks	Y
Putting Green	Y	Grill/Bar	Y
Practice Green	N	Restaurant	N
Spikeless	Y	Locker Room	N
Proshop	F	Showers	N

Management:	
Manager	Greg Hubbard
Professional	Mark Foley

Manitou Ridge Golf Course features one of the highest points in Ramsey County offering panoramic views of the metropolitan area. There are a number of elevation changes on the course including the 17th, a great downhill golf hole hitting over a pond. For the most part the course was in very good shape which provided for an enjoyable round at a very good price. The course is well suited for beginner to intermediate golfers.

Rating   100.38

Course Rating

Tees	Grade 3.53
Ability Levels	2.5
Condition	4
Signs / Hole Maps	4
Ball Washers	4
Benches	4.5
Fairways	**3.9**
Condition	4
Yardage Markers	3.5
Pin Indicators	4
Rough	4
Watered / Drainage	4.5
Greens	**4.45**
Condition	4.5
Speed	4
Size and Variety	5
Slope	4.5
Fringe	4.5
Layout	**3.98**
Par 3's	4
Par 4's	4
Par 5's	3
Strategic Trouble	4
Bunkers	4.5
Enough Space	4
Walkability	4.5
Amenities	**3.28**
Driving Range	3.5
Practice Green	4
Water on Course	3
Port-O-Potties	4
Locker Rooms	1
Pro Shop	4
Grill & Bar	4.5
Weather Shelter	1
Golf Carts	3
Overall	**3.75**
Enjoyable	4
Challenging / Fair	3.5
Reservations	3.5
Scenery	4
Gimmicky Holes	5
Weather Monitor	1
Value	**4.5**
Overall	**100.38**

Hole	Blue	White	Red	Par	Men Handicap	Women Handicap
1	325	312	307	4	16	10
2	397	380	365	4	10	4
3	368	353	338	4	2	2
4	382	357	288	4	6	6
5	503	472	445	5	4	8
6	420	405	389	4	8	12
7	150	138	125	3	18	18
8	361	335	310	4	14	14
9	302	280	255	4	12	16
Out	3208	3032	2822	36		
10	205	192	105	3	9	17
11	425	404	385	4	1	5
12	389	382	375	4	15	7
13	173	166	159	3	17	15
14	368	358	339	4	5	1
15	368	358	338	4	11	9
16	538	485	420	5	3	3
17	189	157	119	3	13	13
18	538	500	406	5	7	11
In	3193	3002	2646	35		
Total	6401	6034	5468	71		
Slope	116	113	119			
Rating	70.4	68.8	71.6			

Hole Commentary

1. This dogleg turns right at 100 yards FG. OB along left side of hole, but favor that side of the fairway. Bunkers left, right and over the green.
2. Very straight hole over a hill with OB along left side of hole. Bunkers guard left and right side of green.
3. Avoid hitting ball left down the hill, can make for tough recovery shot. Water fronts the green on the left side.
4. Ravine to the right off the tee box but a very open tee shot. Bunkers left and right of the green with trouble over.
5. Bunker on the right is at 250 yards FG. No trouble until you reach the green where a bunker guards front left of the green.
6. Bunker on the right from 185-165 yards FG. Green guarded by bunker over left side of green so don't go over.
7. Bunkers guard both left and right side of the green with mounds over the green.
8. Bunker on right is at the dogleg at 110 yards FG. Approach shot is uphill, take enough club. Three bunkers surround green.
9. Downhill and short par 4 with the fairway sloping right to left. Favor left side of fairway and avoid water on right which gets close around 80 yards FG. Water right and bunkers left of the green.
10. Longer par 3 over water with the only trouble being long and right.
11. Wide open driving hole on this longer par 4. Green is to the left side of the fairway and has no real trouble around it.
12. Favor right side of the fairway on tee shot. Stay away from trees and it's an easy hole. Bunker guards front right of green.
13. Bunkers guard this large green in the front left and right side of the green.
14. OB left of the fairway. Fairway slopes to the left so favor right side. Most level area for approach is at 200 yards FG, past that and you'll have an uphill lie. Take extra club on uphill approach shot to a fairly open green.
15. Favor the right side of the fairway to avoid trees on left at 135 yards FG. OB left of the fairway. Not much trouble around this green.
16. OB along entire left side of the hole. Bunker on the left at 275 yards FG and on the right at 190 yards FG. Don't want to go too far over this green.
17. Straight downhill tee shot to a green protected by water in front and right. Wind will determine if you need less club. Two bunkers guard over the green.
18. OB along left side of hole. Plenty of room to hit right. Bunkers guard both left and right side of the green. Don't go over the green.

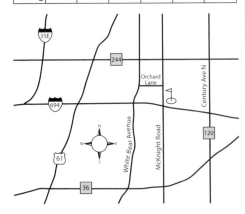

From I-694 take White Bear Avenue north 0.4 miles to Orchard Lane. Go east 1/2 mile to McKnight Road. Go south 0.4 mile, course is on the left.

Meadowbrook Golf Club

201 Meadowbrook Road
Hopkins, MN 55343
952-929-2077
www.minneapolisparks.com

Course Information

Reservations:	4 days in advance www.teemaster.com		
2000 Fees:	**9**	**18**	**Comments**
Weekdays	$17.00	$24.00	
Weekends	$17.00	$26.00	9 hole > 2pm
Twilight	$17.00	$17.00	After 5 pm
Seniors	N/A	$15.00	* see other
Power Cart	$13.00	$24.00	
Pull Cart	$2.00	$3.00	
Club Rental	$4.00	$7.50	
Credit cards	Visa Mastercard		
Checks	Local Checks Only		
Rain Check	18 hole<4 holes, 9 hole<13 holes		
Other	M-Th < 1pm, w/ 2 or 4-some is $27.50 including cart. *Sr. rate w/ patron card M-Th < 11am.		
Leagues:	Mon - Thur		

Amenities:			
Driving Range	Y	Snacks	Y
Putting Green	Y	Grill/Bar	Y
Practice Green	N	Restaurant	N
Spikeless	Y	Locker Room	Y
Proshop	B	Showers	Y

Management:	
Manager	Scott Nelson
Professional	None

Meadowbrook is one of the Minneapolis city courses. The course is set amidst mature trees and rolling hills. Water comes into play on 13 holes, most notably the 5th hole which requires a lay-up in front of the creek on a downhill, blind tee shot. The course was in better than average condition with fast greens. Most of the greens were round and about the same size. The course will challenge golfers of all ability levels.

Rating   90.95

Course Rating

Tees	Grade 3.45
Ability Levels	4
Condition	3.5
Signs / Hole Maps	1
Ball Washers	4
Benches	4.5

Fairways	3.45
Condition	3.5
Yardage Markers	3.5
Pin Indicators	3
Rough	3.5
Watered / Drainage	4

Greens	3.23
Condition	4
Speed	3
Size and Variety	2.5
Slope	3
Fringe	3.5

Layout	3.8
Par 3's	4
Par 4's	4
Par 5's	3.5
Strategic Trouble	3
Bunkers	3.5
Enough Space	4
Walkability	5

Amenities	3.03
Driving Range	1
Practice Green	4
Water on Course	3
Port-O-Potties	3
Locker Rooms	5
Pro Shop	1
Grill & Bar	3.5
Weather Shelter	3.5
Golf Carts	4.5

Overall	3.55
Enjoyable	3.5
Challenging / Fair	3.5
Reservations	3
Scenery	3.5
Gimmicky Holes	5
Weather Monitor	3

Value	4.0
Overall	**90.95**

Hole	Blue	White	Yellow	Red	Par	Men Handicap	Women Handicap
1	512	497	462	398	5	7	5
2	162	154	144	119	3	17	17
3	322	306	298	234	4	11	11
4	462	452	441	405	5	9	7
5	442	381	367	354	4	3	1
6	187	178	167	120	3	13	13
7	398	389	352	310	4	5	9
8	363	326	319	226	4	15	15
9	450	440	324	313	4	1	3
Out	3298	3123	2874	2481	36		
10	389	369	343	282	4	6	6
11	367	356	319	275	4	12	12
12	349	344	309	271	4	14	14
13	126	123	120	118	3	18	16
14	494	487	420	358	5	10	10
15	416	394	333	279	4	2	4
16	135	121	107	102	3	16	18
17	409	399	366	328	4	4	2
18	546	536	449	442	5	8	8
In	3231	3129	2766	2455	36		
Total	6529	6252	5640	4936	72		
Slope	132	130	M 124 W 127	119			
Rating	72.0	70.7	M 67.9 W 72.7	68.8			

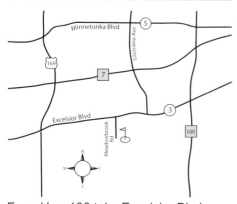

From Hwy 100 take Excelsior Blvd. west 1.25 miles to Meadowbrook Road. Go south 1/4 mile, course is on the left. From Hwy 169 take Excelsior Blvd east 1.25 miles to Meadowbrook Road. Follow directions above.

Hole Commentary

1. Straightforward par 5 with a bunker at the top of the first hill at 240 yards FG. On your second shot there's water from 160-140 yards FG on the right side. Green is guarded by bunker in front left of green.
2. Slightly downhill par 3 with bunkers front left and right of the green. Water left of green.
3. Uphill par 4 with little trouble on your drive. Take enough club on the uphill approach and avoid bunker on left side of green.
4. Bunker on the right side of the fairway at 214 yards FG on this par 5. Uphill approach requires extra club to reach this unprotected green.
5. Creek runs across the fairway at 150 yards FG. Plan to hit your tee shot to 160-150 yard FG keeping in mind that the tee shot is downhill. Not a lot of trouble around the green.
6. Slightly downhill par 3, but the wind is typically in your face so club selection is difficult. Bunkers in front of and over the green.
7. Plan to hit your tee shot to the left side around 165 yards FG to avoid an uphill or sidehill lie. Don't go too far over this green.
8. Downhill par 4 with water on the left from 120-50 yards FG. Bunkers guard front left and right side of the green.
9. Elevated tee shot with trees on both sides of the fairway. Water on left side at 240 yards FG. Bunker guards left side of the green.
10. Wide open tee shot, favor right side of fairway. Uphill approach requires extra club. Green guarded by bunker in front right side.
11. Avoid left side of fairway with water left from 200-100 yards FG. There is OB in all directions except short around green.
12. Water to the left of this hole from 200-150 yards FG. Approach shot is uphill and blind. Look for pin location from tee box. Bunker guards front of green.
13. Bunkers front, left and right of green don't leave much room for error.
14. Tee shot must avoid trees on right and water over the hill on the left from 175-150 yards FG. Bunker in front of green.
15. Water to the right from 130-100 yards FG. Favor center to right side of fairway to prevent being blocked by trees on left side. Two bunkers guard right side of the hole.
16. Short par 3, well guarded by bunkers so accuracy is essential.
17. Water over the hill on the left from 170-100 yards FG and on the right from 150-100 yards FG. Bunker guards front left side of the green.
18. Elevated tee shot must avoid water both left and right that end at 240 yards FG. Past the water there is little trouble on the hole with trees left and right of the fairway.

114

Mississippi Dunes Golf Links

10351 Grey Cloud Trail
Cottage Grove, MN 55016
651-768-7611
www.mississippidunes.com

Course Information

Reservations:	7 days in advance www.teemaster.com		
2000 Fees:	9	18	Comments
Weekdays	$20.00	$36.00	
Weekends	$25.00	$42.00	9 hole > 2pm
Twilight	N/A	$20/25	wkday/wkend
Seniors	N/A	N/A	
Power Cart	$9.00	$14.00	per person
Pull Cart	$3.00	$3.00	
Club Rental	N/A	$15/30	
Credit cards	Visa Mastercard Discover AmEx		
Checks	Any		
Rain Check	18 hole<3 hole, 9 hole<13 holes		
Other	M-F<9:00am: $25. Twilight > 6 pm: $15 - 18 holes, $10 - 9 holes		
Leagues:	Various		

Amenities:			
Driving Range	Y	Snacks	Y
Putting Green	Y	Grill/Bar	Y
Practice Green	Y	Restaurant	Y
Spikeless	Y	Locker Room	Y
Proshop	F	Showers	Y

Management:	
Manager	Greg Doebler
Professional	Dave Tentis

Mississippi Dunes is an exciting newer course, built in 1995. It is a links-style course with lots of mounds, sand and bends. It also has lots of trees which make for an interesting mix. The greens are mostly elevated. Try and play this course with someone who knows it, there are a lot of blind shots with trouble near the greens. You won't play too many courses like this with 6 par 3's, par 4's and par 5's, The course will challenge golfers of all ability levels.

Rating   105.15

Course Rating

Tees	Grade **4.0**
Ability Levels	5
Condition	4
Signs / Hole Maps	1
Ball Washers	5
Benches	4

Fairways	**4.75**
Condition	4.5
Yardage Markers	5
Pin Indicators	5
Rough	4
Watered / Drainage	5

Greens	**4.75**
Condition	5
Speed	5
Size and Variety	4
Slope	5
Fringe	4

Layout	**3.9**
Par 3's	4.5
Par 4's	3
Par 5's	4.5
Strategic Trouble	3
Bunkers	4
Enough Space	5
Walkability	4

Amenities	**4.3**
Driving Range	5
Practice Green	4
Water on Course	4
Port-O-Potties	4
Locker Rooms	4
Pro Shop	4
Grill & Bar	5
Weather Shelter	4
Golf Carts	5

Overall	**4.45**
Enjoyable	5
Challenging / Fair	4
Reservations	4
Scenery	5
Gimmicky Holes	4
Weather Monitor	4

Value	**4.0**
Overall	**105.15**

Hole	Black	Blue	White	Gold	Par	Handicap
1	407	366	330	302	4	7
2	146	138	126	111	3	15
3	489	464	444	379	5	13
4	241	209	177	140	3	9
5	399	383	355	321	4	1
6	187	166	146	124	3	5
7	575	566	515	429	5	3
8	520	506	487	377	5	11
9	120	106	91	77	3	17
Out	3084	2904	2671	2260	35	
10	454	436	413	332	4	2
11	537	484	467	453	5	18
12	219	208	168	137	3	6
13	547	534	476	396	5	12
14	515	515	510	444	5	8
15	390	379	338	285	4	14
16	294	281	262	190	4	16
17	219	207	175	130	3	10
18	435	418	368	337	4	4
In	3610	3462	3177	2694	37	
Total	6694	6366	5848	4954	72	
Slope	135	132	M 128 W 125	115		
Rating	73.1	71.6	M 69.3 W 74.9	69.9		

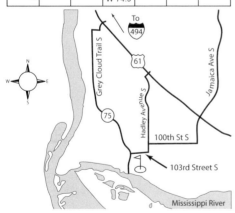

From I-494 take Hwy 61 south to the 80th Street/Grange exit. Go right at the light then left on Hadley Avenue S for 2.2 miles to 103rd Street S. Go west 1/2 mile to Grey Cloud Trail. Entrance to course is on the left.

Hole Commentary

1. Best tee shot is a control club faded to right side of fairway. Mound on front-left will make approach from left side somewhat blind.
2. Want to hit this short par 3 green. Nice view of Mississippi River to the right.
3. Aim between the 2 oaks at top of hill. Too long past the oaks will put you in waste bunkers in the fairway. The smart shot is to lay up for an accurate chip to the green, don't go over!
4. Green is extremely large, with many undulations. Take pin position into account, as it could mean the difference in a club.
5. Dog-leg left, aim for the mound in the center of the fairway with fairway wood. Approach shot is lined by trees on both sides.
6. Don't miss this green left, as it is a long sloping hill and you will have a blind 2nd shot.
7. There are thick trees and rough on the right and left side. Fairway splits, forming a highland left and lowland right. Left side of the fairway sets up the best look at the green.
8. Hit over the markerstone on your drive. Fairway bends right, with trouble on both sides. Safe 2nd shot is to the left and beware of bunker at 85 yards FG. One less club for approach.
9. Nothing fancy about this hole – play your wedge shot into the green.
10. Three large fairway "pit" bunkers at about 220 yards FT. Aim just right or over them if you have confidence in your distance.
11. Fairway ends at 260 FT and resumes shortly after. Green starts up hill from the water, so will play longer. Sprinkler heads will tell you distance to the water and the green. Green is undulating, sloping back to front.
12. Green slopes left to right. Clear prairie grass on your way to the green. Avoid the pot bunker on the front left.
13. Favor the right side of this hole, as there is OB on the left. Avoid the pot bunkers with the railroad ties on the back. Best 2nd shot is a lay up just short of the mounds 100 yards FG.
14. Aim straight off the tee between bunkers. Best approach from left side, but that shot is guarded by a large bunker about 100 yards FG.
15. Fairway does an S. Play the tee shot like a dogleg left. Too far left and you will find water. If you drive straight, you may end up in a waste bunker. Best approach to green from left side.
16. With fairway bunkers, you want to hit a club you can control. Approach green straight on. Don't go long or you'll be in the trees.
17. Waste bunker for the first 75 yards to penalize a poor tee shot. Avoid going long or right of this green, as the trees are thick.
18. Hit your drive to the top of the hill. Once there, you will have a great view of the green for your downhill approach. Take the elevation into account in your club selection.

Monticello
Country Club
1209 Golf Course Road
Monticello, MN 55362
763-295-4653

Course Information

Reservations:	5 days in advance		
2000 Fees:	9	18	Comments
Weekdays	$18.50	$28.75	
Weekends	$18.50	$39.50	
Twilight	N/A	N/A	
Seniors	N/A	N/A	
Power Cart	$16.00	$27.00	
Pull Cart	$3.00	$3.00	
Club Rental	$12.50	$12.50	
Credit cards	Visa Mastercard		
Checks	Local Checks Only		
Rain Check	18 hole<4 holes, 9 hole<13 holes		
Other	Mon & Wed < 1pm, $22.50 or $140 for a foursome with carts		
Leagues:	Tues, Thur, Sat		

Amenities:			
Driving Range	Y	Snacks	Y
Putting Green	Y	Grill/Bar	Y
Practice Green	N	Restaurant	Y
Spikeless	Y	Locker Room	Y
Proshop	F	Showers	Y

Management:	
Professional	Jon Foucault
Manager	Rick Traver

Monticello Country Club is a place to get away from the Twin Cities, without having to drive too far. The course is surrounded by trees and countryside. Although it is not a long course it will challenge you with strategic trouble on many holes throughout the course. There are some holes which allow you to swing away and take your shot at birdie while others require more patience. The course will challenge golfers of all ability levels.

Rating 92.20

Course Rating

	Grade
Tees	**3.95**
Ability Levels	4
Condition	4
Signs / Hole Maps	3
Ball Washers	4
Benches	5
Fairways	**3.15**
Condition	3.5
Yardage Markers	2
Pin Indicators	4
Rough	3
Watered / Drainage	4
Greens	**4.35**
Condition	4
Speed	5
Size and Variety	4
Slope	4
Fringe	5
Layout	**3.65**
Par 3's	3
Par 4's	4
Par 5's	3
Strategic Trouble	4
Bunkers	3
Enough Space	4
Walkability	5
Amenities	**3.35**
Driving Range	2
Practice Green	3
Water on Course	4
Port-O-Potties	4
Locker Rooms	4
Pro Shop	4
Grill & Bar	5
Weather Shelter	2
Golf Carts	4
Overall	**3.35**
Enjoyable	3
Challenging / Fair	3
Reservations	3
Scenery	4
Gimmicky Holes	5
Weather Monitor	3
Value	**3.0**
Overall	**92.20**

Hole	Black	Blue	Yellow	Green	Par Men	Men Handicap	Par Women	Women Handicap
1	337	323	295	272	4	15	4	11
2	390	390	358	333	4	5	4	3
3	221	210	179	165	3	9	3	13
4	534	514	498	448	5	3	5	1
5	356	346	340	289	4	11	4	9
6	370	345	320	258	4	13	4	7
7	166	158	140	124	3	17	3	15
8	401	382	364	310	4	7	4	5
9	444	433	411	375	4	1	5	17
Out	3219	3101	2905	2574	35		36	
10	185	185	166	134	3	18	3	18
11	426	391	370	322	4	6	4	8
12	502	479	469	426	5	10	5	6
13	387	380	362	283	4	8	4	10
14	174	163	145	110	3	14	3	16
15	512	512	494	406	5	2	5	2
16	355	355	340	265	4	12	4	12
17	167	162	146	134	3	16	3	14
18	532	508	475	431	5	4	5	4
In	3240	3135	2967	2511	36		36	
Total	6459	6236	5872	5085	72		71	
Slope	125	M 123 W 130	M 119 W 126	117				
Rating	71.7	M 70.6 W 76.1	M 68.9 W 74.0	69.8				

Hole Commentary

1. Good starting hole, straight away. Two mounds guard front right and left of green.
2. Slight dogleg left. Favor the right side of fairway for best approach to the green. Shots hit left will kick right off hillside toward green.
3. Big ridge separates front ? and back ? of this long green on this lengthy par 3. Be sure you know where the pin is located.
4. Tee shot favoring the left side of the fairway gives you the only chance to reach the green in two. Overhanging trees on the right force a lay-up if your tee shot goes right.
5. 90° dogleg left. Aim just right of trees on left and hit to 150 yards FG. Trees that you see straight ahead of you are about 170 FG. Bail out right on approach and hill will kick ball back to the left. Right of the green is water.
6. Hit your tee shot to 100 - 80 yards FG favoring left side to avoid overhanging tree on right.
7. Avoid trees on left. Pot bunkers guard front and right of green.
8. More room to hit your tee shot than it appears. Aim just left of small tree on hill straight away which looks like it is in the middle of fairway. Right is better than left.
9. Get out the big lumber! Hit all you have in the bag just to right of trees in front of you to set up a long approach to this lengthy par 4.
10. Straightforward par 3.
11. Dogleg left, aim at very left edge of fairway for best approach to hole. Anything right is okay but will be longer to the hole.
12. Avoid water on the right side which is reachable. Hit to the left of the bridge crossing the water, there is no water left of the bridge. Water to the right of the green on approach.
13. Straight away par 4, water on right is reachable so stay left of that. Two tiered green, know where the pin is and hit that level or you'll have a tough putt.
14. Large green with many undulations. Severe break right to left so be sure to hit your ball to the proper level.
15. Favor the right side of the fairway on this slight dogleg right. Water guards the front of the green so if you for it in two and miss, miss long and right.
16. Aim for middle to right of fairway on this slight dogleg right. Good chance to make a birdie.
17. Some room over the hole to the left but if you miss it, miss short. Most of the time this hole plays into the wind so you may need an extra club.
18. Aim just to the left of the two bunkers guarding the right side of the fairway on this dogleg right par 5. Reachable if you hit a good drive. Great way to finish the round.

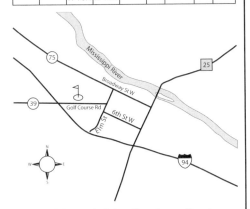

Take I-94 north 24 miles from the I-694/I-494 split to Hwy 25. Go north 1/4 mile to 6th Street. Go west 1/2 mile to Elm Street. Take a right on Elm and a left on Golf Course Road (CR 39). The course is on the right.

New Prague Golf Club

400 Lexington Avenue South
New Prague, MN 56071
952-758-3126
www.newpraguegolf.com

Course Information

Reservations:	1 week in advance www.teemaster.com		
2000 Fees:	9	18	Comments
Weekdays	$15.00	$27.00	
Weekends	$17.00	$32.00	
Twilight	$11.00	$22.00	> 3pm
Seniors	$11.00	$22.00	every day
Power Cart	$16.00	$27.00	
Pull Cart	$3.00	$3.00	
Club Rental	N/A	N/A	
Credit cards	Visa Mastercard		
Checks	Any		
Rain Check	18 hole<6 holes, 9 hole< 14 holes		
Other			
Leagues:	Mon - Thur		

Amenities:			
Driving Range	Y	Snacks	Y
Putting Green	Y	Grill/Bar	Y
Practice Green	N	Restaurant	Y
Spikeless	Y	Locker Room	Y
Proshop	F	Showers	Y

Management:	
Manager	Scott Proshek
Professional	Rob Giesen

If you want to enjoy an afternoon walking a course, visit New Prague Golf Club. Rolling hills and mature trees are abundant on the course. While not extremely challenging it is a fun course to play and will give you a chance to score well. The course is well kept and very scenic. Because it is not in the Metro it is usually easy to get on the course. The course is well suited for beginner to intermediate golfers.

Rating   95.40

Course Rating

Tees	Grade 3.95
Ability Levels	4
Condition	4
Signs / Hole Maps	3
Ball Washers	4
Benches	5
Fairways	**3.7**
Condition	4
Yardage Markers	3
Pin Indicators	4
Rough	4
Watered / Drainage	4
Greens	**4.25**
Condition	4
Speed	4
Size and Variety	5
Slope	4
Fringe	5
Layout	**3.70**
Par 3's	3.5
Par 4's	3
Par 5's	3.5
Strategic Trouble	3
Bunkers	4
Enough Space	5
Walkability	5
Amenities	**3.35**
Driving Range	3
Practice Green	4
Water on Course	4
Port-O-Potties	3
Locker Rooms	2
Pro Shop	3
Grill & Bar	4
Weather Shelter	4
Golf Carts	3
Overall	**3.65**
Enjoyable	3
Challenging / Fair	3
Reservations	5
Scenery	4
Gimmicky Holes	5
Weather Monitor	3
Value	**3.5**
Overall	**95.40**

Hole	Blue	White	Gold	Red	Par	Men Handicap	Women Handicap
1	443	456	443	372	5/4	3	7
2	295	277	277	233	4	7	9
3	396	373	359	319	4	13	1
4	351	351	351	291	4	9	3
5	201	187	176	148	3	15	13
6	545	499	486	402	5	1	5
7	151	140	140	132	3	17	17
8	336	318	306	272	4	11	15
9	356	345	345	306	4	5	11
Out	3074	2946	2883	2475	36/35		
10	345	334	322	299	4	14	10
11	550	536	408	408	5	2	8
12	164	145	145	131	3	16	16
13	536	524	420	420	5	6	14
14	196	178	178	115	3	18	18
15	335	325	325	280	4	8	2
16	355	343	343	260	4	12	12
17	400	385	322	282	4	4	4
18	407	375	365	338	4	10	6
In	3288	3145	2828	2533	36		
Total	6362	6091	5711	5008	72/71		
Slope	126	M 124 W 131	M 120 W 126	118			
Rating	69.9	M 68.8 W 74.6	M 67.1 W 72.5	68.6			

From Hwy 169 take Hwy 21 south 10 miles to Hwy 13/19. Go east 0.8 miles to Lexington Ave. S., south to the course. From I-35 W take CR 70 (turns into CR 8) west 10.5 miles to Hwy 13. Go south 6 miles to Hwy 13/19. Go west 3.2 miles to Lexington Ave. S., south to the course.

Hole Commentary

1. Fairly short par 5 (long par 4 from blue tees). Favor right side of fairway but avoid bunker on right 225 yards FG and water on left starting at 175 FG.
2. Shorter par 4 which is tougher than it looks. Avoid water 65 yards FG on left. Be sure to leave ball below hole on small green.
3. Favor left side of fairway on drive to avoid trees on right. Left and over are OB.
4. Easy hole when you drive ball in fairway. Large green, just stay out of bunkers.
5. Par is a good score on this long par 3. Do not go over this green or left.
6. OB runs along the left of this par 5. Bunkers left and right at 260 yards FG are the only trouble on the drive. Don't go over green.
7. Pay attention to wind direction. Tough to recover if you go over this well bunkered green.
8. Nice dogleg left which requires tee shot past the corner to have an approach to green. Aim just right of left treeline to 100 - 80 yards FG. Don't go left or over the green.
9. Not a long hole but once again the approach shot is more difficult since the green is very well bunkered.
10. Avoid bunker on the right side of fairway which runs from 150-120 yards FG. Small green makes accuracy important on approach shot. Hit to middle of green.
11. Toughest hole on the course. Three shots are usually required since the hole plays uphill into a prevailing wind. Aim second shot just right of trees on left to get closer to the hole.
12. Over and left are OB. Club selection dependent on wind direction, good birdie hole.
13. This par 5 can play very short since it's downhill and downwind. Aim just left of trees on right side and ball will roll downhill. Errant shots left will find wildflowers. Can run the ball up on the green.
14. Long uphill par 3 which requires one or two extra clubs, especially into the wind. Know where the pin is since green is two-tiered.
15. Can be a tough par 4 with prevailing wind even though it is a shorter hole. Bunker guards right side of fairway at 130 yards FG. Best to aim at left side of fairway.
16. Dogleg right which offers risk/reward. Long hitters can go over part of water but that brings double bogey into play. Water runs from 165 - 105 yards FG. Best play is just left of water and hit to about 100 yards FG. Bunker on right side is at 105 yards FG.
17. Longer par 4 requires tee shot over water. Best shot is to favor right side of fairway to avoid clump of trees guarding left side of green.
18. Narrow par 4 with OB along right side of hole. Small green can be hard to hit, one less club is better than one more.

120

Oak Glen Golf Club

1599 McKusik Road
Stillwater, MN 55082
651-439-6963

Course Information

Reservations:	3 days in advance		

2000 Fees:	9	18	Comments
Weekdays	$15.00	$25.00	
Weekends	$15.00	$30/25	<1pm, >1pm
Twilight	N/A	$17/23	Walk/Ride
Seniors	N/A	$32.00	w/ cart weekday
Power Cart	$14.00	$24.00	
Pull Cart	$2.00	$2.00	
Club Rental	$6.00	$12.00	
Credit cards	Visa Mastercard		
Checks	Any		
Rain Check	Prorated		
Other			

Leagues:	Mon, Tues, Thur		

Amenities:			
Driving Range	Y	Snacks	Y
Putting Green	Y	Grill/Bar	Y
Practice Green	N	Restaurant	N
Spikeless	Y	Locker Room	Y
Proshop	F	Showers	Y

Management:			
Manager	Mark Larson		
Professional	Greg Stang		

Oak Glen Golf Club offers one of the best values in the Twin Cities Area. The course is always in very good condition with very quick greens. The layout of the course offers good variety. Water comes into play on 9 holes and the bunkers are well placed to catch errant shots. Some holes offer risk and reward, playing them smart is never a bad idea. It was a very enjoyable course to play and a very good value. The course will challenge golfers of all ability levels.

Rating   105.18

Course Rating

	Grade
Tees	**3.68**
Ability Levels	3
Condition	4
Signs / Hole Maps	3.5
Ball Washers	4
Benches	5
Fairways	**3.85**
Condition	4
Yardage Markers	3.5
Pin Indicators	4
Rough	3.5
Watered / Drainage	4.5
Greens	**4.6**
Condition	4.5
Speed	4.5
Size and Variety	5
Slope	4.5
Fringe	4.5
Layout	**4.15**
Par 3's	4.5
Par 4's	4
Par 5's	3.5
Strategic Trouble	4
Bunkers	4
Enough Space	4.5
Walkability	5
Amenities	**3.65**
Driving Range	3
Practice Green	5
Water on Course	3.5
Port-O-Potties	3
Locker Rooms	5
Pro Shop	3.5
Grill & Bar	4
Weather Shelter	1
Golf Carts	3
Overall	**4.15**
Enjoyable	4
Challenging / Fair	4
Reservations	4
Scenery	4
Gimmicky Holes	5
Weather Monitor	5
Value	**5.0**
Overall	**105.18**

Hole	Blue	White	Red	Par	Men Handicap	Women Handicap
1	368	348	334	4	6	6
2	488	480	455	5	2	2
3	140	130	105	3	16	16
4	328	323	290	4	14	14
5	408	395	340	4	8	10
6	136	126	106	3	18	18
7	441	416	353	4	4	12
8	501	490	433	5	10	4
9	406	388	365	4	12	8
Out	3216	3096	2781	36		
10	406	388	353	4	1	7
11	498	486	464	5	13	3
12	183	175	150	3	11	17
13	356	350	335	4	15	11
14	509	502	447	5	3	1
15	420	370	300	4	7	13
16	218	185	155	3	5	5
17	358	358	306	4	17	15
18	410	400	335	4	9	9
In	3358	3214	2845	36		
Total	6574	6310	5626	72		
Slope	131	128	130			
Rating	72.4	71.3	73.4			

Hole Commentary

1. Water left from 160 yards FG to the green and far right. OB right inside 100 yards FG. U-shaped green requires accurate approach shot.
2. Water left and a bunker right at 250 yards FG. Right of fence is OB. Bunker on right 80 yards FG. Don't miss over or right.
3. Downhill par 3 to a large green protected by bunkers left and right.
4. OB along right side of hole. Long hitters can cut corner over left side of fairway but beware of bunkers left and right of fairway at 100 yards FG. Water right from 80 yards FG to the green. Best shot is to 100 yards FG.
5. Dogleg right with OB along right side. Aim for right to center of fairway. Bunker on left from 150-120 yards FG. Bunker over the green and water left of the green.
6. Short par three well protected by bunkers.
7. Long par 4 with a bunker at 200 yards FG. Bunkers front left and right of green with trouble over the green.
8. OB along left side of this par 5. Bunkers on left at 260 yards and 80 yards FG. Approach is uphill to a green surrounded by bunkers, take extra club. OB left of green.
9. Bunker on right side of fairway from 160-150 yards FG. Bunkers left and right of green.
10. Water along left side of hole. Largest landing area at 150 yards FG, inside that and fairway narrows quickly. Creek crosses fairway at 100 yards FG, with water right of fairway.
11. OB left of fairway. Bunkers left and right from 270 – 255 yards FG. Big hitters aim over top of bunker on left, otherwise aim just right of that bunker. Don't go over this green.
12. Slight uphill par 3 so take enough club. Three bunkers guard the putting surface.
13. Dogleg left par 4 with bunkers right at 160-150 yards FG and left from 160-120 yards FG. OB left of the hole. Favor left side of fairway. Water fronts the green on right from 50 yards FG to green. Cannot go left or over this green.
14. Favor right side of fairway. OB along entire left side of hole and right inside of 200 yards FG. Bunkers left and right at 260 yards FG. From 200-100 yards FG there's not much fairway and it slopes severely right to left.
15. Not much trouble once you cross the creek. Bunkers front left and right of green.
16. Long downhill par 3 to a fairly large green. Water front, right and over the green.
17. Straight uphill par 4 with OB along left side of hole. Favor right side of fairway. Left and over green are OB. Bunkers front left and right.
18. Severe dogleg left with OB along left side of hole. Can cut some distance off hole by hitting over left side of rough but beware of OB. Bunkers on left from 170-140 yards FG. Don't miss the green right or left.

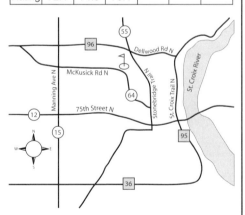

From I-694 take Hwy 36 east 5 miles to Manning Trail (CR 15). Go north 2.5 miles to McKusik Rd. (CR 64). Go east 1.6 miles, course is on the left.

Oak Marsh Golf Club

526 Inwood Avenue North
Oakdale, MN 55
651-730-8886
www.wpgolf.com

Course Information

Reservations:	7 days in advance		
	www.teemaster.com		
2000 Fees:	9	18	Comments
Weekdays	N/A	$24.00	
Weekends	N/A	$29.00	
Twilight	N/A	$17.00	
Seniors	N/A	$26.00	$22 walking
Power Cart	$17.00	$25.00	$17 twilight
Pull Cart	N/A	$3.00	
Club Rental	N/A	$11.00	$8 twilight
Credit cards	Visa Mastercard		
Checks	Any		
Rain Check	18 hole<6 holes, 9 hole<15 holes		
Other			
Leagues:	Mon - Thur		

Amenities:			
Driving Range	Y	Snacks	Y
Putting Green	Y	Grill/Bar	Y
Practice Green	Y	Restaurant	Y
Spikeless	Y	Locker Room	Y
Proshop	F	Showers	N

Management:	
Manager	Steve Whillock
Professional	Drew Ekstrom

Opened in 1996, Oak Marsh is relatively short course measuring only 6184 yards from the back tees. The course was generally in very nice shape. There are not that many trees on the course but plenty of marsh land to contend with. Most of the course is fairly open but a few holes will challenge your shot making ability. There is a nice practice facility where you can tee up from either end of the range. The course is well suited for beginner to intermediate golfers.

Rating 101.75

Course Rating

Tees	Grade 4.18
Ability Levels	5
Condition	4
Signs / Hole Maps	2.5
Ball Washers	4
Benches	4.5

Fairways	3.35
Condition	3.5
Yardage Markers	2.5
Pin Indicators	4
Rough	4
Watered / Drainage	3.5

Greens	4.1
Condition	4
Speed	4
Size and Variety	4.5
Slope	4
Fringe	4

Layout	4.0
Par 3's	4.5
Par 4's	4
Par 5's	3
Strategic Trouble	4.5
Bunkers	4
Enough Space	4
Walkability	4

Amenities	3.98
Driving Range	5
Practice Green	4.5
Water on Course	3
Port-O-Potties	3.5
Locker Rooms	3
Pro Shop	4
Grill & Bar	4.5
Weather Shelter	3
Golf Carts	4.5

Overall	4.18
Enjoyable	4.5
Challenging / Fair	4
Reservations	3.5
Scenery	4
Gimmicky Holes	5
Weather Monitor	4

Value	4.5
Overall	101.75

Hole	Blue	White	Gold	Red	Par	Men Handicap	Women Handicap
1	503	474	442	399	5	5	5
2	396	349	287	206	4	1	7
3	170	155	130	115	3	13	13
4	417	405	366	327	4	9	15
5	444	416	405	342	4	3	3
6	136	128	107	88	3	17	17
7	486	472	445	422	5	7	1
8	198	187	164	140	3	11	11
9	357	327	312	285	4	15	9
Out	3107	2913	2658	2324	35		
10	305	293	263	243	4	10	12
11	521	503	469	455	5	6	2
12	458	433	406	371	4	2	4
13	218	190	170	149	3	12	8
14	328	314	279	245	4	18	14
15	178	149	135	117	3	16	16
16	479	441	428	380	5	4	6
17	202	184	126	105	3	14	18
18	388	373	339	259	4	8	10
In	3077	2880	2615	2324	35		
Total	6184	5793	5273	4648	70		
Slope	117	113	109	108			
Rating	69.3	67.5	65.2	66.2			

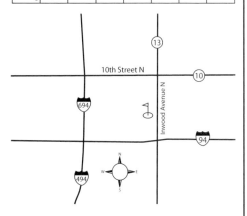

From I-94 take the Inwood Avenue/ Radio Drive exit. Go north 0.4 miles, the course is on the left.

Hole Commentary

1. The bunkers on the left are at 260 and 100 yards FG respectively on this par 4. OB both left and right on the hole.
2. Make sure you check the yardage to reach the 150-yard mark and don't come up short. Approach shot is over marsh with a bunker back right. Water surrounds this green.
3. Waste area right. Hitting to a very large green. Bunkers front right and middle left.
4. OB left and waste area right on this par 4. Favor left side of fairway. Water right of green and OB on left side of green on approach.
5. Favor right side of fairway with waste area to the left side. Water left of fairway from 150 - 100 yards FG.
6. Two pot bunkers over and one left of green.
7. The fairway curves behind the bunker on the left at 240 yards FG and in front on the bunker on the right at 215 yards FG. Water on the left runs from 180 - 100 yards FG and cuts close to the fairway at 150 yards FG.
8. Big bunker in the front right portion of the green on this long par 3. Better to miss left.
9. Grass bunker on the right from 160 - 130 yards FG. Bunker front left of green and grass bunkers over and right of green.
10. Short and tempting par 4. OB left of fairway with bunkers on the left from 110 yards FG to the green. Water on right from 100 yards FG to the green, getting closer to the fairway all the way to the hole. Best shot is to 100 yards FG for a short wedge shot.
11. Left of fence on left is OB. Fairway narrows at 240 yards FG. Can roll the ball onto green with OB well over the green.
12. Two bunkers on left side at 250 and 225 yards FG respectively. Bunker front right of green with no other trouble around green.
13. Long par 3 with water on the left and a bunker guarding front left of green.
14. No reason not to hit driver on this short par 4. Not much trouble on this hole.
15. Grass bunker front left of green with water far left. Plenty of room to the right.
16. Short par 5 with plenty of trouble. Bunkers left at 250 and 225 yards FG. After bunkers, water starts on left, cutting close to fairway at 150 yards FG. Fairway ends at 110 yards FG and starts up 30 yards later. With bunkers surrounding green, cannot roll ball onto green.
17. Pot bunker guards right of green with a large bunker in front of green and water left of green. Some room to hit over the green.
18. Fairway is split by the bunker at 170 yards FG. There is about 20 yards of fairway left of the bunker. The fairway narrows around 130 yards FG. Safest shot is right of bunker but anyone could hit left of bunker and have a shorter approach shot.

Oneka Ridge
Golf Course
5610 North 120th Street
White Bear Lake, MN 55110
651-429-2390

Course Information

Reservations:	4 days in advance		
2000 Fees:	9	18	Comments
Weekdays	$15.50	$25.50	
Weekends	$17.00	$27.50	
Twilight	N/A	$11.00	After 6:30pm
Seniors	$14.50	$20.00	M-F < noon
Power Cart	$15.00	$26.00	
Pull Cart	$3.00	$3.00	
Club Rental	$12.00	$18.00	
Credit cards	Visa Mastercard Discover		
Checks	Any		
Rain Check	18 hole<5 holes, 9 hole<14 holes		
Other			
Leagues:	Various		

Amenities:			
Driving Range	Y	Snacks	Y
Putting Green	Y	Grill/Bar	Y
Practice Green	Y	Restaurant	N
Spikeless	Y	Locker Room	N
Proshop	S	Showers	N

Management:	
Manager	Kristin Jaques
Professional	Brad Rekstad

Opened in 1995, Oneka Ridge features rolling terrain, strategic bunkering and water on 11 of the 18 holes. It also features the longest par 3 in the Twin Cities, # 13 measuring a whopping 255 yards from the back tees. The grass was in good shape but the yardages were poorly marked. Most of the holes are wide open but there are a few that require accurate shot making. The course is well suited for beginner to intermediate golfers.

Rating   91.90

Course Rating

Tees	Grade 3.78
Ability Levels	3.5
Condition	4
Signs / Hole Maps	3
Ball Washers	4
Benches	5

Fairways	3.05
Condition	4
Yardage Markers	2
Pin Indicators	3
Rough	3.5
Watered / Drainage	3

Greens	3.8
Condition	3.5
Speed	4
Size and Variety	4
Slope	4
Fringe	3

Layout	3.7
Par 3's	4
Par 4's	4
Par 5's	3
Strategic Trouble	4
Bunkers	3
Enough Space	3
Walkability	5

Amenities	3.55
Driving Range	4
Practice Green	5
Water on Course	4
Port-O-Potties	3
Locker Rooms	1
Pro Shop	3
Grill & Bar	4
Weather Shelter	1
Golf Carts	4

Overall	3.38
Enjoyable	3.5
Challenging / Fair	3
Reservations	3
Scenery	3.5
Gimmicky Holes	5
Weather Monitor	2

Value	3.5
Overall	**91.90**

Hole	Blue	White	Red	Par	Men Handicap	Women Handicap
1	310	298	229	4	16	12
2	185	174	112	3	6	18
3	410	399	294	4	2	6
4	497	486	408	5	12	8
5	489	481	445	5	14	4
6	424	416	371	4	4	2
7	324	289	240	4	8	14
8	343	334	317	4	10	10
9	141	135	121	3	18	16
Out	3123	3012	2537	36		
10	483	473	445	5	13	3
11	373	366	318	4	7	11
12	396	386	322	4	5	7
13	255	235	167	3	3	5
14	307	294	281	4	17	9
15	181	161	116	3	15	17
16	350	340	291	4	9	15
17	343	300	246	4	11	13
18	549	494	443	5	1	1
In	3237	3049	2629	36		
Total	6360	6061	5166	72		
Slope	119	116	114			
Rating	70.8	69.5	69.7			

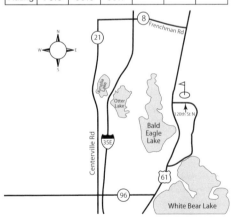

From I-35E take CR 8 (exit 123) east 1.9 miles to Hwy 61. Go south 2.5 miles to 120th Street N. (CR 81). Go east 1/2 mile, the course is on the left.

Hole Commentary

1.   Dogleg left, you can see green through the trees on the left. The creek is 200 yards FG straight ahead and runs to the left past the fairway. Cutting the corners will lead to trouble. Hit to left side to between 150-100 yards FG.

2.   Tee box protected, look to the flag for wind speed and direction. Take enough club.

3.   OB along right side of hole with plenty of room to the left. Bunker front right of green.

4.   Dogleg left par 5 with plenty of room to hit left. Right of the fairway is OB. Favor left side of fairway.

5.   Water sits behind the stand of trees to the left so stay right of that. Water and trees run from 220-130 yards FG on left. Cannot miss green left or over.

6.   Dogleg right par 4. Aim for left side of trees on far side of fairway with a fade.

7.   An arrow marks the left side of the pond on the right of the fairway. Long hitters can hit over that but most people aim just left of the arrow. The water end at 80 yards FG. Long green slopes away from you in the back.

8.   Dogleg left par 4 with OB on the entire left side. You can try to cut the corner, but come up short and you are OB. Hole turns left at 150 yards FG and that should be your target area. Large trees right of fairway make for very difficult recovery shot.

9.   Short par 3 over water with trouble over green.

10.   Reachable dogleg right par 5. Aim for the right side of the fairway, plenty of area to hit to. Bunker right of green. Don't go over this green.

11.   Hole doglegs right with water on the right side of the fairway off the tee box. Aim for center to left side of fairway for best look at green. Don't miss this green long.

12.   Water on the right runs from 160-100 yards FG. Bunker right of green.

13.   Very long par 3 with a multi-level green. Make sure you end up below the hole.

14.   Tee shot to 130-100 yards FG leaves the flattest approach. Left of the fairway is OB. Creek runs in front of green at 50 yards FG. Bunker right with trouble left and long.

15.   Other than the pot bunker left of green there is plenty of area to hit to.

16.   Aim over the 150 yard stake on the left side. Water to the right at 150 yards FG. Not a large green to hit with trouble in all directions.

17.   OB along the entire right side of the fairway. Can hit over top of trees on left if you are a long hitter, just don't miss right and end up OB. Smart play is to hit into wedge range.

18.   Favor far left side of fairway, left rough is ok. Anything right will kick right and be blocked by trees on right. Need to be inside 200 yards FG to have clean shot at green from right.

126

Phalen Park Golf Course

1615 Phalen Drive
St. Paul, MN 55106
651-778-0413
www.ci.stpaul.mn.us/depts/parks

Course Information

Reservations:	Weekdays - 1 week in advance Weekend - Thursday morning www.teemaster.com		
2000 Fees:	9	18	Comments
Weekdays	$18.00	$25.00	
Weekends	$18.00	$25.00	
Twilight	N/A	$16.00	After 4pm
Seniors	*	*	avail w/ permit
Power Cart	$15.00	$23.00	
Pull Cart	$3.00	$3.00	
Club Rental	$6.00	$6.00	
Credit cards	Visa Mastercard		
Checks	Any		
Rain Check	18 hole<9 holes, 9 hole<14 holes		
Other			
Leagues:	Mon - Fri		

Amenities:			
Driving Range	Y	Snacks	Y
Putting Green	Y	Grill/Bar	Y
Practice Green	Y	Restaurant	N
Spikeless	Y	Locker Room	Y
Proshop	S	Showers	Y

Management:	
Professional	Nora McGuire
Manager	Nora McGuire

Phalen Park is one of the St. Paul City golf course. Originally built in the 1920's it was redesigned and enlarged in the 1970's. Although it was enlarged, it is a relatively short course and is a little bit crowded. With bunkers, mature trees and some water you can find trouble if you mishit. It was an enjoyable course with nice scenery. This course is well suited for beginner to intermediate golfers.

Rating   92.60

Course Rating

Tees	Grade 3.1
Ability Levels	2
Condition	4
Signs / Hole Maps	2
Ball Washers	4
Benches	5

Fairways	3.4
Condition	3.5
Yardage Markers	3
Pin Indicators	4
Rough	3.5
Watered / Drainage	3

Greens	3.98
Condition	4
Speed	4
Size and Variety	4
Slope	4
Fringe	3.5

Layout	3.48
Par 3's	3.5
Par 4's	3
Par 5's	2
Strategic Trouble	4
Bunkers	3
Enough Space	5
Walkability	5

Amenities	3.38
Driving Range	3
Practice Green	4.5
Water on Course	2.5
Port-O-Potties	3
Locker Rooms	5
Pro Shop	3
Grill & Bar	4
Weather Shelter	1
Golf Carts	3

Overall	3.95
Enjoyable	4
Challenging / Fair	3
Reservations	5
Scenery	4
Gimmicky Holes	5
Weather Monitor	3

Value	4.0
Overall	**92.60**

Hole	Blue	White	Par	Handicap	Red	Par	Handicap
1	361	349	4	11	325	4	11
2	351	344	4	13	322	4	5
3	209	195	3	9	165	3	15
4	510	495	5	3	468	5	1
5	345	333	4	15	281	4	13
6	370	358	4	7	333	4	9
7	415	408	4	1	406	5	3
8	152	144	3	17	122	3	17
9	337	325	4	5	299	4	7
Out	3050	2951	35		2721	36	
10	359	346	4	14	323	4	12
11	506	485	5	6	412	5	2
12	176	164	3	16	135	3	18
13	372	360	4	12	332	4	10
14	394	379	4	2	351	4	6
15	363	351	4	8	322	4	8
16	167	154	3	18	139/113	3	16
17	404	391	4	4	374/322	4	4
18	310	300	4	10	280	4	14
In	3051	2930	35		2668/2590	35	
Total	6101	5881	70		5389/5311	71	
Slope	120	118			125		
Rating	68.9	67.8			70.7		

Hole Commentary

1. Bunkers on the right side of the fairway at 150 and 115 yards FG and one on the left at 120 yards FG. Bunkers left and right of green.
2. Uphill par 4 with a bunker on the right from 150-120 yards FG. Fairway gets narrow inside 100 yards FG. Bunker guards right of green.
3. Long par 3 with large bunkers guarding front left and right of the green. Over the green is trouble.
4. Dogleg left par 5. The corner is at 240 yards FG. Long hitters favor left side, others favor center to right side of fairway. Bunkers front and left of green with tree trouble over green.
5. This par 4 is a 90° dogleg to the right which turns right at 125 yards FG. Best shot is to aim just left of trees on right. Bunkers guard front left and right of green.
6. Bunker on the right side of the fairway from 150-125 yards FG. Stray too far left or right and there's tree trouble.
7. Favor left side of fairway. Pond in front of green from 115-40 yards FG. Bunkers guard front left and right of green.
8. Downhill par 3 surrounded by bunkers. Wind direction will determine club selection.
9. Trees which over hang left side are at 170 yards FG. Aim just right of those trees. Bunker guards front left of green and over is trouble.
10. Favor the left side of fairway to avoid being blocked by trees. Get past 150 yards FG for best angle to green. Bunker on left is at 125 yards FG. Don't go long or left of this green.
11. Favor right to center of fairway to have a chance to go for green in two. Hole doglegs left. Bunkers guard front left and right of green.
12. Short downhill par 3 with bunker guarding left side of green. Water and bunker right and trees over this green cause trouble.
13. Dogleg left par 4 with a bunker at the turn on the right from 135-110 yards FG. Favor left side to cut some distance. Bunkers guard front left and right of green.
14. Dogleg to the right with water on the left from 230-170 yards FG. Favor left side of fairway to avoid being blocked by trees. Don't go over this green.
15. Dogleg left par 4. The hole turns at 150 yards FG where the tree on the left side sits. Hit ball to 135-110 yards FG to have a good shot at green.
16. Par 3 going over water. Bunkers right and left and water in front guard green.
17. Favor left side of fairway on this dogleg right par 4. Hole turns at 150 yards FG.
18. Short, dogleg right par 4. Last big tree on right where hole turns is at 100 yards FG. Too far right and you'll be blocked by the trees on the right. Bunkers front, left and right of green.

From I-35E take Larpenteur Avenue east 1 block to McMenemy St. Go south 1 block to Wheelock Parkway. Go east 1.8 miles to Phalen Drive. Go north, the course is on the left.

Pheasant Acres Golf Club

10705 County Road 116
Corcoran, MN 55374
763-428-8244

Course Information

Reservations:	Weekdays - Saturday Weekend - Tuesday		

2000 Fees:	9	18	Comments
Weekdays	$16.00	$24.00	
Weekends	$16.00	$27.00	
Twilight	N/A	$15.00	
Seniors	N/A	$15.00	M-Th < 11am
Power Cart	$8.00	$12.00	Per person
Pull Cart	$3.00	$3.00	
Club Rental	$6.00	$10.00	
Credit cards	Visa Mastercard		
Checks	Any		
Rain Check	18 hole<3 holes, 9 hole<12 holes		
Other			

Leagues:	Mon, Wed, Thur

Amenities:			
Driving Range	Y	Snacks	Y
Putting Green	Y	Grill/Bar	Y
Practice Green	N	Restaurant	N
Spikeless	Y	Locker Room	Y
Proshop	F	Showers	N

Management:	
Professional	Steve Fessler
Manager	Steve Fessler

Pheasant Acres has been making strides to improve the level of golf for its patrons. They are currently renovating a few of the holes to add some challenge and to speed up play. The course is pretty flat with only a few elevation changes. Most of the holes are wide open and allow you to swing away. With the addition of new tee boxes and redesigned holes, the course is only going to get better. The course is well suited for beginner to intermediate golfers.

Rating 93.20

Course Rating

	Grade
Tees	**3.28**
Ability Levels	2.5
Condition	4
Signs / Hole Maps	2
Ball Washers	4
Benches	5
Fairways	**3.95**
Condition	3.5
Yardage Markers	4.5
Pin Indicators	4
Rough	3.5
Watered / Drainage	4
Greens	**3.5**
Condition	3.5
Speed	3.5
Size and Variety	3
Slope	4
Fringe	4
Layout	**3.55**
Par 3's	3.5
Par 4's	3.5
Par 5's	3
Strategic Trouble	3
Bunkers	3.5
Enough Space	4
Walkability	5
Amenities	**3.88**
Driving Range	3.5
Practice Green	4
Water on Course	4.5
Port-O-Potties	4.5
Locker Rooms	2
Pro Shop	4
Grill & Bar	4
Weather Shelter	4.5
Golf Carts	4
Overall	**3.53**
Enjoyable	3.5
Challenging / Fair	3
Reservations	3
Scenery	3.5
Gimmicky Holes	5
Weather Monitor	5
Value	**4.0**
Overall	**93.20**

Hole	Blue	White	Gold	Red	Par	Men Handicap	Women Handicap
1	325	306	300	287	4	13	13
2	344	334	330	324	4	11	7
3	145	120	115	110	3	17	17
4	516	504	440	436	5	3	3
5	137	126	120	116	3	15	15
6	415	395	325	322	4	5	9
7	380	345	335	272	4	9	11
8	492	482	478	403	5	7	1
9	441	431	370	370	4/5	1	5
Out	3195	3043	2813	2640	36/37		
10	390	380	375	305	4	6	6
11	400	384	378	292	4	2	4
12	339	331	327	238	4	18	16
13	210	200	165	160	3	8	8
14	341	336	315	247	4	14	10
15	505	495	490	412	5	4	2
16	206	196	136	132	3	12	18
17	385	376	370	289	4	10	14
18	360	348	333	323	4	16	12
In	3136	3046	2889	2398	35		
Total	6331	6089	5702	5038	71/72		
Slope	117	116	110	115			
Rating	69.9	69.0	66.4	68.6			

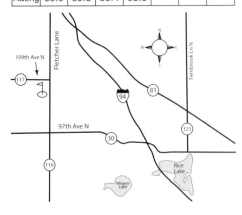

From I-94 take 95th Avenue North, west 3 miles to Fletcher Lane (CR 116). Go north 1.25 miles, the course is on the left.

Hole Commentary

1. Water on the left ends at 150 yards FG. Bunkers left and right front of green.
2. OB on the far right of the fairway. Bunkers guard front left and right of the green.
3. Short downhill par 3, but don't let it fool you. Water surrounds a green that is very wide but shallow.
4. Aim for the left side of the fairway as OB runs along the right side of the fairway. Not much trouble on your approach shot other than OB far right of the green.
5. Take a little extra club for the uphill to avoid coming up short. Bunker right front of green.
6. OB all along the right side of the hole. Anything on the left side is fine. Bunker guards front right of green. There is OB over and right of this multi-tiered green.
7. Bunker on the right at 130 yards FG. Right and over this green are both trouble.
8. Dogleg right par 5. Aim at left side of fairway but must get past 225 FG to avoid trees on the right.
9. Long par 4 with water in front of the green from 50 - 30 yards FG. Other than the water there is no trouble around the green.
10. Water runs along the entire left side of the fairway. There is also water to the right of the hole at 120 yards FG. Bunker guards front left of green.
11. Tough par 4 with trees splitting the fairway at 170 – 160 yards FG. Water on the left from 110 – 90 yards FG. Approach shot is uphill and requires an extra club. Don't miss this green left or long.
12. Straightforward par 4 with a bunker on the left at 120 yards FG and one to the right at 100 yards FG. Don't go over the green.
13. Long, tough, uphill par 3. Definitely need at least 1 extra club to reach this green.
14. OB runs along the right side of this hole. Not much other trouble on this hole. Green has two levels on it so pay attention to pin location.
15. Water cuts across almost the entire fairway at 220 yards FG. Water also on the right starting 250 yards FG and running into OB on the right. Water cuts across the fairway once again 20 yards FG. Don't miss the green to the right.
16. Long but straightforward par 3 with water right and left of the green.
17. Anything center to left of the fairway is a good shot on this on this hole. Don't miss this green left or long. Right side of green is guarded by a bunker.
18. Long finishing par 4 with water both left and right of the fairway. Water on the left ends at 150 yards FG and water on right goes from 125 – 80 yards FG. Bunker guards left side of the green.

Pioneer Creek

705 Copeland Road
Maple Plain, MN 55359
952-955-3982

Course Information

Reservations:	7 days in advance		

2000 Fees:	9	18	Comments
Weekdays	$16.00	$28.00	
Weekends	N/A	$35.00	
Twilight	N/A	$25/16	
Seniors	$15/20	$21/27	with, w/out cart
Power Cart	$8.00	$16.00	
Pull Cart	$2.00	$4.00	
Club Rental	$10.00	$15.00	
Credit cards	Visa Mastercard		
Checks	Local Checks Only		
Rain Check	18 hole<4 holes, 9 hole<13 holes		
Other			

Leagues:	Mon - Fri

Amenities:			
Driving Range	Y	Snacks	Y
Putting Green	Y	Grill/Bar	Y
Practice Green	N	Restaurant	N
Spikeless	Y	Locker Room	N
Proshop	B	Showers	N

Management:	
Manager	Mark Ellingson
Professional	Mark Ellingson

Opened in 2000, Pioneer Creek was well planned with 5 different tee boxes to hit from. The course curves through the Pioneer Creek valley with water in coming into play on 10 holes. There are a number of elevation changes which afford you beautiful views of the creek, trees and rolling hills. A new "log cabin" clubhouse will be open for the 2002 season. It is worth the drive and the price is very reasonable. The course will challenge golfers of all ability levels.

Rating   106.83

Course Rating

Tees	Grade 4.75
Ability Levels	5
Condition	4.5
Signs / Hole Maps	5
Ball Washers	4
Benches	5

Fairways	3.2
Condition	2.5
Yardage Markers	3
Pin Indicators	4
Rough	3.5
Watered / Drainage	4

Greens	4.33
Condition	4
Speed	4
Size and Variety	5
Slope	4.5
Fringe	5

Layout	4.53
Par 3's	4
Par 4's	5
Par 5's	4.5
Strategic Trouble	5
Bunkers	4
Enough Space	4.5
Walkability	4.5

Amenities	4.08
Driving Range	5
Practice Green	5
Water on Course	3.5
Port-O-Potties	3
Locker Rooms	4
Pro Shop	4
Grill & Bar	4
Weather Shelter	1
Golf Carts	5

Overall	4.63
Enjoyable	4.5
Challenging / Fair	4.5
Reservations	5
Scenery	5
Gimmicky Holes	4.5
Weather Monitor	4

Value	4.5
Overall	106.83

Hole	Championship	Back	Middle	Executive	Front	Par	Handicap
1	501	490	478	462	427	5	7
2	374	364	355	329	283	4	15
3	195	186	170	161	126	3	9
4	389	369	351	329	280	4	11
5	446	426	403	379	359	4	3
6	374	364	342	325	272	4	13
7	425	389	359	336	296	4	5
8	204	187	170	123	98	3	17
9	558	533	518	509	443	5	1
Out	3466	3308	3146	2953	2584	36	
10	437	413	384	354	340	4	2
11	369	359	355	296	267	4	10
12	371	356	331	296	282	4	12
13	208	198	184	171	155	3	14
14	597	558	539	525	435	5	8
15	440	417	398	360	325	4	6
16	310	296	286	263	221	4	18
17	182	164	151	130	101	3	16
18	573	549	517	492	437	5	4
In	3487	3310	3145	2887	2563	36	
Total	6953	6618	6291	5840	5147	72	
Slope	134	131	128	124	118		
Rating	72.7	71.1	69.7	67.6	68.9		

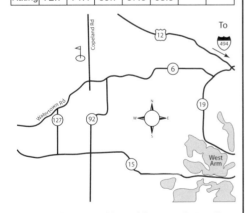

From I-494 take Hwy 12 west 8.5 miles to CR 6. Go west 6.5 miles on CR 6 to Copeland Road. Go north, the course is on the left.

Hole Commentary

1. Favor center to left side of the fairway on this short, downhill par 5. Either lay-up short of 150 yards FG or inside 90 yards FG. Cannot go right or long of this green.
2. Spit fairway with small area on left and larger area right. Hitting from right is better angle to green. Bunker on left is 150 yards FG. Bunker right and over green.
3. Water guards the right side of the green on this par 3. Plenty of room long and left.
4. Trees along the right side of hole. Tree on left side at 120 yards FG, fairway gets tight inside of there. Bunkers left and right of green.
5. Downhill par 4 with 220 yards to clear bunker on left. Aim for the 150 yard pole. Creek runs in front of green with a bunker left.
6. Favor left side of fairway, but avoid marsh to left of the hole from 200-130 yards FG. Bunker right is at 110 yards FG. Green is elevated so take enough club.
7. Straight away par 4 with bunkers left and right from 175-135 yards FG.
8. Bunkers guard front left and back right of the green. Plenty of green to hit to.
9. Water left of fairway past bunker on left. Aim just right of bunker on left. Smart play on second is to lay up to 150 yards FG. The only fairway over creek is to the left.
10. Dogleg left with a creek left of the fairway. Bunker right of fairway at 160 yards FG. Pond just in front of green.
11. Favor left side of fairway but be careful of water on left side of fairway. A bunker and water left of fairway at 150 yards FG. Water surrounds green except for right side.
12. Tight driving hole with trees left and right. There is hazard along right side of hole. Hit a club off the tee that will get you in the middle of the fairway from 150-135 yards FG.
13. Longer par 3 with plenty of area to miss right, long and short.
14. About 250 yards FT to water on right side of fairway. Fairway is split by bunker from 160-120 yards FG. Bunker left of fairway from 120-100 yards FG.
15. Cannot see green until you're inside of 180 yards FG. Bunkers left and right at 150 yards FG. Creek runs behind and right of green.
16. Driver not a smart play on this hole. Anything right of the fairway is hazard. Inside of 50 yards FG is the flattest area but it is very narrow. Water left and behind long green.
17. Downhill par 3 but don't come up short. Water and a bunker right of the green.
18. Trees on the left are 210 yards FT. Fairway ends at 210 yards FG and starts up again at 150 yards FG. Favor right side of fairway on 2nd shot. Know where the pin is as the green has two levels.

Prestwick Golf Club

9555 Wedgewood Drive
Woodbury, MN 55125
651-731-4779
www.prestwick.com

Course Information

Reservations:	5 days in advance www.teemaster.com		
2000 Fees:	9	18	Comments
Weekdays	$26.00	$44.00	
Weekends	$29.00	$49.00	
Twilight	N/A	$26.00	4 hrs < dark
Seniors	*	*	* see other
Power Cart	$15.00	$30.00	
Pull Cart	$3.50	$3.50	
Club Rental	$15.00	$15.00	
Credit cards	Visa Mastercard Discover AmEx		
Checks	Local Checks Only		
Rain Check	18 hole<3 holes, 9 hole<13 holes		
Other	Senior rates available with membership		
Leagues:	Wed		

Amenities:

Driving Range	Y	Snacks	Y
Putting Green	Y	Grill/Bar	Y
Practice Green	Y	Restaurant	N
Spikeless	Y	Locker Room	Y
Proshop	F	Showers	N

Management:

Manager	Paul Lambert
Professional	Tom Wahl

Prestwick is one of the premiere public golf courses in the Twin Cities area. Everything from the tee boxes to the greens are kept in pristine condition. Not only are the greens in good condition but they are fast. Finding your yardage quickly is not a problem. The course offers a great variety in the layout of the holes with a number of significant elevation changes, affording you a view of the surrounding area. The course will challenge golfers of all ability levels.

Rating   108.08

Course Rating

Tees	Grade 4.75
Ability Levels	5
Condition	5
Signs / Hole Maps	4
Ball Washers	4
Benches	5
Fairways	**4.4**
Condition	4.5
Yardage Markers	4.5
Pin Indicators	4.5
Rough	4
Watered / Drainage	4
Greens	**4.58**
Condition	4.5
Speed	5
Size and Variety	4
Slope	4.5
Fringe	5
Layout	**4.45**
Par 3's	4
Par 4's	4.5
Par 5's	4
Strategic Trouble	4.5
Bunkers	4.5
Enough Space	5
Walkability	5
Amenities	**4.45**
Driving Range	5
Practice Green	5
Water on Course	4
Port-O-Potties	4
Locker Rooms	5
Pro Shop	4
Grill & Bar	4
Weather Shelter	3
Golf Carts	4
Overall	**4.03**
Enjoyable	4.5
Challenging / Fair	4
Reservations	3
Scenery	3.5
Gimmicky Holes	5
Weather Monitor	4
Value	**4.0**
Overall	**108.08**

Hole	Blue	White	Gold	Red	Par	Men Handicap	Women Handicap
1	345	330	290	290	4	13	13
2	396	374	338	311	4	9	7
3	180	148	135	115	3	17	15
4	534	487	426	417	5	3	3
5	442	429	341	335	4	1	5
6	174	161	122	96	3	15	17
7	400	390	317	314	4	5	9
8	336	321	265	240	4	11	11
9	506	494	471	408	5	7	1
Out	3313	3134	2705	2511	36		
10	409	392	387	328	4	10	10
11	389	378	350	310	4	8	8
12	331	307	291	266	4	14	16
13	408	386	371	334	4	2	6
14	161	147	137	135	3	18	18
15	419	409	382	327	4	4	2
16	569	519	433	428	5	6	4
17	200	180	178	173	3	16	14
18	500	480	460	440	5	12	12
In	3386	3198	2989	2701	36		
Total	6699	6332	5694	5212	72		
Slope	128	125	M 119 W 125	120			
Rating	72.7	71.1	M 68.2 W 73.3	70.8			

From I-494 take Lake Street east 4 miles to Wedgewood Drive. Go south 1/2 mile to the course.

Hole Commentary

1. OB along the right side of the hole and bunkers on the right from 130-90 yards FG. Water to the right of the green.
2. Aim at center of fairway on this dogleg right and beware of OB right of hole. Plenty of room left. Bunker guards front left side of green.
3. Bunker guards left side of the green on this mid-length par 3.
4. Narrow driving hole with OB both left and right of the fairway. Approaching the green, bunkers guard both front and left side of green.
5. Long par 4 with bunkers on the left side from 220-150 yards FG. Bunker on right at 190 yards FG. Very deep green with bunkers right and left front of green and water over.
6. Tee shot over water with bunkers both left and right of the green.
7. Water just off the tee box with OB both left and right of the fairway. Favor left to center of fairway. Bunker guards front right side of green.
8. OB right of the fairway and water left. Pick a club that gets you safely to the landing area.
9. Shorter par 5 that is reachable by longer hitters with two good shots. On approach avoid the bunker on the right at 80 yards FG and the water on the left that runs from 130 yards FG to the green.
10. Favor the right side of the fairway on your drive. Bunkers on the right starting at 200 yards FG with water left. Approaching the green there is water from 100 yards FG to the green and two bunkers left of the green.
11. Approach is uphill so take extra club. Bunker on left is at 130 yards FG.
12. Bunkers on the left from 140 yards FG to the green. Placement more important than length on this hole. Deep green with a bunker front right.
13. Aim just right of the bunkers on the left that start at 210 yards FG. Water on the right starts at 165 yards FG. Bunker guards front left side of the green.
14. Wind makes club selection more difficult on this hole. Bunkers front left and right of green.
15. Favor left side of fairway but be aware of OB along left side. Approach shot is uphill and requires extra club. Bunkers both front left and front right of the green.
16. This hole should be played as a three shot hole. Second shot should set up comfortable third shot with a wedge. OB left of hole to the water which runs all the way to the green.
17. Tough uphill par 3 to a large green with a bunker left of green. Par is a good score.
18. Shorter par 5 with bunkers on the left from 300-250 yards FG. Two bunkers on the right as you approach the green and one bunker left of the green.

The Refuge Golf Club

21250 Yellow Pine Street
Oak Grove, MN 55011
763-753-8383
www.refugegolfclub.com

Course Information

Reservations:	7 days in advance		
	www.teemaster.com		
2000 Fees:	9	18	Comments
Weekdays	$40.00	$75.00	
Weekends	$40.00	$75.00	
Twilight	N/A	$40.00	After 4 pm
SeniorsJr.	N/A	N/A	
Power Cart	Incl.	Incl.	
Pull Cart	Incl.	Incl.	
Club Rental	N/A	$25.00	
Credit cards	Visa Mastercard AmEx		
Checks	Any		
Rain Check	18 hole<4 holes, 9 hole<13 holes		
Other			
Leagues:	Various		

Amenities:			
Driving Range	Y	Snacks	Y
Putting Green	Y	Grill/Bar	Y
Practice Green	Y	Restaurant	Y
Spikeless	Y	Locker Room	Y
Proshop	F	Showers	Y

Management:	
Manager	Joe Sidoti
Professional	Patty Lynn

Spread out over 350 acres of woodlands and wetlands, The Refuge is one of the most scenic golf courses in the Twin Cities area. Aside from being scenic it also offers some of the best golf around. Although carved out of wetlands, the designers and builders were environmentally conscious and impacted very little of the natural environment. A new clubhouse opening in 2002 will be the envy of other clubs. The golf course will challenge golfers of all ability levels, but beginning golfers may find the course intimidating.

Rating   104.98

Course Rating

Tees	Grade **4.85**
Ability Levels	5
Condition	4.5
Signs / Hole Maps	5
Ball Washers	5
Benches	5
Fairways	**3.75**
Condition	4
Yardage Markers	3
Pin Indicators	4
Rough	4
Watered / Drainage	4.5
Greens	**4.55**
Condition	4.5
Speed	4
Size and Variety	5
Slope	5
Fringe	5
Layout	**4.58**
Par 3's	5
Par 4's	5
Par 5's	4
Strategic Trouble	4.5
Bunkers	5
Enough Space	5
Walkability	3
Amenities	**3.78**
Driving Range	4
Practice Green	5
Water on Course	4
Port-O-Potties	1
Locker Rooms	5
Pro Shop	4
Grill & Bar	4.5
Weather Shelter	1
Golf Carts	5
Overall	**4.88**
Enjoyable	5
Challenging / Fair	4.5
Reservations	5
Scenery	5
Gimmicky Holes	5
Weather Monitor	5
Value	**3.5**
Overall	**104.98**

Hole Commentary

Hole	Black	Green	Grey	Gold	Purple	Par	Men Handicap	Women Handicap
1	333	322	314	293	271	4	11	9
2	531	494	468	452	427	5	13	5
3	142	140	133	117	103	3	17	17
4	406	384	375	356	310	4	5	1
5	508	491	465	425	387	5	3	7
6	195	183	175	161	145	3	15	15
7	408	395	386	318	248	4	7	3
8	163	149	142	132	127	3	9	13
9	510	464	403	347	286	5	1	11
Out	3196	3022	2861	2601	2304	36		
10	387	367	358	337	301	4	10	2
11	370	356	347	331	299	4	6	10
12	503	483	463	443	416	5	14	14
13	380	363	354	337	303	4	4	4
14	207	192	167	157	141	3	16	18
15	359	340	291	278	256	4	8	8
16	184	164	144	121	97	3	12	16
17	426	405	367	319	275	4	2	12
18	522	496	467	448	427	5	18	6
In	3338	3166	2958	2771	2515	36		
Total	6534	6188	5819	5372	4819			
Slope	139	136	M 133 W 133	M 129 W 128	121			
Rating	71.9	70.4	M 68.7 W 73.9	M 66.7 W 71.4	68.4			

1. Take care not to overdrive the fairway to left into the water, look at the card to determine how far you can hit your drive. Bunkers front left and right of green, don't go over.
2. Bunkers on left from 240 - 210 yards FG. Favor right side of fairway as hole turns left at 150 yards FG. Green is large.
3. Water all around this green so accuracy is essential on this short par 3.
4. Sharp dogleg left with OB right. Aim left of bunker on right at 135 yards FG. Big hitters aim just right of trees on left.
5. More landing area than it appears. Going for green in two is not the best play, hit your approach to set up a short wedge shot. Trouble all around the green, especially left and over.
6. Long par 3 with plenty of area to hit to. The green is well bunkered with hazard right.
7. Trees left and right as you hit over wetlands. Plenty of landing area. Bunkers both left and right with hazard left of the green.
8. Long carry over wetlands to a very large green with not much room to miss the green.
9. The tee shot is critical with a long carry over wetlands. Tee shots hit too far and left may end up OB. To reach green in two, must be all carry. Don't miss right or over.
10. Aim just right of trees on left, long hitters can hit over right side of trees with no trouble over them. Marsh on right from 150 – 80 yards FG.
11. Favor left side of fairway. 150 yard mark is just over wetlands. Don't go over this green.
12. The dogleg sits at 240 yards FG. Hitting a draw can be an advantage but trying to hit too far will result in high scores. Bunkers guard approach on right side.
13. Trees along the right and wetlands left demand an accurate tee shot. A creek cuts across the fairway at 100 yards FG. There is no room to bail out anywhere around the green.
14. Don't go over the green on this challenging long par 3. Large bunker guards front left side.
15. This fairway goes away from you diagonally to the right. Aim for tallest tree straight away with a slight fade. Largest landing area is at 130 yards FG.
16. The only place to miss here is to the left on this par 3. Right can be OK.
17. Fairly long carry over wetlands to a very generous landing area on this longer par 4. Bunkers guard left and right front of the green with long native grass over the green
18. Aim right of the trees on the left side of the fairway. Green is reachable in two with a long drive. Bunkers guard the approach on the left side with bunkers left and right of green. Don't miss the green left or over.

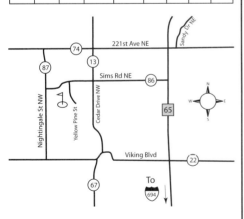

From I-694 take Hwy 65 (Central Ave.) north 20 miles to Sims Road. Go west 3.3 miles to Yellow Pine Street. Turn left, the course is on the right.

Ridges at Sand Creek

21775 Ridges Drive
Jordan, MN 55352
952-492-2644
www.ridgesatsandcreek.com

Course Information

Reservations:	7 days in advance		

2000 Fees:	9	18	Comments
Weekdays	$17.00	$29.00	
Weekends	N/A	$34.00	
Twilight	N/A	N/A	
Seniors	$10.50	$18.00	
Power Cart	$7.50	$13.00	
Pull Cart	$4.00	$4.00	
Club Rental	$6.00	$10.00	
Credit cards	Visa Mastercard Disc AmEx		
Checks	Any		
Rain Check	Ask		
Other			

Leagues:	None

Amenities:			
Driving Range	Y	Snacks	Y
Putting Green	Y	Grill/Bar	Y
Practice Green	N	Restaurant	Y
Spikeless	Y	Locker Room	N
Proshop	F	Showers	N

Management:	
Manager	Mike Malone
Professional	Tom Bakke

Opened in 2000, Ridges at Sand Creek was nominated for the best new course in 2001. The course is spread out over 170 acres with 11 holes carved through the woods and the other 7 holes laid out links style. Features that you will come across include the winding Sand Creek, natural wetlands, rolling terrain, elevated tees, undulating greens, and numerous strategically placed bunkers. This is one of the best values in the Twin Cities and well worth the drive. The course will challenge golfers of all ability levels.

Rating   109.53

Course Rating

Tees	Grade 4.4
Ability Levels	5
Condition	4
Signs / Hole Maps	5
Ball Washers	4
Benches	3

Fairways	4.05
Condition	4
Yardage Markers	3.5
Pin Indicators	4
Rough	5
Watered / Drainage	5

Greens	4.68
Condition	4
Speed	5
Size and Variety	5
Slope	5
Fringe	4.5

Layout	4.3
Par 3's	4.5
Par 4's	4
Par 5's	5
Strategic Trouble	4
Bunkers	4.5
Enough Space	5
Walkability	3

Amenities	3.8
Driving Range	5
Practice Green	4.5
Water on Course	3
Port-O-Potties	3
Locker Rooms	2
Pro Shop	4
Grill & Bar	5
Weather Shelter	2
Golf Carts	5

Overall	4.73
Enjoyable	5
Challenging / Fair	4.5
Reservations	5
Scenery	5
Gimmicky Holes	4
Weather Monitor	4

Value	5.0
Overall	109.53

Hole	Black	Blue	White	Gold	Red	Par	Men Handicap	Women Handicap
1	550	530	505	485	430	5	5	3
2	415	390	360	345	308	4	13	11
3	180	160	135	120	101	3	17	17
4	447	392	382	342	302	4	1	9
5	202	186	170	173	122	3	15	15
6	425	405	380	360	323	4	9	7
7	518	504	481	465	420	5	7	5
8	430	404	372	347	294	4	11	13
9	452	437	402	373	335	4	3	1
Out	3619	3408	3187	3010	2635	36		
10	600	573	535	521	461	5	4	2
11	219	182	160	140	125	3	12	16
12	394	364	343	301	285	4	10	10
13	459	444	426	353	339	4	2	8
14	297	285	280	271	260	4	14	12
15	110	104	90	87	75	3	18	18
16	559	537	482	471	424	5	6	6
17	163	154	142	132	116	3	16	14
18	516	496	470	453	416	5	8	4
In	3317	3139	2928	2729	2501	36		
Total	6936	6547	6115	5739	5136	72		
Slope	133	129	M 125 W 131	M 122 W 126	119			
Rating	73.0	71.3	M 69.3 W 75.2	M 67.6 W 73.2	69.8			

Hole Commentary

1. Water left from 200 – 150 yards FT. OB right of fairway. Bunker on left is 262 yards FT. Collection area right of green.
2. It's 272 yards FT to the water which runs all the way behind the green. Favor left side of fairway, it narrows inside 150 yards FG.
3. Nice par 3 with a couple of bunkers guarding the front of this green.
4. Fairly straight hole with a creek running far right of fairway. Big bunker guards front left side of the elevated green.
5. A tough par 3 with the creek along the left side. Wide but shallow green.
6. You can try to cut a little distance off this dogleg left but you must get inside 200 yards FG. Creek runs just in front of green with plenty of trouble over the green.
7. Aim just left of the bunker on right. Bunker left at 100 yards FG and center of the fairway at 80 yards FG on your second shot. A drop-off left of green can make for difficult shots.
8. Fairway splits at the bunker, out 250 yards FT. Right side is safer. Fairway slopes left. Not a big green with water left and over green.
9. Water at 283 yards FT. Aim just left of bunker on right at 233 yards FT. There is water right of that bunker. The creek crosses fairway at 130 yards FG.
10. A long par 5 with OB left of fairway. Aim just left of bunker on right at 230 yards FG. Water on left at 190 yards FG and bunkers on the right at 135 yards FG. Don't go over this green.
11. Short and straightforward par 3.
12. You must hit past 240 yards FT if you hit ball down left side of fairway. Inside 150 yards FG you have a great view of the hole. Water runs in front of the hole. Don't go over green.
13. The creek is 150 yards FG with trees right and left of green.
14. A lot of trouble around the green so if you go for the green, you have to hit it. Smart play is to hit tee shot 200 yards FT.
15. 15th hole is a very short par 3. Very wide but shallow green surrounded by bunkers.
16. Bunkers left and right from about 250 – 290 yards FT. Favor left side of fairway, too far right will be tree trouble. Don't go over green.
17. Downhill par 3 with a bunker to the left and water to the right.
18. Fairly straightforward hole with a bunker out at 200 yards FT on the right. Water comes into play at 270 yards FT on the right and 296 yards FT on the left. Once you get past the creek it's wide open to the uphill green. Multi-level green, important to know where the pin is.

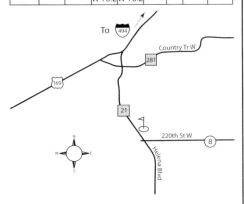

To 494

Country Tr W

281

169

21

220th St W

8

Helena Blvd

From I-494 take Hwy 169 south 21 miles to Jordan. Go south 3 miles on Hwy 21, the course is on the left.

River Oaks Municipal Golf Course

11099 South Highway 61
Cottage Grove, MN 55016
651-438-2121

Course Information

Reservations:	Weekdays - prior Friday Weekend - Wednesday		
2000 Fees:	9	18	Comments
Weekdays	$17.00	$25.00	
Weekends	$18.00	$28.00	
Twilight	N/A	$11.00	F, Sa, Su > 5pm
Seniors.	$13.00	$16.50	
Power Cart	$18.00	$26.50	$12/$18 Sr.
Pull Cart	$2.50	$2.50	
Club Rental	N/A	$9.00	
Credit cards	Visa Mastercard		
Checks	Any		
Rain Check	Ask		
Other	Senior rates available weekdays<3pm, weekends>3pm		
Leagues:	Various		

Amenities:			
Driving Range	Y	Snacks	Y
Putting Green	Y	Grill/Bar	Y
Practice Green	N	Restaurant	N
Spikeless	Y	Locker Room	N
Proshop	F	Showers	N

Management:	
Manager	Bruce Anderson
Professional	Bruce Anderson

Set on the bluffs overlooking the Mississippi River valley, River Oaks offers some incredible views. Numerous elevation changes, 57 bunkers and 3 ponds add to the challenge of the course. You may be lucky enough to see a wild turkey or deer as you play your round. The golf is very good and the scenery and wildlife even better. The course will challenge golfers of all ability levels.

Rating   99.80

Course Rating

Tees	Grade 3.95
Ability Levels	4
Condition	4
Signs / Hole Maps	3
Ball Washers	4
Benches	5
Fairways	**4.1**
Condition	4
Yardage Markers	4
Pin Indicators	4
Rough	4
Watered / Drainage	5
Greens	**3.75**
Condition	4
Speed	4
Size and Variety	3
Slope	4
Fringe	3
Layout	**3.7**
Par 3's	3
Par 4's	4
Par 5's	3
Strategic Trouble	4
Bunkers	4
Enough Space	4
Walkability	4
Amenities	**4.0**
Driving Range	4
Practice Green	5
Water on Course	5
Port-O-Potties	4
Locker Rooms	2
Pro Shop	3
Grill & Bar	4
Weather Shelter	3
Golf Carts	3
Overall	**3.95**
Enjoyable	3
Challenging / Fair	4
Reservations	5
Scenery	4
Gimmicky Holes	5
Weather Monitor	4
Value	**4.5**
Overall	**99.80**

Hole	Blue	White	Red	Par	Handicap
1	506	471	406	5	4
2	408	388	318	4	2
3	385	362	316	4	10
4	158	141	119	3	18
5	364	347	329	4	12
6	325	298	276	4	14
7	164	152	141	3	16
8	359	335	283	4	8
9	399	376	314	4	6
Out	3068	2870	2502	35	
10	408	384	346	4	5
11	388	367	339	4	15
12	193	169	129/105	3	7
13	571	490	432	5	3
14	334	319	250	4	17
15	405	377	340	4	13
16	207	180	143	3	11
17	413	381	321	4	9
18	496	481	422	5	1
In	3415	3148	2722	36	
Total	6483	6018	5224	71	
Slope	131	127	128		
Rating	71.4	69.5	70.5		

From I-494 take Hwy 61 south 9.25 miles, the course is on the right.

Hole Commentary

1. Straight par 5 with a bunker at 250 yards FG on left side of the fairway. OB runs on the right side so don't go right.
2. Bunker on the right of fairway from 150 - 130 yards FG. Plenty of room on the left so just aim for the middle of the fairway and swing away. Don't go over.
3. Out of bounds runs far left but favor the left side as opposed to the right side to avoid the trees on the right.
4. Take an extra half club on this uphill par 3 to avoid coming up short. Bunkers guard the entire back of the green.
5. Aim over or just right of the 150 yard marker on the left side of the fairway. The bunker runs from 150 - 130 yards FG. Water runs along the right side and juts in at the 150 yard marker on the right.
6. Water runs along the entire right side of the fairway. Smart play is to hit a club down the middle to a comfortable distance for approach.
7. Just don't go over on this mid-range par 3.
8. Aim at the left side of fairway for the best approach to the green. Plenty of room to the right so swing away.
9. Straight par 4. Bunker on the left from 145 - 125 yards FG.
10. Follow directions on the sign. Aim just left of the trees on the right. Once you get past the dogleg the fairway runs downhill and the ball will run down and to the right. Hit the ball 200 yards FT and you will end up inside 150 FG.
11. Hole is located straight over the bunker on the right that runs from 150 - 125 yards FG. Aim just left of the bunker on the right.
12. Very interesting par 3 over water. Plenty of room left and long, just don't be short or right.
13. Double dogleg, nearly impossible to reach in two. Favor left side of fairway on tee shot and second shot to avoid being blocked out by trees on the right side. The very left side of the fairway is the only place to go for green in two.
14. There is no advantage to going over the bunkers on the right since trees in front of the green block your ball. Hit ball to right middle of fairway from 100 - 75 yards FG.
15. Favor the left side of the fairway but be aware of bunkers on the left from 170 - 125 yards FG. Plenty of room right.
16. Long par three to a two tiered green. Hit to the correct level to avoid a treacherous putt.
17. Dogleg left par 4 with bunkers guarding the left side of the fairway from 150 - 125 yards FG. Aim just right of bunkers on the left.
18. Play the hole smart and hit your tee shot to 260-240 yards FG just to the right of the bunker on the left. The green is located in line with the power line pole to the left. Play smart and finish the round on a good note.

Rum River Hills Golf Club

16659 St. Francis Blvd.
Ramsey, MN 55303
763-753-3339

Course Information

Reservations:	4 days in advance www.teemaster.com		
2000 Fees:	9	18	Comments
Weekdays	$17.00	$25.00	
Weekends	$17.00	$29.00	
Twilight	N/A	$12.00	< 6pm
Seniors	$8.00	$16.00	* see other
Power Cart	$12.00	$24.00	
Pull Cart	$3.00	$3.00	
Club Rental	$8.00	$8.00	
Credit cards	Visa Mastercard Discover		
Checks	Any		
Rain Check	Pro-rated		
Other	Sr. rates < 10 am M-F & >4 pm on Sa, Su. & holidays		
Leagues:	Tues, Wed		

Amenities:			
Driving Range	Y	Snacks	Y
Putting Green	Y	Grill/Bar	Y
Practice Green	N	Restaurant	Y
Spikeless	Y	Locker Room	Y
Proshop	F	Showers	Y

Management:	
Manager	Jeff Tollette
Professional	Jeff Tollette

Trouble abounds at Rum River Hills. Whether is it out of bounds, water, or bunkers – you are bound to find trouble. The course is very short so you will want to hit your long irons and metal woods off the tees to keep the ball in play. If you can play smart you should score very well. The course needs to be kept in better shape as the grass from tee to green was not in very good condition. This course is well suited for beginner to intermediate golfers.

Rating   78.80

Course Rating

Tees	Grade 3.05
Ability Levels	2
Condition	2
Signs / Hole Maps	5
Ball Washers	5
Benches	5
Fairways	**2.0**
Condition	2
Yardage Markers	2
Pin Indicators	1
Rough	3
Watered / Drainage	3
Greens	**2.4**
Condition	2
Speed	2
Size and Variety	3
Slope	3
Fringe	3
Layout	**3.23**
Par 3's	3.5
Par 4's	3.5
Par 5's	3
Strategic Trouble	3
Bunkers	3
Enough Space	2
Walkability	5
Amenities	**3.0**
Driving Range	2
Practice Green	4
Water on Course	3
Port-O-Potties	3
Locker Rooms	3
Pro Shop	2
Grill & Bar	4
Weather Shelter	2
Golf Carts	4
Overall	**2.95**
Enjoyable	3
Challenging / Fair	2
Reservations	3
Scenery	3
Gimmicky Holes	5
Weather Monitor	3
Value	**3.5**
Overall	**78.80**

Hole	Black	Blue	White	Red	Par	Men Handicap	Women Handicap
1	413	400	343	270	4	1	9
2	525	510	489	436	5	11	11
3	352	348	326	272	4	5	5
4	160	142	132	132	3	17	17
5	416	403	388	362	4	3	3
6	200	190	162	151	3	13	13
7	372	358	310	310	4	9	1
8	303	293	280	202	4	7	7
9	368	348	340	328	4	15	15
Out	3109	2992	2770	2463	35		
10	374	366	336	288	4	14	16
11	410	400	383	336	4	12	10
12	517	507	495	423	5	6	6
13	411	401	388	347	4	2	4
14	118	108	95	89	3	18	18
15	327	322	310	254	4	4	2
16	161	153	147	140	3	16	14
17	420	391	372	313	4	10	12
18	461	451	442	371	5	8	8
In	3199	3099	2968	2561	36		
Total	6308	6091	5738	5024	71		
Slope	117	115	112	120			
Rating	71.0	70.0	68.4	69.6			

Hole Commentary

1. Fade is best shot off tee on this dogleg right but beware of water on right. Straight off the tee may find trees on left side of fairway.
2. Waste bunkers right and left of fairway on this dogleg right. Trees at corner may block off second shot. Set up for a good 3rd shot since fairway narrows and slopes to water from 75 yards in. A long, running 2nd shot will be wet.
3. Dogleg right. Trees along right side, Rock-creek on left side. Play a fade tee shot. Need to cross water as you approach the green.
4. Rock-bed to the right, large hill to the left. Cart path may come into play just left of green.
5. Large waste bunker at inside corner with another awaiting long drives through the corner. It's 250 yards to the corner. Approach is downhill, take one less club. OB over green.
6. Long, straight par 3. OB tight on the left side. Very hard to judge pin position.
7. Water all over on this hole. Play an accurate iron 200 yards FT on the left side of the fairway. Green protected by bunkers.
8. Take a 170 club off the tee and play to left side. Water is at about 190. Probably have a downhill lie for approach to peninsula green.
9. Waste bunkers up and down the right and left side. OB far left. Approach the green from the left side of the fairway.
10. Slight dogleg right. A slice will end up OB on the left. Approach green from right side. Don't go over or right.
11. Waste bunkers at the corner on right and left side. Favor right side of fairway to avoid trees. OB far right and left. Large fairway bunker on left side at the corner 250 yards FT.
12. Difficult par 5 not reachable in 2 because of water from 75 yards FG to the hole. OB about 250 yards FT on right side and OB on the left side. Safety is to the left side as you approach the water / marsh. OB left and long of green.
13. Green is downhill from fairway. Fairway narrows from 275-200 yards FG. OB left and right, large bunker left. Play to left side of fairway to avoid trees on approach.
14. Hole surrounded by bunkers and trouble long. Don't take too much club as tee box is sheltered from the wind by trees.
15. Smart play is a control club off the tee, as there is OB left and treeline right. A creek cuts in front of the green so do not lay up too far.
16. OB left and water right. Green is long front to back, so choose club wisely.
17. Hit at least 200 yards FT to reach corner, 250 yards is better. Water left, trees right.
18. Need to hit it at least 220 yards FT to the corner on this sharp dogleg right. Waste bunkers and trees at the corner. Approach green from the right side of the fairway to avoid water from about 75 yards FG to the green.

From I-494 take Hwy 169 north 8.5 miles to Hwy 47 (Ferry Street). Go north 5 miles, course is on the right.

Rush Creek Golf Club

7801 Troy Lane
Maple Grove, MN 55311
763-494-8844
www.rushcreek.com

Course Information

Reservations:	14 days in advance		
	www.teemaster.com		

2000 Fees:	9	18	Comments
Weekdays	N/A	Ask	*
Weekends	N/A	Ask	*
Twilight	N/A	Ask	*
Seniors	N/A	N/A	
Power Cart	N/A	$15.00	
Pull Cart	N/A	N/A	
Club Rental	N/A	$30.00	

Credit cards	Visa Mastercard AmEx Diners
Checks	Any
Rain Check	Ask
Other	Stadium pricing depends on time of day and time of year. Call or visit website for pricing.

Leagues:	None

Amenities:			
Driving Range	Y	Snacks	Y
Putting Green	Y	Grill/Bar	Y
Practice Green	N	Restaurant	Y
Spikeless	Y	Locker Room	Y
Proshop	F	Showers	Y

Management:	
Manager	Ed and Lori Money
Professional	Derek Stendahl

Rush Creek is spread out over 260 acres of rolling prairie and natural marshes. From the minute you arrive you will be pampered by the friendly staff. The experience is somewhat akin to going to a spa, where every little detail is perfect. The price is steep but it is worth it to experience it at least once. Be sure to play from the appropriate tee box or you may not enjoy the experience. The course will challenge golfers of all ability levels.

Rating   105.70

Course Rating

Tees	Grade 4.9
Ability Levels	5
Condition	5
Signs / Hole Maps	5
Ball Washers	4
Benches	5

Fairways	4.75
Condition	4.5
Yardage Markers	5
Pin Indicators	5
Rough	4
Watered / Drainage	5

Greens	4.98
Condition	5
Speed	5
Size and Variety	5
Slope	5
Fringe	4.5

Layout	4.63
Par 3's	5
Par 4's	5
Par 5's	4.5
Strategic Trouble	4.5
Bunkers	4.5
Enough Space	4.5
Walkability	4

Amenities	4.13
Driving Range	5
Practice Green	5
Water on Course	3
Port-O-Potties	3
Locker Rooms	5
Pro Shop	3.5
Grill & Bar	4
Weather Shelter	2
Golf Carts	5

Overall	4.85
Enjoyable	5
Challenging / Fair	5
Reservations	5
Scenery	5
Gimmicky Holes	5
Weather Monitor	2

Value	2.5
Overall	**105.70**

Hole	Gold	Blue	Silver	Green	Par	Men Handicap	Women Handicap
1	428	399	366	309	4	7	7
2	532	532	492	423	5	5	5
3	196	173	152	133	3	17	17
4	336	322	322	270	4	13	15
5	417	383	345	319	4	9	9
6	340	340	314	246	4	15	11
7	203	187	187	163	3	11	13
8	609	581	525	489	5	3	3
9	452	418	401	364	4	1	1
Out	3513	3335	3104	2716	36		
10	575	522	507	403	5	8	4
11	410	410	373	334	4	14	8
12	186	164	164	132	3	12	10
13	345	345	314	228	4	6	12
14	378	359	310	277	4	16	14
15	171	143	128	115	3	18	18
16	462	409	409	344	4	4	6
17	411	384	384	341	4	10	16
18	569	569	530	427	5	2	2
In	3507	3305	3119	2601	36		
Total	7020	6640	6223	5317	72		
Slope	137	M 136 W 143	M 131 W 138	M 119 W 127			
Rating	74.2	M 72.1 W 78.8	M 70.0 W 76.4	M 66.2 W 71.1			

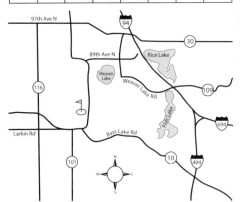

From I-494 take Bass Lake Road (CR 9) west 4 miles to CR 101. Go north 0.7 miles, the course is on the left.

Hole Commentary

1.   Water along left side of fairway. Bunkers left and right of green. Favor right side of green.
2.   Water left and pines trees right of the fairway. Accuracy is essential on approach. Fairway narrows inside 150 yards FG, bunker at 130 yards FG. Long green surrounded by trouble.
3.   Don't be fooled by the yardage, this uphill hole requires an extra club.
4.   Bunkers right at 132 and 82 yards FG and left at 122 yards FG. Approach is only a pitch but green rises 25 feet from the 150-yard pole. Green slopes off on all sides.
5.   Hole is 35 below tee box with trees left and right of fairway and water left. Two bunkers in front of green and a large bunker on left side.
6.   Tee shot must be placed atop plateau. Approach shot must carry bunkers in front of green yet hold this shallow, multi-tiered green.
7.   Tees are 30 feet above a green protected by an overhanging tree on the left, water right and three bunkers around the narrow green.
8.   Long fairway bunker on left side 243 yards FT catches many tee shots. Pond guards landing area on left on second shot. Small green with bunker front and water left of green.
9.   Two bunkers on the right are at 220 and 171 yards FG respectively. Approach is downhill over pond. Don't miss right with water and bunker right of green.
10.   Favor left side of fairway to avoid bunkers and wetlands on the right. Narrow approach area to a green that can be reached with two good shots. Bunker on left is 40 yards FG. Green is multi-tiered with water to the right.
11.   Tee shot that can carry bunkers and pond on left will result in shorter approach, must hit to 180 yards FG. Approach must be accurate to a green that slopes away from you.
12.   Downhill tee shot to a wide but shallow green surrounded by marsh.
13.   Difficult hole requires accurate tee shot. Approach shot must carry water starting 90 yards FG and hold the wide but shallow green. Bunker left at 140 yards FG.
14.   Trees right and left. Bunkers guard front left of a punchbowl shaped green. Bunker on right at 140 yards to hole. OB right of the hole.
15.   Short uphill par 3. Huge bunker short of green and bunkers both left and right of green.
16.   Long downhill hole with bunkers on left side of fairway at 195 and 155 yards FG.
17.   Sloping fairway downhill to landing area. Bunker on left from 160 - 125 yards FG. Hit your ball to left side and fairway will kick it back to the right. Two bunkers guard front of green.
18.   First two shots are played over portions of the marsh on the left. There is room to hit to the right. Two bunkers guard the front of the green.

Sanbrook Golf Course

2181 NE County Road 5
Isanti, MN 55040
763-444-9904

Course Information

Reservations:	7 days in advance		

2000 Fees:	9	18	Comments
Weekdays	$12.00	$19.00	
Weekends	$16.00	$24.00	
Twilight	N/A	N/A	
Seniors	$9.00	$13.00	
Power Cart	$12.00	$20.00	
Pull Cart	$2.00	$2.00	
Club Rental	$3.00	$3.00	
Credit cards	Visa Mastercard		
Checks	Local Checks Only		
Rain Check	18 hole<4 holes, 9 hole<13 holes		
Other			

Leagues:	Varies		

Amenities:			
Driving Range	Y	Snacks	Y
Putting Green	Y	Grill/Bar	N
Practice Green	N	Restaurant	N
Spikeless	Y	Locker Room	N
Proshop	B	Showers	N

Management:			
Manager	Pat Zimba		
Professional	None		

Sanbrook Golf Course is a very flat and unassuming course. Most of the holes are straight and they all kind of look alike. There are a number of water hazards and some trees to add challenge to the course but for the most part it is wide open. The fairways were not in great shape with weeds and some bare patches. If you like playing wide open golf, this is a good course for you. The course is well suited for beginner to intermediate golfers.

Rating   81.23

Course Rating

Tees	Grade 3.05
Ability Levels	3
Condition	3
Signs / Hole Maps	3
Ball Washers	3
Benches	3.5

Fairways	2.2
Condition	2
Yardage Markers	2.5
Pin Indicators	1
Rough	2.5
Watered / Drainage	4

Greens	3.475
Condition	3.5
Speed	3.5
Size and Variety	3
Slope	4
Fringe	3.5

Layout	2.85
Par 3's	3.5
Par 4's	2.5
Par 5's	2.5
Strategic Trouble	3
Bunkers	1
Enough Space	3.5
Walkability	5

Amenities	2.475
Driving Range	2.5
Practice Green	3
Water on Course	2.5
Port-O-Potties	3
Locker Rooms	1
Pro Shop	2
Grill & Bar	1
Weather Shelter	2
Golf Carts	4

Overall	3.425
Enjoyable	3
Challenging / Fair	2.5
Reservations	5
Scenery	3
Gimmicky Holes	5
Weather Monitor	4

Value	3.5
Overall	81.23

Hole	Back	Front	Women	Par	Men Handicap	Women Handicap
1	444	407	288	4	15	1
2	617	591	426	5	11	3
3	138	123	103	3	17	5
4	542	531	474	5	7	11
5	288	273	258	4	5	9
6	185	175	165	3	9	17
7	389	374	283	4	3	7
8	326	316	306	4	13	15
9	368	356	301	4	1	13
Out	3297	3146	2604	36		
10	601	582	425	5	6	8
11	281	264	219	4	12	18
12	131	112	97	3	4	12
13	513	493	404	5	2	6
14	315	295	254	4	14	16
15	305	291	269	4	8	2
16	139	124	109	3	18	10
17	410	395	342	4	16	14
18	393	382	329	4	10	4
In	3088	2938	2448	36		
Tot	6385	6084	5052	72		
Slope	118	115	114			
Rating	70.1	68.7	68.6			

Hole Commentary

1. A very straight par 4. OB runs along the left side with trees to the right. There is water just in front and right of green.
2. You tee off over a little creek. The hole is very straight with OB running all along the left side of the hole. Water in front of the green from 75 - 50 yards FG where it really juts in.
3. Shorter par 3 over water. Don't go to the right of the green or long.
4. Field on left and trees along the right side. The green itself is completely surrounded by pine trees, there's no real area to bailout.
5. A short dogleg to the left par 4. It is 120 yards to the landing area. Water on the right starting at 140 yards and water along the left side as you approach hole make cutting the corner risky.
6. A longer par 3 hitting out of the chute of trees. Be aware of the wind direction.
7. It is 150 yards to carry the water. If you hit too far right there is water all the way up to 150 yards and there is water along the entire left side of the fairway. The green is two-tiered and slopes back to front and left to right.
8. A very straight hole, not much to this hole. No trouble around the green either.
9. It's a 200 yard carry off the tee to clear the water. A creek runs along the left side and crosses the fairway at 150 yards from green.
10. Trouble along the entire right side of this hole. Favor left side of the fairway to avoid being blocked out by trees on the right on your second shot and approach. Tree trouble on the left from 280 - 200 yards FG. Inside of 200 yards FG you have a good look at the hole.
11. Another very straight hole. Water on the right side from 100 yards FG to the green. Don't go right or over the green.
12. A short par 3 over the creek into a stand of trees. Not much room to miss this green except for short, any other direction will be in the trees.
13. Aim for the small bush toward the right side of fairway in the distance, it is the 150 yard marker. There is no reason or advantage to trying to cut the corner. There is water on the left side from 120 - 100 yards FG.
14. Favor left side of fairway but beware of water inside of 100 yards FG on the left side. Birch trees on right will block you from the green. Trouble all around this green.
15. 145 yards to carry the water on the tee shot. Not much trouble all around this green unless you go long and left.
16. Short par 3. Not much trouble on this hole.
17. Straight forward hole. Green is comma shaped, back right pin placement is tough.
18. 175 yards to carry the water. A small marshy area to the right on this easy finishing hole.

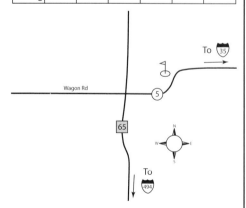

From I-694 take Hwy 65 north 29 miles to CR 5. Go east 1 mile, course is on the left. From I-35 take CR 95 (exit 147) west 0.8 miles until CR 5 splits off. Continue east 10.2 miles on CR 5, course is on the right.

Sawmill Golf Club

11177 McKusick Road
Stillwater, MN 55082
651-439-7862

Course Information

Reservations:	4 days in advance		
	www.ezlinks.com		

2000 Fees:	9	18	Comments
Weekdays	$16.00	$29.00	
Weekends	N/A	$37.00	
Twilight	N/A	$25.00	weekend
Seniors	$15.00	$22.00	
Power Cart	$14.00	$26.00	
Pull Cart	$2.00	$3.00	
Club Rental	$8.00	$8.00	
Credit cards	Visa Mastercard AmEx		
Checks	Any		
Rain Check	18 hole<4 holes, 9 hole<12 holes		
Other	Memberships available		

Leagues:	Mon, Tues, Thur

Amenities:			
Driving Range	Y	Snacks	Y
Putting Green	Y	Grill/Bar	Y
Practice Green	N	Restaurant	N
Spikeless	Y	Locker Room	Y
Proshop	S	Showers	Y

Management:	
Manager	Greg Shulze
Professional	Greg Shulze

Sawmill Golf Club is set amidst trees, water and beautiful scenery. This course is very well kept with great greens and nice fairways. While not being extremely long, the course is very challenging. Accuracy is required to avoid the trees and water. Hitters who can hit long and stay in the fairways will be rewarded. If you are not hitting the ball straight, it could be a long day. This course is a little known gem in the Twin Cities area. This course will challenge golfers of all ability levels.

Rating   102.15

Course Rating

	Grade
Tees	**4.6**
Ability Levels	5
Condition	4
Signs / Hole Maps	5
Ball Washers	4
Benches	5
Fairways	**3.9**
Condition	4
Yardage Markers	3
Pin Indicators	4
Rough	5
Watered / Drainage	5
Greens	**4.25**
Condition	4
Speed	4
Size and Variety	5
Slope	4
Fringe	5
Layout	**3.85**
Par 3's	4
Par 4's	4
Par 5's	3
Strategic Trouble	4
Bunkers	4
Enough Space	4
Walkability	4
Amenities	**4.0**
Driving Range	4
Practice Green	5
Water on Course	4
Port-O-Potties	3
Locker Rooms	5
Pro Shop	3
Grill & Bar	4
Weather Shelter	3
Golf Carts	3
Overall	**4.15**
Enjoyable	5
Challenging / Fair	4
Reservations	3
Scenery	4
Gimmicky Holes	4
Weather Monitor	4
Value	**4.0**
Overall	**102.15**

Hole	Blue	White	Gold	Par	Handicap	Red	Par	Handicap
1	478	469	457	5	11	426	5	13
2	326	306	296	4	9	286	4	7
3	172	152	150	3	15	145	3	15
4	389	378	355	4	5	346	5	3
5	202/164	175/154	138	3	17	107	3	17
6	405	371	321	4	7	292	4	1
7	588	576	564	5	1	412	5	5
8	173	156	139	3	13	116	3	11
9	425	325	320	4	3	278	4	9
Out	3158/3120	2908/2887	2740	35		2408	36	
10	401	384	379	4	6	374	4	4
11	441	434	390	4	2	382	4	2
12	300	288	281	4	16	257	4	14
13	180	159	142	3	14	123	3	12
14	372	361	347	4	8	310	4	6
15	415	335	303	4	12	249	4	18
16	140	125	120	3	18	115	3	16
17	558	488	438	5	4	422	5	10
18	445	355	344	4	10	286	4	8
In	3252	2929	2744	35		2518	35	
Total	6410/6372	5837/5816	5484	70		4926	71	
Slope	119	116	113			122		
Rating	69.9	68.1	68.8			66.8		

Hole Commentary

1. Need to be aware of tree on right side of fairway, as it will block your approach to the green. Creek in front of green prevents running ball onto green.
2. Favor right side of fairway since it slopes left. Hit tee shot to 150-120 yards FG for best approach.
3. Avoid the bunker short of the green and the hole is fairly easy.
4. Can hit over hill but fairway narrows with water left and OB right. Smart play is to 170 yards FG. Take extra club on approach shot.
5. Forget about the water and just hit your shot to the yardage indicated.
6. Favor right side of fairway as it slopes left. Hit to between 140-120 yards FG for best approach shot.
7. Tricky dogleg right par 5. Best shot is a fade of 200-220 yards FT, longer for a good fade hitter but tree trouble lurks left and right. Avoid trouble left of green if you go for it in two.
8. Do not go over or short right on this par 3.
9. Short par 4 but there is trouble. Creek runs at 215 yards FT. Best shot is to 120 yards FG for short approach shot. Can go over creek but must be accurate.
10. Creek runs 80 yards FG. Best shot is from 120-100 yards FG. Do not go over this green.
11. Favor right side of fairway as it slopes left. Largest landing area is from 200-150 yards FG. Over this green is not good.
12. Trouble all along the left side of this hole. Best shot is about 190-200 yards FT which leaves short approach shot.
13. May need a little extra club to reach this green depending on the wind.
14. Very narrow driving area. Hit tee shot to 150-120 yards FG for the best approach shot.
15. Largest landing area is at about 120 yards FG. Green is well bunkered and long and narrow.
16. Very pretty par 3 but beware of the OB on the left, it will cost you.
17. OB runs all along the left side of this hole and the right side is the driving range. Plenty of room to swing away and put yourself in a good position to reach this long and narrow green in two.
18. Favor the right side of the fairway since it slopes down to the left. Hit tee shot to 150 yards FG for the best approach shot.

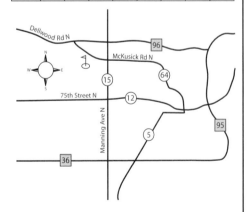

From I-694 take Hwy 36 east 5 miles to Manning Avenue N (CR 19). Go north 2.5 miles to McKusick Road (CR 64). Go west 1 mile, course is on the left.

Shamrock Golf Club
19625 Larkin Road
Corcoran, MN 55340
763-478-9977

Course Information

| Reservations: | Weekday - 1st come/1st served |
| | Weekends - Reservations taken |

2000 Fees:	9	18	Comments
Weekdays	$16.50	$23.50	
Weekends	$18.00	$27.00	
Twilight	N/A	N/A	
Seniors	$12.00	$15.00	
Power Cart	$13.00	$24.00	
Pull Cart	$3.00	$3.00	
Club Rental	$4.50	$4.50	

Credit cards	None
Checks	Local Checks Only
Rain Check	18 hole<5 holes, 9 hole<14 holes
Other	

Leagues:	Mon - Thur

Amenities:			
Driving Range	N	Snacks	Y
Putting Green	Y	Grill/Bar	N
Practice Green	N	Restaurant	N
Spikeless	Y	Locker Room	N
Proshop	S	Showers	N

Management:	
Manager	Rick Deziel
Professional	None

Shamrock Golf Course attempts to make up for its lack of bunkers and other strategic trouble by having extremely narrow fairways. Although the fairways are narrow, the rough is very fair and is not much of a penalty. With little trouble on the course you can swing away on most holes and find yourself in a position to hit the green on your approach shot. The course was in average shape and somewhat boring but if you are looking to practice your game, this is a great course for doing so. The course is well suited for beginner to intermediate golfers.

Rating　　76.48

Course Rating

Tees	Grade
	2.88
Ability Levels	2.5
Condition	3
Signs / Hole Maps	2
Ball Washers	4
Benches	4

Fairways	3.15
Condition	3.5
Yardage Markers	3
Pin Indicators	2.5
Rough	3
Watered / Drainage	4

Greens	3.0
Condition	3.5
Speed	3
Size and Variety	2
Slope	3
Fringe	4

Layout	2.65
Par 3's	2.5
Par 4's	2
Par 5's	2.5
Strategic Trouble	2.5
Bunkers	1.5
Enough Space	4
Walkability	5

Amenities	2.08
Driving Range	1
Practice Green	3
Water on Course	2.5
Port-O-Potties	3
Locker Rooms	1
Pro Shop	2
Grill & Bar	1.5
Weather Shelter	1
Golf Carts	2.5

Overall	2.8
Enjoyable	2.5
Challenging / Fair	2
Reservations	3
Scenery	3
Gimmicky Holes	5
Weather Monitor	3

Value	3.0
Overall	**76.48**

Hole	Blue	White	Par	Handicap	Red	Par	Handicap
1	542	533	5	5	510	5	1
2	414	404	4	1	394	5	5
3	377	357	4	9	337	4	17
4	159	149	3	17	140	3	11
5	360	350	4	13	305	4	13
6	466	451	5	15	436	5	3
7	380	358	4	11	351	4	9
8	224	215	3	3	211	4	15
9	386	376	4	7	366	4	7
Out	3308	3193	36		3050	38	
10	361	346	4	10	326	4	10
11	408	396	4	2	338	4	6
12	318	308	4	16	283	4	14
13	158	148	3	14	123	3	16
14	514	484	5	4	464	5	4
15	340	325	4	12	310	4	12
16	144	129	3	18	114	3	18
17	368	358	4	8	331	4	8
18	504	484	5	6	454	5	2
In	3115	2978	36		2743	36	
Total	6423	6171	72		5793	74	
Slope	111	108			115		
Rating	69.8	69.0			72.1		

Hole Commentary

1.   Par 4 with water all along the right side of the hole. Trees along the left make this a tight driving hole. Uphill approach to the green requires extra club.

2.   OB far right of the hole should not come into play. Uphill approach shot requires extra club.

3.   OB along the right side of this hole. Very straightforward hole with no trouble around the green.

4.   Straightforward hole with no trouble around the green.

5.   Another easy hole, no trouble.

6.   Dogleg left with trees both left and right of the fairway. No trouble around green.

7.   Straightforward hole with little trouble.

8.   Long par three to a smaller green. No trouble around the green if you miss it.

9.   Dogleg right par 4 with water to the right at 200 yards FG.

10. Favor the right side of the fairway with OB all along the left side of the hole.

11. Favor the right side of the fairway with OB all along the left side of the hole. Water cuts across the fairway at 125 yards FG. No trouble around the green.

12. OB along the left side of the hole. Trees left and right at 100 yards FG. Bunker guards front of the green.

13. Water all along the right side of the green so don't miss right or long.

14. Favor the left side of the fairway as it slopes left to right. Willow tree on left side at 180 yards FG can block out approach shots.

15. Straightforward hole with little trouble.

16. Bunker guards front of the green, but no other trouble around the green. Green slopes away from you slightly.

17. Water cuts in from the left side of the fairway at 100 yards FG.

18. Water just 100 yards FT both left and right. Favor the left side of the fairway as it slopes left to right.

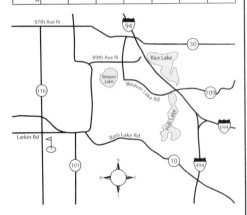

From I-494 take Bass Lake Road (CR10) west 4.6 miles to Larkin Road. Take Larkin road 1/4 mile, the course is on the left.

Southern Hills Golf Club

18950 Chippendale Avenue
Farmington, MN 55024
651-463-4653

Course Information

Reservations:	7 days in advance www.ezlinks.com		
2000 Fees:	9	18	Comments
Weekdays	$18.00	$26.00	
Weekends	N/A	$34.00	
Twilight	N/A	$21.00	
Seniors	N/A	$19.00	M-F < 3:30
Power Cart	$17.00	$27.00	
Pull Cart	$3.75	$3.75	
Club Rental	$9.00	$9.00	
Credit cards	Visa Mastercard		
Checks	Any		
Rain Check	18 hole<5 holes, 9 hole<14 holes		
Other			
Leagues:	Wed, Thur		

Amenities:			
Driving Range	Y	Snacks	Y
Putting Green	Y	Grill/Bar	Y
Practice Green	N	Restaurant	N
Spikeless	O	Locker Room	N
Proshop	S	Showers	N

Management:	
Manager	Lynn Rosendahl
Professional	Lynn Rosendahl

Southern Hills Golf Club combines gently rolling hills, water hazards and natural beauty to create an enjoyable round of golf. From tee to green the grass was in better than average condition. The layout of the course offers you a nice variety in the holes, especially the par 3's. Not far from the metro area and usually easier to get on, it is worth the drive. The course will challenge golfers of all ability levels.

Rating   95.15

Course Rating

Tees	Grade 3.4
Ability Levels	3
Condition	4
Signs / Hole Maps	2
Ball Washers	4
Benches	4.5

Fairways	3.75
Condition	3.5
Yardage Markers	4
Pin Indicators	4
Rough	3
Watered / Drainage	4

Greens	3.8
Condition	4
Speed	3
Size and Variety	5
Slope	4
Fringe	2

Layout	3.95
Par 3's	4.5
Par 4's	4
Par 5's	3.5
Strategic Trouble	4
Bunkers	3
Enough Space	4
Walkability	5

Amenities	3.2
Driving Range	3
Practice Green	3.5
Water on Course	4
Port-O-Potties	3.5
Locker Rooms	1
Pro Shop	3
Grill & Bar	4
Weather Shelter	2.5
Golf Carts	4

Overall	4.05
Enjoyable	4
Challenging / Fair	4
Reservations	5
Scenery	3
Gimmicky Holes	5
Weather Monitor	3

Value	4.0
Overall	**95.15**

Hole	Blue	White	Red	Par	Men Handicap	Women Handicap
1	504	489	422	5	7	1
2	194	180	132	3	9	9
3	317	297	240	4	13	11
4	174	159	135	3	17	15
5	369	361	296	4	11	13
6	435	421	316	4	1	3
7	376	363	311	4	15	17
8	206	196	164	3	5	7
9	472	462	403	5	3	5
Out	3047	2928	2419	35		
10	417	411	341	4	2	2
11	163	155	121	3	18	18
12	547	534	446	5	6	6
13	351	339	258	4	12	12
14	407	383	312	4	8	10
15	147	128	119	3	16	16
16	366	358	277	4	14	14
17	355	347	264	4	10	8
18	514	490	413	5	4	4
In	3267	3145	2551	36		
Total	6314	6073	4970	71		
Slope	126	124	116			
Rating	70.5	69.4	68.7			

Hole Commentary

1. Creek runs along the right side of the fairway from 250 yards FG to the green and runs in front of the green.
2. Downhill par 3. The wind tends to push the ball right. Do not go over or right of green.
3. Favor the right side of the fairway on this uphill par 4. Green guarded by bunkers front and right of the green. Over the green is the driving range and left is down a big hill.
4. The wind is usually in your face on this par 3. Over and left of the green are trouble.
5. Favor left side of fairway on tee shot but keep in mind OB is far left. Past 150 yards FG the fairway slopes down to the hole. Creek over the green.
6. Trees on left, but you must hit to left side. Approach is over creek with water along the right. Trouble over the green.
7. Favor left side of fairway as everything slopes right. Wide but shallow green with bunker guarding front left of green.
8. Tough uphill par 3. Long is okay because of natural backstop over green. Easy to leave short, take extra club or two.
9. Green is actually located toward clubhouse. Fairway narrows from 250-200 yards FG with bunkers on both sides. Water front and left of green.
10. Straight uphill par 4 with OB far right. Take extra club on uphill approach shot with natural backstop over green.
11. Downhill par 3. Cannot go over green but bunkers guard short.
12. Dogleg right par 5. Long hitters aim left of trees on right. May be in rough but good angle to green. Others hit over women's tee box to fairway. Marsh on left at 250 yards FG. Pin tucked around hill on left, don't go over.
13. Straight par 4 with bunker on the left at 150 yards FG and right at 100 yards FG. Favor left side of fairway for best angle to green.
14. OB all along right side of fairway. Hole doglegs severely left after 150 yards FG. Long hitters can cut yardage off by hitting over mounds on left. Will be in rough but cut some distance. Can't go right of the green.
15. Short downhill par 3 to a multi-level green. Need to know where the pin is.
16. Hit left of the rocks. Approach shot has water all along the right side of the green.
17. Creek runs all along the right side of the hole. Favor left side of fairway as it slopes to the right. Bunkers run from 120-80 yards FG on the left side of the fairway. Green guarded in front and right by water.
18. Aim toward left side of fairway. Right is trees and water. Creek dissects fairway at 150 yards. Bunkers run along right side from 100 yards FG.

From I-35 take CR 70 (exit 72) east 4 miles. Follow the signs for CR 50 and take it east 4 miles to Hwy 3. Go north 2.3 miles, course is on the right.

Stonebrooke Golf Club

2693 South County Road 79
Shakopee, MN 55379
952-496-3171
www.stonebrooke.com

Course Information

Reservations:	3 days in advance		
2000 Fees:	9	18	Comments
Weekdays	N/A	$39.00	
Weekends	N/A	$46.00	
Twilight	N/A	$29.00	* see other
Seniors	N/A	N/A	
Power Cart	N/A	$28.00	
Pull Cart	N/A	$5.00	
Club Rental	N/A	$19/30	
Credit cards	Visa Mastercard		
Checks	Any		
Rain Check	18 hole<4 holes, 9 hole<12 holes		
Other	Twilight >2pm, super twilight >5:30pm - $25.00		
Leagues:	Mon - Thur		

Amenities:			
Driving Range	Y	Snacks	Y
Putting Green	Y	Grill/Bar	Y
Practice Green	Y	Restaurant	N
Spikeless	O	Locker Room	Y
Proshop	F	Showers	Y

Management:	
Manager	Einar Odland
Professional	Einar Odland

Water abounds on Stonebrooke as it comes into play on 14 of the 18 holes. The most interesting of the water holes is the par 4 eighth hole which includes a 200 yard carry over the lake followed by a boat ride to the fairway. With trees, bunkers, water and wetland, Stonebrooke has challenges and natural beauty on every hole. It is the perfect setting for a peaceful and fun round of golf. The course will challenge golfers of all ability levels.

Rating   101.10

Course Rating

Tees	Grade **4.6**
Ability Levels	5
Condition	4
Signs / Hole Maps	5
Ball Washers	4
Benches	5

Fairways	**3.3**
Condition	5
Yardage Markers	3
Pin Indicators	1
Rough	3
Watered / Drainage	4

Greens	**4.5**
Condition	4
Speed	5
Size and Variety	5
Slope	4
Fringe	4

Layout	**4.33**
Par 3's	3.5
Par 4's	4.5
Par 5's	5
Strategic Trouble	5
Bunkers	4
Enough Space	4
Walkability	4

Amenities	**3.75**
Driving Range	4
Practice Green	5
Water on Course	3
Port-O-Potties	3
Locker Rooms	4
Pro Shop	3
Grill & Bar	3
Weather Shelter	3
Golf Carts	4

Overall	**3.9**
Enjoyable	4
Challenging / Fair	4
Reservations	3
Scenery	4
Gimmicky Holes	4
Weather Monitor	5

Value	**3.5**
Overall	**101.10**

Hole	Championship	Regular	Forward	Par	Handicap
1	544	512	440	5	4
2	168	155	129	3	16
3	367	344	310	4	14
4	172	153	136	3	12
5	550	519	377	5	2
6	415	373	325	4	8
7	148	125	110	3	18
8	406	355	195	4	10
9	411	379	346	4	6
Out	3181	2915	2368	35	
10	351	332	309	4	15
11	229	187	152	3	9
12	526	494	405	5	7
13	188	165	141	3	17
14	410	383	334	4	5
15	404	377	291	4	3
16	327	301	278	4	13
17	595	533	444	5	1
18	393	382	311	4	11
In	3423	3154	2665	36	
Total	6604	6069	5033	71	
Slope	133	128	120		
Rating	72.4	70.0	69.9		

Hole Commentary

1. Intimidating tee shot with a creek running at 220 yards FG. There is more room right than left off the tee. Fairway slopes right to left so aim at the right side on your approach.
2. Very long green so know where the pin is and choose your club accordingly.
3. Aim just left of the power pole keeping in mind that the shed on the left is OB. Water on right doesn't come into play on the tee shot.
4. The marsh is a ball magnet so aim for the center of the green.
5. It's 160 yards FT to carry marsh. The upper fairway is the safe but may leave you blocked FG. The lower fairway affords a straight shot to the hole but runs along side creek. The creek runs in front of green at 100 yards.
6. Aim at the right side of the fairway since the fairway slopes down to the left. A creek runs down the left side of the hole so going a little right is better than left.
7. Nice, short par three over water. Enjoy!
8. From the white tees its 200 yards FT to carry the water. Best shot is 225-230 yards FT just left of trees on right. For big hitters green is reachable but the risk is not worth reward.
9. Aim right of bunker on left side on this straightforward par 4.
10. This hole doglegs 90° at the bunker straight ahead 220 yards FT. Hit your shot to 100-80 yards FG or if your feeling lucky hit a big draw and the ball will roll down toward the green. Beware of trees on the left and OB long.
11. Take one extra club and use the hill as a backstop on this long par 3.
12. Aim just left of the far bunker for the safe play as water runs along the fairway on the left. Green may be reachable in two with plenty of bail out area except long.
13. Hard to see the putting surface so trust the yardage on the card.
14. Aim just left of the pine tree on the right. The longer the drive, the narrower the fairway. A creek crosses the fairway at 120 yards FG so stay short of that.
15. Favor the left side for a shorter second shot to this peninsula green. Don't go left or long on your approach.
16. OB left of fairway. Bunker on right is at 100 yards FG, bunker on left is at 130 yards FG and another bunker guards the front right of the green. Fairway slopes to the left so aim at the right side and the ball will run down to the left.
17. Aim just left of the bunker on the right. The two trees straight ahead are on the left side of the fairway. A creek runs in front of the green from 80 yards on the right to 40 yards on left.
18. Water left and a bunker right on this nice finishing hole. Take an extra club on the blind uphill approach shot.

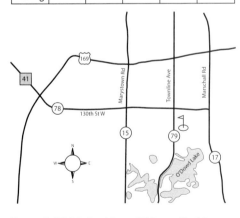

From I-494 take Hwy 169 south 10 miles to Marschall Road (CR 17). Go south 1.1 miles to 130th Street W (CR 78). Go west 3/4 mile to Townline Road (CR 79). Go south 1/4 mile, course is on the left.

StoneRidge Golf Club

13600 North Hudson Blvd
Stillwater, MN 55082
651-436-4653
www.stoneridgegc.com

Course Information

Reservations:	1 week in advance		
2000 Fees:	9	18	Comments
Weekdays	$40.00	$69.00	
Weekends	$50.00	$79.00	
Twilight	N/A	N/A	
Seniors	N/A	N/A	
Power Cart	$20.00	$30.00	
Pull Cart	N/A	N/A	
Club Rental	N/A	$25.00	
Credit cards	Visa Mastercard AmEx		
Checks	Any		
Rain Check	18 hole<3 holes, 9 hole<13 holes		
Other	Memberships available		
Leagues:	Member leagues only		

Amenities:			
Driving Range	Y	Snacks	Y
Putting Green	N	Grill/Bar	Y
Practice Green	Y	Restaurant	Y
Spikeless	Y	Locker Room	Y
Proshop	F	Showers	

Management:	
Manager	Jeanne McGrath
Professional	Keith Kalny

One of the first thing you will notice at Stone Ridge, which opened for play in 2000, is the lack of huge houses. This links style course incorporates water, rough and unbelievable bunkers to add challenge to the game. You would probably fare better from the bunkers themselves than the long grass surrounding the bunkers. With beautiful fairways, fast greens and plenty of scenery this course is destined to become one of the nicest in the Twin Cities. The course will challenge golfers of all ability levels.

Rating   93.85

Course Rating

Tees	Grade 4.1
Ability Levels	5
Condition	5
Signs / Hole Maps	1
Ball Washers	2
Benches	5

Fairways	3.3
Condition	4
Yardage Markers	2
Pin Indicators	4
Rough	3
Watered / Drainage	4

Greens	4.4
Condition	4
Speed	4
Size and Variety	5
Slope	5
Fringe	5

Layout	3.88
Par 3's	4.5
Par 4's	4
Par 5's	4
Strategic Trouble	4
Bunkers	4
Enough Space	3
Walkability	3

Amenities	3.6
Driving Range	4
Practice Green	5
Water on Course	2
Port-O-Potties	2
Locker Rooms	5
Pro Shop	4
Grill & Bar	4
Weather Shelter	1
Golf Carts	5

Overall	4.65
Enjoyable	4.5
Challenging / Fair	5
Reservations	5
Scenery	5
Gimmicky Holes	4
Weather Monitor	3

Value	2.5
Overall	**93.85**

Hole	Black	Burgundy	White	Green	Par	Handicap
1	335	309	301	248	4	17
2	516	503	468	421	5	13
3	360	350	328	318	4	7
4	575	565	532	443	5	3
5	462	447	429	320	4	1
6	401	396	370	314	4	5
7	168	156	135	124	3	11
8	364	348	324	253	4	9
9	152	144	130	109	3	15
Out	3333	3218	3017	2550	36	
10	420	410	362	339	4	6
11	502	489	457	422	5	18
12	480	458	426	382	4	2
13	331	305	278	250	4	16
14	191	182	162	119	3	12
15	440	429	395	334	4	8
16	237	224	197	144	3	10
17	552	526	437	383	5	14
18	473	453	386	324	4	4
In	3626	3476	3100	2697	36	
Total	6959	6694	6117	5247	72	
Slope	133	130	126	117		
Rating	73.3	72.3	70.0	68.6		

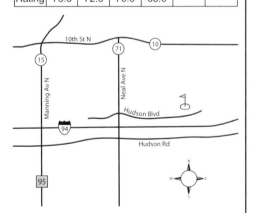

From I-94 take Manning Avenue south 1 block to Hudson Road. Go east 1 mile to Neal Avenue. Go north to the frontage road (Hudson Blvd. N). Go east, course is on the left.

Hole Commentary

1. Nice opening downhill par 4. Can drive the hole but smart play is to lay-up to a comfortable distance for a wedge approach and a good start. Don't go too far over the green.
2. Favor the middle of the fairway on this slight dogleg right par 5. Keep the ball in the fairway and this is a fairly simple par 5. If you go for the green in two, miss right if at all.
3. Just hit a controlled club to about 150-120 yards FG. Bunker on right covers most of fairway and ends at 100 yards FG.
4. Long par 5 where right is not good off tee box. Favor left side but avoid bunkers from 310-280 yards FG. Lay-up to 150 yards or 100 yards FG. No place to miss this green.
5. Favor middle of fairway and avoid bunkers along left side. Can't go left or right of green.
6. Bunkers along entire left side of fairway so favor right side. Long green with many undulations, know where the pin is.
7. Deceptively deep green, looks small. Front pin is a sucker pin. Aim for middle of green.
8. Uphill par 4 with bunkers on left side. Requires 1 or 2 extra clubs on approach to this two-tiered green which is well bunkered.
9. Bunkers surround this deep green. Know where pin is located to avoid long putts.
10. The fairway falls off at 130 yards FG. Aim for right side of fairway. Water left of green with a little room over.
11. Aim just left of trees on right side. At 170 yards FG the bunker on right pinches in. On 2nd shot aim just left of 150-yard mark and set up your pitch to green. Green nearly impossible to hit in two because of bunkers.
12. Intimidating tee shot on this hole, favor left side of fairway. Bunkers on left start at 170 yards FG. Bunkers guard this green well.
13. Short uphill par 4 that is reachable by long hitters but is well guarded. Favor left side of fairway and lay-up to about 80 yards FG.
14. Wind will affect this tee shot. Cannot go over or right of this green.
15. Tee shot looks intimidating but its fairly open. Aim just left of the small trees on the right, cannot go right of those trees. Elevated green so make sure you get to the green.
16. Longer par 3 with sand all along the left side of the hole. Long and right are okay. Wind could change club selection 1 or 2 clubs.
17. Fairly straight par 5 with OB running entire right side of the hole and bunkers on the left. Fairway narrows at 150 yards FG. Tough to run ball up to hole, need to fly it on this small green if you go for it in two.
18. Favor left side of fairway to avoid bunkers on right. Green is well guarded on left side so favor right side of green. Back pin placement is tough to get back to.

Sundance Golf Club
15240 North 113th Avenue
Maple Grove, MN 55369
763-420-4700

Course Information

Reservations:	Weekdays - 1 week in advance Weekend - Tuesday		
2000 Fees:	9	18	Comments
Weekdays	$16.50	$26.00	
Weekends	$17.00	$30.00	9 hole > 3pm
Twilight	N/A	$25.00	wknd > 4 w/cart
Seniors	$11.00	$16.00	M-F < 11am
Power Cart	$16.00	$25.00	
Pull Cart	$3.00	$3.00	
Club Rental	$7.00	$10.00	
Credit cards	Visa Mastercard AmEx		
Checks	Any		
Rain Check	18 hole<3 holes, 9 hole<12 holes		
Other			
Leagues:	Mon - Thur		

Amenities:			
Driving Range	Y	Snacks	Y
Putting Green	Y	Grill/Bar	Y
Practice Green	N	Restaurant	Y
Spikeless	Y	Locker Room	N
Proshop	F	Showers	N

Management:	
Manager	David Leyse
Professional	David Leyse

Sundance is not a long course and many of the holes are wide open. Water does come into play on 10 holes with 36 bunkers ready to catch errant shots. There are not many trees on the course and the rough is very playable. There was nothing really wrong with the course but nothing stood out about it either. The pace of play is usually fairly quick so you it may be a good course to play if you are in a hurry. The course is well suited for beginner to intermediate golfers.

Rating   87.93

Course Rating

	Grade	Comments
Tees	**3.3**	
Ability Levels	3	
Condition	3.5	
Signs / Hole Maps	2	
Ball Washers	4	
Benches	5	
Fairways	**3.6**	
Condition	3.5	
Yardage Markers	3.5	
Pin Indicators	4	
Rough	3	
Watered / Drainage	4	
Greens	**3.6**	
Condition	4	
Speed	3	
Size and Variety	3.5	
Slope	4	
Fringe	4	
Layout	**3.63**	
Par 3's	3	
Par 4's	3.5	
Par 5's	3	
Strategic Trouble	3.5	
Bunkers	4	
Enough Space	4	
Walkability	5	
Amenities	**3.15**	
Driving Range	4	
Practice Green	3	
Water on Course	3	
Port-O-Potties	3	
Locker Rooms	1	
Pro Shop	4	
Grill & Bar	4	
Weather Shelter	4	
Golf Carts	3	
Overall	**3.63**	
Enjoyable	3.5	
Challenging / Fair	3	
Reservations	5	
Scenery	3.5	
Gimmicky Holes	5	
Weather Monitor	1	
Value	**3.0**	
Overall		**87.93**

Hole	Blue	White	Par	Handicap	Red	Par	Handicap
1	403	395	4	1	381	5	14
2	203	189	3	5	123	3	16
3	328	306	4	9	241	4	12
4	332	325	4	15	293	4	6
5	331	318	4	11	304	4	8
6	499	487	5	7	472	5	2
7	386	368	4	3	330	4	4
8	342	323	4	13	278	4	10
9	281	272	4	17	245	4	18
Out	3105	2983	36		2667	37	
10	334	321	4	14	249	4	13
11	170	145	3	16	119	3	17
12	408	400	4	4	330	4	3
13	398	396	4	8	342	4	5
14	577	567	5	10	431	5	11
15	390	372	4	2	346	4	7
16	361	336	4	12	321	4	9
17	120	120	3	18	107	3	15
18	552	552	5	6	494	5	1
In	3310	3209	36		2739	36	
Total	6415	6192	72		5406	73	
Slope	126	124			124		
Rating	70.7	69.6			71.5		

Hole Commentary

1. Water on the right from 180 – 50 yards FG with a small pond far left of fairway. Two bunkers guard front of green.
2. Downhill par 3 with water guarding in front of green and OB over the green.
3. Slight dogleg left with OB far left of fairway. Favor left side of fairway and hit to 100 – 70 yards FG. Water runs just in front of and right of green. OB over green.
4. Water just off to the left of the tee. Bunkers left and right from 120 – 90 yards FG.
5. Water on left starts at 120 yards FG and as you get closer to the hole it get closer to the fairway. OB over the green, two bunkers right of green and water left of green make accuracy essential on the approach shot.
6. OB along the entire left side of this hilly par 5. Bunker on right from 75 – 40 FG. Bunker guards front left of green.
7. Very straightforward hole with OB far left of the fairway. Bunker over the green.
8. Short par 4 with no reason not to hit driver. Bunkers front left and right of green. Even poor drives leave you with a decent approach shot.
9. Smart play is to hit to a yardage you feel comfortable hitting a wedge from. Trouble surrounds the green so trying to drive the green can result in high scores.
10. Dogleg right past the trees. Most people who try to hit over the trees end up with high scores. Hole is directly over trees about 10 yards from left edge of trees. Best play is just left of the trees to set up a wedge shot. Bunker on left sits at 100 yards FG.
11. Par 3 with bunkers surrounding the green.
12. Dogleg right par 4 with bunker on the right at 175 yards FG and bunker on left at 165 yards FG. Bunkers in front left and right of green as well as over the green.
13. Water on left ends at 150 yards FG. Favor right side of fairway, plenty of area to hit to over there. OB over the hole.
14. Trees along left of hole are OB, plenty of area to hit right. Two bunkers sit 20 yards FG. No trouble around the green
15. Hazard all along the left side of hole. Aim just left of bunker on right side which is at 140 yards FG. OB over the green.
16. Downhill par 4 with water left of fairway at 150 yards FG so avoid left side of fairway. Cannot see putting surface on approach but left and long are big trouble.
17. Hitting over a pond with OB over the green. Not much area to miss the green.
18. From the tee you cannot see water that dissects fairway at 230 yards FG on the left. Approach shot is uphill to the green and requires extra club to reach a green with not much trouble other than long.

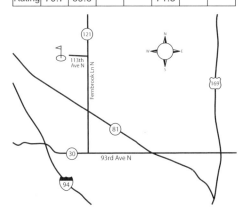

From I-94 go east 1.25 miles on 95th Avenue Fernbrook Lane N (CR 121). Go north 2.5 miles to 113th Avenue N. Go west 1/2 mile to the course.

Tanners Brook Golf Club

5810 190th Street
Forest Lake, MN 55025
651-464-2300
www.tannersbrook.com

Course Information

Reservations:	3 days in advance		
2000 Fees:	9	18	Comments
Weekdays	$15.00	$25.00	
Weekends	$17.00	$28.00	
Twilight	N/A	$20/25	Walk/Ride
Seniors	N/A	$20/25	Walk/Ride, M-Th
Power Cart	$6.00	$10.00	per person
Pull Cart	$3.00	$3.00	
Club Rental	$7.00	$14.00	
Credit cards	Visa Mastercard Disc AmEx		
Checks	Any		
Rain Check	18 hole<5 holes, 9 hole<13 holes		
Other			
Leagues:	Tues - Thur		

Amenities:			
Driving Range	Y	Snacks	Y
Putting Green	Y	Grill/Bar	Y
Practice Green	N	Restaurant	N
Spikeless	O	Locker Room	N
Proshop	S	Showers	N

Management:	
Manager	Jaime McGovern & John Dunlap
Professional	Mark Fitzenberger

Tanners Brook is spread out over 220 acres with water and wetlands on 17 out of 18 holes. One of the more scenic par 3's in the Twin Cities has to be the 17th hole overlooking the wetlands. This is another of the newer courses being built without large houses sur-rounding it. Some of the grass still needs to grow in a little but overall the course was in very good condition. The course will chal-lenge golfers of all ability levels.

Rating   98.53

Course Rating

	Grade
Tees	**3.55**
Ability Levels	4
Condition	3.5
Signs / Hole Maps	2
Ball Washers	4
Benches	4
Fairways	**3.95**
Condition	4
Yardage Markers	4
Pin Indicators	4
Rough	3.5
Watered / Drainage	4
Greens	**3.85**
Condition	4
Speed	3.5
Size and Variety	4
Slope	4
Fringe	4
Layout	**3.95**
Par 3's	4
Par 4's	4
Par 5's	3.5
Strategic Trouble	4
Bunkers	3.5
Enough Space	4.5
Walkability	4.5
Amenities	**3.4**
Driving Range	4
Practice Green	5
Water on Course	4
Port-O-Potties	3
Locker Rooms	1
Pro Shop	2
Grill & Bar	2
Weather Shelter	1
Golf Carts	4
Overall	**3.98**
Enjoyable	4
Challenging / Fair	4
Reservations	3
Scenery	4
Gimmicky Holes	5
Weather Monitor	4.5
Value	**4.5**
Overall	**98.53**

Hole	Blue	White	Red	Par	Men Handicap	Women Handicap
1	399	374	339	4	10	4
2	381	344	303	4	18	16
3	197	173	150	3	14	10
4	556	512	425	5	8	6
5	413	395	322	4	4	12
6	382	364	293	4	12	8
7	405	367	294	4	16	18
8	215	194	148	3	6	14
9	570	538	446	5	2	2
Out	3518	3261	2720	36		
10	453	423	412	4	3	7
11	198	179	144	3	9	9
12	398	370	296	4	5	13
13	180	155	127	3	13	15
14	409	389	327	4	1	1
15	389	367	330	4	15	11
16	529	505	435	5	11	3
17	155	128	113	3	17	17
18	506	490	428	5	7	5
In	3217	3006	2612	35		
Total	6735	6267	5332	71		
Slope	130	126	124			
Rating	72.6	70.5	70.8			

Hole Commentary

1. Water down to the right off the tee box. Bunkers left of fairway at 150 yards and right at 120 yards FG. Water on left all the way to the hole. Bunkers guard front and over green.
2. Fairly open driving hole. Creek runs along left side of green with a big bunker on the right. There is trouble over the green.
3. A long par 3 with two bunkers left and one bunker guarding front right side of green.
4. Bunker is at 250 yards FG. Approaching the green, a large bunker guards the front of a green with a hump in the middle.
5. Longer par four, very straight with water down on the right and quite a few bunkers in the hitting zone. Trouble over the green.
6. Favor left side of fairway on this dogleg right to avoid being blocked by tree on to the right. Water left of very long green
7. Bunker on the right at 150 yards FG. Green sits behind a hill with water left and over. Want to be on right side of fairway for best approach.
8. Long par 3 with trees over green and water just in front.
9. A long par 5 with trouble along left side on drive until the bunker on the right at 300 yards FG. There is water on the right at 200 yards FG. A creek on the right runs from 165 yards FG to the green. A bunker sits on left side of fairway at 75 yards FG. Water right of green.
10. Trees and OB left of the fairway. Aim just left of bunker on right at 200 yards FG. Tree on left is 60 yards FG. Water left of green.
11. Coming up short on this par 3 is okay just don't be long of this small green.
12. Best view of the hole is from left side of fairway just don't go too far left. Bunker guards the front right of the green with some room to bailout over or left but not left and over.
13. Another long par 3 with a bunker guarding left side, two bunkers guarding front right.
14. Favor left side as water on right runs from 200-170 yards FG. Creek runs on the left from 120 yards FG to the green. Water left of green
15. Pond on the left from 230-150 yards FG. Bunker runs from 120-90 yards FG. Bunker guards right side of the green with trouble over green.
16. Wide open tee shot. Usually plays as a 3 shot hole. Marsh on left at 270 yards FG and 220 yards FG. Trees are OB all the way to the hole. Water just right of green with OB left.
17. Short par 3 with water on left side of green.
18. Very straightforward par 5. Approaching the green there is water to the left and in front of the green. Bunker in front of green and to the right of green. Have to fly your ball onto green, cannot roll it up.

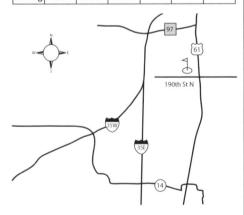

From I-35 take CR 97 (exit 129) east 2 miles to Hwy 61. Go south 2 miles to 190th Street N. Go west, the course is on the right.

Theodore Wirth Golf Club

1300 Theodore Wirth Parkway
Minneapolis, MN 55422
612-522-4584
www.minneapolisparks.com

Course Information

Reservations:	4 days in advance www.teemaster.com		
2000 Fees:	9	18	Comments
Weekdays	$17.00	$24.00	
Weekends	$17.00	$26.00	9 hole>2pm
Twilight	N/A	$17.00	After 4pm
Seniors	N/A	$15.00	w/ patron card
Power Cart	$13.00	$24.00	
Pull Cart	$2.00	$3.00	
Club Rental	$4.00	$7.50	
Credit cards	Visa Mastercard Discover AmEx		
Checks	Local Checks Only		
Rain Check	18 hole<3 holes, 9 hole<12 holes		
Other	M-Th < 1pm, w/ 2 or 4-some is $27.50 including cart.		
Leagues:	Wed		

Amenities:			
Driving Range	N	Snacks	Y
Putting Green	Y	Grill/Bar	Y
Practice Green	N	Restaurant	N
Spikeless	O	Locker Room	Y
Proshop	B	Showers	Y
Management:			
Manager	Bill Baughton		
Professional	None		

Theodore Wirth Golf Course is one of the oldest public golf courses in the state of Minnesota. The front nine of Wirth is beautifully set around Bassett Creek with several scenic views of the Minneapolis downtown skyline. The back nine is very hilly with elevation changes on almost every hole. The elevation changes make club selection difficult, short is better than long on most of the holes. The course will challenge golfers of all ability levels.

Rating 88.98

Course Rating

Tees	Grade 3.4
Ability Levels	4
Condition	3
Signs / Hole Maps	2
Ball Washers	4
Benches	4
Fairways	**3.1**
Condition	3
Yardage Markers	2
Pin Indicators	4
Rough	4
Watered / Drainage	4
Greens	**3.65**
Condition	4
Speed	4
Size and Variety	3
Slope	3
Fringe	4
Layout	**3.35**
Par 3's	3
Par 4's	3.5
Par 5's	3
Strategic Trouble	3
Bunkers	4
Enough Space	4
Walkability	3
Amenities	**2.53**
Driving Range	1
Practice Green	3
Water on Course	2.5
Port-O-Potties	2
Locker Rooms	5
Pro Shop	3
Grill & Bar	3
Weather Shelter	2
Golf Carts	3
Overall	**3.53**
Enjoyable	3
Challenging / Fair	3
Reservations	4
Scenery	4
Gimmicky Holes	5
Weather Monitor	3.5
Value	**4.0**
Overall	**88.98**

Hole	Blue	White	Gold	Red	Par	Handicap Men	Handicap Women
1	378	368	313	230	4	7	7
2	489	471	441	368	5	1	1
3	333	311	270	232	4	13	13
4	224	195	178	153	3	15	15
5	446	410	361	316	4	3	3
6	492	471	446	392	5	11	11
7	397	363	350	307	4	9	9
8	160	140	120	100	3	17	17
9	391	374	308	308	4	5	5
Out	3310	3103	2787	2406	36		
10	380	370	303	303	4	8	8
11	358	346	335	335	4	12	14
12	518	471	461	461	5	2	2
13	422	410	342	342	4	4	6
14	372	367	358	358	4	14	12
15	491	485	436	436	5	6	4
16	180	175	156	156	3	16	16
17	407	402	391	391	4	10	10
18	146	143	125	125	3	18	18
In	3274	3169	2907	2907	36		
Total	6584	6272	5694	5313	72		
Slope	132	129	M 123 W 126	122			
Rating	72.7	71.2	M 67.9 W 73.4	71.3			

Hole Commentary

1. Straightforward hole that doglegs slightly to the left. Creek runs in front of hole at 50 yards FG.
2. This hole runs away from the tee box to the left with red stakes along entire left side of hole. Favor middle to right side of fairway. Long and right of green are trouble on approach.
3. Elevated tee box with water running along left side of hole, favor middle to right side of fairway. Bunker guards front left of green. Don't go over this green.
4. Hole tends to play into the wind so choose club carefully. Trouble over and left of green.
5. Uphill par 4 with marsh running along left side of hole. Favor center to left side of fairway to avoid being blocked out by trees on the right side. Trouble over this green.
6. Blind tee shot as hole goes downhill. Fairway runs left of the tree at 220 yards FG. Can go right of tree and hit from rough, just don't end up behind tree. Elevated green has trouble all around it.
7. Longer hitters can favor left side of fairway otherwise hit to middle. Approach is to elevated green and may require extra club.
8. Slightly downhill par 3 with bunker guarding front right of green. Over green is tree trouble.
9. Elevated tee shot with water on left of hole from 210-140 yards FG and water on right from 160-60 yards FG. Bunkers guard front left and front right of green.
10. Uphill par 4 with hazard along right side of hole. Approach shot is uphill with uphill lie. Take 1 or 2 extra clubs.
11. Bunker on right side at 150 yards FG where hill begins to slope down toward hole. Past 100 yards FG and you'll have bad downhill lie. Try to hit center of fairway. Don't go over the green.
12. Severe dogleg left par 5 with water along entire left side of hole. Favor right side of fairway to avoid being blocked by trees on left. Creek runs across fairway at 150 yards FG.
13. Uphill par 4, need to hit it as far up hill as possible. Uphill approach typically into wind so 1 or 2 extra clubs may be required.
14. Downhill par 4 where length is not as important as accuracy. Don't get stuck behind trees on right or left. Don't go over this green.
15. Uphill par 5 where the right side of the fairway is preferred. On second shot favor left side of fairway. Large bunker over green to catch errant shots, past that is big trouble.
16. Downhill par 3 with bunker guarding right side of green.
17. Tight, downhill driving hole. Favor left side of fairway. Hole doglegs right at 150 yards FG which is best place to hit tee shot.
18. Short finishing par 3 with bunker over the green. Better off being short than long.

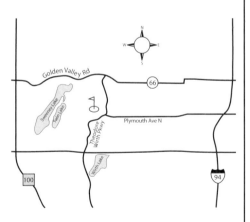

From I-94 take Hwy 55 west 2 miles to Theodore Wirth Parkway. Go north 0.7 miles, the course is on the left.

Timber Creek Golf Course

9750 County Road 24
Watertown, MN 55388
952-955-3600

Course Information

Reservations:	4 days in advance		
2000 Fees:	9	18	Comments
Weekdays	$15.00	$22.00	M - Th
Weekends	$17.00	$28.00	
Twilight	N/A	$10.00	After 6pm
Seniors	$11.00	$16.00	* see other
Power Cart	$16.00	$24.00	$9/$17 Sr.
Pull Cart	$3.00	$3.00	
Club Rental	$12.00	$12.00	
Credit cards	Visa Mastercard		
Checks	Any		
Rain Check	Pro-rated		
Other	Senior rate M-Th < 1pm, F < 10am		
Leagues:	Mon - Thur		

Amenities:			
Driving Range	Y	Snacks	Y
Putting Green	Y	Grill/Bar	Y
Practice Green	Y	Restaurant	N
Spikeless	Y	Locker Room	Y
Proshop	B	Showers	Y

Management:	
Manager	Stepahnie Wren
Professional	Frank Freer

Timber Creek is a fairly wide open course, however, water, trees and bunkers coming into play on many holes to penalize wayward shots. If you keep the ball in play, the course is not long and will yield some good scores. Enjoy the quiet atmosphere away from the buzz of the city. Being outside the metro area it is usually easier to get on the course. If you are looking for a relaxing, peaceful round of golf this is a good course to try. The course is well suited for beginner to intermediate golfers.

Rating 92.70

Course Rating

Tees	Grade 3.7
Ability Levels	4
Condition	4
Signs / Hole Maps	2
Ball Washers	4
Benches	4

Fairways	3.4
Condition	3
Yardage Markers	3
Pin Indicators	4
Rough	4
Watered / Drainage	4

Greens	3.1
Condition	3.5
Speed	3.5
Size and Variety	2
Slope	3
Fringe	3

Layout	3.8
Par 3's	3.5
Par 4's	4
Par 5's	3.5
Strategic Trouble	4
Bunkers	3
Enough Space	4
Walkability	5

Amenities	2.95
Driving Range	4
Practice Green	4
Water on Course	2
Port-O-Potties	2
Locker Rooms	3
Pro Shop	2
Grill & Bar	3
Weather Shelter	1
Golf Carts	3

Overall	3.3
Enjoyable	3
Challenging / Fair	3
Reservations	3
Scenery	4
Gimmicky Holes	4
Weather Monitor	4

Value	4.5
Overall	**92.70**

Hole	Black	Blue	White	Women	Par	Men Handicap	Women Handicap
1	477	475	470	445	5	13	3
2	205	190	180	160	3	5	7
3	410	405	370	310	4	1	1
4	390	365	344	325	4	15	13
5	385	380	375	290	4	9	15
6	170	150	130	115	3	17	17
7	405	390	380	340	4	3	11
8	515	505	498	435	5	11	5
9	385	380	370	335	4	7	9
Out	3342	3240	3117	2755	36		
10	376	370	360	346	4	4	4
11	354	350	340	295	4	8	14
12	344	335	330	300	4	12	12
13	480	465	455	415	5	14	8
14	205	165	150	140	3	16	16
15	540	515	480	430	5	10	10
16	160	150	140	120	3	18	18
17	410	395	365	310	4	2	2
18	410	405	400	310	4	6	6
In	3279	3150	3020	2666	36		
Total	6621	6390	6137	5421	72		
Slope	128	125	M123 W134	125			
Rating	71.8	70.8	M69.7 W75.0	71.0			

Hole Commentary

1. Avoid the bunker on the right at 250 yards FG and the bunker on the left at 170 yards FG on this slight dogleg left par 5. Right on approach shot brings trees and creek into play.
2. Don't go over this long par 3. Running the ball on in windy conditions is a good idea.
3. Favor left side of fairway to avoid being blocked out by trees on right. Creek runs just in front of green on right to 100 yards FG on left side of fairway. Long is better than short.
4. Bunkers at 150 yards FG right and left are the only trouble on the drive on this slight dogleg left par 4. Trouble over this green.
5. Uphill tee shot on a par 4 which doglegs right at 150 yards FG. Must hit tee shot to right side of fairway for good approach to green. Pond and bunker guard right side of green.
6. Tee shot through trees to a large double green. Hit it too long and you'll be on the 12th green with a long putt ahead of you.
7. Avoid water on left from 120 - 100 yards FG on the tee shot. Take 1/2 extra club on uphill approach shot.
8. Hit away on this straight away par 5. Avoid bunker on right at 250 yards FG. Can go for the green in two but must avoid water on right and over green on approach shot.
9. Another narrow fairway on this undulating par 4. Avoid bunker on right on tee shot and leave the ball below the hole.
10. Favor left side of fairway to avoid being blocked out by trees on right. Over and left of green are both trouble.
11. Aim just to the left of the big tree in front of you. Fairway gets wide and turns to the left at 150 yards FG. Trouble over and right of green.
12. Blind, downhill tee shot on this dogleg right. Hit just left of trees on right side to 120 yards FG. Fairway ends at 100 yards FG with three bunkers. Large double green.
13. Favor left center of fairway for better approach. Too far left or right and you'll be blocked by trees. Best play is to middle with fairway wood, lay-up to a comfortable distance FG and try to hit it close.
14. Slightly downhill par 3 to a good sized green. Trees over and water right of green.
15. Favor right or center of fairway on this par 5. Bunker guards right side of fairway at 250-230 yards FG. Approach shot is downhill with marsh left and over green.
16. Hill acts as backstop over green and bunker guards right side of this par 3.
17. Aim straight over 150 yard marker on right side and ball will roll down hill and give short approach to slightly elevated green.
18. Bunkers guard left and right side of this narrow fairway. Be sure to know where the pin is located because of severe slope on left side.

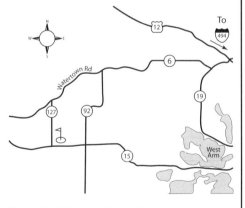

From I-494 take Hwy 12 west 8.5 miles to CR 6. Follow CR 6 west 5.8 miles to CR 92. Go south 3.25 miles to CR 15/24. Go west 1.25 miles, the course is on the left.

University of Minnesota Golf Course

2275 West Larpenteur Avenue
Falcon Heights, MN 55113
612-627-4000

Course Information

Reservations:	5 days in advance www.ezlinks.com		
2000 Fees:	9	18	Comments
Weekdays	N/A	$26.00	
Weekends	N/A	$26.00	
Twilight	N/A	$16.00	
Seniors	N/A	N/A	
Power Cart	$13.00	$26.00	
Pull Cart	N/A	$2.50	
Club Rental	N/A	$10.00	
Credit cards	Visa Mastercard Discover		
Checks	Any		
Rain Check	None (Unless it's lightning)		
Other			
Leagues:	Various		

Amenities:			
Driving Range	Y	Snacks	Y
Putting Green	Y	Grill/Bar	N
Practice Green	Y	Restaurant	N
Spikeless	Y	Locker Room	Y
Proshop	B	Showers	Y

Management:	
Professional	Chris Korbol
Manager	Chris Korbol

The University of Minnesota Golf Course is where the men's and women's golf teams compete. I was disappointed to find only two sets of tee boxes. The course was in average shape and could be improved with a little work. The course has rolling hills, many mature trees and a few water hazards to add to the challenge. The mature trees give it more of a rural feel and can cause problems if you are not hitting the ball straight. The course is well suited for beginner to intermediate golfers.

Rating   84.23

Course Rating

	Grade
Tees	**2.63**
Ability Levels	1.5
Condition	3
Signs / Hole Maps	2
Ball Washers	4
Benches	5
Fairways	**3.9**
Condition	3
Yardage Markers	5
Pin Indicators	4
Rough	4
Watered / Drainage	3
Greens	**3.1**
Condition	4
Speed	3
Size and Variety	2
Slope	3
Fringe	3
Layout	**3.73**
Par 3's	4
Par 4's	3.5
Par 5's	3.5
Strategic Trouble	3.5
Bunkers	3.5
Enough Space	4
Walkability	4.5
Amenities	**3.65**
Driving Range	5
Practice Green	4.5
Water on Course	3
Port-O-Potties	2
Locker Rooms	5
Pro Shop	1
Grill & Bar	3
Weather Shelter	2
Golf Carts	4
Overall	**3.95**
Enjoyable	3.5
Challenging / Fair	4
Reservations	4
Scenery	4.5
Gimmicky Holes	5
Weather Monitor	2.5
Value	**2.5**
Overall	**84.23**

Hole	White	Par	Handicap	Red	Par	Handicap
1	393	4	2	375	4	7
2	163	3	10	130	3	13
3	400	4	6	382	5	9
4	355	4	4	340	4	1
5	150	3	16	135	3	17
6	306	4	18	294	4	11
7	464	5	12	450	5	3
8	185	3	8	178	3	15
9	472	5	14	444	5	5
Out	2888	35		2728	36	
10	339	4	11	281	4	12
11	347	4	13	268	4	16
12	411	4	1	396	5	4
13	525	5	9	430	5	2
14	280	4	17	268	4	14
15	390	4	3	383	4	10
16	374	4	5	361	5	6
17	145	3	15	137	3	18
18	409	4	7	396	5	8
In	3220	36		2920	39	
Total	6108	71		5648	75	
Slope	M 119 W 130			125		
Rating	M 69.5 W 75.5			72.9		

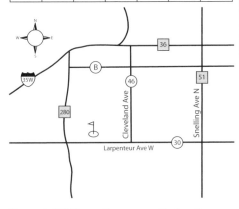

From I-35W south, go south 1 mile on Hwy 280 to Larpenteur Ave. Go west 1/2 mile, course is on the left. From I-35W north, take Cleveland Ave. south 1.25 miles to Larpenteur Ave. Go west 1/3 mile, course is on the right.

Hole Commentary

1.   Fence left of hole is OB. Favor center to left side of fairway. Approach shot is blind to a round green guarded by a bunker front left.
2.   Nice par 3 over a pond to a slightly elevated green.
3.   The dogleg right par 4 goes downhill severely from 175 - 100 yards FG. Bunkers guard back right side of green.
4.   Longer, slightly uphill par 4. Green is guarded by a bunker on front left side. Do not miss over this green.
5.   You cannot miss the green anywhere but short on this par 3.
6.   Bunker on left side of fairway at 75 yards FG. Large bunker guards front left side of the green.
7.   Water on left side of hole ends at 230 yards FG. If you want to go for green in two you must favor right side of fairway. Approach shot will be uphill so take enough club.
8.   Slightly uphill par three with trouble left and long.
9.   Water off the tee box to the right ends about 200 yards FT. Bunkers both left and right of fairway from 215-190 yards FG. Bunkers surround this green.
10.   Tight driving hole with large trees left and right and OB on left side of hole. Big bunker on back right side of green. Don't miss long.
11.   The road to the left is OB with large trees to the right and left sides of the fairway. Not a lot of trouble around this green.
12.   Very difficult par 4 with OB along the left side of fairway. Approach shot is uphill so take extra club. Not much room to miss this green.
13.   Dogleg left par 5 with trees on the left guarding against cutting too much of the corner. OB along the entire right side of the hole. Bunker guards right side of the green.
14.   Don't let the distance fool you, trying to drive this green is not a smart play. Best play is to hit to 125-100 yards FG to set up a short wedge shot. OB along the right side of the hole and right of the green.
15.   OB along entire right side of hole. You won't be able to see the putting surface on your approach shot. Bunker guards left side of green with OB left of the green. Don't miss the green long either.
16.   Straight uphill par 4 with mature trees lining the fairway. OB right of the trees on the right. Favor right side of fairway as it slopes to the left. Bunkers guard right and back of green with OB right of green.
17.   Slightly uphill par 3 so take enough club with trouble all around this green.
18.   Fairly open driving hole with trees left and right of the fairway. There is room to miss this green left or right but not a lot of room over.

Valley View Golf Club

23795 Laredo Avenue
Belle Plaine, MN 56011
952-873-4653
www.vvgolf.com

Course Information

Reservations:	7 days in advance		
2000 Fees:	9	18	Comments
Weekdays	$17.00	$23.00	
Weekends	$17.00	$29.00	
Twilight	N/A	$15.00	< 6pm w/ cart
Seniors/Jr.	$8/$15	$14/29	wkday/wkend
Power Cart	$12.00	$24.00	Sr. $6/$10
Pull Cart	$3.00	$3.00	
Club Rental	$8.00	$12.00	
Credit cards	Visa Mastercard		
Checks	Any		
Rain Check	18 hole<4 holes, 9 hole<9 holes		
Other	Sr. Special: $24 - 18 holes w/cart wkdays < noon		
Leagues:	Various		

Amenities:			
Driving Range	Y	Snacks	Y
Putting Green	Y	Grill/Bar	N
Practice Green	Y	Restaurant	N
Spikeless	Y	Locker Room	N
Proshop	B	Showers	N

Management:	
Manager	Tim Jochim
Professional	Tim Jochim

Valley View is set on the hillside overlooking the surrounding countryside. There are many elevation changes including the par 5 fourteenth hole which drops severely from the approach shot to the green. Most of the course is fairly open but there are plenty of tight spots which can cost you a few strokes. You don't need to be long but keeping the ball in play is a must and can result in a very good score. The course is well suited for beginner to intermediate golfers.

Rating 88.60

Course Rating

Tees	Grade 3.15
Ability Levels	3
Condition	3
Signs / Hole Maps	2
Ball Washers	4
Benches	5

Fairways	3.4
Condition	3
Yardage Markers	3
Pin Indicators	4
Rough	4
Watered / Drainage	4

Greens	3.25
Condition	4
Speed	3.5
Size and Variety	2
Slope	3
Fringe	3

Layout	3.63
Par 3's	3.5
Par 4's	3.5
Par 5's	3
Strategic Trouble	3
Bunkers	4
Enough Space	4
Walkability	5

Amenities	2.75
Driving Range	3
Practice Green	3
Water on Course	3
Port-O-Potties	3
Locker Rooms	2
Pro Shop	3
Grill & Bar	2
Weather Shelter	1
Golf Carts	3

Overall	3.35
Enjoyable	3
Challenging / Fair	3
Reservations	4
Scenery	3
Gimmicky Holes	5
Weather Monitor	3

Value	4.0
Overall	**88.60**

Hole	Blue	White	Yellow	Red	Par	Men Handicap	Women Handicap
1	450	458	440	351	4/5	12	14
2	244	190	170	160	3	14	12
3	545	502	482	438	5	2	4
4	276	258	235	225	4	16	10
5	139	132	129	117	3	18	18
6	374	361	345	254	4	6	16
7	389	376	361	294	4	8	8
8	345	328	322	317	4	10	2
9	235	208	192	161	3	4	6
Out	3005	2805	2676	2317	34/35		
10	410	392	387	384	4	3	1
11	486	454	439	372	5	7	5
12	394	384	374	329	4	13	7
13	150	140	130	125	3	15	15
14	538	523	512	411	5	9	11
15	130	118	110	100	3	17	17
16	440	422	411	323	4	1	13
17	380	356	346	288	4	5	3
18	376	360	282	272	4	11	9
In	3394	3149	2991	2604	36		
Total	6309	5954	5667	4921	70/71		
Slope	121	117	N/A	113			
Ratin	70.1	68.5	N/A	68.4			

Hole Commentary

1. Aim to the very right side of the fairway. The hole starts going downhill at 200 yards FG. A bunker guards the left of the green and the hill on the right can be used as a backstop.
2. Wind affects the ball on this par 3 so club selection is crucial. Don't go over or left.
3. Aim over the pine trees on the left side of the fairway since there is OB right. The creek runs at 40 yards in front of green so choose your second shot carefully.
4. The bunker is 187 yards FT and 85-90 yards FG. Hit the ball in the fairway and use an extra half club on the uphill approach shot.
5. Don't go left. Use the hill on the right to kick the ball back to the green if necessary. Take a half a club less for being downhill.
6. Do not go left as a creek runs the entire length of the fairway on that side.
7. Aim just to the left of the mound on the right side of the fairway for a great approach.
8. Aim just to the right of the bunker on the left side of the fairway. Take an extra club on this uphill approach shot to a sloping green.
9. Long and tough par 3. Depending on the wind could be as much as two or three extra clubs. Aim left and use the hill.
10. Aim at the right side of the fairway since the fairway slopes and kicks balls left. Avoid the water which is in the front left of the green.
11. Water on the right of this uphill par 5 is at 225 yards FG. One or two extra clubs are needed on the uphill approach.
12. Aim just to the right of the candy cane pole (water marker) on the left. Long hitters beware of water at 275 yards FT straight away.
13. Nothing to this straight par 3.
14. Aim just right of the trees on the left and hit your tee shot to the top of the plateau from 250-225 yards FG. Downhill approach requires less club. Beware of water on right.
15. Take an extra club on this uphill par 3.
16. Tough driving hole with trees right and OB left. Right side of fairway gives best approach but smarter play is to aim at the tall tree just to the left of the fairway since the fairway slopes left. Depending on the pin location the big tree in front of the green can block your approach.
17. The widest landing area is at 150 yards FG on this hole. Don't go farther than 120 yards FG or you'll find trouble. Easy to come up short on second shot so take an extra half club.
18. Aim just to the right of the tree in front of you. There is no need to hit the driver just get the ball in the fairway and set up your approach shot. A backstop over the green will stop some balls and a bunker guards the right side.

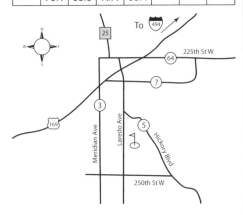

From I-494 take Hwy 169 south 28 miles to Laredo Avenue (CR 5/55). Go south 1.2 miles, course is on the left.

Valleywood
Golf Course

4851 125th Street West
Apple Valley, MN 55124
952-953-2323

Course Information

Reservations:	5 days in advance		
	www.teemaster.com		
2000 Fees:	9	18	Comments
Weekdays	$18.00	$27.00	
Weekends	$21.0	$34.00	
Twilight	N/A	N/A	
Seniors	$14.00	$21.00	M-Th
Power Cart	$15.00	$28.00	
Pull Cart	$4.00	$4.00	
Club Rental	$15.00	$15.00	
Credit cards	Visa Mastercard Discover		
Checks	Any		
Rain Check	18 hole<4 holes, none > 10th hole		
Other			
Leagues:	Tues - Thur		

Amenities:			
Driving Range	Y	Snacks	Y
Putting Green	Y	Grill/Bar	Y
Practice Green	N	Restaurant	N
Spikeless	Y	Locker Room	N
Proshop	F	Showers	N

Management:	
Manager	Rick Dodge
Professional	Jim Zinck

Valleywood Golf Course combines rolling hills, mature trees, water hazards and bunkers to create a fun golf experience. Water come into play on 12 of the 18 holes. The three par 5's are all relatively short and reachable with two good shots. The course feels secluded and affords you an opportunity to enjoy nature. The course could be better maintained in areas but overall was in good shape. The course will challenge golfers of all ability levels.

Rating   87.53

Course Rating

Tees	Grade 3.03
Ability Levels	2
Condition	3
Signs / Hole Maps	3.5
Ball Washers	4
Benches	5
Fairways	**3.5**
Condition	3
Yardage Markers	4
Pin Indicators	3
Rough	4
Watered / Drainage	4
Greens	**3.65**
Condition	3.5
Speed	3.5
Size and Variety	4
Slope	4
Fringe	3
Layout	**3.4**
Par 3's	3
Par 4's	3.5
Par 5's	3
Strategic Trouble	3.5
Bunkers	2.5
Enough Space	4
Walkability	5
Amenities	**2.73**
Driving Range	2.5
Practice Green	3
Water on Course	3
Port-O-Potties	3
Locker Rooms	1.5
Pro Shop	3.5
Grill & Bar	3
Weather Shelter	2
Golf Carts	3
Overall	**3.8**
Enjoyable	3.5
Challenging / Fair	4
Reservations	4
Scenery	3.5
Gimmicky Holes	4.5
Weather Monitor	3.5
Value	**3.5**
Overall	**87.53**

Hole	Championship	MGA	Par	Handicap	Forward	Par	Handicap
1	354	320	4	8	318	4	4
2	157	148	3	16	126	3	7
3	393	385	4	6	225	4	18
4	490	463	5	12	458	5	9
5	326	308	4	14	275	4	13
6	333	323	4	10	280	4	6
7	180	160	3	18	130	3	15
8	443	431	4	4	308	4	17
9	463	454	4	2	420	5	12
Out	3139	2992	35		2540	36	
10	386	380	4	5	340	4	2
11	171	133	3	17	110	3	16
12	480	469	5	11	265	4	8
13	204	138	3	15	100	3	14
14	361	353	4	13	335	4	11
15	513	495	5	1	403	5	1
16	400	380	4	9	320	4	3
17	421	406	4	3	401	5	5
18	381	370	4	7	330	4	10
In	3318	3124	36		2604	36	
Tot	6457	6116	71		5144	72	
Slope	123	121			122		
Rating	70.6	68.9			71.5		

Hole Commentary

1. Best shot is to favor left side of fairway and hit to 160-140 yards FG. Very long green with bunker to left.
2. Bunkers guard front left and right of green. Don't go left or over green.
3. This hole doglegs 90° left past the trees on the left side. Aim just right of trees on left. The fairway ends at 160 yards FG. A big draw could get you very close to the hole.
4. A very reachable par 5. Aim for the flag out in the fairway. OB far left of the fairway. Green located downhill so consider that when selecting a club. Can't go left or over the green.
5. Dogleg left par 4. Hole located over smaller trees on left side. Best shot is over or just right of those trees. Very wide but shallow green.
6. Tough driving hole. Where the hill slopes up toward green is 100 yards FG and that's a good spot to aim at. Favor left side to avoid tree trouble. Blind approach shot.
7. Watch out for the wind. Far right pin location is tough. Don't want to be short.
8. Blind tee shot. Aim to the right of the flag in the fairway. Long hitters can hit further right of the flag. No trouble around the green.
9. Favor the center of the fairway on this par 5. Bunkers on left from 225-200 yards FG and 150-130 yards FG. Don't go over.
10. Pole in fairway sits at 170 yards FG. Water on right side from 150 FG yards to the hole. Aim just left of trees on right. Don't go over.
11. Uphill par 3 generally plays into wind. Could require a couple extra clubs, depending on wind. Don't go over green.
12. Favor left side of fairway over forward tee box. OB runs along left side of hole. On approach need to be accurate due to trouble left and right and the fact that the green slopes front to back.
13. Par 3 over water. Long is better than short on this wide but shallow green.
14. Favor right side of fairway with OB all along left side. Approach shot is somewhat blind so take a look at pin location.
15. Aim down middle of fairway on this par 5. Fairway ends at 200 yards FG. Approach over pond to small green bunkered in front left.
16. Hitting a long fade will result in easier hole. Aim just left of trees on right and hit to 150 yards FG. Can't miss green short, long or right.
17. This is another 90° dogleg left hole with water all along left side. Smart play is to favor left side of fairway and hit to 200-150 yards FG, don't go past 150 yards FG. Approach is uphill so take a little extra club. Over green is trouble.
18. One last 90° dogleg left which turns left at 150 yards FG. Aim just right of trees on left and hit to about 150 yards FG. Big draw can get you closer to green. Bunker guards over green.

From I-35E take Cliff Road (CR 32) east 1.6 miles to Pilot Knob Road (CR 31). Go south 1.5 miles to McAndrews Road (CR 38). Go east 1/3 mile, the course entrance is on the left.

Viking Meadows Golf Club

1788 Viking Boulevard
East Bethel, MN 55011
763-434-4205
www.vikingmeadows.com

Course Information

Reservations:	Weekdays - 1 week		
	Weekend - Tuesday		
2000 Fees:	9	18	Comments
Weekdays	$17.00	$23.00	
Weekends	$19.00	$26.00	
Twilight	$15.00	$20.00	> 4pm Sa,Su
Seniors	N/A	$19.00	M-Th w/cart
Power Cart	$14.00	$21.00	
Pull Cart	$1.50	$1.50	
Club Rental	$6.00	$6.00	
Credit cards	Visa Mastercard		
Checks	Any		
Rain Check	Pro-rated		
Other			
Leagues:	Various		

Amenities:			
Driving Range	Y	Snacks	Y
Putting Green	Y	Grill/Bar	Y
Practice Green	N	Restaurant	N
Spikeless	Y	Locker Room	Y
Proshop	S	Showers	N

Management:	
Manager	Cedar Management
Professional	None

Viking Meadows has made an effort over the past few years to improve the quality of the course. The course is very flat with few elevation changes and for the most part is wide open. There are a few holes where you need to use caution on your drives but many holes allow you to swing away. It was a course where nothing was wrong with it, but nothing about it stood out. The course is well suited for beginner to intermediate golfers.

Rating   90.75

Course Rating

Tees	Grade 3.25
Ability Levels	2
Condition	3
Signs / Hole Maps	5
Ball Washers	4
Benches	5

Fairways	3.45
Condition	4.5
Yardage Markers	2
Pin Indicators	4
Rough	3.5
Watered / Drainage	3.5

Greens	3.78
Condition	5
Speed	4
Size and Variety	2
Slope	3
Fringe	4.5

Layout	3.9
Par 3's	4
Par 4's	5
Par 5's	3
Strategic Trouble	4
Bunkers	3
Enough Space	3
Walkability	5

Amenities	2.98
Driving Range	3
Practice Green	3.5
Water on Course	3.5
Port-O-Potties	3
Locker Rooms	2
Pro Shop	2
Grill & Bar	2
Weather Shelter	3
Golf Carts	3

Overall	3.45
Enjoyable	3
Challenging / Fair	3
Reservations	5
Scenery	3
Gimmicky Holes	5
Weather Monitor	2

Value	3.5
Overall	90.75

Hole	Blue	White	Par	Handicap	Red	Par	Handicap
1	293	275	4	10	255	4	14
2	338	320	4	8	320	4	10
3	414	399	4	4	364	4	6
4	190	174	3	12	145	3	18
5	558	538	5	2	491	5	2
6	323	317	4	18	263	4	12
7	323	308	4	14	298	4	8
8	183	174	3	16	143	3	16
9	459	453	5	6	442	5	4
Out	3081	2968	36		2721	36	
10	430	415	4	5	350	4	7
11	465	453	4	7	394	5	3
12	230	220	3	3	170	3	15
13	364	352	4	13	300	4	9
14	140	128	3	17	118	3	17
15	500	490	5	1	455	5	1
16	317	307	4	11	267	4	13
17	334	322	4	15	296	4	11
18	503	483	5	9	463	5	5
In	3283	3170	36		2813	37	
Total	6364	6138	72		5534	73	
Slope	124	122			121		
Rating	70.6	69.6			71.4		

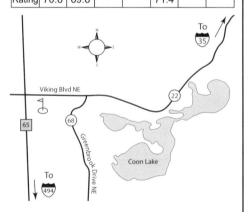

From I-494 take Hwy 65 north 17.5 miles to Viking Blvd. Go east, the course is on the right. From I-35 take Viking Blvd. (exit 135) west 13.5 miles, course is on the right.

Hole Commentary

1. It is 173 yards FT to the water on the first hole. Hole is located just past clump of birches on left side. Best tee shot is to hit about 210 yards FT and favor right side. Going for green is risky with trouble left and long.
2. Creek runs in front of the green at about 60 yards FG. Best shot is to lay-up to 100-80 yards FG in center or right side of fairway.
3. Water runs at 200 yards FG. Do not go over this green.
4. Blind shot to this par 3 green with a creek over the green. Short, left or right are okay.
5. Slight dogleg left par 5. Very wide open unless you reach the trees on the far right. Swing away! Can reach green in two by avoiding trees right and left. Small pond guards front left of the green.
6. Creek runs at 170 yards FG and along right side of hole. No room over the green.
7. Hitting back over the creek which runs at 150 yards FG. Not much trouble on the approach to the green.
8. Do not miss this green right or long right.
9. Dogleg right par 5 with water on both the left and right side of fairway. If you are a long hitter you can hit just to left of big tree in front of you to about 200 yards FG, longer for a fade. Creek dissects fairway at 100 yards FG.
10. Tough uphill par 4 with tree trouble both left and right. Tree on left and trees right are at 200 yards FG. OB over the green.
11. Another tough par 4 dogleg left with bunker at 230 yards FG. Green is actually behind sheds on left. Best shot is over or just right of bunker.
12. Long par 3 with plenty of trouble. Come up short or left if anything.
13. Dogleg right par 4. Hit just left of trees on the right and beware of the bunkers which guard the fairway left and right at 150 yards FG.
14. Shorter par 3 but watch out for the wind if you hit the ball high.
15. Trouble all along the left and right side of this hole. Creek runs across the fairway at 110 yards FG.
16. Shorter par 4 but plenty of trouble right and some left. Can have tree trouble if you hit too far right. A pond sits at 100 yards FG on left side.
17. Trouble all along the left and right side. The further you hit the ball the more trouble comes into play on the right side. Lots of trouble surrounding this green so be accurate on your approach.
18. One last chance to swing away on this par 5. The only trouble on this hole is if you hit way right. This hole should be a great birdie opportunity to finish the round.

Wild Marsh Golf Club

1710 Montrose Blvd.
Buffalo, MN 55313
763-682-4476
www.wildmarsh.com

Course Information

Reservations:	1 week in advance		

2000 Fees:	9	18	Comments
Weekdays	$25.00	$37.00	
Weekends	N/A	$43.00	
Twilight	N/A	$28.00	after 4pm
Seniors	N/A	$27.00	M-Th < noon
Power Cart	N/A	Incl.	
Pull Cart	N/A	N/A	
Club Rental	N/A	$12.00	
Credit cards	Visa Mastercard AmEx		
Checks	Any		
Rain Check	18 hole<5 holes, 9 hole<13 holes		
Other			

Leagues:	Various

Amenities:			
Driving Range	N	Snacks	Y
Putting Green	Y	Grill/Bar	Y
Practice Green	N	Restaurant	Y
Spikeless	Y	Locker Room	Y
Proshop	S	Showers	Y

Management:	
Manager	Joe Malone
Professional	Andrew DeGuise

Wild Marsh was redesigned and opened in the summer of 2000. They did a great job with this course. It is set amidst acres of marsh and wetlands with numerous bridges crossing the marshes. As pretty as the marshes are, you won't be singing their praises if you hit into them, which isn't hard to do. The course is very challenging and the bentgrass fairways and greens are in terrific shape. It's a little longer drive to get to but well worth it, one of the best values around. This course will challenge golfers of all ability levels.

Rating   105.10

Course Rating

Tees	Grade 4.3
Ability Levels	5
Condition	4
Signs / Hole Maps	3
Ball Washers	4
Benches	5

Fairways	4.25
Condition	4.5
Yardage Markers	4
Pin Indicators	5
Rough	3
Watered / Drainage	4

Greens	4.25
Condition	4
Speed	4
Size and Variety	5
Slope	5
Fringe	2

Layout	4.48
Par 3's	4
Par 4's	4.5
Par 5's	4.5
Strategic Trouble	5
Bunkers	5
Enough Space	5
Walkability	3

Amenities	3.1
Driving Range	1
Practice Green	5
Water on Course	3
Port-O-Potties	3
Locker Rooms	3
Pro Shop	3
Grill & Bar	5
Weather Shelter	1
Golf Carts	5

Overall	4.6
Enjoyable	5
Challenging / Fair	4
Reservations	5
Scenery	5
Gimmicky Holes	4
Weather Monitor	4

Value	4.5
Overall	105.10

Hole	Blue	White	Gold	Red	Par	Handicap
1	379	367	334	325	4	9
2	421	394	334	218	4	5
3	351	324	296	255	4	13
4	155	144	133	122	3	15
5	415	397	382	300	4	3
6	353	323	310	148	4	7
7	578	547	523	489	5	1
8	150	134	123	94	3	17
9	347	338	319	309	4	11
Out	3149	2968	2758	2260	35	
10	416	400	380	348	4	4
11	345	277	249	232	4	10
12	424	370	316	212	4	2
13	218	199	183	97	3	12
14	387	348	323	301	4	6
15	380	359	329	282	4	8
16	159	140	119	86	3	18
17	535	502	473	402	5	14
18	492	469	443	410	5	16
In	3356	3064	2815	2370	36	
Total	6505	6032	5573	4630	71	
Slope	139	134	M 130 / W 131	120		
Rating	72.4	70.2	M 68.1 / W 73.0	67.7		

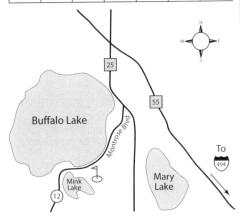

From I-494 take Hwy 55 west 25 miles to Hwy 25. Go south 1.1 miles to Montrose Blvd. (CR 12). Go west 1.6 miles, the course is on the left.

Hole Commentary

1.   Favor right side of fairway. Bunkers on right at 150 yards FG. Trees over green make club selection on downhill approach important.
2.   Tee shot over the marsh to a hole which doglegs right. Bunker at 150-130 yards FG. Multi-tiered green makes knowing pin position very important on approach shot.
3.   Favor left side of fairway and hit ball to 125-100 yards FG. Short shots are blocked by trees on right. Take a little extra club on uphill approach to long but narrow green.
4.   Shorter par 3 which has multiple breaks depending on where tee shot ends up.
5.   Cutting too much off the corner brings double-bogey or worse into play. Hit tee shot to 160-130 yards FG, middle of fairway. Over and left on approach are trouble.
6.   Long carry over marsh on this pretty hole. Fairway starts at 160 yards FG. Take extra club on approach or you'll come up short.
7.   Long par 5 with water on right side of hole. Staying right makes it play shorter but brings water into play. Safe play is middle of fairway, lay-up to about 120 yards FG. Fairway ends at 100 yards FG but is sloped at that point.
8.   Short par 3 with a lot of trouble. Water left and long, bunkers short and right.
9.   Favor left side of fairway on uphill par 4. Bunker on left at 110-90 yards FG . Hit front of green as green slopes front to back.
10.   Straight away par 4. Uphill approach shot requires extra club. Don't go left or long.
11.   Shorter dogleg left par 4 where accuracy is more important than length. Widest areas of fairway are at 120 yards and 80 FG. Bunkers guard right side and trees guard left side of fairway. Trouble over green.
12.   Tee shot over marsh on this dogleg left par 4. Marsh ends at 200 yards FG but runs along entire left side of hole. Bunker on right runs from 160-140 yards FG so aim left of that. Approach is uphill and requires 1/2 extra club.
13.   Long par 3 over marsh with bailout area right. Usually requires extra club for wind.
14.   Trees all along left side so favor right side of fairway. Approach is slightly downhill with bunker guarding right front of green.
15.   Favor right side of fairway as hill kicks ball to left. Aim left of bunker on right at 150 yards FG. No trouble long on this hole.
16.   Downhill par 3 which is easy to leave ball short of hole. Know wind direction.
17.   Reachable par 5 which requires tee shot to right or right center of fairway. Downhill approach can be run up to green but there is no bail out area for errant shots.
18.   Aim just left of bunker on right side of fairway. Approach shot is uphill with bunker guarding left and right of green, over is ok.

Wilds Golf Club

3151 Wilds Ridge
Prior Lake, MN 55372
952-445-4455
www.golfthewilds.com

Course Information

Reservations:	14 days 4 or more players 5 days twosome or threesome www.teemaster.com		
2000 Fees:	9	18	Comments
Weekdays	N/A	$99.00	
Weekends	N/A	$99.00	
Twilight	N/A	$50.00	
Seniors	N/A	N/A	
Power Cart	N/A	Incl.	
Pull Cart	N/A	N/A	
Club Rental	N/A	$30.00	
Credit cards	Visa Mastercard Discover		
Checks	Any		
Rain Check	Ask		
Other	Sunrise sp: $75 M-Th <8am. Weekend sp: $75 Sa-Su > 1pm. Evenings: $30 starts 2 hrs 10 min before sunset.		
Leagues:	None		

Amenities:			
Driving Range	Y	Snacks	Y
Putting Green	Y	Grill/Bar	Y
Practice Green	Y	Restaurant	Y
Spikeless	Y	Locker Room	N
Proshop	F	Showers	N

Management:	
Professional	Shad Gordon
Manager	Michael Regan

The Wilds is another course to go to if you are looking for some pampering. From the moment you arrive, there is always someone willing to help you. With multiple ability levels, you can decide how much challenge you are looking for. The holes are interesting, the course is in great shape and the greens are fast. If you want to splurge on a round of golf, this is the place. This course will challenge golfers of all ability levels.

Rating   94.50

Course Rating

Tees	Grade **4.55**
Ability Levels	5
Condition	5
Signs / Hole Maps	2
Ball Washers	5
Benches	5

Fairways	**4.05**
Condition	4.5
Yardage Markers	3
Pin Indicators	5
Rough	4
Watered / Drainage	4

Greens	**4.15**
Condition	4
Speed	4
Size and Variety	4
Slope	5
Fringe	4

Layout	**4.08**
Par 3's	4
Par 4's	4.5
Par 5's	3.5
Strategic Trouble	5
Bunkers	4
Enough Space	4
Walkability	3

Amenities	**3.75**
Driving Range	5
Practice Green	4
Water on Course	2
Port-O-Potties	3
Locker Rooms	5
Pro Shop	4
Grill & Bar	4
Weather Shelter	1
Golf Carts	5

Overall	**4.35**
Enjoyable	5
Challenging / Fair	4
Reservations	4
Scenery	4
Gimmicky Holes	4
Weather Monitor	5

Value	**2.0**
Overall	**94.50**

Hole	Weiskopf	Championship	Wilds	Forward	Par	Men Handicap	Women Handicap
1	406	372	360	317	4	9	15
2	517	484	471	401	5	5	11
3	170	152	148	103	3	17	17
4	340	292	286	237	4	15	13
5	478	429	400	370	4	1	5
6	460	433	398	363	4	3	1
7	174	167	159	148	3	13	3
8	540	529	518	372	5	11	9
9	378	353	345	247	4	7	7
Out	3463	3211	3085	2558	36		
10	433	410	381	253	4	6	8
11	224	180	160	134	3	10	14
12	553	520	508	391	5	14	4
13	165	156	137	129	3	16	12
14	475	445	433	369	4	4	10
15	378	355	348	299	4	12	16
16	330	295	285	202	4	18	18
17	560	545	530	415	5	8	2
18	444	421	409	345	4	2	6
In	3562	3327	3191	2537	36		
Total	7025	6538	6276	5095	72		
Slope	140	131	M 124 W 136	M 117 W 126			
Rating	74.7	72	M 69.0 W 74.7	M 65.4 W 70.2			

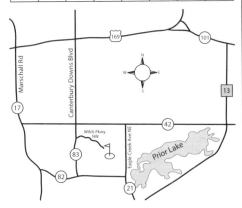

From I-494 take Hwy 169 south 8.2 miles to Canterbury Road (CR 83). Go south 3 miles to Wilds Parkway. Go east 3/4 mile to the course.

Hole Commentary

1. Aim for the teepee. The tee box is positioned to send your tee shot into the water. Aim left and let the hill kick the ball right.
2. Short par 5 dogleg left. Aim just right of the bunkers on the left. A long drive over the hill could end up at 150 yards FG for the approach.
3. Do not go left or long on this par 3.
4. Uphill par 4 which is reachable by big hitters but bunkers guard the green. Smart play is to hit your tee shot to a comfortable yardage for your approach to a two-tiered green.
5. Very long and tough par 4. The approach shot requires a long, high shot to clear the front bunkers. Aim just over the bunkers and let the ball run to the green. Over is okay.
6. Split fairway. The left fairway gives a great look at the hole but is harder to hit. The right fairway gives a blind shot to the hole but is easier to hit. Do not go left on your approach!
7. Carry over the marsh on this uphill par 3. There are not many bail out areas.
8. Favor the left side of the fairway to get a better look at the hole on your approach. The green is guarded by water long and left and a bunker to the right. If you choose to go for it in two, rolling it up is a good idea.
9. This hole is set up by a good tee shot. The approach is a blind shot over bunkers with plenty of room long so take an extra club to avoid the front bunkers.
10. Long downhill par 4. Not much trouble on the drive but be sure you know where the pin is on the approach to this long green.
11. Depending on the wind, this long downhill par 3 can play one or two clubs less or it can play the yardage on the card.
12. Favor the right side of the fairway on the drive for the best angle to the green. All shots to the green will kick right off the hill.
13. Take an extra club or two on this uphill par three.
14. Favor the left side of the fairway for a shorter approach shot but beware of going too far left.
15. Best shot is to hit a club to about 120 yards FG. Bunker guard the right side of this fairway and water guards the right side as you approach the green.
16. For long hitters this hole is reachable but the best play is to hit your tee shot to a comfortable yardage for the approach shot.
17. Uphill par 5 all the way. Right side of fairway gives the best approach but anything in the fairway is acceptable. Bunker guards the entire front left side of the green.
18. Great view of the Minneapolis Skyline on this tough finishing hole. Avoid the water on the right and be happy to finish your round with par.

Willinger's Golf Club

6900 Canby Trail
Northfield, MN 55057
952-440-7000

Course Information

Reservations:	Weekdays - 7 days		
	Weekends - 4 days		

2000 Fees:	9	18	Comments
Weekdays	N/A	$37.00	M-W
Weekends	N/A	$42.00	
Twilight	N/A	$29.00	$32 wknd
Seniors	N/A	$33.00	Mon-Wed
Power Cart	$14.00	$28.00	
Pull Cart	$2.50	$2.50	
Club Rental	N/A	$15/30	
Credit cards	Visa	Mastercard	
Checks	Any		
Rain Check	Ask		
Other			

Leagues:	None

Amenities:			
Driving Range	Y	Snacks	Y
Putting Green	Y	Grill/Bar	Y
Practice Green	Y	Restaurant	Y
Spikeless	Y	Locker Room	Y
Proshop	F	Showers	Y

Management:	
Manager	Howie Samb
Professional	Scott Reuter

Willingers has been one of the best kept golf secret in the state, but word is getting out. The course is scenic, challenging and incredibly well kept. The 12th hole is one of the most picturesque golf holes in Minnesota. If you don't hit the ball straight you'd better bring some extra balls. Marsh land, water, trees and bunkers will add strokes to your score quickly. Precision is the key to scoring well at Willingers. It is well worth the drive. The course will challenge golfers of all ability levels.

Rating   103.25

Course Rating

Tees	Grade 4.75
Ability Levels	5
Condition	5
Signs / Hole Maps	4
Ball Washers	4
Benches	5

Fairways	3.55
Condition	3.5
Yardage Markers	3
Pin Indicators	4
Rough	4
Watered / Drainage	4

Greens	3.9
Condition	3.5
Speed	4
Size and Variety	4
Slope	4
Fringe	5

Layout	3.88
Par 3's	3.5
Par 4's	4
Par 5's	3
Strategic Trouble	4
Bunkers	4
Enough Space	5
Walkability	4

Amenities	4.25
Driving Range	4
Practice Green	5
Water on Course	4
Port-O-Potties	4
Locker Rooms	5
Pro Shop	3
Grill & Bar	4
Weather Shelter	4
Golf Carts	4

Overall	4.3
Enjoyable	5
Challenging / Fair	4
Reservations	4
Scenery	4
Gimmicky Holes	5
Weather Monitor	2

Value	4.5
Overall	103.25

Hole	Black	Blue	White	Red	Par	Handicap
1	399	374	353	310	4	5
2	504	487	472	417	5	7
3	185	165	127	96	3	11
4	430	392	374	318	4	3
5	330	305	295	245	4	17
6	530	504	474	443	5	1
7	188	180	156	104	3	9
8	384	362	350	308	4	13
9	380	356	331	292	4	15
Out	3330	3125	2932	2533	36	
10	370	339	331	282	4	12
11	390	354	334	294	4	10
12	445	425	405	365	4	2
13	362	345	325	288	4	14
14	183	166	155	123	3	16
15	503	472	440	409	5	8
16	419	386	365	339	4	6
17	143	121	101	93	3	18
18	566	500	471	440	5	4
In	3381	3108	2927	2633	36	
Total	6711	6233	5859	5166	72	
Slope	140	136	132	130		
Rating	73.3	71.1	69.4	71.6		

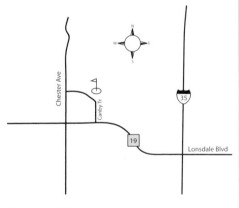

Take I-35W south 19 miles from the I-35E/I-35W split to Hwy 19, exit 69. Go west 1.6 miles to Canby Trail. Go north to the course.

Hole Commentary

1. Intimidating opening hole but if you forget about the water it can be an easy hole. There is plenty of landing area so hit the ball to 150 yards FG and you'll have a nice approach.
2. Trees to the left and marsh to the right so accuracy is more important than distance. Water on the right runs from 180-150 yards FG. Green slopes right and left away from the middle of the green.
3. Tee box tends to send balls right into a watery grave on this slightly downhill par 3.
4. Aim just to the right of tree on left. Big hitters can go over tree but beware of water.
5. Short par 4 where a driver is not necessary. Avoid the bunkers and put ball in good position for approach shot.
6. The further you hit the drive, the less area there is to land the ball. Edge of water is 230 yards FG. Smart play for second shot is to lay up to about 100 – 120 yards FG.
7. Tee shot over marsh on this tough par 3. Beware of the wind when you select a club.
8. Hit your drive just right of the trees on the left (follow cart path). Big hitters be sure not to over-drive fairway which ends at 100 yards FG.
9. Don't try to hit it over the bunkers on the left which run from 120-80 yards FG. Aim just right of them for the best approach.
10. Straight, uphill par 4. Nothing to do here but swing away!
11. From the tee it looks like a dogleg left but it actually goes right. Hit your tee shot to about 140-130 yards FG. Hitting down the hill can get you in a lot of trouble and there is little reward even if you hit a good drive.
12. Very scenic downhill par 4. Aim just to the right of the trees on the left and take an extra club on your uphill approach shot.
13. Need to hit it right toward the water to avoid being blocked by the trees on the right on your approach shot. Past 150 yards FG the hole opens up to shots from the right side of the fairway.
14. Water on the left is a ball magnet on this pretty par 3.
15. Aim just to the right of the tree on the left and use a club that you can hit straight, distance is not as important as accuracy. Marsh on the left starts at 225 FG and water juts out across the fairway at 130 yards FG.
16. Avoid the bunkers on the right which end at 130 yards FG. Uphill approach shot will require one extra club.
17. Long is better than short on this downhill par 3.
18. Favor the right side of the fairway on your drive. Best lay-up is to 100 yards FG. If you do go for it, it's better to bail out right than left.

Applewood Hills
Golf Course
11840 60th Street North
Stillwater, MN 55082
651-439-7276

Course Information

Reservations:	4 days in advance		
2000 Fees:	9	18	Comments
Weekdays	$12.00	$22.00	
Weekends	$14.00	$24.00	
Twilight	N/A	$22.00	Sa, Sun > 4pm
Seniors	$10.00	$20.00	M-Th <3:30 PM
Power Cart	$12.00	$20.00	
Pull Cart	$2.00	$3.00	
Club Rental	$8.00	$12.00	
Credit cards	Visa Mastercard		
Checks	Local Checks Only		
Rain Check	18 hole<3 holes, 9 hole<12 holes		
Other	Twilight rate includes cart		
Leagues:	Mon - Fri		

Amenities:			
Driving Range	Y	Snacks	Y
Putting Green	Y	Grill/Bar	Y
Practice Green	N	Restaurant	Y
Spikeless	Y	Locker Room	Y
Proshop	S	Showers	N

Management:	
Manager	Paul Gruebner
Professional	John Scanlan

Hole	Blue	White	Red	Par	Men Handicap	Women Handicap
1	129	118	107	3	18	18
2	152	145	128	3	12	13
3	161	139	137	3	10	7
4	155	139	121	3	16	15
5	145	134	123	3	8	9
6	308	300	205	4	6	11
7	220	209	156	3	2	3
8	256	247	224	4	14	5
9	327	318	216	4	4	2
Out	1853	1749	1417	30		
10	330	318	298	4	9	1
11	381	361	315	4	1	4
12	138	128	118	3	17	14
13	159	146	133	3	13	12
14	339	323	313	4	3	6
15	342	330	302	4	5	8
16	153	140	130	3	15	16
17	260	250	234	4	7	10
18	155	146	132	3	11	17
In	2257	2142	1975	32		
Total	4110	3891	3392			
Slope	92	91	94			
Rating	59.1	58.2	59.1			

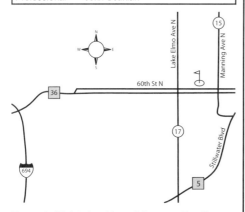

From I-694 take Hwy 36 east 5 miles to Manning Avenue (CR 15). Take a left and an immediate left on the frontage road. Course is 1/3 mile on the right.

179

Dwan Golf Club
3301 West 110th Street
Bloomington, MN 55431
952-563-8702

Course Information

Reservations:	1 day in advance		

2000 Fees:	9	18	Comments
Weekdays	$14.00	$22.00	
Weekends	$14.00	$22.00	
Twilight	N/A	N/A	
Seniors	N/A	N/A	
Power Cart	$11.00	$22.00	
Pull Cart	$2.00	$2.00	
Club Rental	N/A	N/A	
Credit cards	Visa Mastercard		
Checks	Any		
Rain Check	9 hole equivalent if 9 or less played		
Other	Patron rates available		

Leagues:	None

Amenities:			
Driving Range	N	Snacks	Y
Putting Green	Y	Grill/Bar	Y
Practice Green	N	Restaurant	N
Spikeless	Y	Locker Room	Y
Proshop	B	Showers	Y

Management:	
Manager	Rick Sitek
Professional	Rick Sitek

Hole	Blue	White	Red	Par	Handicap
1	325	320	294	4	7
2	325	300	245	4	17
3	495	485	440	5	9
4	145	129	96	3	15
5	380	373	342	4	1
6	195	181	147	3	3
7	370	344	293	4	5
8	175	168	125	3	11
9	350	340	310	4	13
Out	2760	2640	2292	34	
10	355	347	319	4	4
11	125	120	111	3	18
12	480	450	390	5	8
13	335	327	280	4	10
14	380	373	290	4	6
15	170	160	110	3	12
16	330	321	287	4	14
17	415	409	329	4	2
18	135	128	110	3	16
In	2725	2635	2226	34	
Total	5485	5275	4518	68	
Slope	110	108	108		
Rating	64.8	64.4	65.0		

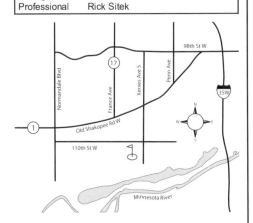

From I-35W take 98th Street west 1.3 miles to Xerxes Avenue. Go south 1.5 miles to West 110th Street. Go west 1 block, course is on the left.

Gem Lake Hills
Golf Course
4039 Scheuneman Road
White Bear Lake, MN 55110
651-429-8715

Course Information

Reservations:	3 days in advance		

2000 Fees:	9	18	Comments
Weekdays	$9.00		$10 Exec
Weekends	$9.50		$10.50 Exec
Twilight	N/A		
Seniors	$8.00		
Power Cart	N/A		
Pull Cart	$2.00		
Club Rental	$6.00		
Credit cards	None		
Checks	Any		
Rain Check	Before the 4th hole		
Other			

Leagues:	Mon - Fri

Amenities:			
Driving Range	N	Snacks	Y
Putting Green	Y	Grill/Bar	N
Practice Green	N	Restaurant	N
Spikeless	O	Locker Room	N
Proshop	B	Showers	N

Management:	
Manager	Tony Carlson
Professional	Jim Edgell

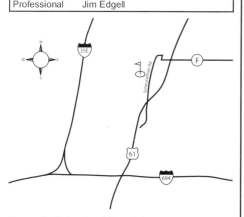

From I-694 take Hwy 61 north 2 miles to CR F. Go west (follow the little jog) to Scheuneman Road. Go south 1/4 mile, course is on the right.

Hole	White	Par	Handicap	Red	Par	Handicap
1	182	3	3	167	3	3
2	216	3	1	214	4	2
3	144	3	9	124	3	9
4	163	3	4	157	3	4
5	189	3	2	175	3	1
6	180	3	6	170	3	6
7	154	3	7	146	3	7
8	160	3	8	155	3	8
9	174	3	5	159	3	5
Par 3	1562	27		1467	28	
Slope	71			70		
Rating	26.9			27.6		
10	173	3	6	148	3	7
11	280	4	7	215	4	4
12	132	3	9	122	3	9
13	140	3	8	133	3	8
14	314	4	1	252	4	1
15	161	3	5	126	3	5
16	308	4	2	209	4	2
17	154	3	4	121	3	6
18	142	3	3	118	3	3
Exec	1804	30		1444	30	
Slope	82			89		
Rating	28.4			28.5		
Total	3366	57		2911	58	
Slope	77			80		
Rating	55.3			56.1		

Hayden Hills Executive Golf

13150 Deerwood Lane
Dayton, MN 55327
763-421-0060

Course Information

Reservations:	3 days in advance		

2000 Fees:	9	18	Comments
Weekdays	$13.00	$19.00	
Weekends	$15.00	$22.00	
Twilight	N/A	N/A	
Seniors	$10.00	$15.00	wkday < 3pm
Power Cart	*	*	* same as
Pull Cart	$2.00	$2.00	grees fees
Club Rental	$5.00	$5.00	
Credit cards	Visa Mastercard		
Checks	Local Checks Only		
Rain Check	Before 5 holes		
Other			

Leagues:	Tues, Wed		

Amenities:			
Driving Range	N	Snacks	Y
Putting Green	Y	Grill/Bar	Y
Practice Green	N	Restaurant	N
Spikeless	Y	Locker Room	N
Proshop	B	Showers	N

Management:	
Manager	Judy Chapman
Professional	None

Hole	Yardage	Par	Handicap
1	193	4	5
2	149	3	9
3	208	4	3
4	93	3	17
5	127	3	15
6	130	3	13
7	158	3	7
8	133	3	11
9	230	4	1
Out	1421	30	
10	187	4	10
11	124	3	16
12	137	3	14
13	233	4	6
14	152	3	12
15	176	3	8
16	120	3	18
17	251	4	4
18	468	5	2
In	1848	32	
Total	3269	62	
Slope	M 69 W 74		
Rating	M 54.2 W 56.0		

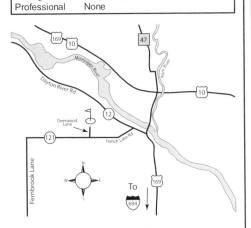

From I-694 take Hwy 169 north 7.6 miles to Dayton Road (CR 12). Go west 0.4 miles to French Lake Road (CR 121). Go west 1.4 miles to Deerwood Lane N. Go north 1/4 mile to the course.

Lone Pine Country Club

15451 Howard Lake Road
Shakopee, MN 55379
952-445-3575

Course Information

Reservations:	1 week in advance		

2000 Fees:	9	18	Comments
Weekdays	$15.00	$22.00	
Weekends	$16.00	$25.00	
Twilight	N/A	N/A	
Seniors	$12.00	$18.00	weekdays
Power Cart	$12.00	$22.00	$14/$24 wkend
Pull Cart	$3.00	$3.00	
Club Rental	$5.00	$5.00	
Credit cards	None		
Checks	Local Checks Only		
Rain Check	None		
Other			

Leagues:	Mon - Fri

Amenities:			
Driving Range	Y	Snacks	Y
Putting Green	Y	Grill/Bar	Y
Practice Green	N	Restaurant	N
Spikeless	N	Locker Room	N
Proshop	B	Showers	N

Management:	
Manager	Betty McKush
Professional	Greg McKush

Hole	White	Par	Handicap	Red	Par	Handicap
1	265	4	9	240	4	7
2	135	3	17	120	3	17
3	315	4	7	280	4	5
4	490	5	1	430	5	1
5	330	4	5	220	4	9
6	450	5	3	430	5	3
7	170	3	13	145	3	11
8	175	3	11	130	3	13
9	145	3	15	125	3	15
Out	2475	34		2120	34	
10	175	3	14	150	3	14
11	310	4	10	275	4	10
12	140	3	16	120	3	16
13	280	4	12	260	4	12
14	415	4	4	410	5	4
15	350	4	8	315	4	8
16	380	4	6	350	4	6
17	505	5	2	440	5	2
18	125	3	18	115	3	18
In	2680	34		2435	35	
Total	5155	68		4555	69	
Slope	108			115		
Rating	65.3			66.3		

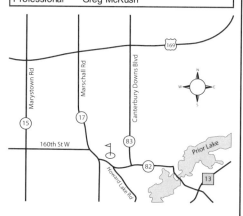

From I-494 take Hwy 169 south 10 miles to Marschall Road (CR 17). Go south 3.75 miles to CR 82. Go east, the course is on the left.

Parkview Golf Club

1310 Cliff Road
Eagan, MN 55123
651-454-9884
www.parkviewgolf.com

Course Information

Reservations:	1 week in advance	

2000 Fees:	9	18	Comments
Weekdays	$13.50	$21.00	
Weekends	$15.50	$24.00	
Twilight	N/A	N/A	
Seniors	$12.50	$17.00	Tu-F < 4pm
Power Cart	$11.00	$18.00	
Pull Cart	$2.50	$2.50	
Club Rental	$7/$14	$7/$14	
Credit cards	Visa Mastercard		
Checks	Any		
Rain Check	18 hole<3 holes, 9 hole<12 holes		
Other			

Leagues:	Mon - Thur

Amenities:			
Driving Range	N	Snacks	Y
Putting Green	Y	Grill/Bar	N
Practice Green	N	Restaurant	N
Spikeless	Y	Locker Room	Y
Proshop	B	Showers	N

Management:	
Manager	Ken Severson
Professional	None

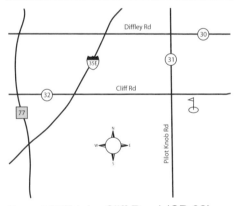

From I-35E take Cliff Road (CR 32) east 2 miles, the course is on the right.

Hole	Back	Par	Handicap	Forward	Par	Handicap
1	378	4	7	368	4	1
2	200	3	9	188	3	5
3	157	3	15	152	3	11
4	148	3	17	136	3	15
5	276	4	11	270	4	7
6	362	4	3	251	4	13
7	218	3	1	209	4	17
8	191	3	13	171	3	9
9	339	4	5	331	4	3
Out	2269	31		2076	32	
10	360	4	2	343	4	2
11	135	3	16	130	3	10
12	208	3	4	200	4	18
13	521	5	8	431	5	6
14	160	3	12	144	3	12
15	332	4	14	322	4	8
16	110	3	18	98	3	14
17	166	3	10	115	3	16
18	305	4	6	274	4	4
In	2297	32		2057	33	
Total	4566	63		4133	65	
Slope	96			99		
Rating	61.2			63.8		

Rich Valley Golf Course
3855 145th Street East
Rosemount, MN 55068
651-437-4653

Course Information

Reservations:	7 days in advance		
2000 Fees:	9	18	Comments
Weekdays	$13.00	$21.00	
Weekends	$13.00	$21.00	
Twilight	N/A	N/A	
Seniors	$10.00	$14.00	M - F < 1pm
Power Cart	$11.00	$22.00	
Pull Cart	$2.00	$2.00	
Club Rental	$5.00	$5.00	
Credit cards	Visa Mastercard		
Checks	Any		
Rain Check	18 hole<5 holes, 9 hole<14 holes		
Other			
Leagues:	Mon - Thur		

Amenities:			
Driving Range	Y	Snacks	Y
Putting Green	Y	Grill/Bar	Y
Practice Green	N	Restaurant	N
Spikeless	Y	Locker Room	N
Proshop	B	Showers	N

Management:	
Manager	Ray or Rosie Rahn
Professional	Sue Bremer

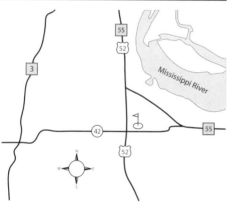

From I-35E take CR 42 east 13 miles, the course is on the left.

Hole	Men	Par	Women	Par	Handicap
1	348	4	335	4	5
2	184	3	172	3	7
3	137	3	125	3	8
4	373	4	364	4	4
5	234	3	226	4	3
6	258	4	229	4	9
7	540	5	434	5	1
8	223	3	160	3	6
9	451	5	366	5	2
Red	2748	34	2411	35	
1	414	4	403	5	1
2	201	3	191	3	6
3	124	3	116	3	9
4	507	5	383	5	2
5	170	3	159	3	7
6	358	4	348	4	4
7	135	3	123	3	8
8	269	4	193	4	5
9	363	4	353	4	3
White	2541	33	2269	34	
1	350	4	317	4	3
2	100	3	85	3	9
3	464	5	346	5	2
4	137	3	124	3	7
5	278	4	252	4	5
6	327	4	259	4	6
7	109	3	95	3	8
8	438	5	370	5	1
9	335	4	280	4	4
Blue	2538	35	2128	35	
R/W	5289	67	4680	69	
Rating	63.7		65.1		
Slope	95		99		
W/B	5079	68	4397	69	
Rating	63.0		63.7		
Slope	98		98		
B/R	5286	69	4539	70	
Rating	64.1		64.4		
Slope	100		101		

Begin Oaks Golf

5635 Yucca Lane
Plymouth, MN 55446
763-559-7574

Course Information

Reservations: 5 days in advance

2000 Fees:	9	18	Comments
Weekdays	$18.00		
Weekends	$18.00		
Twilight	N/A		
Seniors	N/A		
Power Cart	$7.00		
Pull Cart	$2.00		
Club Rental	*		* $1/club
Credit cards	Visa Mastercard		
Checks	None		
Rain Check	None after 3 holes		
Other			

Leagues:	Mon - Thur

Amenities:			
Driving Range	Y	Snacks	Y
Putting Green	Y	Grill/Bar	Y
Practice Green	N	Restaurant	N
Spikeless	Y	Locker Room	N
Proshop	S	Showers	N

Management:	
Manager	Judy Begin
Professional	Judy Begin

Hole	Blue	White	Red	Par	Handicap
1	335	319	270	4	8
2	322	242	223	4	4
3	155	124	110	3	7
4	321	300	277	4	6
5	150	130	110	3	9
6	290	262	200	4	5
7	285	245	211	4	3
8	322	290	255	4	2
9	375	315	297	4	1
Total	2555	2227	1953	34	
Slope	107	M 102 W 104	98		
Rating	32.3	M 31.1 W 32.9	31.4		

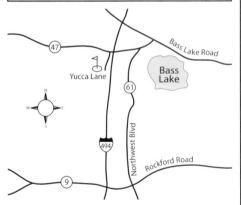

From I-494 take Bass Lake Road (CR 10) east 1/2 mile to Northwest Blvd. (CR 61). Go south 1/4 mile to CR 47. Go west 0.4 mile to Yucca Lane N (just past the 494 underpass). Go south to the course.

Brockway Golf Club

13500 South Robert Trail
Rosemount, MN 55068
651-423-5222

Course Information

Reservations:	1 week in advance		
2000 Fees:	9	18	Comments
Weekdays	$16.00		
Weekends	$16.00		
Twilight	$14.00		
Seniors	$11.00		$14.00 wkend
Power Cart	$15.00		
Pull Cart	$2.00		
Club Rental	$8.00		
Credit cards	None		
Checks	Any		
Rain Check	Before completing 5 holes		
Other			
Leagues:	Mon - Thur		

Amenities:			
Driving Range	Y	Snacks	Y
Putting Green	Y	Grill/Bar	N
Practice Green	N	Restaurant	N
Spikeless	O	Locker Room	N
Proshop	B	Showers	N

Management:	
Manager	Julie Lenertz
Professional	Jim Manthis

Hole	Blue	White	Red	Par	Men Handicap	Women Handicap
1	328	313	263	4	5	5
2	161	155	146	3	3	9
3	330	325	309	4	6	3
4	382	373	269	4	4	7
5	272	263	253	4	9	8
6	209	200	185	3	2	1
7	482	477	383	5	1	4
8	555	530	479	5	7	2
9	186	179	174	3	8	6
Total	2905	2815	2461	35		
Slope	117	116	109			
Rating	34.0	33.5	34.0			

From I-35E go west 7.75 miles on CR 42 to Hwy 3. Go north 1.6 miles, the course is on the right.

Buffalo Heights Golf Course

905 South Highway 25
Buffalo, MN 55313
763-682-2854

Course Information

Reservations:	5 days in advance		
2000 Fees:	9	18	Comments
Weekdays	$13.50		
Weekends	$15.50		
Twilight	N/A		
Seniors	$10.50		M - F < noon
Power Cart	$15.00		
Pull Cart	$2.50		
Club Rental	$6.00		
Credit cards	Visa Mastercard Discover		
Checks	Local Checks Only		
Rain Check	Before completing 3 holes		

Leagues:	Tues - Fri

Amenities:			
Driving Range	N	Snacks	Y
Putting Green	Y	Grill/Bar	Y
Practice Green	N	Restaurant	Y
Spikeless	N	Locker Room	N
Proshop	F	Showers	N

Management:	
Manager	Tom Gomilak, III
Professional	Tom Gomilak, III

Hole	Men Blue/White	Par	Handicap	Women Gold/Blue	Par	Handicap
1	343	4	13/16	329/343	4	7/12
2	365	4	9/8	241/365	4	13/10
3	158/162	3	17/18	148/158	3	17/18
4	441/475	4/5	1/12	431/441	5	1/4
5	314/175	4/3	15/10	201/314	4	15/6
6	339/349	4	7/6	276/339	4	3/8
7	325	4	11/14	240/325	4	11/14
8	517/442	5/4	5/2	442/517	5	5/2
9	390/399	4	3/4	302/390	4/5	9/16
Out/In	3192/ 3035	36/ 35		2924/ 3192	37/38	
Total	6227	71		6116	75	
Slope O/I/T	123/117 120			119/129 124		
Rating O/I/T	35.3/34.7 70.0			35.2/38.5 73.7		

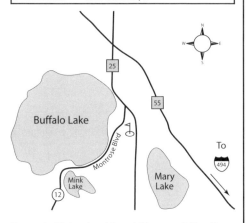

From I-494 take Hwy 55 west 25 miles to Hwy 25. Go south 1.5 miles, course is on the right.

Castlewood Golf Course

7050 Scandia Traill North
Forest Lake, MN 55025
651-464-6233

Course Information

Reservations:	Reservations taken		
2000 Fees:	9	18	Comments
Weekdays	$10.75		
Weekends	$11.75		
Twilight	N/A		
Seniors	$8.75		
Power Cart	$13.00		
Pull Cart	$3.00		
Club Rental	$7.50		
Credit cards	Visa Mastercard		
Checks	Any		
Rain Check	Before completing 3 holes		
Other			
Leagues:	Mon - Thur		

Amenities:			
Driving Range	N	Snacks	Y
Putting Green	Y	Grill/Bar	Y
Practice Green	N	Restaurant	Y
Spikeless	O	Locker Room	N
Proshop	Γ	Showers	N

Management:	
Manager	Mike Olson
Professional	Tom Lynch

Hole	Blue	White	Par	Red	Handicap
1	558	528	5	415	1
2	363	353	4	343	3
3	383	375	4	315	4
4	349	344	4	340	6
5	531	501	5	387	2
6	149	139	3	126	9
7	356	341	4	315	5
8	260	250	4	245	7
9	217	212	3	120	8
Tot	3166	3043	36	2656	
Slope	130	128		132	
Rating	35.8	35.5		35.4	

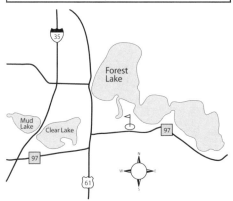

From I-35 take Hwy 97 east 3.3 miles. The course is on the left.

Fort Snelling
Golf Course
Building 175
Fort Snelling, MN 55111
612-726-9331
www.minneapolisparks.com

Course Information

Reservations:	4 days in advance
	www.teemaster.com

2000 Fees:	9	18	Comments
Weekdays	$14.50		
Weekends	$14.50		
Twilight	$10.50		After 6pm
Seniors	$10.50		
Power Cart	$10.00		
Pull Cart	$1.50		
Club Rental	$4.00		
Credit cards	Visa Mastercard Discover AmEx		
Checks	Any		
Rain Check	Before completing 4 holes		
Other			

Leagues:	Mon - Fri

Amenities:			
Driving Range	N	Snacks	Y
Putting Green	Y	Grill/Bar	Y
Practice Green	N	Restaurant	N
Spikeless	Y	Locker Room	Y
Proshop	B	Showers	Y

Management:	
Manager	Scott Nelson
Professional	None

Hole	Yardage	Men Par	Men Handicap	Women Par	Women Handicap
1	410	4	1	5	3
2	280	4	9	4	9
3	375	4	4	4	2
4	200	3	2	3	6
5	313	4	6	4	5
6	461	5	5	5	1
7	228	4	8	4	8
8	270	4	7	4	4
9	145	3	3	3	7
Total	2682	35		36	
Slope		102		109	
Rating		32.5		33.9	

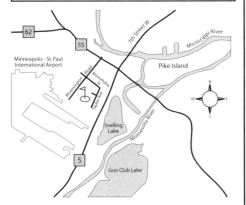

From I-494 take Hwy 5 east 2.4 miles to Hwy 55. Go west (north) to the first exit. At the bottom of the ramp go right. Continue to Minnehaha Ave. (stop sign). Go left and take the next right to the course.

Highland Park
Executive Course

1797 Edgcumbe Road
St. Paul, MN 55116
651-699-6082
www.ci.stpaul.mn.us/depts/parks

Course Information

Reservations:	First come / first served		
2000 Fees:	9	18	Comments
Weekdays	$16.00		
Weekends	$16.00		
Twilight	N/A		
Seniors	$10.50		Avail w/ Sr. card
Power Cart	$15.00		
Pull Cart	$3.00		
Club Rental	$5.00		
Credit cards	Visa Mastercard		
Checks	Local Checks Only		
Rain Check	Before completing 3 holes		
Other			
Leagues:	Various		

Amenities:			
Driving Range	A	Snacks	Y
Putting Green	Y	Grill/Bar	A
Practice Green	N	Restaurant	N
Spikeless	O	Locker Room	N
Proshop	B	Showers	N

Management:	
Manager	Bob Cotie
Professional	Bob Cotie

Hole	Blue	White	Red	Par	Men Handicap	Women Handicap
1	477	467	438	5	3	3
2	185	175	111	3	4	9
3	320	306	306	4	9	8
4	384	371	371	4	2	1
5	316	306	306	4	7	7
6	397	362	335	4	1	2
7	170	160	160	3	5	6
8	345	330	330	4	6	4
9	328	317	317	4	8	5
Total	2922	2794	2764	35		
Slope	114	111	114			
Rating	34.1	33.5	35.3			

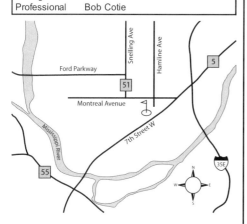

From I-35E go west 1/3 mile on 7th
Street W. to Montreal Avenue (CR 51).
Go west 0.4 miles to Hamline Ave. Go
south, the course is on the right.

Lost Spur Golf Course

2750 Sibley Memorial Highway
Eagan, MN 55128
651-454-5681
www.wpgolf.com

Course Information

Reservations:	7 days in advance www.teemaster.com		
2000 Fees:	9	18	Comments
Weekdays	$16.00		
Weekends	$16.00		
Twilight	N/A		
Seniors	$13.00		M-Th <11am
Power Cart	$16.50		
Pull Cart	$3.00		
Club Rental	$4.00		
Credit cards	Visa Mastercard		
Checks	Any		
Rain Check	Before completing 4 holes		
Other			
Leagues:	Tue, Wed, Thur		

Amenities:

Driving Range	Y	Snacks	Y
Putting Green	Y	Grill/Bar	Y
Practice Green	N	Restaurant	N
Spikeless	Y	Locker Room	Y
Proshop	F	Showers	Y

Management:

Manager	Ken Norland
Professional	Ken Norland

From I-494 take Pilot Knob Road south 1/2 mile to Highview Avenue. Go west 1/2 mile to Hwy 13. Go north 1/4 mile, course is on the right.

Hole	White	Par	Handicap	Red	Par	Handicap
1	346/352	4	1/2	338/346	4	2/1
2	253/260	4	15/16	246/253	4	9/8
3	157/161	3	9/7	144/157	3	11/10
4	296/276	4	4/11	271/271	4	7/6
5	302/305	4	13/14	254/302	4	12/4
6	212/216	3	8/6	208/212	4	17/18
7	435/440	5	5/3	418/421	5	5/3
8	145/165	3	12/10	136/165	3	15/13
9	240/250	4	17/18	225/255	4	16/14
In/Out	2401/2425	34		2240/2382	35	
Total	4836	68		4622	70	
Slope	117			124		
Rating	63.4			66.8		

River's Edge Country Club

1455 County Road 27
Watertown, MN 55388
952-955-2223

Course Information

Reservations:	7 days in advance		
2000 Fees:	9	18	Comments
Weekdays	$12.00		
Weekends	$14.00		
Twilight	N/A		
Seniors	N/A		
Power Cart	$14.00		
Pull Cart	$2.00		
Club Rental	$5.00		
Credit cards	Visa Mastercard		
Checks	Any		
Rain Check	Before completing 4 holes		
Other	M-F < noon, $13 w/cart, $8 walking		
Leagues:	Mon - Thur		

Amenities:			
Driving Range	N	Snacks	Y
Putting Green	Y	Grill/Bar	Y
Practice Green	N	Restaurant	Y
Spikeless	Y	Locker Room	N
Proshop	F	Showers	N

Management:	
Manager	Tom Hollander
Professional	Tom Hollander

Hole	Blue	White	Red	Par	Men Handicap	Women Handicap
1	487	482	434	5	3	1
2	330	315	265	4	6	6
3	295	292	276	4	7	4
4	479	469	410	5	2	2
5	423	418	321	4	1	3
6	126	120	100	3	9	8
7	195	169	108	3	4	9
8	257	253	219	4	8	5
9	266	263	206	4	5	7
Total	2809	2743	2287	36		
Slope	N/A	N/A	N/A			
Rating	33.6	M33.3 W35.8	33.2			

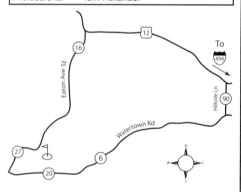

From I-494 take Hwy 12 west 18 miles to Delano. Where Hwy 12 turns right, stay straight on CR 30. In 1 block turn south on CR 16 and go 5 miles, the course is on the left.

Woodland Creek Golf Club

3200 South Coon Creek Drive
Andover, MN 55304
763-323-0517

Course Information

Reservations:	7 days in advance		
2000 Fees:	9	18	Comments
Weekdays	*		* see other for
Weekends	*		rate schedule
Twilight	N/A		
Seniors	N/A		
Power Cart	$10.00		
Pull Cart	$3.00		
Club Rental	$5.00		
Credit cards	Visa Mastercard AmEx Discover		
Checks	Local Checks Only		
Rain Check	Before completing 5 holes		
Other	M-F: open-8am $6, 8-10am $8, 10am-noon $10, noon-close $13 Sa-Su: open-7 $7, 7-9am $9 9am-close $15		
Leagues:	Mon - Thur		

Amenities:			
Driving Range	Y	Snacks	Y
Putting Green	Y	Grill/Bar	N
Practice Green	N	Restaurant	N
Spikeless	O	Locker Room	N
Proshop	S	Showers	N

Management:	
Manager	Tom Weber
Professional	Tom Weber

Hole	Men	Women	Par	Men Handicap	Women Handicap
1	471	388	5	3	2
2	300	285	4	8	6
3	415	323	4	2	3
4	156	91	3	9	9
5	465	401	5	1	1
6	337	253	4	6	4
7	362	299	4	4	7
8	187	120	3	7	8
9	353	287	4	5	5
East	3046	2447	36		
1	359	281	4	6	5
2	145	138	3	9	8
3	330	240	4	5	6
4	390	305	4	2	2
5	476	401	5	1	1
6	171	122	3	8	9
7	469	396	5	4	4
8	304	248	4	7	7
9	409	375	4	3	3
West	3053	2506	36		
Total	6099	4953	72		
Slope	110	114			
Rating	68.7	69.0			

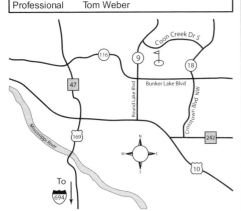

From I-494 take Hwy 169 north 8.5 miles to Hwy 10. Go east 1.5 miles to Round Lake Blvd. (CR 9). Go north 2 miles to Coon Creek Drive. Go east 1/3 mile, course is on the right.

Apple Valley Golf Course

8661 West 140th Street
Apple Valley, MN 55124
952-432-4647

Course Information

Reservations::	First come, first served

2000 Fees:	9	18	Comments
Weekdays	$12.00		
Weekends	$13.00		
Twilight	N/A		
Seniors	$11.00		M - F < 4pm
Power Cart	N/A		
Pull Cart	$2.00		
Club Rental	$5.00		
Credit cards	None		
Checks	Local checks only		
Rain Check	Before completing 3 holes		
Other			

Leagues:	Mon, Tue, Thur

Amenities:			
Driving Range	N	Snacks	Y
Putting Green	Y	Grill/Bar	Y
Practice Green	N	Restaurant	N
Spikeless	Y	Locker Room	N
Proshop	S	Showers	N

Management:	
Manager	Joe
Professional	None

Hole	Front	Par
1	244	4
2	115	3
3	251	4
4	149	3
5	117	3
6	243	4
7	266	4
8	242	4
9	143	3
Total	1770	32
Slope	N/A	
Rating	N/A	

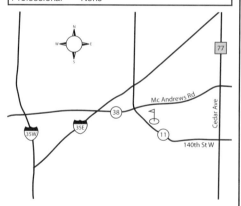

From I-35E take CR 11 (exit 90) south
0.6 miles, the course is on the left.

Arbor Pointe GC

8919 Cahill Avenue
Inver Grove Heights, MN 55076
651-451-9678
www.arborpointegc.com

Course Information

Reservations:	5 days in advance
	www.teemaster.com

2000 Fees:	9	18	Comments
Weekdays	$12.00		
Weekends	$13.00		
Twilight	N/A		
Seniors	$11.00		
Power Cart	$10.00		
Pull Cart	$3.00		
Club Rental	$5.00		
Credit cards	Visa Mastercard		
Checks	Any		
Rain Check	Before completing 4 holes		
Other			

Leagues:	Various

Amenities:			
Driving Range	N	Snacks	Y
Putting Green	Y	Grill/Bar	N
Practice Green	N	Restaurant	N
Spikeless	Y	Locker Room	N
Proshop	B	Showers	N

Management:	
Manager	Curt Hadlern
Professional	Ron Christenson

Hole	Blue	White	Red	Par
1	149	123	105	3
2	125	100	80	3
3	141	135	107	3
4	360	333	296	4
5	305	284	248	4
6	304	300	204	4
7	125	98	85	3
8	392	369	252	4
9	178	153	123	3
Total	2079	1895	1500	31
Slope	107	M 104 W 104	97	
Rating	29.9	M 29.1 W 30.9	28.0	

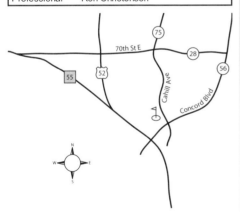

From I-494 take Hwy 52 south 4.4 miles to Concord Blvd. (CR 56). Go east 1/3 mile to Cahill Avenue. Go north, the course is on the left.

Baker National Golf Course - Evergreen

2935 Parkview Drive
Medina, MN 55340
763-473-0800
www.bakernational.com

Course Information

Reservations:	3 days in advance
	www.teemaster.com

2000 Fees:	9	18	Comments
Weekdays	$12.00		
Weekends	$12.00		
Twilight	N/A		
Seniors	$11.00		
Power Cart	N/A		
Pull Cart	$2.00		
Club Rental	$7.75		
Credit cards	Visa Mastercard Discover		
Checks	Any		
Rain Check	Before completing 4 holes		

Leagues:	None

Amenities:			
Driving Range	Y	Snacks	Y
Putting Green	Y	Grill/Bar	Y
Practice Green	Y	Restaurant	N
Spikeless	Y	Locker Room	Y
Proshop	F	Showers	Y

Management:	
Manager	Jeff May
Professional	LisaMasters

Hole	Blue	Red	Par	Handicap
1	163	149	3	6
2	212	161	3	3
3	360	318	4	2
4	125	100	3	9
5	320	250	4	1
6	111	97	3	8
7	255	234	4	4
8	142	126	3	7
9	167	150	3	5
Total	1855	1585	30	
Slope	83	82		
Rating	28.4	28.9		

From I-494, take Highway 55 west 2 miles to CR 24. Go west (south) 8 miles to Parkview Drive (CR 201). Go north 1/2 mile, course is on the left.

Bridges of Moundsview
8920 Coral Sea Street
Moundsview, MN 55449
763-785-9063

Course Information

Reservations: 3 days in advance

2000 Fees:	9	18	Comments
Weekdays	$14.00		
Weekends	$15.00		
Twilight	N/A		
Seniors	-$2.00		
Power Cart	$12.00		$6.00 < noon
Pull Cart	$2.00		
Club Rental	$7.00		
Credit cards	Visa Mastercard		
Checks	Any		
Rain Check	Pro-rated		
Other			

Leagues: Sun - Thur

Amenities:

Driving Range	Y	Snacks	Y
Putting Green	Y	Grill/Bar	N
Practice Green	Y	Restaurant	N
Spikeless	Y	Locker Room	N
Proshop	S	Showers	N

Management:

Manager	Ken Manthis
Professional	Ken Manthis

Hole	Blue	White	Red	Par	Handicap
1	356	329	249	4	2
2	476	455	380	5	1
3	177	155	133	3	8
4	142	121	100	3	9
5	290	266	242	4	4
6	122	98	74	3	6
7	146	123	100	3	7
8	351	333	308	4	3
9	182	156	115	3	5
Total	2242	2038	1701	32	
Slope	95	91	93		
Rating	30.6	29.7	29.3		

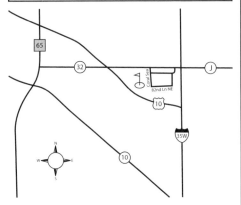

From I-35W take 85th Avenue NE (exit 31B) west 1/2 miles to Coral Sea Street NE. Go south to the course.

Brightwood Hills
Golf Course
1975 Silver Lake Road
New Brighton, MN 55112
651-633-7776

Course Information

Reservations: 7 days in advance
www.teemaster.com

2000 Fees:	9	18	Comments
Weekdays	$11.00		
Weekends	$13.00		
Twilight	N/A		
Seniors	N/A		
Power Cart	$10.00		
Pull Cart	$2.00		
Club Rental	$3.00		
Credit cards	Visa Mastercard		
Checks	Any		
Rain Check	Before completing 3 holes		
Other			

Leagues:	Various

Amenities:			
Driving Range	Y	Snacks	Y
Putting Green	Y	Grill/Bar	N
Practice Green	N	Restaurant	N
Spikeless	Y	Locker Room	N
Proshop	B	Showers	N

Management:
Manager	Mary Burg
Professional	Pat Porte

Hole	White	Red	Par	Handicap
1	281	252	4	3
2	135	124	3	6
3	119	114	3	8
4	175	144	3	1
5	134	120	3	7
6	235	195	4	2
7	90	74	3	9
8	240	211	4	4
9	164	150	3	5
Total	1573	1384	30	
Slope	M 86 W 91	86		
Rating	M 27.6 W 29.0	28.0		

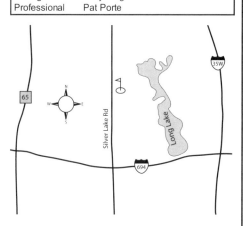

From I-694 take Silver Lake Road
north 1 mile, the course is on the right.

Bunker Hills Executive Golf Course

Hwy 242 and Foley Blvd.
Coon Rapids, MN 55448
763-755-4141

Course Information

Reservations:	First come/ first served		
2000 Fees:	9	18	Comments
Weekdays	$10.00		
Weekends	$10.00		
Twilight	N/A		
Seniors	$5.00		w/ patron card
Power Cart	$13.00		
Pull Cart	$3.00		
Club Rental	$5.00		
Credit cards	Visa Mastercard Discover		
Checks	Any		
Rain Check	Before completing 3 holes		
Other			
Leagues:	Thur		

Amenities:

Driving Range	Y	Snacks	Y
Putting Green	Y	Grill/Bar	Y
Practice Green	Y	Restaurant	Y
Spikeless	Y	Locker Room	Y
Proshop	F	Showers	Y

Management:

Manager	Richard Tollette
Professional	Richard Tollette

Hole	Men	Women	Par	Handicap
1	280	260	4	1
2	360	325	4	3
3	155	145	3	7
4	140	130	3	6
5	330	255	4	4
6	240	220	4	5
7	125	115	3	8
8	260	240	4	2
9	110	90	3	9
Total	2000	1780	32	
Slope	N/A	N/A		
Rating	30.7	30.9		

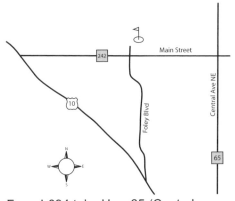

From I-694 take Hwy 65 (Central Avenue) north 9 miles to Hwy 242. Go west 2.25 miles to Foley Blvd. Take a right on Foley and follow the signs to the course.

Chaska Par 30

1207 Hazeltine Boulevard
Chaska, MN 55318
952-448-7454

Course Information

Reservations:	First come, first served		

2000 Fees:	9	18	Comments
Weekdays	$8.00		
Weekends	$9.00		
Twilight	N/A		
Seniors	$7 / $8		Wkday / Wkend
Power Cart	$9.00		
Pull Cart	$1.00		
Club Rental	$3.00		
Credit cards	None		
Checks	Any		
Rain Check	Before completing 4 holes		
Other	Resident rates available		

Leagues:	Tues - Fri

Amenities:			
Driving Range	N	Snacks	Y
Putting Green	Y	Grill/Bar	N
Practice Green	N	Restaurant	N
Spikeless	Y	Locker Room	N
Proshop	B	Showers	N

Management:	
Manager	Whitey Felker
Professional	None

Hole	Men	Women	Par	Handicap
1	129	114	3	8
2	284	262	4	2
3	136	116	3	6
4	104	95	3	9
5	140	111	3	5
6	294	264	4	1
7	156	133	3	4
8	131	101	3	7
9	271	240	4	3
Total	1648	1436	30	
Slope	89	94		
Rating	28.2	28.3		

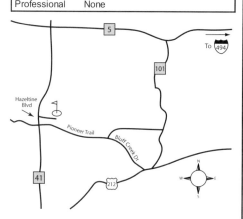

From I-494 take Hwy 5 west 8.25 miles to
Hwy 41. Go south 2 miles to Hazeltine
Blvd. Go east, the course is on the left.

Glen Lake Golf Center

14350 County Road 62
Minnetonka, MN 55345
952-934-8644
www.hennepinparks.org

Course Information

Reservations:	5 days in advance www.teemaster.com		
2000 Fees:	9	18	Comments
Weekdays	$12.50		
Weekends	$12.50		
Twilight	N/A		
Seniors	$10.00		Before 2 pm
Power Cart	$12.00		
Pull Cart	$3.00		
Club Rental	$7.00		
Credit cards	Visa Mastercard Discover		
Checks	Any		
Rain Check	Before completing 4 holes		
Other			
Leagues:	Mon, Tue, Wed, Fri		

Amenities:			
Driving Range	Y	Snacks	Y
Putting Green	Y	Grill/Bar	Y
Practice Green	N	Restaurant	N
Spikeless	N	Locker Room	N
Proshop	B	Showers	N

Management:	
Manager	Troy Nygaard
Professional	Brian Pabst

Hole	Blue	Red	Par	Handicap
1	117	100	3	9
2	147	139	3	8
3	308	285	4	3
4	153	131	3	6
5	273	252	4	4
6	357	326	4	1
7	173/147	129	3	5
8	166/141	119	3	7
9	301	275	4	2
Total	1995/1944	1756	31	
Slope	M 100 W 108	102		
Rating	M 29.7 W 31.8	30.4		

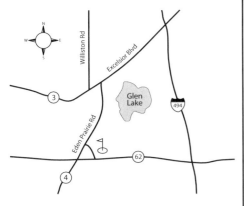

From I-494 take Hwy 62 west 1 mile, the course is on the right.

Inverwood Executive Golf Course

1850 70th Street East
Inver Grove Heights, MN 55077
651-457-3667

Course Information

Reservations:	3 days in advance		
2000 Fees:	9	18	Comments
Weekdays	$12.00		
Weekends	$12.00		
Twilight	N/A		
Seniors	$7.00		M - F < 2pm
Power Cart	$9.00		Sr. cart $7
Pull Cart	$2.75		
Club Rental	$3/$9		
Credit cards	Visa Mastercard		
Checks	In State Checks Only		
Rain Check	Before completing 4 holes		
Other			
Leagues:	Mon, Tue		

Amenities:			
Driving Range	Y	Snacks	Y
Putting Green	Y	Grill/Bar	Y
Practice Green	N	Restaurant	Y
Spikeless	O	Locker Room	Y
Proshop	F	Showers	N

Management:	
Manager	Al McMurchie
Professional	Jim Neitz

Hole	Blue	White	Red	Par	Men Handicap	Women Handicap
1	384	353	305	4	4	2
2	139	108	89	3	8	8
3	125	105	102	3	7	5
4	308	289	266	4	2	3
5	149	136	121	3	9	9
6	116	101	92	3	6	7
7	121	92	75	3	3	6
8	365	329	286	4	1	1
9	150	118	108	3	5	4
Total	1857	1631	1444	30		
Slope	86	M 81 W 87	83			
Rating	28.5	M 27.5 W 28.8	27.7			

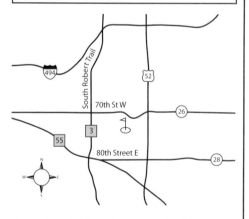

From I-494 take Hwy 3 south 1.75 miles to 70th Street E (CR26). Go east 0.8 miles, the course is on the right.

Kate Haven
Golf Course
8791 Lexington Avenue NE
Circle Pines, MN 55014
651-786-2945

Course Information

Reservations:	7 days in advance		
2000 Fees:	9	18	Comments
Weekdays	$12.00		
Weekends	$14.00		
Twilight	N/A		
Seniors	$10.00		M - F < 3 pm
Power Cart	$12.00		
Pull Cart	$3.00		
Club Rental	$5.00		
Credit cards	Visa Mastercard		
Checks	Local Checks Only		
Rain Check	Before completing 5 holes		
Other			
Leagues:	Mon - Thur		

Amenities:			
Driving Range	N	Snacks	Y
Putting Green	Y	Grill/Bar	N
Practice Green	N	Restaurant	N
Spikeless	Y	Locker Room	N
Proshop	F	Showers	N

Management:	
Manager	Melanie Lundgren
Professional	None

Hole	White	Par	Red	Par	Handicap
1	248	4	188	3	3
2	119	3	119	3	9
3	166	3	145	3	6
4	158	3	116	3	5
5	295	4	186	3	1
6	223	4	179	3	2
7	143	3	131	3	8
8	169	3	124	3	7
9	174	3	114	3	4
Total	1695	30	1302	27	
Slope	80		76		
Rating	27.9		26.9		

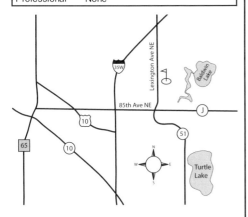

From I-35W north take 85th Ave. NE
(CR J) east 1.1 miles to Lexington
Avenue. Go north 0.4 miles, course is
on the right. From I-35W south take
Lexington Avenue south 2 miles,
course is on the left.

Majestic Oaks
Executive Course
701 Bunker Lake Blvd
Ham Lake, MN 55304
763-755-2142

Course Information

Reservations:	First come / first served

2000 Fees:	9	18	Comments
Weekdays	$7.50		
Weekends	$8.50		
Twilight	N/A		
Seniors	$5.00		
Power Cart	$14.00		
Pull Cart	$3.00		
Club Rental	$10.00		
Credit cards	Visa Mastercard AmEx		
Checks	Any		
Rain Check	Before completing 3 holes		
Other			

Leagues:	None

Amenities:			
Driving Range	Y	Snacks	Y
Putting Green	Y	Grill/Bar	Y
Practice Green	Y	Restaurant	Y
Spikeless	O	Locker Room	Y
Proshop	F	Showers	Y

Management:	
Manager	Bill Folkes
Professional	Bill Folkes

Hole	Black	Par	Handicap	Silver	Par	Handicap
1	180	3	4	175	3	4
2	190	3	2	185	3	2
3	170	3	5	165	3	5
4	325	4	3	320	4	1
5	305	4	8	300	4	3
6	235	3	1	225	4	8
7	160	3	6	155	3	6
8	140	3	7	135	3	7
9	90	3	9	90	3	9
Total	1795	29		1750	30	
Slope	73			81		
Rating	28.1			29.5		

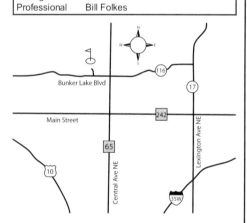

From I-694 take Hwy 65 (Central Avenue) north 15.5 miles to Bunker Lake Blvd. (CR 116). Go west 1/2 mile, course entrance is on the right.

Orono Golf Course

265 Orono Orchard Road
Orono, MN 55391
952-473-9904

Course Information

Reservations:	5 days in advance		

2000 Fees:	9	18	Comments
Weekdays	$11.00		
Weekends	$11.00		
Twilight	N/A		
Seniors	$6.00		Wkdays < noon
Power Cart	$10.50		
Pull Cart	$2.50		
Club Rental	$3.00		
Credit cards	None		
Checks	Local checks only		
Rain Check	Ask		
Other	Weekdays $9 < noon, cart $8.00		

Leagues:	Tue, Wed, Thur		

Amenities:			
Driving Range	N	Snacks	Y
Putting Green	N	Grill/Bar	Y
Practice Green	N	Restaurant	N
Spikeless	O	Locker Room	N
Proshop	B	Showers	N

Management:	
Manager	Ron Steffenhagen
Professional	Doug Erickson

Hole	Yardage	Par	Handicap
1	224	4	7
2	231	4	4
3	124	3	9
4	345	4	3
5	183	3	8
6	248	4	5
7	249	4	6
8	190	3	2
9	345	4	1
Total	2139	33	
Slope	99		
Rating	30.7		

From I-494 take Hwy 12 west 5.6 miles to Orono Orchard Road (on the left under the stone bridge). Go south 0.8 miles, course is on the right.

Pinewood Golf Course

14000 182nd Avenue NW
Elk River, MN 55330
763-441-3451

Course Information

Reservations:	Reservations taken		
2000 Fees:	9	18	Comments
Weekdays	$10.50		
Weekends	$12.50		
Twilight	N/A		
Seniors	$9.50		$10.50 wkends
Power Cart	$10.00		
Pull Cart	$2.00		
Club Rental	$5.00		
Credit cards	None		
Checks	Any		
Rain Check	Ask		
Other			
Leagues:	Mon, Thur, Fri		

Amenities:

Driving Range	Y	Snacks	Y
Putting Green	Y	Grill/Bar	N
Practice Green	N	Restaurant	N
Spikeless	Y	Locker Room	N
Proshop	S	Showers	N

Management:

Manager	Dave Comstock
Professional	Dave Comstock

Hole	Yardage	Par	Handicap
1	290	4	2
2	170	3	3
3	150	3	5
4	125	3	8
5	290	4	4
6	140	3	7
7	390	4	1
8	150	3	6
9	125	3	9
Total	1830	30	
Slope	N/A		
Rating	N/A		

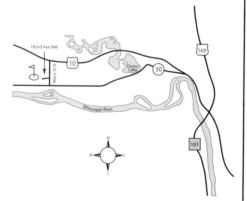

From I-94 take Hwy 101 north 6.75 miles to Hwy 10. Go west 4.25 miles to Waco Street NW. Go south 1/3 mile, course is on the right.

Vikingwoods
Golf Course
1788 Viking Boulevard
East Bethel, MN 55011
763-434-4205
www.vikingmeadows.com

Course Information

Reservations:	First come / first served

2000 Fees:	9	18	Comments
Weekdays	$10.00		
Weekends	$11.00		
Twilight	N/A		
Seniors	$8.00		M - F
Power Cart	$14.00		
Pull Cart	$1.50		
Club Rental	$6.00		
Credit cards	Visa Mastercard Discover		
Checks	Any		
Rain Check	None		
Other			

Leagues:	None

Amenities:			
Driving Range	Y	Snacks	Y
Putting Green	Y	Grill/Bar	Y
Practice Green	N	Restaurant	N
Spikeless	Y	Locker Room	Y
Proshop	B	Showers	N

Management:	
Manager	Cedar Management
Professional	None

Hole	White	Red	Par
1	153	134	3
2	279	268	4
3	105	95	3
4	115	103	3
5	152	142	3
6	261	252	4
7	179	170	3
8	272	260	4
9	139	130	3
Total	1655	1554	30
Slope	93	89	
Rating	28.5	29.6	

From I-494 take Hwy 65 (Central Ave.) north 17.5 miles to Viking Blvd. Go east, the course is on the right. From I-35 take Viking Blvd (exit 135) west 13.5 miles, the course is on the right.

Waters Edge
Golf Course
2693 South County Road 79
Shakopee, MN 55379
952-496-3171
www.stonebrooke.com

Course Information

Reservations:	First come / first served		
2000 Fees:	9	18	Comments
Weekdays	$14.00		
Weekends	$14.00		
Twilight	N/A		
Seniors	$9.00		
Power Cart	$14.00		
Pull Cart	$3.00		
Club Rental	$5.00		
Credit cards	Visa Mastercard		
Checks	Local Checks Only		
Rain Check	None		
Other			
Leagues:	Mon, Tues		

Amenities:

Driving Range	Y	Snacks	Y
Putting Green	Y	Grill/Bar	Y
Practice Green	N	Restaurant	N
Spikeless	O	Locker Room	N
Proshop	B	Showers	N

Management:

Manager	Einar Odland
Professional	Paul Myer

Hole	Blue	Regular	Forward	Par	Handicap
1	112	105	90	3	7
2	171	152	125	3	5
3	203	187	133	3	1
4	105	90	77	3	9
5	309	295	280	4	2
6	272	251	185	4	3
7	106	91	74	3	8
8	155	127	112	3	4
9	292	276	243	4	6
Total	1725	1574	1319	30	
Slope	N/A	N/A	N/A		
Rating	N/A	N/A	N/A		

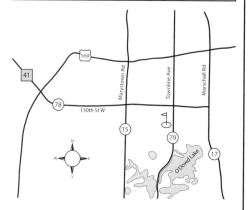

From I-494 take Hwy 169 south 10 miles to Marschall Road (CR 17). Go south 1.1 miles to 130th Street W (CR 78). Go west 3/4 miles to Townline Road (CR 79). Go south 1/3 mile, the course is on the right.

All Seasons Golf
7552 West Point Douglas Road
Cottage Grove, MN 55016
651-459-2135

Course Information

Reservations::	First come, first served		
2000 Fees:	9	18	Comments
Weekdays	$10.00		
Weekends	$10.00		
Twilight	N/A		
Seniors	$9.00		
Power Cart	N/A		
Pull Cart	$2.00		
Club Rental	$5.00		
Credit cards	Visa Mastercard		
Checks	Any		
Rain Check	Before completing 4 holes		
Other			
Leagues:	Mon		

Amenities:			
Driving Range	Y	Snacks	Y
Putting Green	Y	Grill/Bar	N
Practice Green	N	Restaurant	N
Spikeless	N	Locker Room	N
Proshop	F	Showers	N

Management:	
Manager	Bill Barnhart
Professional	Bill Barnhart

Hole	Yardage	Par	Handicap
1	130	3	4
2	72	3	9
3	154	3	1
4	83	3	7
5	122	3	5
6	130	3	3
7	157	3	2
8	71	3	8
9	87	3	6
Total	1006	27	
Slope	N/A		
Rating	N/A		

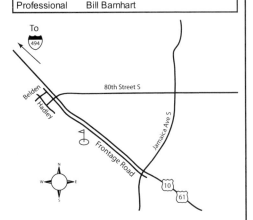

From I-494 take Hwy 61 south 7 miles to the 80th Street exit. Go west to Hadley Ave. S. Go right 1 block to Belden Blvd. S. Go right 1 block to West Point Douglas Rd. Go right 0.8 miles, the course is on the right.

Birnamwood
Golf Course
12424 Parkwood Drive
Burnsville, MN 55337
952-707-6393

Course Information

Reservations:	7 days in advance		
2000 Fees:	9	18	Comments
Weekdays	$9.50		
Weekends	$10.50		
Twilight	N/A		
Seniors	$7.00		
Power Cart	$9.50		
Pull Cart	$2.00		
Club Rental	$3.00		
Credit cards	None		
Checks	Any		
Rain Check	Before completing 5 holes		
Other			
Leagues:	Mon - Thur		

Amenities:

Driving Range	N	Snacks	Y
Putting Green	Y	Grill/Bar	N
Practice Green	N	Restaurant	N
Spikeless	Y	Locker Room	Y
Proshop	B	Showers	N

Management:

Manager	Dan Hill
Professional	None

Hole	Yardage	Par	Handicap
1	122	3	8
2	123	3	7
3	171	3	1
4	139	3	2
5	109	3	9
6	139	3	5
7	165	3	3
8	142	3	6
9	157	3	4
Total	1267	27	
Slope	N/A		
Rating	N/A		

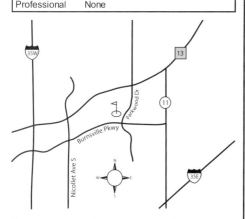

From I-35W take Burnsville Parkway east 1.5 miles to Parkwood Drive. Go north, the course is on the left.

Braemar Executive Course

6364 John Harris Drive
Edina, MN 55439
952-826-6786

Course Information

Reservations:	1 day in advance		
2000 Fees:	9	18	Comments
Weekdays	$11.00		
Weekends	$11.00		
Twilight	N/A		
Senior	N/A		
Power Cart	$12.00		
Pull Cart	$2.00		
Club Rental	$4.00		
Credit cards	Visa Mastercard		
Checks	Any		
Rain Check	Ask		
Other	Patron discounts available		
Leagues:	Mon, Tues, Wed, Fri		

Amenities:			
Driving Range	A	Snacks	Y
Putting Green	Y	Grill/Bar	A
Practice Green	N	Restaurant	A
Spikeless	Y	Locker Room	A
Proshop	A	Showers	A

Management:	
Manager	John Valliere
Professional	Joe Greupner

Hole	Men	Par	Women	Par
1	190	3	185	4
2	110	3	100	3
3	142	3	132	3
4	152	3	140	3
5	326	4	299	4
6	113	3	96	3
7	295	4	288	4
8	144	3	114	3
9	157	3	104	3
Total	1629	29	1458	30
Slope	83		85	
Rating	28.1		28.7	

From I-494 go north 1/2 mile on Hwy 169 to Valley View Road. Go east to the T in the road and follow the signs to the course. You will be on Valley View Road until you hit Braemar Blvd.

Brookland Executive Nine Golf Course

8232 Regent Avenue North
Brooklyn Park, MN 55443
763-561-3850

Course Information

Reservations:	2 days in advance		
2000 Fees:	9	18	Comments
Weekdays	$9.75		
Weekends	$9.75		
Twilight	N/A		
Seniors/Junior	$8.75		
Power Cart	$14.00		
Pull Cart	$2.25		
Club Rental	$4.75		
Credit cards	None		
Checks	Any		
Rain Check	Before completing 7 holes		
Other			
Leagues:	Mon, Tues, Thurs		

Amenities:			
Driving Range	N	Snacks	Y
Putting Green	Y	Grill/Bar	N
Practice Green	N	Restaurant	N
Spikeless	O	Locker Room	N
Proshop	B	Showers	N

Management:	
Manager	Bob Slind
Professional	None

Hole	White	Par	Red	Par	Handicap
1	144	3	144	3	9
2	178	3	178	3	7
3	118	3	118	3	8
4	169	3	169	3	6
5	210	3	210	3	5
6	214	3	214	3	2
7	298	4	261	4	3
8	266	4	221	3	4
9	252	4	186	3	1
Total	1849	30	1701	28	
Slope	85		89		
Rating	29.5		30.3		

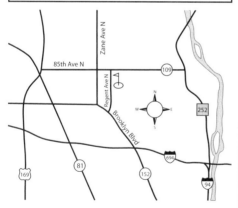

From I-694 take Brooklyn Blvd. (CR 152) north 1.1 miles to Regent Avenue N. Go north 1 mile, the course is on the right.

Brookview Par 3 Course

200 Brookview Parkway
Golden Valley, MN 55426
763-512-2333
www.ci.golden-valley.mn.us/brookviewgolf

Course Information

Reservations:	2 days in advance		
2000 Fees:	9	18	Comments
Weekdays	$8.25		
Weekends	$8.25		
Twilight	N/A		
Seniors	*		* See other
Power Cart	$12.00		
Pull Cart	$2.50		
Club Rental	$6.00		
Credit cards	Visa Mastercard		
Checks	Local Checks Only		
Rain Check	Before completing 4 holes		
Other	Senior discount available with patron card		
Leagues:	Various		

Amenities:			
Driving Range	Y	Snacks	Y
Putting Green	Y	Grill/Bar	Y
Practice Green	N	Restaurant	Y
Spikeless	O	Locker Room	Y
Proshop	S	Showers	Y

Management:	
Manager	Kris Tovson
Professional	Jeff Orthun

Hole	Back	Forward	Handicap	Par
1	137	132	4	3
2	137	130	5	3
3	188	180	2	3
4	116	110	8	3
5	126	120	6	3
6	133	127	7	3
7	173	114	1	3
8	160	121	3	3
9	117	112	9	3
Total	1287	1146		27
Slope	N/A	N/A		
Rating	N/A	N/A		

West of Hwy 100 and east of Hwy 169 on Hwy 55. Take Winnetka Avenue south to Brookview Parkway. Go west 1/2 mile, the course is on the right.

Cedarholm Golf Course

2323 Hamline Avenue
Roseville, MN 55113
651-415-2166
www.ci.roseville.mn.us

Course Information

Reservations:	5 days in advance

2000 Fees:	9	18	Comments
Weekdays	$8.75		
Weekends	$9.25		
Twilight	N/A		
Seniors	$7.50		M-F <3:30 pm
Power Cart	N/A		
Pull Cart	$2.00		
Club Rental	$4.00		
Credit cards	Visa Mastercard		
Checks	Any		
Rain Check	Before completing 5 holes		
Other			

Leagues:	Mon - Fri

Amenities:			
Driving Range	N	Snacks	Y
Putting Green	Y	Grill/Bar	Y
Practice Green	N	Restaurant	N
Spikeless	O	Locker Room	N
Proshop	B	Showers	N

Management:	
Manager	Kevin Elm
Professional	None

Hole	Yardage	Par Men	Par Women	Handicap
1	191	3	4	2
2	186	3	4	1
3	167	3	3	3
4	128	3	3	6
5	154	3	3	5
6	202	3	4	4
7	113	3	3	8
8	112	3	3	9
9	120	3	3	7
Total	1373	27	30	
Slope		N/A	N/A	
Rating		N/A	N/A	

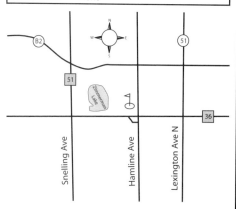

From I-35W take Hwy 36 east 1.5 miles to Hamline Avenue. Go north on Hamline, course is on the west side of Hamline.

Centerbrook
Golf Course
5500 North Lilac Drive
Brooklyn Center, MN 55430
763-561-3239

Course Information

Reservations:	1 week in advance		

2000 Fees:	9	18	Comments
Weekdays	$10.00		
Weekends	$10.50		
Twilight	N/A		
Seniors	$9.00		weekdays
Power Cart	$11.00		
Pull Cart	$2.00		
Club Rental	$4.00		
Credit cards	Visa	Mastercard	
Checks	Any		
Rain Check	Ask		
Other			

Leagues:	Mon - Fri

Amenities:			
Driving Range	N	Snacks	Y
Putting Green	Y	Grill/Bar	N
Practice Green	N	Restaurant	N
Spikeless	O	Locker Room	N
Proshop	S	Showers	N

Management:	
Manager	Arnie Mavis
Professional	None

Hole	Blue	White	Red	Par	Handicap
1	192	182	172	3	3
2	190	180	170	3	1
3	130	120	110	3	8
4	195	185	175	3	2
5	180	170	160	3	4
6	155	145	135	3	5
7	165	137	127	3	7
8	130	120	110	3	9
9	160	150	140	3	6
Total	1497	1389	1299	27	
Slope	N/A	N/A	N/A		
Rating	N/A	N/A	N/A		

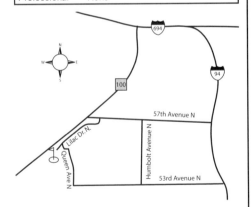

From I-94 take 53rd Avenue west 2/3 mile to Humbolt Ave. N. Go north 1/2 mile to 57th Avenue N. Go west 1/3 mile to Lilac Dr. Go south to the course.

Cimarron Golf Course
901 Lake Elmo Avenue North
Lake Elmo, MN 55042
651-436-6188

Course Information

Reservations:	7 days in advance		
2000 Fees:	9	18	Comments
Weekdays	$9.00		
Weekends	$10.00		
Twilight	N/A		
Seniors	$8.25		Weekdays
Power Cart	N/A		
Pull Cart	$2.00		
Club Rental	$4.00		
Credit cards	None		
Checks	Any		
Rain Check	Before completing 4 holes		
Other			
Leagues:	Mon - Thur		

Amenities:			
Driving Range	N	Snacks	Y
Putting Green	Y	Grill/Bar	N
Practice Green	N	Restaurant	Y
Spikeless	Y	Locker Room	N
Proshop	B	Showers	N

Management:	
Manager	Kyle Howieson
Professional	None

Hole	Men	Women	Par	Handicap
1	198	171	3	2
2	119	100	3	9
3	192	172	3	3
4	181	172	3	4
5	116	92	3	8
6	150	130	3	6
7	160	145	3	5
8	218	189	3	1
9	126	116	3	7
Total	1460	1287	27	
Slope	77	75		
Rating	26.9	26.8		

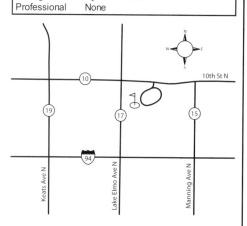

From I-94 take Manning Avenue N
(exit 253) north 1 mile to 10th Street N.
Go west 0.9 miles, turn left just before
the stop sign. Course is 2 blocks on the
right.

Cleary Lake Park
Golf Course
18106 Texas Avenue
Prior Lake, MN 55372
952-447-2171
www.hennepinparks.org

Course Information

Reservations:	2 days in advance
	www.teemaster.com

2000 Fees:	9	18	Comments
Weekdays	$11.00		
Weekends	$11.00		
Twilight	N/A		
Seniors	$9.00		
Power Cart	$11.00		
Pull Cart	$3.00		
Club Rental	$4.00		
Credit cards	Visa Mastercard Discover		
Checks	Any		
Rain Check	Only if lightning		
Other			

Leagues:	Tues, Thur

Amenities:			
Driving Range	Y	Snacks	Y
Putting Green	Y	Grill/Bar	N
Practice Green	N	Restaurant	N
Spikeless	Y	Locker Room	N
Proshop	S	Showers	N

Management:	
Manager	Jenna Tuma
Professional	Brad Rollinson

Hole	Front	Par Men	Par Women	Handicap
1	155	3	3	4
2	118	3	3	8
3	115	3	3	9
4	145	3	3	7
5	157	3	3	6
6	237	3	4	2
7	207	3	3	3
8	209	3	3	5
9	332	4	4	1
Total	1675	28	29	
Slope		N/A	N/A	
Rating		N/A	N/A	

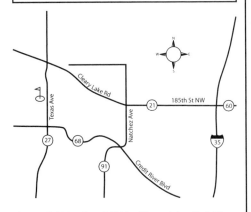

From I-35 take 185th Street (exit 84) west 4.5 miles to Texas Avenue. Go south 1/2 mile, park entrance is on the right.

Country View Golf Course

2926 North Highway 61
Maplewood, MN 55109
651-484-9809

Course Information

Reservations:	First come/first served		
2000 Fees:	9	18	Comments
Weekdays	$8.50		
Weekends	$9.00		
Twilight	N/A		
Seniors	$6.50		weekdays<4pm
Power Cart	N/A		
Pull Cart	$1.50		
Club Rental	$2.50		
Credit cards	None		
Checks	Any		
Rain Check	Before completing 5 holes		
Other	Lighted course, last ticket sold at 9:30pm		
Leagues:	None		

Amenities:			
Driving Range	Y	Snacks	Y
Putting Green	Y	Grill/Bar	N
Practice Green	N	Restaurant	N
Spikeless	O	Locker Room	N
Proshop	B	Showers	N

Management:	
Manager	Judy Mogren
Professional	None

Hole	Yardage	Par
1	143	3
2	135	3
3	155	3
4	136	3
5	170	3
6	124	3
7	167	3
8	118	3
9	152	3
Red	1300	27
1	148	3
2	149	3
3	151	3
4	110	3
5	167	3
6	158	3
7	155	3
8	172	3
9	158	3
White	1368	27
Slope	N/A	N/A
Rating	N/A	N/A

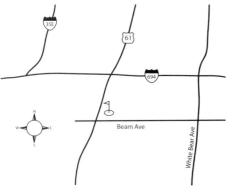

From I-694 take Hwy 61 south 0.7 mile to Beam Avenue. Go east, course is on the left.

Falcon Ridge
Executive Course

33942 Falcon Avenue North
Stacy, MN 55079
651-462-5797 or 877-535-9335
www.falconridgegolf.net

Course Information

Reservations:	First come / first served		
2000 Fees:	9	18	Comments
Weekdays	$7.00		
Weekends	$10.00		
Twilight	N/A		
Seniors	N/A		
Power Cart	$12.00		
Pull Cart	$3.00		
Club Rental	$6.00		
Credit cards	Visa Mastercard Discover		
Checks	Any		
Rain Check	Before completing 4 holes		
Other			
Leagues:	None		

Amenities:

Driving Range	Y	Snacks	Y
Putting Green	Y	Grill/Bar	N
Practice Green	N	Restaurant	N
Spikeless	Y	Locker Room	N
Proshop	S	Showers	N

Management:

Manager	Patrick Smith
Professional	Patrick Smith

Hole	White	Red	Par	Handicap
1	170	162	3	7
2	143	132	3	6
3	91	76	3	9
4	144	137	3	3
5	129	121	3	5
6	302	281	4	2
7	242	231	4	1
8	149	145	3	8
9	175	166	3	4
Total	1545	1451	29	
Slope	82	80		
Rating	28.7	28.1		

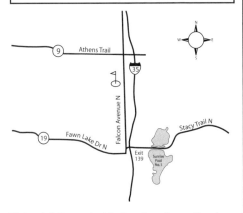

Take I-35 north 12.6 miles from the I-35W/I-35E split to CR 19, exit 139. Go west to Falcon Avenue (CR 78). Go north 3 miles, the course is on the left.

Fred S. Richards
Golf Course

7640 Parklawn Avenue
Edina, MN 55435
952-915-6606

Course Information

Reservations:	2 days in advance		
2000 Fees:	9	18	Comments
Weekdays	$11.00		
Weekends	$11.00		
Twilight	N/A		
Senior	*		* See other
Power Cart	$11.00		
Pull Cart	$2.00		
Club Rental	$6.00		
Credit cards	None		
Checks	Any		
Rain Check	Before teeing off on 4th hole		
Other	Patron and Senior patron discounts available		
Leagues:	Various		

Amenities:			
Driving Range	N	Snacks	Y
Putting Green	Y	Grill/Bar	N
Practice Green	N	Restaurant	N
Spikeless	Y	Locker Room	N
Proshop	B	Showers	N

Management:	
Manager	Bob Favaro
Professional	None

Hole	Back	Middle	Forward	Par	Men Handicap	Women Handicap
1	150	150	150	3	8	4
2	164	137	112	3	6	7
3	298	254	210	4	2	2
4	147	130	100	3	9	9
5	150	142	129	3	7	6
6	200	168	134	3	4	5
7	175	175	170	3	3	3
8	320	299	275	4	1	1
9	182	158	105	3	5	8
Total	1786	1613	1385	29		
Slope		28.0	26.7			
Rating		82	82			

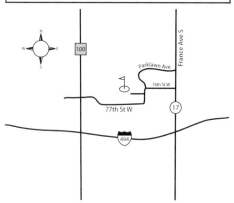

From I-494 take Hwy 100 north 1/3 mile to 77th Street W. Go east 0.7 miles to Parklawn Ave. Go north 1 block, course entrance is on the left.

French Lake Open Golf Club

17500 County Road 81
Maple Grove, MN 55369
763-428-4544

Course Information

Reservations:	Any time		
2000 Fees:	9	18	Comments
Weekdays	$10.00		
Weekends	$12.00		
Twilight	N/A		
Seniors	$8.00		wkday < 3pm
Power Cart	$10.00		
Pull Cart	$1.00		
Club Rental	$3.00		
Credit cards	None		
Checks	Any		
Rain Check	Before completing 3 holes		
Other			
Leagues:	Mon -Thur		

Amenities:			
Driving Range	Y	Snacks	Y
Putting Green	Y	Grill/Bar	Y
Practice Green	N	Restaurant	N
Spikeless	Y	Locker Room	N
Proshop	B	Showers	N

Management:
Manager   Mark Regan
Professional   None

Hole	Men	Women	Par	Handicap
1	243	233	4	5
2	145	100	3	9
3	155	145	3	3
4	277	260	4	4
5	132	101	3	7
6	135	105	3	8
7	121	111	3	6
8	139	129	3	2
9	160	123	3	1
Total	1507	1307	29	
Slope	63.0	67.0		
Rating	26.2	26.0		

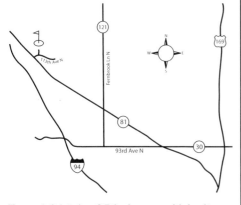

From I-94 take 95th Avenue N (exit 213) 1.2 miles east to Fernbrook Lane. Go north 1.1 miles to CR 81. Go west 2.6 miles to 113th Avenue N. Take a right, course is on the left.

Hyland Greens
Golf Course
10100 Normandale Boulevard
Bloomington, MN 55437
952-948-8868

Course Information

Reservations:	1 week in advance		

2000 Fees:	9	18	Comments
Weekdays	$8.50		Inside $7.00
Weekends	$8.50		Inside $7.00
Twilight	N/A		
Seniors	N/A		
Power Cart	$10.00		
Pull Cart	$1.50		
Club Rental	$5.00		
Credit cards	Visa Mastercard		
Checks	Any		
Rain Check	None		
Other			

Leagues:	Mon - Fri

Amenities:			
Driving Range	Y	Snacks	Y
Putting Green	Y	Grill/Bar	Y
Practice Green	N	Restaurant	N
Spikeless	O	Locker Room	N
Proshop	B	Showers	N

Management:	
Manager	Ali Hassan
Professional	Ali Hassan

Hole	Outside	Handicap	Inside	Handicap	Par
1	173	3	99	8	3
2	158	5	147	3	3
3	145	9	142	4	3
4	193	1	107	6	3
5	143	4	185	1	3
6	184	6	71	9	3
7	132	8	163	2	3
8	174	2	100	7	3
9	136	7	145	5	3
Total	1438		1159		27
Slope	N/A		N/A		
Rating	N/A		N/A		

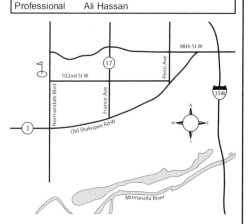

From I-35W go west 3 miles on West 98th Street to Normandale Blvd. (CR 34). Go south 1/2 miles to West 102nd Street. Go west, the course is on the right.

Island Lake Golf Course
1000 Red Fox Road
Shoreview, MN 55126
651-787-0383

Course Information

Reservations:	3 days in advance		

2000 Fees:	9	18	Comments
Weekdays	$11.00		
Weekends	$13.00		
Twilight	$10.00		2 hrs < sunset
Seniors	$10.00		
Power Cart	Incl.		
Pull Cart	Incl.		
Club Rental	$4.00		
Credit cards	None		
Checks	Any		
Rain Check	Before completing 5 holes		
Other			

Leagues:	Mon - Wed

Amenities:			
Driving Range	Y	Snacks	Y
Putting Green	Y	Grill/Bar	Y
Practice Green	Y	Restaurant	N
Spikeless	Y	Locker Room	N
Proshop	B	Showers	N

Management:	
Manager	Dan Farr
Professional	Jason Erickson

Hole	Blue	White	Red	Par	Men Handicap	Women Handicap
1	149	149	139	3	6	7
2	136	126	94	3	9	9
3	96	96	86	3	8	8
4	114	114	97	3	7	5
5	143	143	135	3	2	2
6	208	118	113	3	5	6
7	139	139	134	4	1	4
8	133	133	93	3	3	3
9	305	244	238	4	4	1
Total	1423	1262	1129	29		
Slope	N/A	71	N/A			
Rating	N/A	51.2	N/A			

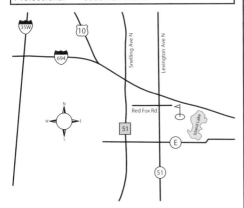

From I-694 take Lexington Avenue
south to stop light. Take Red Fox Road
east, road ends at entrance to course.

Maple Hills Golf Center

905 Parkway Drive
St. Paul, MN 55106
651-776-2226

Course Information

Reservations:	First come / first served		
2000 Fees:	9	18	Comments
Weekdays	$7.50		
Weekends	$9.00		
Twilight	$7.00		
Seniors	$6.50		weekdays
Power Cart	N/A		
Pull Cart	$2.00		
Club Rental	$3.50		
Credit cards	None		
Checks	Any		
Rain Check	Before completing 5 holes		
Other	Lighted course until 10:30pm daily		
Leagues:	Mon - Fri		

Amenities:			
Driving Range	N	Snacks	Y
Putting Green	Y	Grill/Bar	N
Practice Green	N	Restaurant	N
Spikeless	O	Locker Room	N
Proshop	B	Showers	N

Management:	
Manager	Peggy Shea
Professional	None

Hole	White	Red	Par	Handicap
1	167	141	3	3
2	102	97	3	6
3	126	121	3	1
4	108	103	3	9
5	110	105	3	8
6	105	100	3	5
7	150	145	3	2
8	178	151	3	4
9	113	98	3	7
Total	1159	1061	27	
Slope	N/A	N/A		
Rating	N/A	N/A		

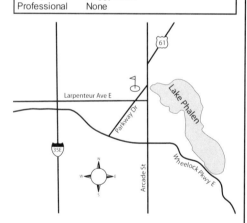

From I-35E take Larpenteur Avenue
east 1 mile to Parkway Drive. Go
north, course is on the left.

Meadowwoods Golf Course

18300 Ridgewood Road
Minnetonka, MN 55345
952-470-4000

Course Information

Reservations:	5 days in advance		
2000 Fees:	9	18	Comments
Weekdays	$10.00		M - Th
Weekends	$11.00		
Twilight	N/A		
Seniors	$8.00		M-F < 4:30
Power Cart	$9.00		
Pull Cart	$2.50		
Club Rental	$5.00		
Credit cards	Visa Mastercard Discover		
Checks	Any		
Rain Check	Full		
Other			
Leagues:	Wed - Thur		

Amenities:

Driving Range	N	Snacks	Y
Putting Green	Y	Grill/Bar	Y
Practice Green	N	Restaurant	N
Spikeless	O	Locker Room	N
Proshop	F	Showers	N

Management:

Manager Shannon Burks
Professional None

Hole	Blue	Yellow	Par	Handicap
1	256	231	4	3
2	161	149	3	7
3	200	170	3	1
4	140	129	3	6
5	160	138	3	5
6	135	125	3	8
7	300	278	4	2
8	180	166	3	4
9	135	106	3	9
Total	1667	1492	29	
Slope	90	90		
Rating	28.1	28.1		

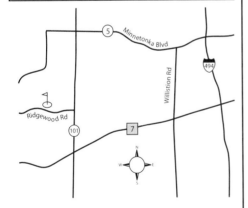

From I-494 take Hwy 7 west 2.6 miles to Hwy 101. Go north 0.7 miles to Ridgewood Road. Go west 1/2 mile, course is on the right.

Mendota Heights Par 3

1695 Dodd Road
Mendota Heights, MN 55118
651-454-9822

Course Information

Reservations:	First come / first served		
2000 Fees:	9	18	Comments
Weekdays	$8.50		
Weekends	$9.50		
Twilight	$7.00		After 7pm
Seniors	$7.00		
Power Cart	$9.00		
Pull Cart	$2.00		
Club Rental	$3.75		
Credit cards	None		
Checks	Any		
Rain Check	Before completing 4 holes		
Other			
Leagues:	Mon - Fri		

Amenities:			
Driving Range	N	Snacks	Y
Putting Green	Y	Grill/Bar	N
Practice Green	N	Restaurant	N
Spikeless	O	Locker Room	N
Proshop	B	Showers	N

Management:	
Manager	Peggy Shea
Professional	None

Hole	White	Red	Par	Handicap
1	140	130	3	4
2	100	90	3	6
3	75	70	3	9
4	165	145	3	2
5	100	90	3	7
6	180	165	3	1
7	125	115	3	5
8	150	130	3	3
9	90	75	3	8
Total	1125	1010	27	
Slope	N/A	N/A		
Rating	N/A	N/A		

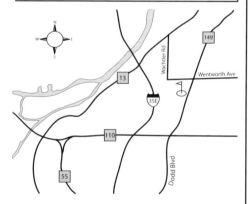

From I-35E take Hwy 110 east 2/3 mile
to Dodd Blvd. Go north 0.8 miles, the
course is on the left.

New Hope Village Golf Course

8130 Bass Lake Road
New Hope, MN 55428
763-531-5178

Course Information

Reservations:	Weekdays - 7 days		
	Weekend - 3 days		
2000 Fees:	9	18	Comments
Weekdays	$11.00		
Weekends	$11.00		
Twilight	N/A		
Seniors	$10.00		
Power Cart	$8.00		$6 seniors
Pull Cart	$1.00		
Club Rental	$2.00		
Credit cards	Visa Mastercard		
Checks	Any		
Rain Check	Before completing 6 holes		
Other			
Leagues:	Various		

Amenities:			
Driving Range	N	Snacks	Y
Putting Green	Y	Grill/Bar	N
Practice Green	N	Restaurant	N
Spikeless	Y	Locker Room	N
Proshop	S	Showers	N

Management:	
Manager	Jim Corbett
Professional	Tim Drew

Hole	Men	Women	Par	Men Handicap
1	124	124	3	9
2	169	169	3	3
3	130	118	3	7
4	171	153	3	4
5	159	142	3	5
6	128	128	3	6
7	169	127	3	2
8	108	108	3	8
9	231/173	143	3	1
Total	1389/ 1331	1212	27	
Slope	74	71		
Rating	26.7	26.6		

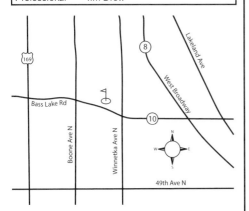

From I-694 take Hwy 169 south 1.75 miles to Bass Lake Road. Go east 0.8 miles, course is on the left.

Oak Glen Short Course

1599 McKusick Road
Stillwater, MN 55082
651-439-6963

Course Information

Reservations:	1 week in advance	

2000 Fees:	9	18	Comments
Weekdays	$9.00		$7.50 < 1pm
Weekends	$9.00		
Twilight	N/A		
Seniors	N/A		
Power Cart	$7.00		
Pull Cart	$2.00		
Club Rental	$6.00		
Credit cards	Visa Mastercard		
Checks	Any		
Rain Check	Pro-rated		
Other			

Leagues:	Wed, Thur

Amenities:			
Driving Range	Y	Snacks	Y
Putting Green	Y	Grill/Bar	Y
Practice Green	N	Restaurant	Y
Spikeless	O	Locker Room	Y
Proshop	F	Showers	Y

Management:	
Manager	Mark Larson
Professional	Greg Stang

Hole	Men	Women	Par	Handicap
1	163	128	3	5
2	163	153	3	4
3	160	135	3	6
4	344	320	4	1
5	165	139	3	3
6	169	159	3	7
7	130	111	3	8
8	336	316	4	2
9	108	99	3	9
Total	1738	1560	29	
Slope	N/A	N/A		
Rating	N/A	N/A		

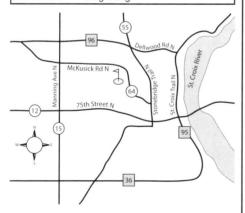

From I-694 take Hwy 36 east 5 miles to Manning Trail (CR 15). Go north 2.5 miles to McKusik Rd. (CR 64). Go east 1.6 miles, course entrance is on the left.

Oakdale Greens

5585 Golfview Avenue North
Oakdale, MN 55128
651-773-3494

Course Information

Reservations:	First come/first served		
2000 Fees:	9	18	Comments
Weekdays	$5.00		Before 4pm
Weekends	$8.00		>4pm weekdays
Twilight	N/A		
Seniors	N/A		
Power Cart	$9.00		
Pull Cart	$2.00		
Club Rental	$3.50		
Credit cards	None		
Checks	Any		
Rain Check	Before completing 4 holes		
Other	Sunday $6 after 6pm		
Leagues:	Mon - Fri		

Amenities:			
Driving Range	N	Snacks	Y
Putting Green	Y	Grill/Bar	Y
Practice Green	N	Restaurant	N
Spikeless	Y	Locker Room	N
Proshop	B	Showers	N

Management:	
Manager	Peggy Shea
Professional	Bruce Johnson

Hole	White	Red	Par	Handicap
1	141	124	3	5
2	143	143	3	6
3	117	112	3	9
4	139	139	3	3
5	148	148	3	1
6	155	145	3	8
7	147	96	3	2
8	174	119	3	4
9	146	109	3	7
Total	1310	1144	27	
Slope	N/A	N/A		
Rating	N/A	N/A		

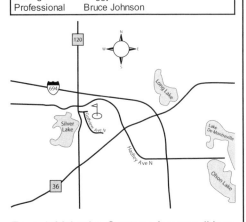

From I-694 take Century Avenue (Hwy 120) south 1/4 mile to 56th Street N. Go east to the course.

Orchard Gardens
Golf Course
1020 West 155th Street
Burnsville, MN 55337
952-435-5771

Course Information

Reservations:	Reservations taken		
2000 Fees:	9	18	Comments
Weekdays	$12.00		
Weekends	$13.00		
Twilight	N/A		
Seniors	-$1.00		M - F < 2pm
Power Cart	$10.00		
Pull Cart	$2.00		
Club Rental	$3.00		
Credit cards	None		
Checks	Any		
Rain Check	None		
Other			
Leagues:	Mon - Thur		

Amenities:			
Driving Range	Y	Snacks	Y
Putting Green	Y	Grill/Bar	N
Practice Green	N	Restaurant	N
Spikeless	Y	Locker Room	N
Proshop	S	Showers	N

Management:	
Manager	Sherri Henry
Professional	Jim Weber

Hole	Yardage	Par Men	Par Women	Handicap
1	140	3	3	9
2	227	3	4	5
3	228	3	4	1
4	160	3	3	2
5	130	3	3	7
6	160	3	3	6
7	200	3	3	4
8	100	3	3	8
9	225	3	4	3
Total	1570	27	29	
Slope	74			
Rating	27.1			

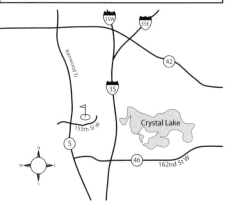

From I-35 take 162nd Street W (CR 46) west 2/3 mile to Kenwood Trail (CR 5). Go north 0.6 miles to 155th Street W. Go east, course in on the left.

Red Oak Golf Club
855 Red Oak Lane
Mound, MN 55364
952-472-3999

Course Information

Reservations:	1 week in advance		

2000 Fees:	9	18	Comments
Weekdays	$8.00		
Weekends	$9.00		
Twilight	N/A		
Seniors	$6.50		Weekdays
Power Cart	$6.00		
Pull Cart	$0.75		
Club Rental	$2.00		
Credit cards	None		
Checks	Any		
Rain Check	Before completing 4 holes		
Other			

Leagues:	Mon, Wed

Amenities:			
Driving Range	N	Snacks	Y
Putting Green	Y	Grill/Bar	Y
Practice Green	N	Restaurant	N
Spikeless	N	Locker Room	N
Proshop	B	Showers	N

Management:	
Manager	David Eidahl
Professional	None

Hole	Yardage	Par	Handicap
1	142	3	3
2	168	3	2
3	113	3	5
4	123	3	6
5	112	3	7
6	94	3	8
7	111	3	9
8	128	3	4
9	217	3	1
Total	1208	27	
Slope	M 25.2 M 25.2		
Rating	M 61 W 62		

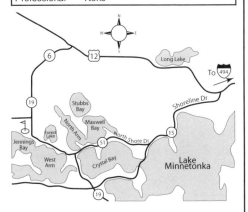

From I-494 take Hwy 12 west 12.5
miles to McCulley Rd. (CR 6). Go south
(CR 6 merges with CR 19) 2.9 miles to
Red Oak Lane. Go west, course is on
the left.

Sanbrook Executive Course

2181 County Road 5
Isanti, MN 55040
763-444-9904

Course Information

Reservations:	2 days in advance		

2000 Fees:	9	18	Comments
Weekdays	$8.50		
Weekends	$9.50		
Twilight	N/A		
Seniors	$6.50		M-F < 3pm
Power Cart	$12.00		
Pull Cart	$2.00		
Club Rental	$3.00		
Credit cards	Visa Mastercard		
Checks	Any		
Rain Check	If rain starts while playing		
Other			

Leagues:	None

Amenities:			
Driving Range	Y	Snacks	Y
Putting Green	Y	Grill/Bar	N
Practice Green	N	Restaurant	N
Spikeless	Y	Locker Room	N
Proshop	S	Showers	N

Management:	
Manager	Pat Zimba
Professional	None

Hole	Men	Women	Par	Men Handicap	Women Handicap
1	197	188	3	4	8
2	373	357	4	1	1
3	189	179	3	2	2
4	159	152	3	5	6
5	131	131	3	7	3
6	271	248	4	8	7
7	169	156	3	3	4
8	156	146	3	6	5
9	129	121	3	9	9
Total	1774	1678	29		
Slope	79	85			
Rating	28.1	29.2			

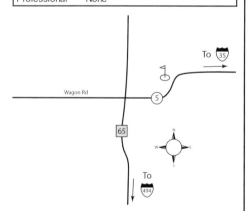

From I-694 take Hwy 65 (Central Ave.) north 29 miles to CR 5. Go east 1 mile, the course is on the left. From I-35 take CR 95 exit 147 west 0.8 miles until CR 5 splits off. Continue east 10.2 miles on CR 5, course entrance is on the right.

Theodore Wirth
Short Course
1301 Theodore Wirth Parkway
Golden Valley, MN 55422
763-522-2818

Course Information

Reservations:	First come / first served		
2000 Fees:	9	18	Comments
Weekdays	$10.00		
Weekends	$10.00		
Twilight	N/A		
Seniors	$8.50		
Power Cart	N/A		
Pull Cart	$1.50		
Club Rental	$4.00		
Credit cards	Visa Mastercard AmEx		
Checks	Any		
Rain Check	Ask		
Other			
Leagues:	None		

Amenities:			
Driving Range	N	Snacks	Y
Putting Green	Y	Grill/Bar	N
Practice Green	N	Restaurant	N
Spikeless	N	Locker Room	N
Proshop	B	Showers	N

Management:	
Manager	Bill Baughton
Professional	None

Hole	Yardage	Par	Handicap
1	114	3	8
2	121	3	6
3	200	3	1
4	104	3	9
5	143	3	4
6	150	3	3
7	161	3	2
8	131	3	5
9	116	3	7
Total	1240	27	
Slope	M 58 W 65		
Rating	N/A		

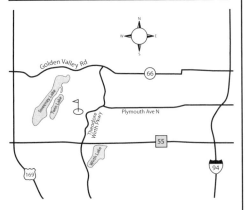

From I-94 take Hwy 55 west 2 miles to Theodore Wirth Parkway. Go north 1/2 mile, course is on the left.

Thompson Oaks

1555 Oakdale Avenue
West St. Paul, MN 55118
651-457-6064

Course Information

Reservations:	7 days in advance		

2000 Fees:	9	18	Comments
Weekdays	$10.00		
Weekends	$12.00		
Twilight	N/A		
Seniors	$8.00		
Power Cart	N/A		
Pull Cart	$3.00		
Club Rental	$3.00		
Credit cards	None		
Checks	Any		
Rain Check	Before completing 4 holes		
Other			

Leagues:	Mon - Thur

Amenities:			
Driving Range	N	Snacks	Y
Putting Green	Y	Grill/Bar	N
Practice Green	N	Restauran	N
Spikeless	Y	Locker Room	N
Proshop	B	Showers	N

Management:	
Manager	Walter Braunig, Jr.
Professional	None

Hole	Blue	White	Red	Par	Men Handicap	Women Handicap
1	125	110	91	3	9	7
2	200	184	143	3	1	5
3	119	117	84	3	8	8
4	143	126	111	3	7	6
5	160	149	87	3	3	9
6	145	131	110	3	6	4
7	285	281	223	4	5	2
8	353	342	295	4	2	1
9	145	137	108	3	4	3
Total	1675	1577	1252	29		
Slope	87	85	77			
Rating	28.8	28.2	26.4			

From I-494 take Hwy 52 north 1.6
miles to Thompson Avenue. Go west
1/4 mile to Oakdale Avenue. Go south,
course is on the right.

Golf Practice Facilities

The following is a listing of some of the golf practice facilities around the Twin Cities area. Many of the courses listed in the book have driving ranges but these are facilities that only have practice facilities. The golf domes and the new open air ranges like Rain, Snow or Shine are open all year.

Airena Golf Dome of Spring Lake Park - All seasons golf dome.
　　　　Spring Lake Park: 763-780-3663
All Seasons Golf Dome - All seasons golf dome.
　　　　Cottage Grove: 651-459-2135
Braemar Golf Dome - Seasonal golf dome.
　　　　Edina: 952-826-6744
Brighton Crossroad Driving Range - Seasonal outdoor driving range.
　　　　New Brighton: 651-638-2170
Bunker Indoor Golf Center - Golf simulators.
　　　　Minneapolis: 612-343-9793
Champions Burnsville Indoor Golf - Golf simulators.
　　　　Burnsville: 952-890-1081
Country Air Driving Range - Seasonal outdoor driving range.
　　　　Lake Elmo: 651-436-6549
Dunham's Driving Range - Seasonal outdoor driving range.
　　　　Lakeville: 952-469-4102
Eagle Lake Golf Center - Seasonal outdoor driving range.
　　　　Plymouth: 763-268-3182
Fore Seasons Golf Dome - All seasons golf dome.
　　　　Long Lake: 952-473-4813
Golf Center - Seasonal golf practice facility.
　　　　Brooklyn Park: 763-424-2929
Goodrich Golf Dome - All seasons golf dome.
　　　　Maplewood: 651-777-0500
Great Northern Golf Range - Seasonal outdoor driving range.
　　　　Ham Lake: 763-434-4109
Highway 8 Driving Range - Seasonal outdoor driving range.
　　　　Forest Lake: 651-462-1162
Lonesome Pine Golf Range - Seasonal outdoor driving range.
　　　　Brooklyn Park: 763-425-9397
Parkers Lake Golf Center - Golf practice facility.
　　　　Plymouth: 763-475-4668
Rain Snow or Shine Golf - All seasons outdoor driving range.
　　　　Newport: 952-445-1500
Rain Snow or Shine Golf - All seasons outdoor driving range.
　　　　Chanhassen: 952-445-1500
Shadow Ridge Golf Driving Range - Seasonal outdoor driving range.
　　　　Lino Lakes: 651-481-7003

Rankings

The following is a complete listing of the final rankings for the 79 courses along with their individual category scores. The courses are grouped by their rating with four golf balls being the best and one golf ball the worst.

Rank	Course	Rating	Tee Box	Fairway	Green	Layout	Amenities	Overall	Value	Cost
1	Ridges at Sand Creek	109.53	4.40	4.05	4.68	4.30	3.80	4.73	5.0	$29.00
2	Chaska Town Course	108.65	4.45	4.25	4.68	4.45	3.90	4.50	4.5	$45.00
3	Prestwick	108.08	4.75	4.40	4.58	4.45	4.45	4.03	4.0	$44.00
4	Pioneer Creek	106.83	4.75	3.20	4.33	4.53	4.08	4.63	4.5	$28.00
5	Rush Creek	105.70	4.90	4.75	4.98	4.63	4.13	4.85	2.5	$95.00
6	Oak Glen	105.18	3.68	3.85	4.60	4.15	3.65	4.15	5.0	$25.00
7	Mississippi Dunes	105.15	4.00	4.75	4.75	3.90	4.30	4.45	4.0	$36.00
8	Wild Marsh	105.10	4.30	4.25	4.25	4.48	3.10	4.60	4.5	$37.00
9	Refuge	104.98	4.85	3.75	4.55	4.58	3.78	4.88	3.5	$75.00
10	Fox Hollow	104.90	4.45	4.25	4.20	3.95	4.18	4.10	4.5	$32.00
11	Links at Northfork	104.60	4.75	4.40	4.30	3.85	4.50	3.95	4.0	$33.00
12	Inverwood	103.70	4.45	3.95	4.05	4.05	3.93	4.20	4.5	$28.00
13	Willingers	103.25	4.75	3.55	3.88	3.88	4.25	4.30	4.5	$37.00
14	Creeksbend	102.85	4.25	3.80	4.10	4.10	3.45	3.80	5.0	$23.00
15	Majestic Oaks Platinum	102.73	4.28	3.55	4.20	4.20	4.48	4.15	4.0	$29.00
16	Bunker Hills	102.65	4.35	3.80	4.10	4.10	3.85	4.10	4.0	$34.00
17	Sawmill	102.15	4.60	3.90	3.85	3.85	4.00	4.15	4.0	$29.00
18	Legends	101.98	4.13	3.35	4.75	4.75	4.50	5.00	3.0	$65.00
19	Oak Marsh	101.75	4.18	3.35	4.00	4.00	3.98	4.18	4.5	$24.00
20	Braemar	101.43	4.03	3.95	4.03	4.03	4.25	3.85	4.0	$30.00
21	Edinburgh	101.25	4.55	4.10	4.25	3.93	4.40	3.90	3.5	$45.00
22	StoneRidge	101.10	4.10	3.30	3.88	3.88	3.60	4.65	2.5	$69.00
23	Manitou Ridge	100.38	3.53	3.90	3.98	3.98	3.28	3.75	4.5	$25.00
24	River Oaks	99.81	3.95	4.10	3.75	3.70	4.00	3.95	4.5	$25.00
25	Eagle Valley	99.70	4.30	4.00	3.30	3.98	3.90	3.90	4.5	$28.00
26	Baker National	99.55	4.40	3.90	4.10	3.50	3.90	4.35	4.0	$32.00
27	Cedar Creek	99.38	4.15	3.95	4.20	3.83	3.35	4.23	4.0	$26.00
28	Dahlgreen	99.25	4.10	3.70	4.30	3.85	3.40	4.15	4.0	$28.00
29	Chisago Lakes	99.05	3.55	3.10	3.80	3.78	4.00	3.90	5.0	$22.00

Rank	Course	Rating	Tee Box	Fairway	Green	Layout	Amenities	Overall	Value	Cost
	◗◗◗ continued									
30	Chomonix	99.05	3.70	3.05	3.90	4.10	3.85	4.15	4.5	$25.00
31	Crystal Lake	98.75	4.45	3.60	4.00	3.75	3.55	4.10	4.0	$26.00
32	Tanners Brook	98.53	3.55	3.95	3.85	3.95	3.40	3.98	4.5	$25.00
33	Keller	97.95	3.80	4.00	4.15	3.95	3.13	3.90	4.0	$27.00
34	Heritage Links	97.25	4.60	2.30	4.25	3.95	3.20	3.65	4.0	$27.00
35	New Prague	95.40	3.95	3.70	4.25	3.70	3.35	3.65	3.5	$27.00
36	Majestic Oaks Gold	95.28	3.55	3.15	3.70	3.73	4.48	3.68	4.0	$24.00
37	Southern Hills	95.15	3.40	3.75	3.80	3.95	3.20	4.05	4.0	$26.00
	◗◗◖									
38	Elk River	94.95	4.08	3.40	3.63	4.00	3.65	4.13	3.5	$31.00
39	Deer Run	94.80	3.60	3.70	3.95	3.83	4.10	3.30	3.5	$29.00
40	Greenhaven	94.80	4.00	3.55	3.30	3.18	3.95	3.90	4.5	$26.50
41	Wilds	94.50	4.55	4.05	4.15	4.08	3.75	4.35	2.0	$99.00
42	Stonebrooke	93.85	4.60	3.30	4.50	4.33	3.75	3.90	3.5	$39.00
43	Brookview	93.68	3.50	4.00	3.73	3.78	3.68	3.83	3.5	$28.00
44	Island View	93.30	3.50	3.90	3.85	3.88	4.20	3.70	3.0	$42.00
45	Pheasant Acres	93.20	3.28	3.95	3.50	3.55	3.88	3.53	4.0	$24.00
46	Timber Creek	92.70	3.70	3.40	3.10	3.80	2.95	3.30	4.5	$22.00
47	Phalen Park	92.60	3.10	3.40	3.98	3.48	3.38	3.95	4.0	$25.00
48	Monticello	92.20	3.95	3.15	4.35	3.65	3.35	3.35	3.0	$28.75
49	Oneka Ridge	91.90	3.78	3.05	3.80	3.70	3.55	3.38	3.5	$25.50
50	Hiawatha	91.43	3.83	3.30	3.35	3.68	3.80	3.65	3.5	$24.00
51	Daytona	91.38	3.93	3.40	3.48	3.63	3.30	3.80	3.5	$26.00
52	Meadowbrook	90.95	3.45	3.45	3.23	3.80	3.03	3.55	4.0	$24.00
53	Viking Meadows	90.75	3.25	3.45	3.78	3.90	2.98	3.45	3.5	$23.00
54	Bellwood Oaks	90.55	3.50	3.30	3.05	3.25	2.35	3.55	5.0	$20.00
55	Columbia	90.20	3.10	3.50	3.65	3.50	3.85	3.60	3.5	$24.00
	◗◗									
56	Theodore Wirth	88.98	3.40	3.10	3.65	3.35	2.53	3.53	4.0	$24.00
57	Hidden Haven	88.60	2.58	3.05	3.80	3.98	2.98	3.73	3.5	$24.00
58	Valley View	88.60	3.15	3.40	3.25	3.63	2.75	3.35	4.0	$23.00
59	Fountain Valley	88.48	2.95	3.35	3.13	3.53	3.30	3.73	4.0	$20.00
60	Sundance	87.93	3.30	3.60	3.60	3.63	3.15	3.63	3.0	$26.00
61	Como	87.56	3.00	3.45	3.33	3.68	2.83	3.98	3.5	$25.00
62	Valleywood	87.56	3.03	3.50	3.65	3.40	2.73	3.80	3.5	$27.00
63	Francis A. Gross	87.50	2.40	3.65	3.28	3.45	3.23	3.65	4.0	$24.00

Rank	Course	Rating	Tee Box	Fairway	Green	Layout	Amenities	Overall	Value	Cost
	continued									
64	Hollydale	87.08	3.10	3.05	3.05	3.40	3.28	3.33	4.0	$23.50
65	Hidden Greens	85.98	3.53	2.70	2.55	3.15	2.85	3.50	4.5	$18.00
66	Falcon Ridge	85.83	2.48	2.85	3.33	3.15	2.63	3.55	4.5	$20.00
67	Bluff Creek	85.60	3.45	3.15	3.20	3.30	2.70	3.55	3.5	$27.00
68	University of Minnesota	84.23	2.63	3.90	3.10	3.73	3.65	3.95	2.5	$26.00
69	Elm Creek	82.10	3.45	2.40	3.00	3.35	2.10	3.35	3.5	$25.00
70	Highland Park	81.75	2.65	3.30	2.78	3.13	3.15	3.30	3.5	$25.00
71	Afton Alps	81.53	2.28	3.15	3.03	2.90	2.68	3.35	4.0	$18.00
72	Sanbrook	81.23	3.05	2.20	3.48	2.85	2.48	3.43	3.5	$19.00
73	Goodrich	81.00	2.98	2.90	2.73	3.75	2.63	3.13	3.0	$24.00
74	Lakeview	79.28	2.90	3.50	2.70	2.78	2.23	3.23	3.5	$22.00
75	Rum River Hills	78.80	3.05	2.00	2.40	3.28	3.00	2.95	3.5	$25.00
76	Greenwood	78.20	2.80	2.55	3.35	3.18	1.90	2.80	3.0	$19.00
77	Carriage Hills	76.90	1.90	2.15	2.95	3.23	2.55	3.10	3.5	$22.00
78	Shamrock	76.48	2.88	3.15	3.00	2.65	2.08	2.80	3.0	$23.50
79	Hampton Hills	75.75	2.85	1.95	2.55	3.38	2.35	2.90	3.0	$21.00

Paul's Picks

Favorite Five
1. Refuge
2. Chaska Town Course
3. Ridges at Sand Creek
4. Rush Creek
5. Legends

Best Bargains
1. Ridges at Sand Creek
2. Oak Glen
3. Pioneer Creek
4. Creeksbend
5. Bellwood Oaks

Worth the Drive
1. Ridges at Sand Creek
2. Refuge
3. Willingers
4. Wild Marsh
5. Pioneer Creek

Twin Cities Fun Facts

The following is a compilation of the shortest, longest, easiest and most difficult holes and courses in the Twin Cities area. A listing for the championship, men's and women's tees is listed for each of the categories.

Par 3's

Championship - Longest
255 - Oneka Ridge (#13)
244 - Valley View (#2)
241 - Mississippi Dunes (#4)
240 - Bunker Hills (#8 gold)
240 - Inverwood (#12)
237 - Stone Ridge (#16)
236 - Braemar (#17)
236 - Highland Park (#17)
235 - Valley View (#9)
230 - Viking Meadows (#12)

Championship - Shortest
91 - Greenwood (#12)
110 - Ridges at Sand Creek (#15)
111 - Greenwood (#14)
112 - Greenwood (#13)
118 - Rum River Hills (#14)
120 - Columbia (#8)
120 - Mississippi Dunes (#9)
120 - Sundance (#17)
122 - Legends (#5)
125 - Fountain Valley (#3)

Men's Longest
235 - Oneka Ridge (#13)
228 - Greenwood (#9)
224 - Stone Ridge (#16)
223 - Hidden Haven (#17)
220 - Highland Park (#17)
220 - Viking Meadows (#12)
220 - Bunker Hills (#8 gold)
219 - Shamrock (#8)
213 - Falcon Ridge (#11)
210 - Monticello (#3)

Men's Shortest
86 - Greenwood (#12)
97 - Greenwood (#14)
102 - Columbia (#8)
104 - Ridges at Sand Creek (#15)
106 - Mississippi Dunes (#9)
107 - Greenwood (#13)
108 - Rum River Hills (#14)
109 - Crystal Lake (#8)
112 - Sanbrook (#12)
115 - Legends (#5)
115 - Fountain Valley (#3)

Women's Longest
197 - Falcon Ridge (#11)
187 - Greenhaven (#17)
186 - Greenwood (#8)
182 - Hampton Hills (#5)
180 - Hidden Greens (#17)
180 - Bunker Hills (#26 east)
180 - Bunker Hills (#16 north)
178 - University of MN (#8)
178 - Deer Run (#6)
177 - Highland Park (#2)

Women's Shortest
70 - Legends (#7)
73 - Legends (#17)
74 - Links at Northfork (#7)
75 - Ridges at Sand Creek (#15)
77 - Mississippi Dunes (#9)
78 - Greenwood (#13)
78 - Chaska Town Course (#4)
80 - Cedar Creek (#4)
82 - Greenwood (#12)
84 - Heritage Links (#14)

Par 4's

Championship Longest
481 - Chaska Town Course (#17)
480 - StoneRidge (#12)
477 - Dahlgreen (#5)
475 - Wilds (#14)
473 - StoneRidge (#18)
466 - Baker National (#1)
465 - Viking Meadows (#11)
463 - Valleywood (#9)
462 - Rush Creek (#16)
462 - StoneRidge (#5)

Championship Shortest
228 - Greenwood (#18)
231 - Lakeview (#14)
234 - Falcon Ridge (#13)
251 - Greenwood (#11)
264 - Lakeview (#12)
270 - Heritage Links (#13)
273 - Lakeview (#13)
276 - Valley View (#4)
281 - Sanbrook (#11)
281 - Sundance (#9)

Men's Longest
465 - Dahlgreen (#5)
458 - StoneRidge (#12)
454 - Valleywood (#9)
453 - Viking Meadows (#11)
453 - StoneRidge (#18)
450 - Chaska Town Course (#17)
447 - StoneRidge (#5)
445 - Braemar (#1)
445 - Wilds (#14)
444 - Ridges at Sand Creek (#13)

Men's Shortest
218 - Greenwood (#18)
222 - Lakeview (#14)
226 - Falcon Ridge (#13)
234 - Greenwood (#11)
244 - Hampton Hills (#10)
245 - Hampton Hills (#13)
251 - Lakeview (#12)
256 - Heritage Links (#13)
258 - Valley View (#4)
259 - Lakeview (#13)

Women's Longest
400 - Hampton Hills (#3)
391 - Theodore Wirth (#17)
390 - Hiawatha (#10)
390 - Bunker Hills (#10)
389 - Manitou Ridge (#6)
388 - Braemar (#15)
385 - Bunker Hills (#19 east)
384 - Valley View (#10)
384 - Braemar (#16)
383 - University of MN (#15)

Women's Shortest
148 - Wild Marsh (#6)
189 - Greenwood (#18)
190 - Mississippi Dunes (#16)
191 - Greenwood (#11)
195 - Stonebrooke (#8)
201 - Chaska Town Course (#13)
202 - Wilds (#16)
202 - Rum River Hills (#8)
204 - Chaska Town Course (#3)
206 - Oak Marsh (#2)
206 - Carriage Hills (#4)

Par 5's

Championship Longest
630 - Elm Creek (#13)
621 - Legends (#16)
617 - Sanbrook (#2)
609 - Rush Creek (#8)
601 - Sanbrook (#10)
600 - Ridges at Sand Creek (#10)
597 - Pioneer Creek (#14)
595 - Stonebrooke (#17)
593 - Legends (#11)
588 - Sawmill (#7)

Championship Shortest
445 - Elm Creek (#18)
449 - Creeksbend (#14)
450 - Creeksbend (#2)
459 - Viking Meadows (#9)
461 - Rum River Hills (#18)
462 - Keller (#9)
462 - Meadowbrook (#4)
465 - Brookview (#2)
465 - Cedar Creek (#12)
465 - Falcon Ridge (#5)

Men's Longest
596 - Legends (#16)
591 - Sanbrook (#2)
582 - Sanbrook (#10)
581 - Rush Creek (#8)
576 - Sawmill (#7)
573 - Ridges at Sand Creek (#10)
573 - Legends (#11)
571 - Greenwood (#17)
569 - Rush Creek (#18)
567 - Sundance (#14)

Men's Shortest
431 - Creeksbend (#2)
434 - Carriage Hills (#2)
437 - Keller (#9)
438 - Creeksbend (#14)
441 - Oak Marsh (#16)
442 - Elm Creek (#5)
445 - Chomonix (#11)
446 - Hidden Haven (#16)
447 - Creeksbend (#8)
447 - Baker National (#6)
447 - Hiawatha (#1)
447 - Hidden Haven (#13)

Women's Longest
510 - Shamrock (#1)
504 - Highland Park (#4)
497 - Chomonix (#1)
494 - Sundance (#18)
491 - Viking Meadows (#5)
489 - Wild Marsh (#7)
489 - Rush Creek (#8)
486 - Heritage Links (#2)
486 - Island View (#3)
481 - Greenwood (#17)

Women's Shortest
288 - Creeksbend (#2)
313 - Legends (#4)
318 - Carriage Hills (#12)
330 - Hollydale (#11)
346 - Sawmill (#4)
350 - Island View (#18)
351 - Daytona (#11)
351 - Valley View (#1)
351 - Carriage Hills (#2)
355 - Goodrich (#13)

Total Yardage

Championship Longest
7025 - Wilds
7020 - Rush Creek
7013 - Majestic Oaks Platinum
6989 - Links at Northfork
6959 - StoneRidge
6953 - Pioneer Creek
6938 - Bunker Hills
6936 - Ridges at Sand Creek
6906 - Legends
6892 - Elk River

Championship Shortest
5468 - Lakeview
5518 - Greenwood
5787 - Falcon Ridge
5821 - Como
6060 - Cedar Creek
6101 - Phalen Park
6144 - Gross
6160 - Hollydale
6184 - Oak Marsh
6228 - Goodrich

Men's Longest
6694 - StoneRidge
6653 - Links at Northfork
6640 - Rush Creek
6619 - Legends
6618 - Pioneer Creek
6573 - Bunker Hills
6561 - Majestic Oaks Platinum
6554 - Eagle Valley
6554 - Elk River
6547 - Ridges at Sand Creek

Men's Shortest
5236 - Lakeview
5438 - Greenwood
5581 - Como
5593 - Afton Alps
5627 - Falcon Ridge
5715 - Cedar Creek
5773 - Elm Creek
5793 - Oak Marsh
5799 - Edinburgh
5806 - Hidden Haven

Women's Longest
5852 - Fountain Valley
5809 - Bunker Hills
5793 - Shamrock
5714 - Chisago Lakes
5707 - Bellwood Oaks
5702 - Braemar
5648 - University of MN
5642 - Columbia
5626 - Oak Glen
5600 - Highland Park

Women's Shortest
4630 - Wild Marsh
4648 - Oak Marsh
4742 - Legends
4791 - Greenwood
4801 - Afton Alps
4805 - Crystal Lake
4815 - Cedar Creek
4848 - Majestic Oaks Gold
4853 - Chaska Town Course
4866 - Creeksbend

Rating

Championship Highest
74.7 - Wilds
74.2 - Rush Creek
73.9 - Baker National
73.9 - Majestic Oaks Platinum
73.7 - Links at Northfork
73.5 - Bunker Hills
73.4 - Chaska Town Course
73.3 - Willingers
73.3 - StoneRidge
73.3 - Legends

Championship Lowest
65.8 - Lakeview
67.2 - Greenwood
68.0 - Falcon Ridge
68.4 - Cedar Creek
68.6 - Como
68.6 - Gross
68.6 - Goodrich
68.9 - Phalen Park
69.0 - Highland Park
69.0 - New Prague

Men's Highest
72.4 - Links at Northfork
72.3 - StoneRidge
72.1 - Rush Creek
72.0 - Wilds
72.0 - Legends
71.8 - Baker National
71.8 - Bunker Hills
71.6 - Mississippi Dunes
71.5 - Dahlgreen
71.4 - Chaska Town Course
71.4 - Eagle Valley
71.4 - Elk River
71.4 - Majestic Oaks Platinum

Men's Lowest
64.9 - Lakeview
66.5 - Greenwood
66.8 - Cedar Creek
67.2 - Carriage Hills
67.2 - Goodrich
67.3 - Afton Alps
67.4 - Como
67.5 - Oak Marsh
67.6 - Gross
67.7 - Hidden Haven

Women's Highest
73.9 - Bunker Hills
73.4 - Oak Glen
73.4 - Fountain Valley
72.9 - University of MN
72.7 - Baker National
72.7 - Braemar
72.7 - Chisago Lakes
72.3 - Chomonix
72.3 - Bellwood Oaks
71.9 - Columbia

Women's Lowest
64.1 - Hidden Haven
65.4 - Cedar Creek
65.9 - Majestic Oaks Platinum
66.2 - Oak Marsh
66.8 - Sawmill
67.1 - Lakeview
67.3 - Greenwood
67.7 - Wild Marsh
67.7 - Gross
68.0 - Elm Creek

Slope

Championship Highest
143 - Legends
140 - Willingers
140 - Wilds
139 - Refuge
139 - Wild Marsh
137 - Rush Creek
135 - Inverwood
135 - Fox Hollow
135 - Mississippi Dunes
135 - Baker National

Championship Lowest
105 - Greenwood
108 - Lakeview
110 - Goodrich
111 - Highland Park
111 - Sanbrook
115 - Falcon Ridge
116 - Manitou Ridge
117 - Cedar Creek
117 - Oak Marsh
117 - Oneka Ridge
117 - Pheasant Acres
117 - Rum River Hills

Men's Highest
140 - Legends
136 - Refuge
136 - Willingers
136 - Rush Creek
134 - Wild Marsh
132 - Mississippi Dunes
131 - Inverwood
131 - Fox Hollow
131 - Pioneer
131 - Baker National
131 - Wilds

Men's Lowest
103 - Greenwood
107 - Goodrich
107 - Lakeview
108 - Carriage Hills
108 - Shamrock
110 - Afton Alps
110 - Highland Park
111 - Hampton Hills
113 - Oak Marsh
113 - Manitou Ridge
114 - Cedar Creek
114 - Falcon Ridge

Women's Highest
131 - Bunker Hills
130 - Willingers
130 - Oak Glen
128 - River Oaks
128 - Edinburgh
128 - Refuge
128 - Baker National
127 - Rush Creek
126 - Wilds
126 - Bellwood Oaks

Women's Lowest
106 - Cedar Creek
108 - Oak Marsh
109 - Greenwood
109 - Lakeview
110 - Greenhaven
111 - Hidden Haven
111 - Francis A. Gross
112 - Chaska Town Course
113 - Majestic Oaks Platinum
113 - Valley View
113 - Goodrich

Greens Fees

The following is a list of which courses will cost you the least green and which courses will take a divot out of your wallet. Both weekday and weekend greens fees are listed. An asterisk means that the cart is included in the greens fee.

Under $20.00

Weekdays
$18.00 Afton Alps
$18.00 Hidden Greens
$19.00 Sanbrook
$19.00 Greenwood

$20.00 - $25.00

Weekdays
$20.00 Bellwood Oaks
$20.00 Falcon Ridge
$20.00 Fountain Valley
$21.00 Hampton Hills
$22.00 Carriage Hills
$22.00 Chisago Lakes
$22.00 Lakeview
$22.00 Timber Creek
$23.00 Creeksbend
$23.00 Valley View
$23.00 Viking Meadows
$23.50 Hollydale
$23.50 Shamrock
$24.00 Columbia
$24.00 Goodrich
$24.00 Francis A. Gross
$24.00 Hiawatha
$24.00 Hidden Haven
$24.00 Majestic Oaks Gold
$24.00 Meadowbrook
$24.00 Oak Marsh
$24.00 Pheasant Acres
$24.00 Theodore Wirth

$25.00 - $30.00

Weekdays:
$25.00 Chomonix
$25.00 Como
$25.00 Elm Creek
$25.00 Highland Park

Under $20.00

Weekends
None

$20.00 - $25.00

Weekends
$22.00 Hidden Greens
$23.00 Afton Alps
$23.00 Greenwood
$23.00 Bellwood Oaks
$24.00 Sanbrook
$24.00 Falcon Ridge
$24.00 Goodrich

$25.00 - $30.00

Weekends
$25.00 Como
$25.00 Fountain Valley
$25.00 Hampton Hills
$25.00 Highland Park
$25.00 Manitou Ridge
$25.00 Phalen Park
$26.00 Chisago Lakes
$26.00 Columbia
$26.00 Francis A. Gross
$26.00 Hiawatha
$26.00 Hidden Haven
$26.00 Lakeview
$26.00 Meadowbrook
$26.00 Viking Meadows
$26.00 Theodore Wirth
$26.00 University of Minnesota
$27.00 Carriage Hills
$27.00 Chomonix
$27.00 Hollydale
$27.00 Keller
$27.00 Pheasant Acres
$27.00 Shamrock
$27.50 Oneka Ridge

$25.00 - $30.00 (cont'd)

Weekdays:

$25.00 Manitou Ridge
$25.00 Oak Glen
$25.00 Phalen Park
$25.00 River Oaks
$25.00 Rum River Hills
$25.00 Tanners Brook
$25.50 Oneka Ridge
$26.00 Cedar Creek
$26.00 Crystal Lake
$26.00 Daytona
$26.00 Southern Hills
$26.00 Sundance
$26.00 University of Minnesota
$26.50 Greenhaven
$27.00 Bluff Creek
$27.00 Heritage Links
$27.00 Keller
$27.00 New Prague
$27.00 Valleywood
$28.00 Brookview
$28.00 Dahlgreen
$28.00 Eagle Valley
$28.00 Inverwood
$28.00 Pioneer Creek
$28.75 Monticello
$29.00 Deer Run
$29.00 Majestic Oaks Platinum
$29.00 Ridges at Sand Creek
$29.00 Sawmill

$30.00 - $35.00

Weekdays

$30.00 Braemar
$31.00 Elk River
$32.00 Baker National
$32.00 Fox Hollow
$33.00 Links at Northfork
$34.00 Bunker Hills

$25.00 - $30.00 (cont'd)

Weekends

$28.00 Brookview
$28.00 Inverwood
$28.00 Majestic Oaks Gold
$28.00 River Oaks
$28.00 Tanners Brook
$28.00 Timber Creek
$29.00 Creeksbend
$29.00 Elm Creek
$29.00 Oak Marsh
$29.00 Rum River Hills
$29.00 Valley View
$29.50 Monticello
$29.75 Greenhaven

$30.00 - $35.00

Weekends

$30.00 Braemar
$30.00 Daytona
$30.00 Oak Glen
$30.00 Sundance
$31.00 Eagle Valley
$32.00 Baker National
$32.00 Cedar Creek
$32.00 New Prague
$33.00 Bluff Creek
$33.00 Crystal Lakes
$33.00 Heritage Links
$33.00 Majestic Oaks Platinum
$34.00 Bunker Hills
$34.00 Elk River
$34.00 Ridges at Sand Creek
$34.00 Southern Hills
$34.00 Valleywood

$35.00 - $40.00

Weekends

$37.00 Sawmill

$35.00 - $40.00

Weekdays
$36.00 Mississippi Dunes
$37.00 Wild Marsh*
$37.00 Willingers
$39.00 Stonebrooke

$40.00 - $50.00

Weekdays
$42.00 Island View
$44.00 Prestwick
$45.00 Chaska Town Course
$45.00 Edinburgh

Over $50.00

Weekdays
$65.00 Legends
$69.00 Stone Ridge
$75.00 Refuge*
$95.00 Rush Creek
$99.00 Wilds*

$40.00 - $50.00

Weekends
$42.00 Fox Hollow
$42.00 Links at Northfork
$42.00 Mississippi Dunes
$42.00 Willingers
$43.00 Wild Marsh*
$45.00 Edinburgh
$46.00 Island View
$46.00 Stonebrooke
$49.00 Chaska Town Course
$49.00 Prestwick

Over $50.00

Weekends
$65.00 Legends
$75.00 Refuge*
$79.00 Stone Ridge
$95.00 Rush Creek
$99.00 Wilds*

The Last Word

Do you have any comments or questions about anything contained in this book? What did you like or dislike about the guide? Did you find a mistake that needs correcting?

Please send or email any comments or questions to:

PK Publishing
PMB 257
4737 County Road 101
Minnetonka, MN 55345
or
paulkangas@tcgolfguide.com

Check out our website at **www.tcgolfguide.com** for updates and ordering information.

All suggestions from you will only help improve this guide in future editions. I hope you enjoyed the Twin Cities Golf Guide!

*Note: All ratings and comments in this book are the opinions of the writer. Courses were rated based on their conditions when they were played. Course conditions change, therefore courses will be re-rated for future editions of the Twin Cities Golf Guide.

Francis A. Gross golf course is under construction and normally plays to a par of 71 so it was included in the regulation courses.